Exercises in Econometrics

EXERCISES IN ECONOMETRICS Volume I

Errata

Page 59:
In the top block row of (2.1.10) "$(D - CA^{-1}B)$" should be "$(D - CA^{-1}B)^{-1}$" where it occurs twice.

Page 75, line 5 from bottom:
The equation "$l = \tilde{u}'\tilde{u}/\hat{u}'\hat{u}$" should be "$l = (\tilde{u}'\tilde{u}/\hat{u}'\hat{u})^{T/2}$".

Exercises in Econometrics

P. C. B. PHILLIPS
Professor of Econometrics, University of Birmingham

M. R. WICKENS
Reader in Econometrics, University of Essex

Volume I

Philip Allan/Ballinger Publishing Company

Published jointly 1978 by

PHILIP ALLAN PUBLISHERS LIMITED
MARKET PLACE
DEDDINGTON
OXFORD OX5 4SE

BALLINGER PUBLISHING COMPANY
17 DUNSTER STREET
HARVARD SQUARE
CAMBRIDGE
MASSACHUSETTS 02138

0 86003 006 7 Volume I
0 86003 009 1 Volume II

Typeset by The Alden Press Ltd, London
Printed in the United States of America

Contents

3. THE MULTIVARIATE LINEAR MODEL *116*

0   **Introduction** *116*

1   Questions *118*

2   **Supplementary Questions** *125*

4. FURTHER ASPECTS OF THE LINEAR MODEL *161*

0   Introduction *161*

1   Questions *161*

4.1 R^2, the variance of an OLS estimate and multicollinearity; 4.2 Multicollinearity
and principal components; 4.3 Specification bias due to omitted variables;
4.4 Conditional and mixed regression; 4.5 The effects of including unnecessary
variables; 4.6 Seasonal variation; 4.7 Deseasonalised models; 4.8 Models with linear
segments; 4.9 Hetcroscedasticity and OLS; 4.10 Properties of OLS with autoregressive
errors; 4.11 Cochrane—Orcutt and ML estimation; 4.12 Asymptotic properties
of the Durbin—Watson statistic; 4.13 Missing observations; 4.14 Covariance model;
4.15 Error components model; 4.16 Comparison of covariance and error components
models; 4.17 Aggregation bias and tests for perfect aggregation; 4.18 Application
of specification bias.

2   **Supplementary Questions** *168*

4.19 Using extraneous information; 4.20 Testing linear restrictions; 4.21 Dummy
variables and the covariance model; 4.22 GLS and tests of linear restrictions;
4.23 Multiple comparisons test; 4.24 Poisson distributed errors; 4.25 Quarterly
dummy variables; 4.26 Models with linear segments; 4.27 Testing for structural change
using recursions; 4.28 An application of testing for autocorrelation and seasonal
variation; 4.29 The finite sample distribution of the MLE of the linear model with
AR(1) errors using Monte Carlo simulations; 4.30 Testing for serial correlation;
4.31 Numerical optimisation methods and AR(1) errors; 4.32 Covariance
analysis; 4.33 Modelling equation and error dynamics.

3   Solutions *177*

5. FURTHER STOCHASTIC MODELS *217*

0   Introduction *217*

1   Questions *217*

5.1 Consistency of MDE in non-linear models; 5.2 MLE and MDE in non-linear
models; 5.3 Asymptotic efficiency of MDE in non-linear models; 5.4 Consistency
of MDE in a non-linear model; 5.5 Asymptotic distribution of MDE in models
non-linear in coefficients; 5.6 Iterative estimation of a linear model with a non-linear

restriction on the coefficients; 5.7 Estimation of the multivariate linear model with
non-linear cross equation restrictions; 5.8 Orthogonal regression; 5.9 Unobservable
variables; 5.10 Estimation of the vintage Cobb—Douglas production function.

5.11 Estimation with a non-linear restriction; 5.12 OLS with errors of measurement;
5.13 Estimation with proxy variables; 5.14 Estimating macro and micro equations
with errors of measurement; 5.15 Estimation of equations with errors in variables
by OLS and instrumental variables; 5.16 Estimation using the method of moments.

6.1 Identifiability and the simultaneous equation bias of OLS; 6.2 Identification
of equations and models using homogeneous restrictions; 6.3 Identification using
non-homogeneous restrictions; 6.4 Identification using cross equation restrictions;
6.5 Identifiability of a given structure; 6.6 Calculation of 2SLS estimates; 6.7 Choice
of instruments in the IV estimator; 6.8 Calculation of a confidence interval for a
2SLS estimate; 6.9 Choice of dependent variable and 2SLS; 6.10 Asymptotic
distribution of OLS; 6.11 Asymptotic distribution of ILS; 6.12 Calculation of LIML
and a test for over identifying restrictions; 6.13 Derivation of FIML, FIML as an
iterated IV estimator, 3SLS as an asymptotically efficient non-iterated estimator;
6.14 3SLS for models with a diagonal error covariance matrix and just-identified

equations; 6.15—6.17 Calculations of FIML for different models; 6.18 Subsystem LIML and subsystem 3SLS; 6.19 Finite sample distribution of an MLE; 6.20 Nagar's approximation to the bias of 2SLS; 6.21 Comparison of the concentration of 2SLS and LIML in finite samples; 6.22 Consistent estimation of a non-linear structural equation; 6.23—6.24 Applied econometrics.

2   Supplementary Questions *281*

6.25 Identification of the Cobb—Douglas production function and factor demand functions; 6.26 Identification of an IS—LM model; 6.27 Calculation of ILS and an IV estimator; 6.28 Identification and estimation; 6.29 Identification with and without non-homogeneous restrictions; 6.30 Equation and model identification; 6.31 Identification using non-homogeneous, cross equation restrictions; 6.32 Calculation of a confidence interval for a 2SLS estimate; 6.33 Related expressions for OLS and 2SLS; 6.34 2SLS and IV estimation; 6.35 Efficient IV estimation for single equations with linear restrictions and for complete models; 6.36 IV estimation with multicollinear instruments and under-identified equations; 6.37 Testing for structural change using 2SLS; 6.38 3SLS as a GLS estimator; 6.39 Asymptotic covariance matrix of 3SLS subject to general linear restrictions; 6.40 ILS and 2SLS and their relationship with 3SLS; 6.41 Systems MDE and FIML; 6.42 MLE for unrestricted and restricted reduced forms; 6.43 Recursive systems and OLS; 6.44 Calculation of an MDE from the unrestricted reduced form; 6.45 Subsystem and single equations LIML as FIML estimators; 6.46 Relationships between LIML and 2SLS; 6.47 Calculation of standard errors for predictions obtained from unrestricted and restricted reduced forms; 6.48 Evaluating macro models; 6.49 Finite sample distribution of an IV estimator.

3   Solutions *291*

7. DYNAMIC MODELS *374*

0   Introduction *374*

1   Questions *374*

7.1 Properties of the OLS estimator of an AR(1) model; 7.2 Properties of a difference equation with AR(1) errors; 7.3 Asymptotic bias of OLS of a difference equation with AR(1) and MA(1) errors; 7.4 MLE of a difference equation with AR(1) errors; 7.5 Asymptotic distribution of the Durbin—Watson statistic and the first order autocorrelation coefficient using OLS and ML estimation on a difference equation with AR(1) errors; 7.6 Local and global identification of a system of difference equations with AR errors; 7.7—7.8 Hatanaka's efficient non-iterative IV estimation for dynamic systems with AR errors; 7.9 Sargan's, Fair's and Hatanaka's estimators for single dynamic equations with AR errors; 7.10 Estimation of polynomial distributed lag models by OLS and restricted least squares and associated tests; 7.11 Polynomial distributed lag models as rational lag models; 7.12 A discrete approximation to system stochastic differential equations; 7.13 Estimation of a differential equation;

2   Supplementary Questions *388*

3   Solutions *401*

APPENDIX *xix*

BIBLIOGRAPHY *xxvi*

INDEX *xxxiii*

Preface

This book provides a set of worked and unworked exercises to supplement
the main textbook material in econometrics. It is written partly for
students who are commencing undergraduate work in econometrics and
who have some prior knowledge of statistics, and partly for students who
are undertaking more advanced undergraduate and graduate instruction.
We also hope that the book will prove useful to teachers by providing
material for classroom discussion and to research workers by going a small
way towards bridging the gap between the textbook and the rapidly
expanding literature in this field.

The book attempts to supplement the existing econometric literature in
two ways. First, in our experience, students very often find that the textbook they are assigned does not prepare them adequately to solve the sort
of problems they face in examinations. They are not shown in a direct
way how the theory can be used to solve such problems and they are not
provided with similar questions which they can attempt on their own.
Second, with the increasing output of econometric research, the coverage
of the established econometrics textbooks is seen to be less complete. This
problem is of particular concern to advanced students searching for a
recent overview of the subject and to beginning research workers who
often feel the need for a simpler introduction to the recent literature,
more particularly in the technical areas.

In this book we provide exercises both on econometric theory and
applied econometrics that cover most of the material in introductory and
advanced econometric textbooks. In addition, we have constructed
problems based on more recent research in order to introduce the reader
to some new results. As far as possible, we have included more than one
question on each topic. We have provided a fairly detailed solution to (at
least) one of these questions; the other questions are intended to be
supplementary and are left either for the reader to answer on his own or
for classroom discussion.

The material within each chapter is organised in the same way. At the
start of each chapter we have a brief introduction to the subject matter of

the chapter and, where this is appropriate, an outline of the notation that is to be used. The next two sections contain all of the questions in the chapter: first, those questions for which worked solutions are provided; and, second, the supplementary questions. The final section in each chapter contains the solutions. The questions and solutions are separated to encourage the reader to attempt the exercises alone before looking at the solutions that are provided. The questions are arranged and the solutions are written to enable the reader to proceed naturally from one question to the next. Knowledge of topics which are treated later in the book is not usually required. Where appropriate, the solution includes some discussion of the relevant econometric theory; and we have made such discussions more detailed in those solutions which relate to more recent research. Naturally, when the theory has already been explained in an earlier solution, it is not repeated, but reference is made to that previous solution. Moreover, to assist those readers who will wish to use the book in conjunction with a textbook, we have given references, as far as possible, to the major textbooks.

Although the questions are arranged in order of their topic, they are not always arranged in order of difficulty. But, when a topic is first introduced, it is usually done through simpler questions; and we have sometimes used numerical exercises to clarify the manipulations that are involved in a particular procedure. Subsequent questions on the same topic then tend to be of increasing difficulty. Therefore, both beginning and advanced students should find questions of interest throughout the book. Some questions deal with various aspects of applied work in econometrics and these questions are included towards the end of each chapter.

The book is divided into two volumes and this has enabled us to cover a fairly wide range of topics in the exercises. Volume I covers most of the usual textbook material dealing with regression techniques and their application in econometrics. Chapter 1 of this volume is concerned with a number of methodological issues that arise in the use of econometric techniques including the underlying concept of an econometric model and fundamental problems such as aggregation, causality and the distinction between recursive and interdependent systems. We also consider the problem of extracting and comparing the sampling distribution of least squares and other estimators in simple bivariate models allowing for serial correlation and errors of measurement. A large part of the remainder of the volume concentrates on methods of estimation and inference that apply to models that are linear in both variables and parameters (Chapters 2 and 4). There are many exercises illustrating standard results on the linear regression model. Most of these are contained in Chapter 2 and a number of extensions dealing with autocorrelated errors, multicollinearity, missing observations and seasonal adjustment are given in Chapter 4. We also consider multiple equation models with across equation parameter restrictions (Chapter 3) and covariance and error component models (Chapter 4). In

Chapter 5 we deal with non-linear regression models and models with errors in variables.

Volume II contains two chapters and deals with models of simultaneous equations (Chapter 6) and dynamic models (Chapter 7). Chapter 6 contains a number of introductory questions on identifiability and the use of single equation estimators such as two stage least squares and limited information maximum likelihood. A number of numerical questions have been included, as in Volume I, to lay out the sequence of manipulations needed to compute estimates and confidence intervals. The remaining questions in Chapter 6 deal with more advanced topics such as identifiability in the presence of cross equation parameter restrictions, systems methods of estimation, some simpler finite sample theory (Nagar's moment approximations and Edgeworth approximations) and an introduction to non-linear simultaneous equations models. Chapter 7 covers problems such as the identification of parameters in dynamic models with serially correlated errors, the consistent estimation of dynamic models with serially correlated errors, distributed lag models, continuous time models and models of markets in disequilibrium, as well as a number of applied questions. Much of the material in Chapter 7 has not yet appeared in textbooks and will, we hope, be of particular interest to advanced students and research workers.

Two major omissions from the book should also be noted: time series regression by spectral methods and the use of Bayesian methods in econometrics. These omissions were made with reluctance through pressure of space and time.

We are greatly indebted to the University of Auckland, the Australian National University and the Universities of Birmingham, Bristol, Essex, London and York for their permission to use questions which have appeared in their examinations. Where we have used questions from these examinations, or adapted them for our purpose here, this has been clearly indicated. Although it is impossible to give due credit to particular people in such cases, we acknowledge with special thanks that the following are among the authors of some of these questions: A.R. Bergstrom, R. Bowden, A. Chesher, J. Durbin, L.G. Godfrey, D.F. Hendry, G. Mizon, A.R. Pagan, J. Richmond, J.D. Sargan and K.F. Wallis. We are also grateful to J. Richmond, W. Barnett, V.B. Hall, E. Maasoumi and M. Prior for their comments on earlier versions of some of the questions and solutions. They are, of course, absolved from blame for any of the errors that remain.

Finally, it is with great pleasure that we thank Mrs Lucy Lowther, Mrs Sheila Ogden and Mrs Phyllis Pattenden for their skill, patience and good spirits in preparing the typescript.

P.C.B. PHILLIPS
M.R. WICKENS
July 1978

List of Symbols and Abbreviations

The following table comprises a list of principal symbols and abbreviations used in the book.

Symbol or Abbreviation	Meaning	Reference
A'	Transpose of the matrix A	
A^*	Complex conjugate transpose of the matrix A	
$AESS_i$	Additional explained sum of squares due to including variable i	p. 76
BAN	Best asymptotically normal	p. 146–147
b_{OLS}	Ordinary least squares estimator	p. 56
b_{GLS}	Generalised least squares estimator	p. 194
BLUE	Best linear unbiased estimator	
CES	Constant elasticity of substitution	
Const.	Constant	
CUAN	Consistent and uniformly asymptotically normal	p. 146
χ_n^2	Chi-squared distribution (or variable) with n degrees of freedom	p. 62

$\chi_n^2(\alpha)$	$P(\chi_n^2 > \chi_n^2(\alpha)) = \alpha$; $100\alpha\%$ significance point of the χ_n^2 distribution	
DW	Durbin—Watson statistic	p. 200
$E(\ )$	Mathematical expectation	
ESS	Explained sum of squares	p. 37
F_{n_1, n_2}	F distribution (or variable) with n_1 and n_2 degrees of freedom	p. 62
$F_{n_1, n_2}(\alpha)$	$P(F_{n_1, n_2} > F_{n_1, n_2}(\alpha)) = \alpha$; $100\alpha\%$ significance point of the F_{n_1, n_2} distribution	p. 63
FIML	Full information maximum likelihood	p. 274
GLS	Generalised least squares	p. 42
H_A	Hypothesis A	
i	$\sqrt{-1}$; complex constant	
$i(x)$	$= (2\pi)^{-1/2} \exp\left(-\frac{1}{2}x^2\right)$; standard normal density	
$I(x)$	$= \int_{-\infty}^{x} i(t)\,dt$; standard normal distribution function	
i_A	$A \times 1$ sum vector each of whose components is unity	p. 167
I_n	Identity matrix of order $n \times n$	p. 167
Im$(\ )$	Imaginary part of a complex quantity	
J_A	$A \times A$ matrix each of whose components is unity	p. 167
LIML	Limited information maximum likelihood	p. 290
ln$(\ )$	natural logarithm	
M_{xx}	$= T^{-1} \sum_{t=1}^{T} x_t x_t'$, sample moment matrix	p. 57

MLE	Maximum likelihood estimator	
$n!$	$= 1, 2, \ldots n; n$ factorial	
$N(\mu, \Sigma)$	Normal distribution with mean vector μ and co-variance matrix Σ	
O( ), o( )	Order of magnitude symbols	Cramér (1946, Ch. 20)
O_p( ), o_p( )	Probability order symbols	p. 107 and Mann and Wald (1943)
OLS	Ordinary least squares	p. 37
$\text{plim}_{T \to \infty}$, plim	Probability limit as $T \to \infty$	
R^2	Coefficient of determination	p. 61
$\bar{R}^2$	Corrected coefficient of determination	p. 61
Re( )	Real part of a complex quantity	
RSS	Residual sum of squares	p. 37
RSS_A	Residual sum of squares from a regression under Hypothesis A	p. 64
$RSS_{y \cdot 123\ldots}$	Residual sum of squares from regression of y on $x_1, x_2, x_3, \ldots$	p. 68
$r_{y1 \cdot 2}$	Partial correlation coefficient between y and χ_1, given χ_2	p. 68
t, n	Integers unless otherwise specified	
T	Integer representing sample size unless otherwise specified	
SE$(\hat{\gamma})$	Standard error of the estimator $\hat{\gamma}$	p. 67

$\text{tr}(A)$	$= \sum_{i=1}^{\min(m,\,n)} a_{ii}$ Trace of the matrix $A = (a_{ij})_{m \times n}$	
TSS	Total sum of squares	p. 62
vec (A)	$nm \times 1$ vector of the components of the $n \times m$ matrix A, by rows	p. xix
$\overline{\text{vec}}\,(A)$	$nm \times 1$ vector of the components of the $n \times m$ matrix A, by columns	p. xxii
V_{OLS}	Covariance matrix of the least squares estimator	p. 193
V_{GLS}	Covariance matrix of the generalised least squares estimator	p. 193
ΔX_t	$= X_t - X_{t-1}$; differencing operator	
LX_t	$= X_{t-1}$; log operator	
$\otimes$	Kronecker matrix product (right hand)	pp. xix–xx
2SLS	Two stage least squares	p. 272
3SLS	Three stage least squares	p. 274

To Emily and Ruth

CHAPTER 1

Concepts, methods and models

0. INTRODUCTION

In this chapter we consider the underlying principles of the econometric method, introduce the concept of an econometric model and illustrate how the theory of probability and the methods of statistical inference can be used in economics. The necessary notation will be given in each question.

1. QUESTIONS

Question 1.1

Econometrics has been defined as follows:

(a) 'The quantitative analysis of actual economic phenomena based on the concurrent development of theory and observations related by an appropriate method of inference', Samuelson (1954).

(b) 'The main objective of econometrics is to give empirical content to *a priori* reasoning in economics', Klein (1962).

(c) 'The aim of econometrics (is) the empirical determination of economic laws. Econometrics rounds off theory by using numerical data to verify the existence of postulated relationships and to define their precise forms', Malinvaud (1966).

In the light of these definitions discuss the nature of econometrics and distinguish the main activities with which it is concerned.

Question 1.2

The model of a certain market is

$$q_t^d = \alpha_0 - \alpha_1 p_t + \alpha_2 y_t + u_{1t} \qquad (1.2.1)$$

$$q_t^s = \beta_0 + \beta_1 p_t + \beta_2 t + u_{2t} \qquad (1.2.2)$$

$$q_t^d = q_t^s = q_t \qquad (1.2.3)$$

where q_t^d is quantity demanded, q_t^s is quantity supplied, q_t is quantity exchanged, p_t is price, y_t is income and u_{1t} and u_{2t} are random disturbances with zero means.

(a) Obtain the reduced form of the above model, interpret it, and explain its usefulness in forecasting.

(b) Find the expected change in q and p that would occur in period one as a result of introducing an excise tax at a rate of $r_t = 1$, where $\alpha_0 = 10$, $\alpha_1 = 0.5$, $\alpha_2 = 0.1$, $\beta_0 = 0$, $\beta_1 = 0.5$, $\beta_2 = 1$, and $y_1 = 100$.

(c) What tax rate is required in order to achieve in period one an expected price of 20? What is the expected value of q_1?

Question 1.3

The model

$$c_{it} = \alpha_i + \beta_i y_{it} + u_{it} \qquad (i = 1, \ldots, n; \quad t = 1, \ldots, T) \qquad (1.3.1)$$

explains the consumption c_{it} of the ith household at time t. The income of the ith household at time t is y_{it} and u_{it} is a disturbance term with zero mean, $E(u_{it}^2) = \sigma_i^2$ and $E(u_{it}u_{js}) = 0$ for all i and j and for $t \neq s$. Denote total consumption and total income at time t by $\bar{c}_t = \Sigma_{i=1}^n c_{it}$ and $\bar{y}_t = \Sigma_{i=1}^n y_{it}$, respectively, and let λ_{it} be the proportion of total income received by the ith household at time t.

(a) Derive the aggregate consumption function at time t and comment on its properties if:
   (i) λ_{it} is non-random; and
   (ii) $\lambda_{it} = \lambda_i + \epsilon_{it}$, where λ_i is non-random, $E(\epsilon_{it}) = 0$, $E(\epsilon_{it}^2) = \omega^2$ and $E(\epsilon_{it}\epsilon_{js}) = 0$ for all i and j and all $t \neq s$.

(b) If $\alpha_1 = 0$ for all i and $\bar{y}_t$ is non-random, derive the mean and variance of

$$b = \sum_{t=1}^T \bar{c}_t \bar{y}_t \bigg/ \sum_{t=1}^T \bar{y}_t^2 \qquad (1.3.2)$$

in cases (i) and (ii) above.

Question 1.4

(a) What do you understand by the following terms in the context of an economic model:

(i) causal relationship,
(ii) recursive model,
(iii) interdependent model?

(b) In the following model Y is real national income, Y^e is expected real national income, E is real private expenditure, E^e is expected real private expenditure and G is real government expenditure. The subscript t or $t-1$ indicates the relevant time period and a bar over a variable indicates that the variable is autonomous (or exogenously determined):

$$Y_t = aY_{t-1} + b \tag{1.4.1}$$
$$E_t^e = cY_t^e + d \tag{1.4.2}$$
$$E_t = E_t^e \tag{1.4.3}$$
$$G_t = \bar{G}_t \tag{1.4.4}$$
$$Y_t = E_t + G_t \tag{1.4.5}$$

Examine each of the relations in the above model for a causal interpretation. Is the model recursive?

Question 1.5

In the model

$$y_t = 3x_t + u_t \qquad (t = 1, 2) \tag{1.5.1}$$

the y_t are observable random variables, the x_t are known to take on the fixed values $x_1 = 1$, $x_2 = 2$, and the u_t are random errors which have the following discrete probability distribution for each value of t:

u_t	Probability
1	$\frac{1}{2}$
−1	$\frac{1}{2}$

(a) If u_1 and u_2 are statistically independent, find the sampling distributions of the following two estimators of the slope coefficient in (1.5.1):

$$a_1 = \sum_{t=1}^{2} y_t \Big/ \sum_{t=1}^{2} x_t \quad \text{and} \quad a_2 = \sum_{t=1}^{2} y_t x_t \Big/ \sum_{t=1}^{2} x_t^2 \tag{1.5.2}$$

Show that $\text{var}(a_1) > \text{var}(a_2)$.

(b) Suppose that u_1 and u_2 are no longer statistically independent but have instead the following joint probability distribution:

(u_1, u_2)	Probability
$(1, 1)$	$\frac{1}{10}$
$(1, -1)$	$\frac{4}{10}$
$(-1, 1)$	$\frac{4}{10}$
$(-1, -1)$	$\frac{1}{10}$

Find the new sampling distributions of the estimators a_1 and a_2 and verify that, in this case, $\mathrm{var}(a_1) < \mathrm{var}(a_2)$.

Question 1.6

In the model

$$y_t = x_t + u_t \qquad (t = 1, 2) \tag{1.6.1}$$

the y_t are observable random variables, and the u_t are serially independent random errors which have the following discrete probability distribution for each value of t:

u_t	Probability
1	$\frac{1}{2}$
-1	$\frac{1}{2}$

The x_t in (1.6.1) are exogenous and take on the fixed values $x_1 = 0$ and $x_2 = 1$. But x_1 is observed with error and we observe instead

$$X_1 = x_1 + v \tag{1.6.2}$$

where v is a random (measurement) error with the following probability distribution

v	Probability
ϵ	$\frac{1}{2}$
$-\epsilon$	$\frac{1}{2}$

where $0 < \epsilon < \frac{1}{3}$, and v is statistically independent of u_1 and u_2.
(a) Find the sampling distributions of the following three estimators of the slope coefficient (of unity) in (1.6.1):

$$a_1 = \frac{y_1 + y_2}{X_1 + x_2}, \quad a_2 = \frac{X_1 y_1 + x_2 y_2}{X_1^2 + x_2^2}, \quad a_3 = \frac{y_2 - y_1}{x_2 - X_1} \tag{1.6.3}$$

(b) Compare the relative concentration of the estimators in (1.6.3) about the true value of the slope coefficient by computing for each estimator the probability that it lies in the following intervals: (i) $[0.75, 1.25]$, and (ii) $[0, 2]$.

Question 1.7

In the following model of a free market for a certain good

$$q^s = 1 + p + u \qquad (1.7.1)$$

$$q^d = 3 - p + v \qquad (1.7.2)$$

$$q^s = q^d \qquad (1.7.3)$$

price, p, is determined in each period so that quantity supplied, q^s, equals quantity demanded, q^d. The random disturbances u and v are statistically independent and have the following probability distributions

u	Probability	v	Probability
1	$\frac{1}{3}$	1	$\frac{1}{3}$
0	$\frac{1}{3}$	0	$\frac{1}{3}$
−1	$\frac{1}{3}$	−1	$\frac{1}{3}$

(a) Find the probability distribution of the free market price p in (1.7.1−3) and determine its expected value.

(b) Suppose the government intervenes in the market by buying (or selling) an amount g of the good to ensure that price is fixed at its expected value (as determined in (a)). What is the probability distribution of g? Find the probability that government purchases of the good are at least as great as private demand, q^d.

Question 1.8

A firm uses the following model to forecast the demand for its product:

$$Q_t = \alpha + \beta Y_t + u_{1t}, \qquad (1.8.1)$$

$$C_t = \gamma + \delta Y_t + u_{2t}, \qquad (1.8.2)$$

$$I_t = \lambda(\theta Y_{t-1} - K_{t-1}) + u_{3t}, \qquad (1.8.3)$$

$$Y_t = C_t + I_t, \qquad (1.8.4)$$

$$K_t = K_{t-1} + I_t, \qquad (1.8.5)$$

where

Q_t = number of units of product demanded in year t,

Y_t = real national income in year t,

C_t = real consumption in year t,

I_t = real investment in year t,

K_t = real stock of capital at the end of year t,

u_{1t}, u_{2t}, u_{3t} = random disturbances in year t.

The disturbances u_{1t}, u_{2t} and u_{3t} are assumed to be normally distributed with zero means and covariance matrix

$$\begin{bmatrix} \sigma_{11} & 0 & 0 \\ 0 & \sigma_{22} & \sigma_{23} \\ 0 & \sigma_{23} & \sigma_{33} \end{bmatrix}.$$

The estimated values of the parameters in this model are: $\alpha = 100$, $\beta = 50$, $\gamma = 10$, $\delta = 0.5$, $\lambda = 0.5$, $\theta = 3$, $\sigma_{11} = 100$, $\sigma_{22} = 1$, $\sigma_{23} = 0.5$, $\sigma_{33} = 1$. The real national income in 1976 was £30 (thousand million) and the real stock of capital at the end of 1976 was £75 (thousand million).

Assuming that the true values of the parameters are equal to the above estimates and treating $Y_{1976} = 30$ and $K_{1976} = 75$ as known non-random numbers, forecast the value of Q_{1977} and find an interval within which there is a 0.95 probability that Q_{1977} will lie.

2. SUPPLEMENTARY QUESTIONS

Question 1.9

(a) A certain market has the following demand and supply functions in each period

$$D = 12 - 3P + 0.1Y + 2U$$

$$S = 5 + P + U$$

$$D = S$$

where D = demand, S = supply, P = price, Y = income and U is a random variable. If $U = 0$ with probability $\frac{1}{4}$ and $U = 1$ with probability $\frac{3}{4}$, and if $Y = 10$, compute the probability that the price exceeds 2
  (i) in 2 periods out of 3,
  (ii) in more than 80 periods out of 100.

(b) A buffer stock authority is set up to stabilise price within the interval $2 \leqslant P \leqslant 2.2$. What is the expected number of interventions by the authority in 100 periods?

(Adapted from University of Essex BA examinations, 1976.)

Question 1.10

In the model

$$y_t = 1 + 2x_t + u_t \qquad (t = 1, 2, 3)$$

the y_t are observable random variables, the x_t are known to take on the fixed values $x_1 = 0, x_2 = 1, x_3 = 2$ and the u_t are serially independent random errors which have the following discrete probability distribution for each value of t:

u_t	Probability
2	$\frac{1}{2}$
-2	$\frac{1}{2}$

(a) Obtain the sampling distributions of the ordinary least squares estimator of the slope coefficient and of the sum of squared residuals from the least squares regression.

(b) Verify that the sum of squared residuals is an unbiased estimator of the variance of the disturbances.

(Adapted from University of Essex MA examinations, 1975.)

Question 1.11

The observable random variables $y_t (t = 1, \ldots, T)$ and non-random quantities x_t satisfy the relation

$$y_t = \beta x_t + u_t \qquad (t = 1, \ldots, T)$$

The u_t are random disturbances each of which has mean zero and variance σ^2 and $E(u_s u_t) = 0$ when $s \neq t$. The estimators $\hat{b}$ and b^* of β are defined by

$$\hat{b} = \sum_{t=1}^{T} y_t \bigg/ \sum_{t=1}^{T} x_t$$

$$b^* = \sum_{t=1}^{T} x_t y_t \bigg/ \sum_{t=1}^{T} x_t^2$$

(a) Show that both $\hat{b}$ and b^* are unbiased estimators of β, but that the variance of $\hat{b}$ is greater than that of b^* except when the x_t are all equal in which case $\hat{b} = b^*$.

(b) Show also that the ratio of the variance of $\hat{b}$ to the variance of b^* is an increasing function of the ratio of the sample variance of the x_t to the squared sample mean of the x_t.

(Adapted from University of Auckland B Com. examinations, 1969.)

Question 1.12

The observable random variables $y_t (t = 1, \ldots, T)$ and non-random quantities $x_t (t = 1, \ldots, T)$ satisfy the relation

$$y_t = \alpha + \beta x_t + u_t \qquad (t = 1, \ldots, T) \tag{1.12.1}$$

The u_t are random disturbances each of which has mean zero and variance σ^2 and $E(u_s u_t) = 0$ when $s \neq t$. It is known that $T = 2n$ for some integer n and the observations $\{(y_t, x_t): t = 1, \ldots, T\}$ are divided into two groups of n with $\bar{x}_a$ and $\bar{x}_b$ denoting the means of the x_t in each group and $\bar{y}_a$ and $\bar{y}_b$ denoting the means of the y_t in each group. It is proposed that the parameter β in (1.12.1) be estimated by

$$\hat{\beta} = (\bar{y}_a - \bar{y}_b)/(\bar{x}_a - \bar{x}_b)$$

(a) Find $E(\hat{\beta})$ and var$(\hat{\beta})$.

(b) How would you allocate the pairs of observations into two groups in order to minimise var$(\hat{\beta})$? Explain why your optimum allocation does minimise var(β).

(Adapted from University of Birmingham B Soc Sc examinations, 1966.)

Question 1.13

In an investigation of the holding of stocks of finished output it is postulated that the level of stocks, Y_t, at the end of any year is a linear function of anticipations of future sales, X_t^*:

$$Y_t = \alpha + \beta X_t^* + u_t \tag{1.13.1}$$

where u_t is a random disturbance. It is further assumed that X_t^* is determined from actual sales, X_t, according to the following adaptive expectations mechanism:

$$X_t^* = X_{t-1}^* + \lambda(X_t - X_{t-1}^*) \qquad \text{(where } 0 < \lambda < 1\text{)} \tag{1.13.2}$$

On the basis of this theory a sample of 61 observations on X and Y is employed in an ordinary least squares regression which yields the following results:

$$Y_t = 73.2 + 0.112\ X_t + 0.620\ Y_{t-1} \qquad R^2 = 0.959 \tag{1.13.3}$$
$$\quad (51.3) \quad (0.024) \qquad (0.005) \qquad\qquad D.W. = 2.13$$

(numbers in parentheses denote standard errors)

(a) Explain how a relationship of the form estimated may be derived from equations (1.13.1) and (1.13.2).

(b) Do you consider ordinary least squares to be an appropriate estimation technique in this problem?

(c) On the presumption that ordinary least squares is an appropriate estimation technique, interpret the information provided in (1.13.3) as to the significance of the coefficients and calculate estimates of the theoretical parameters α, β and λ. Comment on the results you obtain.

(Adapted from University of Essex BA examinations, 1975.)

Question 1.14

In the following model Y is real national income, Y^e is real expected national income, E is real private expenditure, G is real government expenditure, M is real money balances and R is the rate of interest. The superscript $*$ attached to a variable indicates that it is a planned as opposed to an actual or realised value; and a bar over a variable indicates that it is autonomously determined (or exogenous).

$$E_t^* = \bar{A}_t + kY_t^e - aR_{t-1}$$

$$E_t = gE_t^* + (1-g)E_{t-1}$$

$$G_t = \bar{G}_t$$

$$M_t^* = mY_t^e - lR_{t-1}$$

$$M_t = dM_t^* + (1-d)M_{t-1}$$

$$M_t^s = \bar{M}$$

$$R_t = a(M_t - M_t^s)$$

$$Y_t^e = bY_{t-1} + (1-b)Y_{t-1}^e$$

$$Y_t = E_t + G_t$$

(a) Examine each of the relations in the above model for a causal interpretation.

(b) Draw an arrow diagram to indicate the causal links between the variables and indicate whether the model is recursive.

(For a model similar to the above but which is *not* recursive see Laidler, 1973.)

3. SOLUTIONS

Solution 1.1

Each of the quotations in the question provides a concise view of the subject matter of econometrics. Our intention in this solution is to outline in more detail the nature of econometrics and the activities that it involves. We hope to build on the quotations and analyse the more fundamental aspects of econometric model building in our answer. In this way, our discussion will remain generally in the area of the question but is not intended to be a closely argued response to or dissection of the definitions we have quoted in (a), (b) and (c).

Econometrics is a comparatively young branch of economics. It began to develop in a fairly distinct form in the 1930's when the need for a quantitative assessment of the implications of national economic policy decisions became most obvious during the world depression. But many economists had for long been aware of the shortcomings of economic analysis without quantification. One of the most urgent appeals for quantitative information on practical issues of economic policy was made as early as the beginning of this century by Pigou (1908). But it was not until the work of Frisch and Tinbergen in the 1930's and Haavelmo in the early 1940's that a scientific basis for the quantification of economic relations began to appear (see Haavelmo, 1944, in particular).

Since the use of a scientific approach has played such an important role in the development of econometrics it will be helpful to take this as the starting point in our discussion. Braithwaite (1968, p.1) states that

> the function of a science . . . is to establish general laws covering the behaviour of empirical events or objects with which the science in question is concerned, and thereby to enable us to connect together our knowledge of the separately known events, and to make reliable predictions of events as yet unknown.

Popper (1963, p.222) takes a similar view:

> The conscious task before the scientist is always the solution of a problem through the construction of a theory which solves the problem; for example, by explaining unexpected and unexplained observations.

The scientific method consists, first, of formulating a theory or an 'axiomatized deductive system' (Popper, 1963, p.221) — that is, a set of hypotheses arranged in order with 'the hypotheses at the highest level being those which occur only as premises in the system (and) those at the lowest level being those which occur as conclusions in the system' (Braithwaite, 1968, p.12). These conclusions are sometimes known as the predictions of the theory. The theory itself, including its predictions, will have an overall structure resting on axioms and logical reasoning similar to that which characterises the deductive method of pure mathematics and logic. When a theory has been conceived and its logical implications explored, we may wish to examine the ability of the theory to explain observed phenomena. To do so we need to record the predictions of a theory and to compare these with the observed facts which the theory purports to explain.

To proceed in this way in economics, we need numerical observations of the economic quantities in which we are interested and a procedure for measuring the relationships between the various economic quantities that are implied by an underlying economic theory. We must also take account of the fact that a theory and its predictions cannot normally be accepted or rejected with complete confidence (i.e. with a probability of unity) on a given set of data; there is almost always a positive probability of an incorrect decision (or inference) being made. Hence we need rules for testing the validity of the relationships suggested by the theory on the strength of their correspondence with the actual observations. It is with these various procedures that the subject of econometrics is concerned.

To take this discussion any further, it will be helpful to consider the very useful set of guidelines concerning the subject matter of econometrics which were laid out in Haavelmo (1944) and later by Bergstrom (1966). Haavelmo and Bergstrom found it convenient to speak of econometrics in terms of the activities it includes. These are:

(a) the formulation of econometric models;
(b) the estimation and statistical testing of these models with observed data; and
(c) the use of these models for prediction and policy purposes.

To clarify the concept of an econometric model we need to recall the meaning of the term 'model' itself. One definition of a model is 'a simplified representation of a real-world process'. Popper (1959, p.142) believes that a model should be as simple as possible:

> Simple statements, if knowledge is our object, are to be prized more highly than less simple ones because they tell us more; because their empirical content is greater; and because they are better testable.

Friedman (1953, p.14) also expresses this view:

> A hypothesis is important if it 'explains' much by little, that is, if it abstracts the common and crucial elements from the mass of complex and detailed circumstances surrounding the phenomena to be explained and permits valid predictions on the basis of them alone.

The choice of a simple model to explain complex phenomena in the real world may lead to the criticisms that the model is oversimplified and that the assumptions that underlie it are unrealistic. Such criticisms are often made of the models which are developed in economic theory and which we call economic models. Koopmans (1957) argues that the use of models in economics can be defended against such criticisms if we look upon economic theory as a sequence of models

> ... that seek to express in simplified form different aspects of an always more complicated reality. At first, these aspects are formalised as much as feasible in isolation, then in combinations of increasing realism. ... The study of simpler models is protected from the reproach of unreality by the consideration that these models may be prototypes of more complicated subsequent models. The card file of successfully completed pieces of reasoning represented by these models can then be looked upon as the logical core of economics, as the depository of available economic theory. (pp.142–143)

The premises on which each member of this sequence of models rest involve approximations to reality and often comprise what seem to be rather crude simplifications of the objectives behind the behaviour of various economic agents such as consumers and producers in an actual economy. But the models themselves

> ... exhibit in a striking manner the power of deductive reasoning in drawing conclusions which, *to the extent one accepts their premises* [our italics, P–W], are highly relevant to questions of economic policy. In many cases the knowledge these deductions yield is the best we have, either because better approximations have not been secured at the level of the premises, or because comparable reasoning from premises recognised as more realistic has not been

completed or has not yet been found possible. (Koopmans, 1957, p.142).

Friedman (1953) argues that

> . . . the relevant question to ask about the assumptions of a theory is not whether they are descriptively 'realistic', for they never are, but whether they are sufficiently good approximations for the purpose in hand. And this question can be answered only by seeing whether the theory works, which means whether it yields sufficiently accurate predictions. (p.15)

A closely related view has recently been put forward by Fair (1974) who looks on

> . . . a theoretical model . . . as not so much true or false as useful or not useful. The model is useful if it aids in the specification of empirical relationships that one would not normally have thought of from a simpler model and that are in turn confirmed by the data. (p.16)

It is with the 'specification of empirical relationships' that the primary task of econometrics is concerned (activity (a) above). In this activity, the econometrician can be guided by the models which have been developed, in abstract, in economic theory within the particular area under study as well as the evidence that may have accumulated from previous empirical studies in the same area. He must then select the economic ideas that seem appropriate to the phenomena in question and reframe the economic model which embodies these ideas into a form sufficiently precise to be estimated from a series of observations on the relevant variables. Once the model is in this form it becomes known as an econometric model.

To clarify the decisions that need to be made in the passage to an econometric model we note that: (a) the relationships in an economic model often take a form which is too general for statistical fitting; and (b) economic models normally, but not necessarily, exclude random elements in behaviour. In formulating an econometric model, therefore, it is usually necessary to decide which variables should be included explicitly in the model (often this will depend on the statistical data that are available) and what functional form the relationship between these variables should take. The formulation of an econometric model also involves the introduction of random disturbances to allow for random elements in behaviour that are not accounted for in the underlying theory and to allow for errors resulting from the omission of variables (whose individual effects are thought to be unimportant) and from the possible mis-specification of the functional form of the relationships; in addition, the model may involve random errors of measurement in the observable economic variables to account for the inaccuracies that may be present in the statistical data to be used. We will discuss some of these points further in solution 1.2.

Bergstrom (1966 and 1967) has provided useful definitions of the terms 'economic model' and 'econometric model' which express the above ideas in a precise way. With some adaptation his definitions are as follows:

(a) An **economic model** is any set of assumptions and relationships which approximately describe the behaviour of an economy or a sector of an economy.

(b) An **econometric model** is normally composed of two parts: first, a system of equations relating observable economic variables and unobservable random variables called disturbances (representing the outcome of political, social and other events not directly incorporated into the equations themselves) and measurement errors (representing errors of measurement in the observations of the economic variables); second, a set of assumptions about the stochastic properties of the random variables (including perhaps — but not necessarily — their probability distribution).

The subject of estimation and statistical testing which we have given as the second activity in econometrics (see (b) above) suggests a close link with the subject of mathematical statistics. It is, indeed, true that many of the statistical methods in use in econometrics draw heavily on procedures which have been developed in the literature of mathematical statistics and applied in the natural sciences. But there are important differences. In the natural sciences the data are often, but not always (c.f. astronomy), subject to experimental control so that an experiment can, for instance, be designed to highlight the particular effects in which an investigator is interested; and the number of sample observations in which an experiment can often be readily increased (although this is sometimes an expensive process), making established procedures of statistical inference that are based on large samples more reliable. But these conditions frequently do not apply to economic data. An econometrician often has to deal with only a small quantity of data, some of which may well contain large inaccuracies or errors of measurement. The data are rarely subject to experimental control and almost always embody non-economic influences. Moreover, the models that are used in econometrics, typically involve *a priori* parameter restrictions (reflecting the information derived from economic theory which we wish to utilise in the specification of the model) and these restrictions often lead us to rather complicated systems of equations which can best be handled by statistical procedures rather different from those in use in the natural sciences.

Econometric model building is not without its critics. Serious doubts are sometimes expressed about the particular specification of an econometric model on the grounds that it is not an adequate empirical representation of the underlying economic model. It may be thought, for example, that the use of a linear econometric model, or the assumption that the econometric model has a time invariant functional form throughout the sample period, are poor approximations. Another criticism often voiced is that an econometric model is not compatible with the type of data to be used. An econometric model based on an economic model of the individual economic agent or commodity may not be suitable for use with data aggregated over individuals or commodities. Problems may also

occur if the data are aggregated over a period of time longer than that to
which the economic model applies.

Even when an econometric model is found to be compatible with the
data on the basis of conventional (non-predictive) statistical tests, there
may still be problems. The model may, for example, be found to be
compatible with several different (and competing) underlying economic
hypotheses. Alternatively, the data may afford support for different
econometric models. Often an econometric model is found to perform
well on one set of data but to perform badly on another set (for instance,
by poor forecasting). This is frequently important evidence of the
inadequacy of the specification of the econometric model. Predictive tests
such as this should be part of the standard procedures.

The adequacy of conventional predictive and non-predictive statistical
tests and the suitability of the method of estimating the econometric
model may depend critically upon the (often implicitly assumed)
stochastic properties of the disturbances of the model — see the second
part of Bergstrom's definition of an econometric model given above. The
failure of the disturbances to satisfy certain assumptions (such as serial
independence) can invalidate the tests and lead to incorrect inferences. It
can also mean that the estimation technique produces estimates with
undesirable statistical properties.

The recent study by Granger and Newbold (1974) reinforces much of
the textbook advice on this point. To help avoid these problems, tests
should be performed of these assumptions.

An interesting challenge to econometric model building has recently
been issued by those who prefer to use for forecasting purposes time
series modelling techniques that do not necessarily link with econometric
theory, rather than econometric models. In this connection the results of
Cooper (1972), Nelson (1972), Granger and Newbold (1974) and Christ
(1975) are of special interest. The time series modelling approach is to fit
simple parametric models (called ARIMA models — see question 7.16) to
univariate and, more recently, to multivariate economic time series and
then to use these models for prediction. In some cases this approach has
been successful, but not so in others (see Chatfield and Prothero, 1973).
The significance of this challenge for econometricians is not so much that
this type of time series modelling is an alternative to econometric model
building but rather that it should focus more attention in econometrics
on improving the specification of both systems and error dynamics. For a
useful reconciliation of the two approaches, see Wallis (1977).

These considerations do not make the task of an econometrician any
easier but should sharpen awareness of the dangers of over-reaching in
conclusions and encourage acceptance of the view that a model is an
approximation which, at best, will prove useful in explaining observed
data. If it is useful in this way, then the results provide an important
feedback and stimulus to the process of guiding the development of more

realistic models. This refers not only to the underlying economic hypotheses but also the statistical assumptions underlying the construction of the econometric model.

Each of the definitions in the question embody the two aspects of the scientific method we have discussed: first, the *a priori* reasoning required in the development of economic theory as a deductive system and leading to the 'laws' that underlie the construction of an econometric model; and second, the testing of the predictions of such theory by statistical inference using empirical evidence. Thus the econometrician frequently finds that there are two rather different jobs of work to be done: assisting the theorist in the refinement of models and designing tools of statistical inference appropriate to the models to be used. In Malinvaud's words:

> The art of the econometrician consists as much in defining a good model as in finding an efficient statistical procedure. Indeed, this is why he cannot be purely a statistician, but must have a solid grounding in economics. Only if this is so, will he be aware of the mass of accumulated knowledge which relates to the particular question under study and must find expression in the model. Malinvaud (1970b, p.723).

Solution 1.2

Part (a). Substituting equation (1.2.3) into (1.2.1) and (1.2.2) we obtain the 'structural' form of model:

$$q_t = \alpha_0 - \alpha_1 p_t + \alpha_2 y_t + u_{1t} \tag{1.2.4}$$

$$q_t = \beta_0 + \beta_1 p_t + \beta_2 t + u_{2t} \tag{1.2.5}$$

The structural equations (1.2.4) and (1.2.5) embody the *a priori* knowledge derived from economic theory. Thus (1.2.4) is a demand function and (1.2.5) is a supply function. The decision of which variables to include and which to exclude from these equations is made in the light of economic theory. These two equations describe the behaviour of the market. They indicate that quantity and price are determined simultaneously *within* the market. For this reason q and p are called **endogenous** variables. On the other hand, y and t are not determined within the market but outside it. They are called **exogenous** variables.

The disturbances u_{1t} and u_{2t} shift the demand and supply functions randomly. They are called structural disturbances or structural errors. They represent the combined effect of all omissions and errors. In practice it is inevitable that an econometric model such as (1.2.4)–(1.2.5) will be an oversimplification of the ideas that underlie the economic model. Common reasons are that the wrong functional form is chosen or that variables have been omitted or again that the variables included are measured with error. All of these errors are captured by random disturbance terms. Frequently we appeal to the central limit theorem to argue that the disturbances are normally distributed. In principle no single omitted variable or functional error should be so large as to dominate the disturbance term. If it does, then the central limit theorem will not be applicable even approximately. In this case, the variable omitted, for example, should be included explicitly in the structural equation. Of course, the normality of the disturbance term cannot be taken to be either a necessary or a sufficient condition for the satisfactory specification of an equation.

If we want to determine the total effect on an endogenous variable of a change in an exogenous variable we use the reduced form of the model. The reduced form expresses each endogenous variable as a function of the exogenous variables and the structural disturbances. Solving (1.2.4) and (1.2.5) for q and p as a function of y, t, a constant and a disturbance, we obtain the reduced forms

$$q_t = \left(\frac{\alpha_0\beta_1 + \alpha_1\beta_0}{\alpha_1 + \beta_1}\right) + \left(\frac{\alpha_2\beta_1}{\alpha_1 + \beta_1}\right)y_t + \left(\frac{\alpha_1\beta_2}{\alpha_1 + \beta_1}\right)t + \left(\frac{\beta_1 u_{1t} + \alpha_1 u_{2t}}{\alpha_1 + \beta_1}\right)$$

and   (1.2.6)

$$p_t = \left(\frac{\alpha_0 - \beta_0}{\alpha_1 + \beta_1}\right) + \left(\frac{\alpha_2}{\alpha_1 + \beta_1}\right)y_t - \left(\frac{\beta_2}{\alpha_1 + \beta_1}\right)t + \left(\frac{u_{1t} - u_{2t}}{\alpha_1 + \beta_1}\right) \quad (1.2.7)$$

The coefficients of the exogenous variables in the reduced form can be interpreted as (impact) multipliers. Thus $\partial q_t/\partial y_t = \alpha_2\beta_1/(\alpha_1 + \beta_1)$ and $\partial p_t/\partial y_t = \alpha_2/(\alpha_1 + \beta_1)$. It should be noted that $\partial q_t/\partial y_t$ obtained from either (1.2.4) or (1.2.5) measures the partial response of q to changes in y with p, the other exogenous variables and the disturbances held fixed. The term $\partial q_t/\partial y_t$ obtained from the reduced form measures the total change in q_t for a unit change in y_t with the remaining exogenous variables and the disturbances held fixed, but with p_t being allowed to change. Using the demand function (1.2.4), the relationship between the two derivatives is

$$(\partial q_t/\partial y_t)_{\text{RF}} = (\partial q_t/\partial p_t)_{\text{D}} (\partial p_t/\partial y_t)_{\text{RF}} + (\partial q_t/\partial y_t)_{\text{D}}$$

$$= (-\alpha_1)[\alpha_2/(\alpha_1 + \beta_1)] + \alpha_2 = \alpha_2\beta_1/(\alpha_1 + \beta_1) \quad (1.2.8)$$

Using the supply function we obtain

$$(\partial q_t/\partial y_t)_{\text{RF}} = (\partial q_t/\partial p_t)_{\text{S}} (\partial p_t/\partial y_t)_{\text{RF}} + (\partial q_t/\partial y_t)_{\text{S}}$$

$$= (\beta_1)[\alpha_2/(\alpha_1 + \beta_1)] + 0 = \alpha_2\beta_1/(\alpha_1 + \beta_1) \quad (1.2.9)$$

The suffixes in (1.2.8) and (1.2.9) denote the equations from which the derivative is obtained.

In figure 1.2 the above result is shown diagrammatically. S denotes the supply function (1.2.5), and D_0 denotes the demand function (1.2.4)

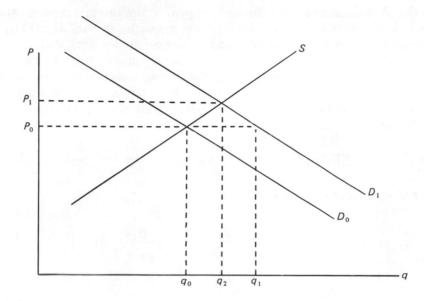

Figure 1.1

before y_t is changed and D_1 is the demand function after y_t is increased by, say, one unit. The distance $q_1 - q_0 = \alpha_2$ shows the change in demand at the original price p_0. The distance $q_1 - q_2$ is the reduction in demand due to the rise in price from p_0 to p_1, namely $\alpha_1 (p_1 - p_0) = \alpha_1 \alpha_2 / (\alpha_1 + \beta_1)$. The distance $q_2 - q_0$ is the total effect on q of a change in y, namely

$$q_2 - q_0 = (q_1 - q_0) - (q_1 - q_2) = \alpha_2 - \alpha_1 \alpha_2 / (\alpha_1 + \beta_1)$$
$$= \alpha_2 \beta_1 / (\alpha_1 + \beta_1).$$

The reduced form is clearly the appropriate model to use for forecasting the value of an endogenous variable for given values of the exogenous variables and the disturbances, as it measures the total effect on the endogenous variable of each of these variables. Since the endogenous variables are random variables we normally predict their *expected* value. The expected value of q_t is obtained by taking the mathematical expectation of the reduced form equation for q, (1.2.6):

$$E(q_t) = \left(\frac{\alpha_0 \beta_1 + \alpha_1 \beta_0}{\alpha_1 + \beta_1} \right) + \left(\frac{\alpha_2 \beta_1}{\alpha_1 + \beta_1} \right) y_t + \left(\frac{\alpha_1 \beta_2}{\alpha_1 + \beta_1} \right) t$$

$$+ \left(\frac{\beta_1 E(u_{1t}) + \alpha_1 E(u_{2t})}{\alpha_1 + \beta_1} \right) \qquad (1.2.10)$$

Part (b). Although a tax rate does not appear in the original model, using economic theory we are able to introduce one without invalidating any evidence that may have been acquired on the original model, such as estimates of the coefficients of the model based on data prior to the introduction of the tax. This is a major advantage of econometric models over conventional statistical models which typically are not specified using economic theory. Introducing the tax affects only the supply function (1.2.5) which becomes

$$q_t = \beta_0 + \beta_1(p_t - r_t) + \beta_2 t + u_{2t}. \tag{1.2.11}$$

The reduced form equations are now

$$q_t = \left(\frac{\alpha_0\beta_1 + \alpha_1\beta_0}{\alpha_1 + \beta_1}\right) + \left(\frac{\alpha_2\beta_1}{\alpha_1 + \beta_1}\right)y_t + \left(\frac{\alpha_1\beta_2}{\alpha_1 + \beta_1}\right)t - \left(\frac{\alpha_1\beta_1}{\alpha_1 + \beta_1}\right)r_t$$

$$+ \left(\frac{\beta_1 u_{1t} + \alpha_1 u_{2t}}{\alpha_1 + \beta_1}\right) \tag{1.2.12}$$

$$p_t = \left(\frac{\alpha_0 - \beta_0}{\alpha_1 + \beta_1}\right) + \left(\frac{\alpha_2}{\alpha_1 + \beta_1}\right)y_t - \left(\frac{\beta_2}{\alpha_1 + \beta_1}\right)t + \left(\frac{\beta_1}{\alpha_1 + \beta_1}\right)r_t$$

$$+ \left(\frac{u_{1t} - u_{2t}}{\alpha_1 + \beta_1}\right) \tag{1.2.13}$$

Substituting into (1.2.12) and (1.2.13) the values of the coefficients and the expected values of u_{1t} and u_{2t} we obtain

$$E(q_t) = 5 + 0.05y_t + 0.5t - 0.25r_t \tag{1.2.14}$$

$$E(p_t) = 10 + 0.1y_t - t + 0.5r_t. \tag{1.2.15}$$

In period one, (1.2.14) and (1.2.15) become

$$E(q_1) = 5 + 0.05(100) + 0.5(1) - 0.25(1) = 10.25$$

$$E(p_1) = 10 + 0.1(100) - (1) + 0.5(1) = 19.5,$$

our required results.

Part (c). In order to find the value of r_t for any target value of $E(p_t)$, we solve (1.2.15) for r_t giving

$$r_t = -20 + 2E(p_t) - 0.2y_t + 2t. \tag{1.2.16}$$

In period one and for a target value of $E(p_1) = 20$, the required tax rate is

$$r_1 = -20 + 2(20) - 0.2(100) + 2 = 2.$$

From (1.2.15)

$$E(q_1) = 5 + 0.05(100) + 0.5(1) - 0.25(2) = 10.$$

In general, the appropriate model for fixed or flexible target policy analysis or for optimal control is the reduced form (see Peston, 1974 and Chow, 1975).

Solution 1.3

Part (a). Aggregating (1.3.1) over all n households we obtain the aggregate consumption function

$$\sum_{i=1}^{n} c_{it} = \sum_{i=1}^{n} \alpha_i + \sum_{i=1}^{n} \beta_i y_{it} + \sum_{i=1}^{n} u_{it} \qquad (t = 1, \dots, T) \tag{1.3.3}$$

or, using the aggregate variables $\bar{c}_t$ and $\bar{y}_t$,

$$\bar{c}_t = \bar{\alpha} + \bar{\beta}_t \bar{y}_t + \bar{u}_t \tag{1.3.4}$$

where $\bar{\alpha} = \sum_{i=1}^{n} \alpha_i$,

$$\bar{\beta}_t = \sum_{i=1}^{n} \beta_i y_{it} \bigg/ \sum_{i=1}^{n} y_{it} = \sum_{i=1}^{n} \beta_i \lambda_{it}, \tag{1.3.5}$$

$\bar{u}_t = \sum_{i=1}^{n} u_{it}$, $E(\bar{u}_t) = 0$, $E(\bar{u}_t^2) = \sum_{i=1}^{n} \sigma_i^2$ and $E(\bar{u}_t \bar{u}_s) = 0$ for all $t \neq s$.
(i) If λ_{it} is non-random then $\bar{\beta}_t$, the 'macro' marginal propensity to consume, is also non-random. $\bar{\beta}_t$ is a weighted average of the time invariant individual marginal propensities to consume β_i. As the weights λ_{it} are dependent on time, $\bar{\beta}_t$ is also time dependent. The aggregate consumption function, equation (1.3.4), is, therefore, an example of a model with a time varying parameter. Only if λ_{it} is independent of time is $\bar{\beta}_t$ a constant and (1.3.4) a conventional linear model with constant coefficients and a disturbance term with zero mean and constant variance.
(ii) If $\lambda_{it} = \lambda_i + \epsilon_{it}$ with λ_i non-random then

$$\bar{\beta}_t = \sum_{i=1}^{n} \beta_i \lambda_i + \sum_{i=1}^{n} \beta_i \epsilon_{it}$$

$$= \beta^* + \epsilon_t^* \tag{1.3.6}$$

where β^* is a constant and ϵ_t^* is a random variable with $E(\epsilon_t^*) \equiv 0$, $E(\epsilon_t^{*2})$

$= \omega^2 \Sigma_{i=1}^n \beta_i^2$ and $E(\epsilon_t^* \epsilon_s^*) = 0$ for all $t \neq s$. Thus $\bar{\beta}_t$ is a serially independent random variable with mean β^* and variance $\omega^2 \Sigma_{i=1}^n \beta_i^2$. Equation (1.3.4) can now be interpreted as a model with a random coefficient. Substituting (1.3.6) into (1.3.4) we obtain

$$\bar{c}_t = \bar{\alpha} + \beta^* \bar{y}_t + u_t^* \tag{1.3.7}$$

where $u_t^* = \bar{u}_t + \epsilon_t^* \bar{y}_t, E(u_t^*) = 0, E(u_t^{*2}) = \Sigma_{i=1}^n \sigma_i^2 + \omega^2 (\Sigma_{i=1}^n \beta_i^2) \bar{y}_t^2$, $E(u_t^* u_s^*) = 0$ for all $t \neq s$ and $E(u_t^* \bar{y}_t) = 0$. The variance of the disturbance term in (1.3.7) is dependent on time and, therefore, heteroskedastic.

Part (b). (i) In this case b, the regression coefficient of $\bar{c}_t$ on $\bar{y}_t$, is

$$b = \sum_{t=1}^T \bar{c}_t \bar{y}_t \Big/ \sum_{t=1}^T \bar{y}_t^2$$

$$= \sum_{t=1}^T (\bar{\beta}_t \bar{y}_t^2 + \bar{u}_t \bar{y}_t) \Big/ \sum_{t=1}^T \bar{y}_t^2 .$$

Since $\bar{y}_t$ is, by assumption, non-random,

$$E(b) = \sum_{t=1}^T \bar{\beta}_t \bar{y}_t^2 \Big/ \sum_{t=1}^T \bar{y}_t^2 = \sum_{t=1}^T \bar{\beta}_t w_t, \tag{1.3.8}$$

where $w_t = \bar{y}_t^2 / \Sigma_{t=1}^T \bar{y}_t^2$. Thus $E(b)$ is a weighted average of the $\bar{\beta}_t$ for $t = 1, \ldots, T$.

The variance of b is

$$E[b - E(b)]^2 = E\left(\sum_{t=1}^T \bar{u}_t \bar{y}_t \Big/ \sum_{t=1}^T \bar{y}_t^2\right)^2$$

$$= \sum_{t=1}^T E(\bar{u}_t^2) \bar{y}_t^2 \Big/ \left(\sum_{t=1}^T \bar{y}_t^2\right)^2 + \sum \sum_{t \neq s} E(\bar{u}_t \bar{u}_s) \bar{y}_t \bar{y}_s \Big/ \left(\sum_{t=1}^T \bar{y}_t^2\right)^2$$

$$= \sum_{i=1}^n \sigma_i^2 \Big/ \sum_{t=1}^T \bar{y}_t^2 . \tag{1.3.9}$$

When $\bar{\beta}_t$ is independent of time and equals $\bar{\beta}$, say, then $E(b) = \bar{\beta}$ but the variance of b is still given by (1.3.9).
(ii) In this case

$$b = \beta^* + \sum_{t=1}^T u_t^* \bar{y}_t \Big/ \sum_{t=1}^T \bar{y}_t^2 .$$

Hence $E(b) = \beta^*$, that is b is an unbiased estimator of β^*, and the variance of b is

$$E(b - \beta^*)^2 = E\left(\sum_{t=1}^{T} u_t^* \bar{y}_t \Big/ \sum_{t=1}^{T} \bar{y}_t^2\right)^2$$

$$= \sum_{t=1}^{T} E(u_t^{*2}) \bar{y}_t^2 \Big/ \left(\sum_{t=1}^{T} \bar{y}_t^2\right)^2 + \sum_{t \neq s} \sum E(u_t^* u_s^*) \bar{y}_t \bar{y}_s \Big/ \left(\sum_{t=1}^{T} \bar{y}_t^2\right)^2$$

$$= \sum_{t=1}^{T} \left[\sum_{i=1}^{n} \sigma_i^2 + \omega^2 \left(\sum_{i=1}^{n} \beta_i^2\right) \bar{y}_t^2\right] \bar{y}_t^2 \Big/ \left(\sum_{t=1}^{T} \bar{y}_t^2\right)^2$$

$$= \left(\sum_{i=1}^{n} \sigma_i^2 \Big/ \sum_{t=1}^{T} \bar{y}_t^2\right) + \left[\omega^2 \left(\sum_{i=1}^{n} \beta_i^2\right) \left(\sum_{t=1}^{T} \bar{y}_t^4\right) \Big/ \left(\sum_{t=1}^{T} \bar{y}_t^2\right)^2\right].$$

As the variance of u_t^* is not constant for all t, b is not an efficient estimator of β^*. We would need to use generalised least squares in order to obtain an efficient estimator (see question 2.12).

Solution 1.4

Part (a). We start our solution with a brief discussion of the meaning of a **causal relationship**. It would be helpful in this respect if we could provide an unambiguous statement about the fundamental concept of causality. While attempts to discuss causality in a very general way have led to much controversy in philosophy, it can still be argued that the concept of causality is of great operational significance in scientific work, particularly in the area of experimental science. In economics the importance of the notion of causality in the construction and use of models has often been emphasized, particularly in the extensive writings of Herman Wold. Fortunately, it seems possible to define more narrowly a concept of causality which is adequate for model building situations in economics. Both Wold (1954) and Simon (1953) have done this and the reader is strongly recommended to consult their articles. Both authors stress that causality is a theoretical concept which must be interpreted in the context of a formal theoretical model. As we have seen in solution 1.1, models in economics involve a set of assumptions and relationships among economic variables which are often expressed in mathematical form as, for instance,

$$y = f(x_1, \ldots, x_n) \tag{1.4.6}$$

Wold then defines this relationship to be causal if the variables $x_1, \ldots, x_n$ would be regarded as the 'cause' variables and y the 'effect' variable in a (fictitious) controlled experiment. In other words, if the relationship (1.4.6) were being investigated by a controlled experiment, the relationship would be said to be causal if the variables $x_1, \ldots, x_n$ were under the experimenter's control and the variable y measured the observed effect of the experiment. Of course, controlled experimentation in economics is virtually impossible so this way of regarding (1.4.6) must remain somewhat abstract.

It is also possible to think of (1.4.6) as a *directed* functional relationship. That is, according to (1.4.6) the variables $y, x_1, \ldots, x_n$ are functionally related and, in addition, the direction of the relationship from $x_1, \ldots, x_n$ to y is an *essential* element of the specification. Otherwise, we might well have written, instead of (1.4.6),

$$x_i = g(y, x_1, \ldots, x_{i-1}, x_{i+1}, \ldots, x_n) \qquad (1.4.7)$$

with the different function $g(\ )$, and x_i now appearing as a dependent variable [under certain conditions on the function $f(\ )$ we *can* write (1.4.6) in the alternative form (1.4.7)]. If (1.4.6) and (1.4.7) are treated as equivalent specifications in a theoretical model then that model attaches a symmetry to the roles of y and the x_i in the relationship (1.4.6). It is this very symmetry which is absent from a causal relationship and indeed the 'common sense' notion of causality. In a causal relationship between a number of variables, direction is an essential component which must be clarified at an early stage in the construction of the model. When the direction of the relationship is specified then the relationship is asymmetrical in much the same way as common sense examples of causality are asymmetrical. We give the following two examples:

pot placed over fire → increase in temperature of water in pot

and

earthquake → burst dam → valley floods.

Each of these examples involves a **chain of causation**. The arrows are an essential part of the reasoning and make the overall statements asymmetric (if we reverse the arrows the statements no longer square with common sense!). We can, in a similar way, build up the concept of causality based on the idea of an asymmetrical functional relationship and Simon (1953) provides a careful treatment of the subject along these lines.

The idea of a chain of causation is very useful when we come to analyse the underlying nature of an economic model. It has been systematically applied by Herman Wold in the development of recursive (or causal chain) systems. A recursive model is one which displays the following features (Wold, 1954, p.172):

(i) The model refers to a sequence of years, months or other time units.
(ii) All relations of the model are causal with two types of variables: endogenous which it is the purpose of the model to explain and exogenous, which are auxiliary. In every relation of the model the effect variable is thus endogenous, while the cause variables are either endogenous or exogenous.
(iii) The model has one, and only one, causal relation for each endogenous variable.
(iv) Given the development of the exogenous variables and a set of initial values for the endogenous variables, the model allows us to calculate, recursively, the development of the endogenous variables.

The nature of the chain of causation in a recursive system can be illustrated by the use of arrow diagrams such as the following:

Recursive model   *Arrow diagram*

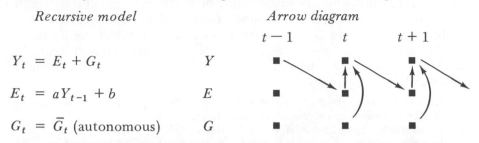

$$Y_t = E_t + G_t \qquad\qquad Y$$

$$E_t = aY_{t-1} + b \qquad\qquad E$$

$$G_t = \bar{G}_t \text{ (autonomous)} \qquad G$$

This model is a simple form of the model given in the question and the variables are as they are defined there. The arrow diagram indicates the causal connections between the variables and the lags that operate in the various relationships. We note that all relations between two variables are unilateral and that all arrows between variables in the same time period are in the same direction. This is consistent with our notion of directed functional relationships. It is easy to see that the model satisfies Wold's criteria (i)–(iv) above and it is, indeed, a recursive system.

Arrow diagrams such as the one we have just employed were used by Tinbergen and Wold in the development of models and the analysis of their underlying features. They were also systematically used in a searching article by Bentzel and Hansen (1954) on the basis for recursive and interdependent systems in economics. In an interdependent system the arrow diagram has quite different features from those that apply in recursive systems. We need only illustrate with the following model, closely related to the one we have just considered:

Interdependent model   *Arrow diagram*

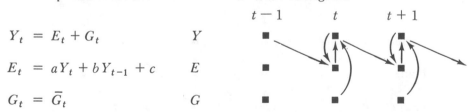

$$Y_t = E_t + G_t \qquad\qquad Y$$

$$E_t = aY_t + bY_{t-1} + c \qquad E$$

$$G_t = \bar{G}_t \qquad\qquad G$$

We notice in the arrow diagram of this model that the arrows between any two variables are not always unidirectional. Between Y and E in any one time period we find two arrows and hence two relations. This means, for example, that E is at once both a cause and an effect of Y.

Consequently, this model cannot be adequately described by a chain of causation. We say that Y and E are jointly and simultaneously determined in this system and the model is described as interdependent. The fact that interdependent models do not embody consistent chains of causation is not in itself a very powerful criticism. These models are best regarded as approximations to the underlying process by which the variables are determined; and, in this process, the time lag between the change in one variable and its influence on another may be sufficiently small (relative to the time unit we are using in the model) for interdependence to be a suitable approximation. There are many other reasons which justify the use of interdependent systems and the reader is urged to consult Bentzel and Hansen (1954) for a detailed discussion. We leave the final word in our general discussion to them:

> On a very abstract level of economic theory there seems to be a very strong case for the recursive type of model. In a certain sense it may be said to be a fundamental type of model in economic theory. Theory on this level is, however, so abstract that it is hardly fit for empirical testing. When we leave the realm of abstract theory and — through elimination of variables, aggregation and other simplifications — move into the realm of more 'realistic' workable models, interdependency may come into the model through several ways. Therefore, on this 'realistic' level of economic theory interdependency does not seem to be an unnatural property of economic models. (Bentzel and Hansen, 1954, p.154.)

Part (b). We notice that the model given by (1.4.1—5) explicitly involves expectations. We assume that these expectations are formed by private individuals in the economy to which the model refers and we observe that the formation of expectations about the values of variables in a certain time period is logically prior to the realisation of the actual values of the variables in that time period. Moreover, economic agents (consumers and producers) will often form plans on the basis of such expectations and these plans too are logically prior to the realisations. These considerations suggest that it is possible to develop a causal chain of expectations through plans through realisations through to expectations for the next period and represent this chain by an arrow diagram as we did in part (a) (this was first done by Bentzel and Hansen, 1954, p.156). We have

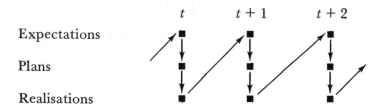

In the model (1.4.1—5) we see that there are no relationships which describe the formation of *plans* on the basis of expectations. But expectations of income are determined via (1.4.1) on the basis of the realised value of income in the last period and expectations of expenditure are formed via (1.4.2) on the basis of income expectations. Expenditure expectations are, in fact, then realised in (1.4.3) and combine with autonomous government expenditures to determine the realised level of income in that period. The arrow diagram for this model is as follows:

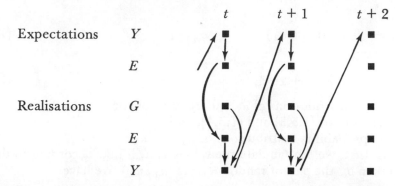

As the arrow schemes make clear this model is, indeed, recursive. The same principle can be applied in more complicated models that involve the formation of plans as well as expectations and for models with many more variables. For a further exercise we refer the reader to supplementary question 1.13.

Remark. Our discussion has concentrated on the nature of recursiveness in the context of economic models. This seems appropriate because it is in the initial formulation of models that the notation of causality must play a primary role. However, recursiveness has important implications in the context of econometric models also and we find that a probabilistic model is recursive only when the random disturbances (that now enter the specification of the model) satisfy certain restrictive conditions. But when these restrictions are satisfied the statistical procedures that are appropriate in the model are greatly simplified. The reader is referred to the excellent discussion in Malinvaud (1970b, pp. 612–614 and pp. 679–681) for further details.

Solution 1.5

Part (a). From the model (1.5.1) and the given values of x_t we see that

$$y_1 = 3 + u_1$$
$$y_2 = 6 + u_2$$

$$\sum_{t=1}^{2} y_t = 9 + (u_1 + u_2)$$

and

$$\sum_{t=1}^{2} x_t y_t = (3 + u_1) + 2(6 + u_2) = 15 + (u_1 + 2u_2)$$

Now $\sum_{t=1}^{2} x_t = 3$ and $\sum_{t=1}^{2} x_t^2 = 5$ so that from the definitions (1.5.2) we have

$$a_1 = 3 + \tfrac{1}{3}(u_1 + u_2) \tag{1.5.3}$$

and

$$a_2 = 3 + \tfrac{1}{5}(u_1 + 2u_2). \tag{1.5.4}$$

The sampling distributions of a_1 and a_2 can now be seen to depend
 (i) on the form of (1.5.3) and (1.5.4), and
(ii) on the probability distributions of u_1 and u_2.
Taking a_1 first, we can tabulate the values a_1 will take according to the
values taken by the pair of random errors (u_1, u_2). We have

a_1	(u_1, u_2)
$3\tfrac{2}{3}$	$(1, 1)$
3	$(1, -1)$
3	$(-1, 1)$
$2\tfrac{1}{3}$	$(-1, -1)$

The sampling distribution of a_1 is then obtained simply by associating a
probability with each value taken by the pair (u_1, u_2) in the above table.
Now u_1 and u_2 are statistically independent, so that

$$P(u_1 = 1, u_2 = 1) = P(u_1 = 1)\,P(u_2 = 1) = \tfrac{1}{2} \times \tfrac{1}{2} = \tfrac{1}{4}$$

$$P(u_1 = 1, u_2 = -1) = P(u_1 = 1)\,P(u_2 = -1) = \tfrac{1}{2} \times \tfrac{1}{2} = \tfrac{1}{4}$$

$$P(u_1 = -1, u_2 = 1) = P(u_1 = -1)\,P(u_2 = 1) = \tfrac{1}{2} \times \tfrac{1}{2} = \tfrac{1}{4}$$

$$P(u_1 = -1, u_2 = -1) = P(u_1 = -1)\,P(u_2 = -1) = \tfrac{1}{2} \times \tfrac{1}{2} = \tfrac{1}{4}$$

Hence the sampling distribution of a is as follows:

a_1	Probability
$3\tfrac{2}{3}$	$\tfrac{1}{4}$
3	$\tfrac{1}{2}$
$2\tfrac{1}{3}$	$\tfrac{1}{4}$

In a similar way we obtain for a_2 the tabulated values

a_2	(u_1, u_2)
$3\tfrac{3}{5}$	$(1, 1)$
$2\tfrac{4}{5}$	$(1, -1)$
$3\tfrac{1}{5}$	$(-1, 1)$
$2\tfrac{2}{5}$	$(-1, -1)$

and, hence, the sampling distribution

a_2	Probability
$3\frac{3}{5}$	$\frac{1}{4}$
$3\frac{1}{5}$	$\frac{1}{4}$
$2\frac{4}{5}$	$\frac{1}{4}$
$2\frac{2}{5}$	$\frac{1}{4}$

From these sampling distributions for a_1 and a_2 we can readily obtain the expected values and variances. We have

$$E(a_1) = (3\frac{2}{3})\frac{1}{4} + (3)\frac{1}{2} + (2\frac{1}{3})\frac{1}{4} = 3$$

$$E(a_2) = (3\frac{3}{5})\frac{1}{4} + (3\frac{1}{5})\frac{1}{4} + (2\frac{4}{5})\frac{1}{4} + (2\frac{2}{5})\frac{1}{4} = 3$$

$$\text{var}(a_1) = E[a_1 - E(a_1)]^2 = (\frac{2}{3})^2\frac{1}{4} + (-\frac{2}{3})^2\frac{1}{4} = \frac{2}{9}$$

$$\text{var}(a_2) = (\frac{3}{5})^2\frac{1}{4} + (\frac{1}{5})^2\frac{1}{4} + (-\frac{1}{5})^2\frac{1}{4} + (-\frac{3}{5})^2\frac{1}{4} = \frac{1}{5}$$

It follows immediately that $\text{var}(a_1) > \text{var}(a_2)$ as required.

Part (b). We can deduce the new sampling distribution of a_1 and a_2 in this case directly from (1.5.3), (1.5.4) and the given joint probability distribution of (u_1, u_2). We have

a_1	Probability
$3\frac{2}{3}$	$\frac{1}{10}$
3	$\frac{8}{10}$
$2\frac{1}{3}$	$\frac{1}{10}$

and

a_2	Probability
$3\frac{3}{5}$	$\frac{1}{10}$
$3\frac{1}{5}$	$\frac{4}{10}$
$2\frac{4}{5}$	$\frac{4}{10}$
$2\frac{2}{5}$	$\frac{1}{10}$

We now obtain for the expected values and variances of a_1 and a_2:

$$E(a_1) = (3\frac{2}{3})\frac{1}{10} + (3)\frac{8}{10} + (2\frac{1}{3})\frac{1}{10} = 3$$

$$E(a_2) = (3\frac{3}{5})\frac{1}{10} + (3\frac{1}{5})\frac{4}{10} + (2\frac{4}{5})\frac{4}{10} + (2\frac{2}{5})\frac{1}{10} = 3$$

$$\text{var}(a_1) = E[a_1 - E(a_1)]^2 = (\frac{2}{3})^2\frac{1}{10} + (\frac{2}{3})^2\frac{1}{10} = \frac{8}{90}$$

and

$$\text{var}(a_2) = E[a_2 - E(a_2)]^2$$
$$= (\frac{3}{5})^2\frac{1}{10} + (\frac{1}{5})^2\frac{4}{10} + (-\frac{1}{5})^2\frac{4}{10} + (-\frac{3}{5})^2\frac{1}{10} = \frac{26}{250}$$

We now see that

$$\text{var}(a_1) = \tfrac{8}{90} = 0.0889 < 0.104 = \tfrac{26}{250} = \text{var}(a_2)$$

as required.

Remark 1. We note from the definitions of a_1 and a_2 in (1.5.2) that, since x_1 and x_2 are fixed, both a_1 and a_2 can be regarded as linear combinations of the observable random variables y_1 and y_2. We therefore refer to a_1 and a_2 as **linear estimators.** Moreover, we see that a_2 is the ordinary least squares estimator of the slope coefficient.

Remark 2. In part (a) where u_1 and u_2 are statistically independent the model (1.5.1) satisfies the assumptions of the classical linear regression model (see Goldberger, 1964, p.162) and, as a result, the least squares estimator a_2 has minimum variance in the class of all linear unbiased estimators (Goldberger, 1964, p.208 and Johnston, 1972, p.22). The fact that $\text{var}(a_1) > \text{var}(a_2)$ as we have seen in part (a) is just an example of this general result. In part (b), a_2 is no longer the linear unbiased estimator which has minimum variance and as we see there the estimator a_1 now has a smaller variance. This is because u_1 and u_2 are correlated [the reader is asked to check for himself that $E(u_1 u_2) \neq 0$] and so the model no longer satisfies the assumptions of the classical linear regression model. In the present case, the linear unbiased estimator with minimum variance is obtained by the use of generalised least squares (Johnston, 1972, p.208–210 and Goldberger, 1964, p.233).

Solution 1.6

Part (a). From equations (1.6.1) and (1.6.2), and using the fact that $x_1 = 0$ and $x_1 = 1$ we see that

$$y_1 = u_1, \quad y_2 = 1 + u_2 \quad \text{and} \quad X_1 = v$$

It now follows from the definitions in (1.6.3) that

$$a_1 = \frac{1 + u_1 + u_2}{1 + v}, \quad a_2 = \frac{1 + u_2 + vu_1}{1 + v^2} \quad \text{and} \quad a_3 = \frac{1 + u_2 - u_1}{1 - v}.$$

$$(1.6.4)$$

We can tabulate the values taken by the estimators in (1.6.4) according to the values assumed by the triple (u_1, u_2, v) in much the same way as we did in solution 1.5. We obtain table 1.6.1.

Table 1.6.1

a_1	a_2	a_3	(u_1, u_2, v)			Probability
$3/(1 + \epsilon)$	$(2 + \epsilon)/(1 + \epsilon^2)$	$1/(1 - \epsilon)$	1	1	ϵ	1/8
$3/(1 - \epsilon)$	$(2 - \epsilon)/(1 + \epsilon^2)$	$1/(1 + \epsilon)$	1	1	$-\epsilon$	1/8
$1/(1 + \epsilon)$	$\epsilon/(1 + \epsilon^2)$	$-1/(1 - \epsilon)$	1	-1	ϵ	1/8
$1/(1 - \epsilon)$	$-\epsilon/(1 + \epsilon^2)$	$-1/(1 + \epsilon)$	1	-1	$-\epsilon$	1/8
$1/(1 + \epsilon)$	$(2 - \epsilon)/(1 + \epsilon^2)$	$3/(1 - \epsilon)$	-1	1	ϵ	1/8
$1/(1 - \epsilon)$	$(2 - \epsilon)/(1 + \epsilon^2)$	$3/(1 + \epsilon)$	-1	1	$-\epsilon$	1/8
$-1/(1 + \epsilon)$	$-\epsilon/(1 + \epsilon^2)$	$1/(1 - \epsilon)$	-1	-1	ϵ	1/8
$-1/(1 - \epsilon)$	$\epsilon/(1 + \epsilon^2)$	$1/(1 + \epsilon)$	-1	-1	$-\epsilon$	1/8

The probabilities in the final column of table 1.6.1 are obtained by noting that u_1, u_2 and v are statistically independent so that, for instance,

$$P(u_1 = 1, u_2 = 1, v = \epsilon) = P(u_1 = 1)P(u_2 = 1)P(v = \epsilon) = (\tfrac{1}{2})^3 = \tfrac{1}{8}$$

We can extract from table 1.6.1 the following sampling distributions for a_1, a_2 and a_3 (tables 1.6.2–4).

Table 1.6.2

a_1	Probability
$3/(1 - \epsilon)$	1/8
$3/(1 + \epsilon)$	1/8
$1/(1 - \epsilon)$	1/4
$1/(1 + \epsilon)$	1/4
$-1/(1 + \epsilon)$	1/8
$-1/(1 - \epsilon)$	1/8

Table 1.6.3

a_2	Probability
$(2 + \epsilon)/(1 + \epsilon^2)$	1/4
$(2 - \epsilon)/(1 + \epsilon^2)$	1/4
$\epsilon/(1 + c^2)$	1/4
$-\epsilon/(1 + \epsilon^2)$	1/4

Table 1.6.4

a_3	Probability
$3/(1 - \epsilon)$	1/8
$3/(1 + \epsilon)$	1/8
$1/(1 - \epsilon)$	1/4
$1/(1 + \epsilon)$	1/4
$-1/(1 + \epsilon)$	1/8
$-1/(1 - \epsilon)$	1/8

Part (b). We are asked to find $P(0.75 < a_i < 1.25)$ for $i = 1, 2, 3$. We must first find the values of a_i (for each i) which lie inside the interval $[0.75, 1.25]$. From tables 1.6.2–4, we see that the values assumed by the a_i depend on ϵ, and ϵ by assumption satisfies the inequality $0 < \epsilon < \tfrac{1}{5}$. There is a corresponding inequality for each value taken by the a_i. To find these inequalities we must first carry out some simple manipulations.

We start with a_1. Since $0 < \epsilon < \tfrac{1}{5}$ we deduce that

$$1 > 1 - \epsilon > \frac{4}{5} \quad \text{so that} \quad 1 < \frac{1}{1 - \epsilon} < \frac{5}{4}$$

$$1 < 1 + \epsilon < \frac{6}{5} \quad \text{so that} \quad 1 > \frac{1}{1 + \epsilon} > \frac{5}{6}$$

and it follows also that

$$3 < \frac{3}{1 - \epsilon} < \frac{15}{4} \quad \text{and} \quad 3 > \frac{3}{1 + \epsilon} > \frac{5}{2}$$

From these inequalities we now have

$$P(0.75 \leqslant a_1 \leqslant 1.25)$$
$$= P[a_1 = 1/(1-\epsilon)] + P[a_1 = 1/(1+\epsilon)]$$
$$= \tfrac{1}{4} + \tfrac{1}{4} = \tfrac{1}{2}$$

and

$$P(0 \leqslant a_1 \leqslant 2)$$
$$= P[a_1 = 1/(1-\epsilon)] + P[a_1 = 1/(1+\epsilon)]$$
$$= \tfrac{1}{2}.$$

Turning to the sampling distribution of a_2, we note that $0 < \epsilon < \tfrac{1}{5}$ implies that

$$1 < 1 + \epsilon^2 < \frac{26}{25}$$

so that

$$\frac{25}{26} < \frac{1}{1+\epsilon^2} < 1. \tag{1.6.5}$$

Moreover

$$2 < 2 + \epsilon < \frac{11}{5} \quad \text{and} \quad \frac{9}{5} < 2 - \epsilon < 2 \tag{1.6.6}$$

Using the rule that if $a < b$, $c < d$ and a, b, c, d are positive then $ac < bd$ we deduce the following inequalities from (1.6.5) and (1.6.6)

$$\frac{25}{13} < \frac{2+\epsilon}{1+\epsilon^2} < \frac{11}{5} \tag{1.6.7}$$

and

$$\frac{45}{26} < \frac{2-\epsilon}{1+\epsilon^2} < 2. \tag{1.6.8}$$

We can sharpen the first inequality in (1.6.7) by noting that

$$2\epsilon^2 - \epsilon = \epsilon(2\epsilon - 1)$$

is negative when $0 < \epsilon < \tfrac{1}{5}$. Thus

$$2\epsilon^2 - \epsilon < 0$$

and, adding $2 + \epsilon$ to both sides, we have

$$2 + 2\epsilon^2 < 2 + \epsilon$$

or

$$2 < \frac{2+\epsilon}{1+\epsilon^2}.$$

Combining this last inequality with (1.6.7) we obtain

$$2 < \frac{2+\epsilon}{1+\epsilon^2} < \frac{11}{5}.$$ (1.6.7′)

We also have

$$0 < \frac{\epsilon}{1+\epsilon^2} < \frac{1}{5}$$ (1.6.9)

and

$$-\frac{1}{5} < -\frac{\epsilon}{1+\epsilon^2} < 0.$$ (1.6.10)

From these inequalities we now deduce that

$$P(0.75 \leqslant a_2 \leqslant 1.25) = 0$$

since (1.6.7–10) indicate that a_2 never takes on a value in the interval $[0.75, 1.25]$; and we see that the only values taken by a_2 which lie in the interval $[0, 2]$ are $(2-\epsilon)/(1+\epsilon^2)$ and $\epsilon/(1+\epsilon^2)$, so that

$$P(0 \leqslant a_2 \leqslant 2)$$
$$= P[a_2 = (2-\epsilon)/(1+\epsilon^2)] + P[a_2 = \epsilon/(1+\epsilon^2)]$$
$$= \tfrac{1}{4} + \tfrac{1}{4} = \tfrac{1}{2}.$$

Finally, turning to a_3 we see from tables 1.6.2 and 1.6.3 that the sampling distributions of a_1 and a_3 are identical. Hence

$$P(0.75 \leqslant a_3 \leqslant 1.25) = P(0.75 \leqslant a_1 \leqslant 1.25) = \tfrac{1}{2}$$

and

$$P(0 \leqslant a_3 \leqslant 2) = P(0 \leqslant a_1 \leqslant 2) = \tfrac{1}{2}.$$

We can now tabulate our results on the relative concentration of the three estimators in table 1.6.5.

Table 1.6.5

Interval	Probability that estimator takes a value in the interval:		
	a_1	a_2	a_3
[0.75, 1.25]	$\tfrac{1}{2}$	0	$\tfrac{1}{2}$
[0, 2]	$\tfrac{1}{2}$	$\tfrac{1}{2}$	$\tfrac{1}{2}$

Remark. We see from the table 1.6.5 that both a_1 and a_3 give a higher probability than a_2 of obtaining a very accurate estimate [i.e. on an estimate close to unity, the true value of the slope coefficient in (1.6.1)]. But they also give a higher probability than a_2 of making a very large error. We can see this from the sampling distributions given in tables 1.6.2–4; we can, in fact, deduce the following from the inequalities we have obtained above:

$$P(|a_1 - 1| > 1.25) = \tfrac{1}{2}, \qquad\qquad (1.6.11)$$

$$P(|a_2 - 1| > 1.25) = 0,$$

$$P(|a_3 - 1| > 1.25) = \tfrac{1}{2}, \qquad\qquad (1.6.12)$$

and the reader may like to check these for himself.

In choosing between two estimators such as a_1 and a_2 we must first decide the relative importance of errors of estimation of different magnitudes. If we attached great importance to a very accurate estimate but were not greatly troubled by the prospect of making a large error then we might well select a_1 or a_3 in this context; but note from (1.6.11–12) that the probability of making a large error is itself large in this case and this must make a_1 and a_3 less attractive.

Solution 1.7

Part (a). The model (1.7.1–3) is a simple case of simultaneous equations model (we will discuss such models in detail in Chapter 6). The quantity exchanged between sellers and buyers of the good in the market and the price at which the exchange takes place is determined jointly by the three equations (1.7.1), (1.7.2) and (1.7.3). We can then solve this system of equations for price, p, and quantity exchanged $q = q^d = q^s$. We have

$$1 + p + u = 3 - p + v$$

so that

$$p = 1 + \tfrac{1}{2}(v - u) \qquad\qquad (1.7.4)$$

and then

$$q = 3 - p + v = 2 + \tfrac{1}{2}(u + v).$$

We can now determine the probability distribution of the free market price p from equation (1.7.4) and the given probability distributions of the random disturbances u and v. Using the fact that u and v are statistically independent, we obtain

p	(u, v)		Probability
1	1	1	$\tfrac{1}{9}$
$\tfrac{1}{2}$	1	0	$\tfrac{1}{9}$
0	1	−1	$\tfrac{1}{9}$
$\tfrac{3}{2}$	0	1	$\tfrac{1}{9}$
1	0	0	$\tfrac{1}{9}$
$\tfrac{1}{2}$	0	−1	$\tfrac{1}{9}$
2	−1	1	$\tfrac{1}{9}$
$\tfrac{3}{2}$	−1	0	$\tfrac{1}{9}$
1	−1	−1	$\tfrac{1}{9}$

and thus

p	Probability
2	$\frac{1}{9}$
$\frac{3}{2}$	$\frac{2}{9}$
1	$\frac{3}{9}$
$\frac{1}{2}$	$\frac{2}{9}$
0	$\frac{1}{9}$

The expected value of p is

$$\bar{p} = E(p) = (2)\tfrac{1}{9} + (\tfrac{3}{2})\tfrac{2}{9} + (1)\tfrac{3}{9} + (\tfrac{1}{2})\tfrac{2}{9}$$
$$= 1.$$

Part (b). If the government now intervenes by purchases or sales of g to ensure that price remains at the fixed value $\bar{p}$ the model becomes

$$q^s = 1 + \bar{p} + u \tag{1.7.5}$$

$$q^d = 3 - \bar{p} + v \tag{1.7.6}$$

$$q^s - q^d - g = 0 \tag{1.7.7}$$

This system determines the extent of government sales or purchases g and substituting (1.7.5) and (1.7.6) in (1.7.7) we obtain

$$g = (1 + \bar{p} + u) = (3 - \bar{p} + v)$$
$$= -2 + 2\bar{p} + u - v$$

and when $\bar{p} = E(p) = 1$ as in part (a) we have

$$g = u - v \tag{1.7.8}$$

The probability distribution of g is now as follows:

g	(u, v)		Probability
0	1	1	$\frac{1}{9}$
2	1	−1	$\frac{1}{9}$
−1	0	1	$\frac{1}{9}$
0	0	0	$\frac{1}{9}$
1	0	−1	$\frac{1}{9}$
−2	−1	1	$\frac{1}{9}$
−1	−1	0	$\frac{1}{9}$
0	−1	−1	$\frac{1}{9}$

or

g	Probability
2	$\frac{1}{9}$
1	$\frac{2}{9}$
0	$\frac{3}{9}$
-1	$\frac{2}{9}$
-2	$\frac{1}{9}$

We can now deduce the probability that g is at least as great as private demand q^d, i.e.

$$P(g \geqslant q^d) = P(g \geqslant 3 - \bar{p} + v)$$
$$= P(u - v \geqslant 2 + v)$$
$$= P(u - 2v \geqslant 2)$$

since $g = u - v$ from (1.7.8) and $\bar{p} = 1$. But $u - 2v \geqslant 2$ if and only if $v = -1$ and either $u = 0$ or $u = 1$. Hence

$$P(u - 2v \geqslant 2) = P(u = 0, v = -1) + P(u = 1, v = -1)$$
$$= \tfrac{1}{9} + \tfrac{1}{9} = \tfrac{2}{9}.$$

Solution 1.8

To forecast Q_{1977} on the basis of the known (and fixed) values $Q_{1976} = 30$ and $K_{1976} = 75$ we must first express Q_{1977} as a function of these fixed values and the random disturbances which occur in equations (1.8.1–3). We can achieve this by successively substituting for Y_t (and then C_t and I_t) in (1.8.1) until we obtain Q_t as a linear combination of Y_{t-1}, K_{t-1} and the random disturbances u_{1t}, u_{2t} and u_{3t}. To put it another way, we derive the reduced form equation for Y_t.

From (1.8.1) and (1.8.4) we have

$$Q_t = \alpha + \beta(C_t + I_t) + u_{1t}$$

and using (1.8.3) this becomes

$$Q_t = \alpha + \beta C_t + \beta\lambda\theta Y_{t-1} - \beta\lambda K_{t-1} + \beta u_{3t} + u_{1t}. \qquad (1.8.6)$$

Now from (1.8.2) and (1.8.4) we have

$$C_t = \gamma + \delta(C_t + I_t) + u_{2t}$$

so that, assuming $0 < \delta < 1$,

$$C_t = \frac{\gamma}{1 - \delta} + \frac{\delta}{1 - \delta} I_t + \frac{1}{1 - \delta} u_{2t} \qquad (1.8.7)$$

Then, using (1.8.3) for I_t in (1.8.7), we get

$$C_t = \frac{\gamma}{1-\delta} + \frac{\delta\lambda\theta}{1-\delta}Y_{t-1} - \frac{\delta\lambda}{1-\delta}K_{t-1} + \frac{\delta}{1-\delta}u_{3t} + \frac{1}{1-\delta}u_{2t}$$
$$(1.8.8)$$

and substituting (1.8.8) directly for C_t into (1.8.6) we find that

$$
\begin{aligned}
Q_t &= \alpha + \frac{\gamma\beta}{1-\delta} + \frac{\beta\delta\lambda\theta}{1-\delta}Y_{t-1} - \frac{\beta\delta\lambda}{1-\delta}K_{t-1} \\
&\quad + \beta\lambda\theta Y_{t-1} - \beta\lambda K_{t-1} + u_{1t} + \beta u_{3t} \\
&\quad + \frac{\beta\delta}{1-\delta}u_{3t} + \frac{\beta}{1-\delta}u_{2t} \\
&= \alpha + \frac{\gamma\beta}{1-\delta} + \frac{\beta\lambda\theta}{1-\delta}Y_{t-1} - \frac{\beta\lambda}{1-\delta}K_{t-1} \\
&\quad + u_{1t} + \frac{\beta}{1-\delta}u_{2t} + \frac{\beta}{1-\delta}u_{3t}.
\end{aligned}
\qquad (1.8.9)
$$

By assumption $Y_{1976} = 30$ and $K_{1976} = 75$ are considered to be fixed and non-random and the disturbances are normally distributed. It follows, therefore, from (1.8.9) that Q_{1977} is itself normally distributed with mean value

$$E(Q_{1977}) = \alpha + \frac{\gamma\beta}{1-\delta} + 30\frac{\beta\lambda\theta}{1-\delta} - 75\frac{\beta\lambda}{1-\delta} \qquad (1.8.10)$$

and variance

$$
\begin{aligned}
\mathrm{var}(Q_{1977}) &= \mathrm{var}\left\{u_{1t} + \frac{\beta}{1-\delta}(u_{2t} + u_{3t})\right\} \\
&= \mathrm{var}\left\{u_{1t} + \left(\frac{\beta}{1-\delta}\right)^2 \mathrm{var}(u_{2t} + u_{3t})\right\}
\end{aligned}
\qquad (1.8.11)
$$

(since, by assumption, u_{1t} is uncorrelated with u_{2t} and u_{3t})

$$= \sigma_{11} + \left(\frac{\beta}{1-\delta}\right)^2 (\sigma_{22} + 2\sigma_{23} + \sigma_{33}). \qquad (1.8.12)$$

To obtain a point forecast of Q_{1977} we can use the mean value (1.8.10) above which, when we substitute the given parameter values (assumed in the question to be the true values), becomes

$$\hat{Q}_{1977} = 100 + \frac{500}{1/2} + 30\left(\frac{75}{1/2}\right) - 75\left(\frac{25}{1/2}\right)$$

$$= 100 + 1{,}000 + 4{,}500 - 3{,}700 = 1{,}850.$$

On the assumption of normality, an interval within which there is a 95% probability that Q_{1977} will lie is just

$$E(Q_{1977}) \pm 1.96[\mathrm{var}(Q_{1977})]^{1/2}$$

$$= 1{,}850 \pm 1.96\left[\sigma_{11} + \left(\frac{\beta}{1-\delta}\right)^2 (\sigma_{22} + 2\sigma_{23} + \sigma_{33})\right]^{1/2}$$

and using the given values for the parameters, this becomes

$$1{,}850 \pm 1.96(100 + 30{,}000)^{1/2}$$

$$= 1{,}850 \pm 1.96(173.4935)$$

$$= (1509.9528, 2190.0472).$$

Remark. We should observe that the above forecast and prediction interval for Q_{1977} are **conditional** on the given values of the variables Y_{1976} and K_{1976}. Moreover, the assumption that the true values of the parameters in the model are known is an important simplification. In practice, these parameter values will not be known and must be estimated from sample observations of the variables. The estimates so obtained will then have a sampling distribution which we will need to consider in constructing a prediction interval for Q_{1977}. We will discuss this type of difficulty in solution 7.15 below.

CHAPTER 2

The linear model

0. INTRODUCTION

In this chapter we are concerned with single equations which are linear both in variables and in coefficients or which can be rewritten in this way. We shall make extensive use of the following notation throughout the chapter: the linear model will be written in the form

$$y = X\beta + u \qquad (2.0.1)$$

where y is a $T \times 1$ vector of observations on the dependent variable, X is a $T \times k$ matrix of observations on k *non-random* explanatory variables, β is a $k \times 1$ vector of coefficients, u is a $T \times 1$ vector of random disturbances and $k < T$. Further information about the definitions of these variables will be given in the questions when it is required. On occasion the linear model (2.0.1) will be written alternatively as

$$y_t = \sum_{i=1}^{k} \beta_i x_{it} + u_t \qquad (t = 1, \ldots, T) \qquad (2.0.2)$$

where y_t is the tth element of y, x_{it} is the itth element of X', β_i is the ith element of β and u_t is the tth element of u; (2.0.2) will also be written in the form

$$y_t = x_t'\beta + u_t \qquad (t = 1, \ldots, T)$$

where $x_t' = (x_{1t}, x_{2t}, \ldots, x_{kt})$ is the tth row of X.

A number of abbreviations are used in this chapter. For example, ordinary least squares is often written as OLS, the residual sum of squares of a regression is written RSS, the explained sum of squares is written ESS and the maximum likelihood estimator is sometimes written MLE. Sometimes it will be assumed that u is a normally distributed vector with zero mean and covariance matrix $\sigma^2 I_T$; we then say that u is $N(0, \sigma^2 I_T)$.

37

1. QUESTIONS

Question 2.1

(a) Estimate by OLS the linear model

$$y_t = \alpha + \beta x_{1t} + \gamma x_{2t} + u_t, \qquad (t = 1, \ldots, T) \tag{2.1.1}$$

given the following sample moment matrix

	$y - \bar{y}$	$x_1 - \bar{x}$	$x_2 - \bar{x}_2$
$y - \bar{y}$	2000	100	90
$x_1 - \bar{x}_1$	100	10	5
$x_2 - \bar{x}_2$	90	5	5

and sample means $\bar{y} = 1200$, $\bar{x}_1 = 100$ and $\bar{x}_2 = 50$, obtained from $T = 100$ observations.
(b) If the u_t are distributed as independent $N(0, \sigma^2)$ variables, estimate σ^2.
(c) Estimate the covariance matrix of the estimates of α, β and γ and hence find the standard errors of these estimates.
(d) Calculate R^2 and $\bar{R}^2$.

Question 2.2

In the linear model $y = X\beta + u$ it is assumed that u is $N(0, \sigma^2 I_T)$.
(a) Derive appropriate tests of the hypothesis: $H_0 : \beta = 0$ against $H_1 : \beta \neq 0$ in the following two cases: (i) when σ^2 is known, and (ii) when σ^2 is unknown.
(b) For the model of question (2.1), test the hypothesis

$$H_0 : \alpha = \beta = \gamma = 0$$

against the alternative

$$H_1 : \alpha, \beta, \gamma \neq 0$$

(i) when σ^2 is known to be 400, and (ii) when σ^2 is unknown.
(c) Suppose that you are given estimates of the coefficient vector β and σ^2 as well as R^2 uncorrected for the constant term, how would you then perform the test in c(ii)?

Question 2.3

In the linear model

$$y = X_1\beta_1 + X_2\beta_2 + u \tag{2.3.1}$$

u is $N(0, \sigma^2 I_T)$, β_1 is a $k_1 \times 1$ vector, β_2 is a $k_2 \times 1$ vector and
$X = (X_1 \vdots X_2)$ is a $T \times k$ matrix with $k = k_1 + k_2$.
(a) Derive a test of the hypothesis $H_0 : \beta_2 = 0, \beta_1 \neq 0$ against
$H_1 : \beta_1, \beta_2 \neq 0$. Show *with proof* how the test statistic is distributed.
(b) Relate this test to the likelihood ratio test.
(c) For the model of question (2.1) test the hypotheses

$$H_0 : \alpha \neq 0, \beta = \gamma = 0$$

and

$$H_1 : \alpha, \beta \neq 0, \gamma = 0$$

against

$$H_2 : \alpha, \beta, \gamma \neq 0$$

Question 2.4

In the model

$$y_t = \beta_0 + \beta_1 x_{1t} + \beta_2 x_{2t} + u_t \qquad (t = 1, \dots, T) \tag{2.4.1}$$

$E(u_t) = 0$, $E(u_t u_s) = \sigma^2$ for $t = s$ and zero for $t \neq s$.
(a) Show that $r_{y1.2}^2$, the squared partial correlation coefficient between
y and x_1, given x_2, can be interpreted as the proportional reduction in
the residual sum of squares due to adding x_1 given that x_2 is already an
included regressor. Hence obtain an expression for $r_{y1.23\dots k}^2$.
(b) Show for the general linear model that an additional regressor
increases $\bar{R}^2$ only if its t statistic is greater than unity. What significance
has this for maximising $\bar{R}^2$?
(c) For the model of question (2.1) find the partial correlation of y with
x_2 given x_1 and verify that these data satisfy (b) above for x_2.

Question 2.5

(a) Show how it is possible to use b, the OLS estimator of β in the linear
model $y = X\beta + u$, to provide a more efficient estimator of β when it is
known that β satisfies the independent linear constraints $R\beta = r$.
(b) For the model of question (2.1), test the hypothesis $H_0 : \alpha \neq 0$,
$5\beta = \gamma$ against $H_1 : \alpha \neq 0$, $5\beta \neq \gamma$ if the u_t are distributed as independent
$N(0, \sigma^2)$ variables.

Question 2.6

(a) Show how the test for the significance of an additional set of

explanatory variables in a regression can be used to test for structural
change. State clearly any assumptions you make.
(b) What problems may arise in using this test? Explain how they can be
overcome.

Question 2.7

Instead of estimating the vectors of coefficients β_1 and β_2 from the linear
model

$$y = X_1\beta_1 + X_2\beta_2 + u, \tag{2.7.1}$$

where the disturbance u has mean zero, it is decided to use OLS on the
following equation:

$$y = X_1^*\beta_1 + X_2\beta_2 + u^* \tag{2.7.2}$$

where X_1^* are the residuals of the regression of X_1 on X_2.
(a) Show that the resulting estimator of β_2 is identical to the regression
coefficients of y on X_2.
(b) Obtain an expression for the bias of this estimator of β_2.
(c) Prove that the OLS estimator of β_1 obtained from (2.7.2) is identical
to the OLS estimator of β_1 obtained from (2.7.1).

(Adapted from University of Essex BA examinations 1975)

Question 2.8

(a) Explain how the Gauss—Doolittle pivotal condensation method for
inverting a matrix can be used to provide a computational algorithm for
OLS.
(b) Describe how you would use this method in stepwise regression.
(c) Illustrate your answer to (b) for the general linear model

$$y = X_1\beta_1 + X_2\beta_2 + u$$

where X_1 is a $T \times k_1$ matrix and X_2 a $T \times k_2$ matrix.
(d) The following sample moment matrix is based on $T = 12$ observations

	$x_1 - \bar{x}_1$	$x_2 - \bar{x}^2$	$y - \bar{y}$
$x_1 - \bar{x}_1$	1	1	2
$x_2 - \bar{x}_2$	1	4	5
$y - \bar{y}$	2	5	10

Without estimating β_1 and β_2, use the Gauss—Doolittle method to test the
significance of β_1 and β_2 for the model

$$y_t = \alpha + \beta_1 x_{1t} + \beta_2 x_{2t} + u_t, \qquad (t = 1, \ldots, T)$$

where the u_t are distributed as independent $N(0, \sigma^2)$ variables.

Question 2.9

(a) Prove that the OLS estimators of β_1 in the following linear models are identical

$$y_t = x_t\beta_1 + t\beta_2 + u_t \tag{2.9.1}$$

$$y_t^* = x_t^*\beta_1 + u_t^* \qquad (t = 1, \ldots, T) \tag{2.9.2}$$

where y_t^* and x_t^* are de-trended y_t and x_t, obtained by regressing y_t and x_t on t and setting y_t^* and x_t^* equal to the respective residuals.
(b) Hence, show how it is possible to estimate β_1 in

$$y_t = x_{1t}\beta_1 + x_{2t}\beta_2 + u_t \tag{2.9.3}$$

using the regression equation

$$y_t^* = x_{1t}^*\beta_1 + u_t^*. \tag{2.9.4}$$

which is a linear transformation of (2.9.3).
(c) How is the significance test for the hypothesis $\beta_1 = 0$ in (2.9.2) related to that for $\beta_1 = 0$ in (2.9.1) if the u_t are distributed as independent $N(0, \sigma^2)$ variables.

Question 2.10

The dependent variable y is regressed on a constant term and the $k + 1$ independent variables $x_1, x_2, \ldots, x_{k+1}$ using the observations

$$y_t, x_{1t}, \ldots, x_{k+1,t} \qquad (t = 1, \ldots, T)$$

The coefficient of determination R_1^2 is calculated from this regression. Another regression is run, this time using only the first k independent variables $x_1, \ldots, x_k$. The coefficient of determination R_2^2 is calculated from this second regression.
(a) Show that $R_1^2 \geq R_2^2$.
(b) Find an exact relation between R_1^2 and R_2^2. Under what condition is $R_1^2 = R_2^2$?

Question 2.11

In the linear regression model $y = X\beta + u$, the matrix $X = (i \vdots Z)$ where i is the sum vector $i' = (1, 1, \ldots, 1)$ and Z is a matrix of T observations on k independent variables. Ignoring the constant term in this model, an

investigator obtains the least squares regression equation $y = Zb + \hat{u}$
where $b = (Z'Z)^{-1}Z'y$.
(a) Show that $y'y = b'Z'Zb + \hat{u}'\hat{u}$.
(b) Construct a numerical example in which

$$R^2 = 1 - \frac{\hat{u}'\hat{u}}{\sum\limits_{t=1}^{T}(y_t - \bar{y})^2} < 0 \qquad (2.11.1)$$

where $\bar{y}$ is the sample mean of $y_1, \ldots, y_T$.
(c) Using your answer to part (a), suggest a modified goodness of fit
measure R_m^2, which satisfies

$$0 \leqslant R_m^2 \leqslant 1$$

(d) If the true model were $y = Z\beta_z + u$ where β_z is the vector of the last k
components of β, would it still be possible to obtain a negative R^2 in the
regression $y = Zb + \hat{u}$?

(University of Essex MA examinations 1974)

Question 2.12

In the linear model

$$y = X\beta + u \qquad (2.12.1)$$

X is a $T \times k$ matrix, $E(u) = 0$, $E(uu') = \Sigma$ and Σ is a known non-singular
matrix.
(a) Obtain the generalised least squares (GLS) estimator of β and show
that it is a best linear unbiased estimator (BLUE).
(b) Examine the efficiency of the OLS estimator of β when each of the
k columns of X is also an eigenvector of $\Sigma(k < T)$.
(c) Find a matrix of $k(<T)$ explanatory variables X for which OLS is
BLUE when

$$\Sigma = \sigma^2 \begin{bmatrix} 1 & -1 & 0 & \cdots & 0 & 0 \\ -1 & 2 & -1 & \cdots & 0 & 0 \\ \cdot & \cdot & \cdot & \cdots & \cdot & \cdot \\ 0 & 0 & 0 & \cdots & 2 & -1 \\ 0 & 0 & 0 & \cdots & -1 & 1 \end{bmatrix}$$

and comment on Σ.

Question 2.13

(a) Derive the best linear unbiased predictor of $y_t (t = T + 1, \ldots, T + R)$ for the linear model $y_t = x_t' \beta + u_t$ with observations $t = 1, \ldots, T$ and where the u_t are distributed as independent $N(0, \sigma^2)$ variables.
(b) Find the covariance matrix of the forecast errors.
(c) Hence, construct a 95% confidence interval for a one-period ahead forecast based on the estimated model

$$\hat{y}_t = 100 + 5x_{1t} - 2x_{2t},$$

where

$$X'X = \begin{bmatrix} 10 & 10 & 20 \\ 10 & 20 & 0 \\ 20 & 0 & 90 \end{bmatrix}$$

$s = 3, T = 10, x_{1, T+1} = 1$ and $x_{2, T+1} = 2$ (s^2 is the unbiased estimator of σ^2 based on the OLS residuals).

Question 2.14

If the r component column vector $\hat{y}_F$ is the best linear unbiased predictor of y_F based on the linear model $y = X\beta + u$ where u is $N(0, \sigma^2 I_T)$,
(a) derive a test of the hypothesis $H_0 : E(\hat{y}_F - y_F) = 0$ against $H_1 : E(\hat{y}_F - y_F) \neq 0$; and
(b) compare this test with the Chow test for structural change.

Question 2.15

(a) Define the term 'consistent estimator'.
(b) For the linear model

$$y = X\beta + u \tag{2.15.1}$$

where $E(u) = 0$ and $E(uu') = \sigma^2 I_T$ show that the condition

$$\lim_{T \to \infty} \frac{X'X}{T} = M,$$

where M is finite and non-singular, is sufficient but not necessary for the consistency of b, the OLS estimator of β.
(c) Prove the consistency of the OLS estimator of β in the linear model

$$y_t = \alpha + \beta t + u_t \qquad (t = 1, \ldots, T) \tag{2.15.2}$$

where $E(u_t) = 0, E(u_t^2) = \sigma^2$ and $E(u_t u_s) = 0$ for $t \neq s$.

Question 2.16

(a) Stating carefully any assumptions that you make, derive the asymptotic distribution of the least squares estimator of β in the linear model

$$y = X\beta + u \qquad (2.16.1)$$

where $E(u) = 0$ and $E(uu') = \sigma^2 I_T$.
(b) Evaluate this distribution when

$$\lim_{T \to \infty} \frac{X'X}{T} = \begin{bmatrix} 1 & 1 \\ 1 & 2 \end{bmatrix} \qquad (2.16.2)$$

(c) Obtain the asymptotic distribution of the OLS estimator of β in the model

$$y_t = \alpha + \beta t + u_t \qquad (t = 1, \ldots, T) \qquad (2.16.3)$$

where $E(u_t) = 0$, $E(u_t^2) = \sigma^2$ and $E(u_t u_s) = 0$ for $t \neq s$.

Question 2.17

The demand for Ceylon tea in the US is assumed to be determined by the equation

$$\ln Q = \beta_0 + \beta_1 \ln P_C + \beta_2 \ln P_I + \beta_3 \ln P_B + \beta_4 \ln Y + u \qquad (2.17.1)$$

where Q = imports of Ceylon tea into the US
$\quad\quad P_C$ = price of Ceylon tea
$\quad\quad P_I$ = price of Indian tea
$\quad\quad P_B$ = price of Brazilian coffee
$\quad\quad Y$ = disposable income

The following OLS estimates were obtained from $T = 22$ observations:

$$\ln Q = \underset{(2.000)}{2.837} - \underset{(0.987)}{1.481} \ln P_C + \underset{(0.690)}{1.181} \ln P_I + \underset{(0.134)}{0.186} \ln P_B$$

$$+ \underset{(0.370)}{0.257} \ln Y$$

$$\text{RSS} = 0.4277 \qquad (2.17.2)$$

$$\ln Q + \ln P_C = -\underset{(0.820)}{0.738} + \underset{(0.155)}{0.199} \ln P_B + \underset{(0.165)}{0.261} \ln Y$$

$$\text{RSS} = 0.6788 \qquad (2.17.3)$$

The figures in parentheses are standard errors.
(a) Test the hypothesis $H_0: \beta_1 = -1, \beta_2 = 0$ and $\beta_0, \beta_3, \beta_4 \neq 0$ against $H_1: \beta_i \neq 0$ $(i = 1, \ldots, 4)$.

(b) Discuss the economic implications of these results.

Question 2.18

The following equation has been estimated by OLS:

$$\ln\frac{Q}{L} = \underset{(0.504)}{1.551} + \underset{(0.266)}{0.654}\ln W - \underset{(0.0403)}{0.0286}\ln Q \qquad R^2 = 0.50 \qquad (2.18.1)$$

where Q = output, L = labour, W = product wage and the figures in parentheses are standard errors. It was derived from the marginal productivity condition for labour from the CES production function

$$Q = A[\alpha L^{-\rho} + (1-\alpha)K^{-\rho}]^{-\nu/\rho} \qquad (2.18.2)$$

where K = capital stock, on the assumption that labour is paid its marginal product.

(a) From (2.18.1) obtain estimates of σ, the elasticity of substitution between labour and capital, and of ν, the degree of returns to scale.

(b) Test the following hypotheses: (i) $H_0 : \sigma = 1$ against $H_1 : \sigma \neq 1$; and (ii) $H_0^* : \nu = 1$ against $H_1^* : \nu \neq 1$. You may assume that the covariance between the estimates of the coefficients of $\ln W$ and $\ln Q$ is zero.

Question 2.19

In a study of investment plans and realisations in UK manufacturing industries since 1955 the following results were obtained by least squares regressions:

$$A_t = \text{const} - \underset{(6.24)}{54.60}\, C_{t-1}, \qquad R^2 = 0.89; DW = 2.50 \qquad (2.19.1)$$

$$I_t - A_t = \text{const} - \underset{(4.44)}{19.96}\,(C_t - C_{t-1}), \qquad R^2 = 0.68; DW = 2.31 \qquad (2.19.2)$$

$$I_t = \text{const} + \underset{(0.10)}{0.88}\, A_t - \underset{(5.15)}{16.32}\,(C_t - C_{t-1}),$$
$$R^2 = 0.90; DW = 1.65 \qquad (2.19.3)$$

$$I_t = \text{const} - \underset{(3.64)}{50.08}\, C_{t-1} - \underset{(3.32)}{14.60}\,(C_t - C_{t-1}),$$
$$R^2 = 0.96; DW = 2.61 \qquad (2.19.4)$$

where A_t = the investment that firms anticipate they will complete in
year t; these plans are held at the end of year $t-1$;
I_t = actual investment in year t, i.e. the realisation of the plans;

C_t = a measure of the average level of under-utilisation of capacity
in year t, the greater is C_t the more *under-utilised* is existing
productive capacity;

and the figures in parentheses are standard errors.

(a) Interpret these results and assess whether or not knowledge of firms'
anticipated investment is helpful in explaining actual investment.

(b) Discuss any policy implications of these results for maintaining a
steady level of investment.

Source: Smyth and Briscoe (1969).

(Adapted from University of Bristol B Sc. examinations, 1971.)

Question 2.20

Three hypotheses have been advanced to explain price formation:

A. The theory of marginal cost pricing which asserts that changes in prices
(Δp) are due to changes in unit labour costs (ΔULC), changes in unit
material costs (ΔUMC), changes in the ratio of unfilled orders to sales
$[\Delta(O/S)]$ and the level of capacity utilisation (CU).

B. The theory of target return pricing in which price changes are due to
changes in standard or normal unit labour costs (ΔULC^N), changes in
standard unit material costs (ΔUMC^N), changes in the standard capital–
output ratio $[\Delta(K/Q)]$ and changes in target rates of return ($\Delta\pi$).

C. The theory of full cost pricing which explains price changes by ΔULC^N
and ΔUMC^N only.

The following equations were estimated by OLS for manufacturing
industries in the US 1954(1)–1965(1):

$$\Delta p = \text{const} + \underset{(1.69)}{0.068\ \Delta ULC} + \underset{(3.00)}{0.072\ \Delta UMC} + \underset{(5.72)}{0.0005\ CU}$$

$$+ \underset{(2.00)}{0.127\ \Delta(O/S)_{-1}}$$

$$\bar{R}^2 = 0.583 \tag{2.20.1}$$

$$\Delta p = \text{const} + \underset{(2.70)}{0.235\ \Delta ULC^N} + \underset{(2.11)}{0.085\ \Delta(ULC - ULC^N)}$$

$$+ \underset{(2.52)}{0.155\ \Delta ULC^N_{-1}} + \underset{(2.98)}{0.065\ \Delta UMC} + \underset{(3.08)}{0.0003\ CU}$$

$$+ \underset{(2.21)}{0.141\ \Delta(O/S)_{-1}}$$

$$\bar{R}^2 = 0.654. \tag{2.20.2}$$

The figures in parentheses are t statistics.

(a) Discuss briefly the economic reasoning behind these specifications of the three theories.

(b) Evaluate the three hypotheses.

(*Source:* Eckstein and Fromm, 1968).

2. SUPPLEMENTARY QUESTIONS

Question 2.21

Consider the linear model

$$y_t = \beta_0 + \beta_1 x_{1t} + \beta_2 x_{2t} + u_t \qquad (t = 1, \ldots, T)$$

where $\beta_1 + \beta_2 = 0$ and the u_t $(t = 1, \ldots, T)$ are serially independent random disturbances with zero mean and variance σ^2. From observations of y_t, x_{1t} and x_{2t} over $T = 103$ periods the following sample moments matrix has been calculated:

	$y - \bar{y}$	$x_1 - \bar{x}_1$	$x_2 - \bar{x}_2$
$y - \bar{y}$	390	30	-20
$x_1 - \bar{x}_1$	30	20	10
$x_2 - \bar{x}_2$	-20	10	10

Using these data, calculate the best linear unbiased estimates of β_1 and β_2. Find the standard errors of your parameter estimates.

Question 2.22

In the model

$$y_t = \alpha + \beta x_t + u_t \qquad (t = 1, \ldots, T) \qquad (2.22.1)$$

x_t is a non-random exogenous variable and the u_t are serially uncorrelated random disturbances with zero mean and variance σ^2 for each value of t.

The following sample moments have been calculated from 10 observations of y_t and x_t:

$$\Sigma y_t = 8 \quad \Sigma x_t = 40 \quad \Sigma y_t^2 = 26 \quad \Sigma x_t^2 = 200 \quad \Sigma y_t x_t = 20$$

where the summations are over $t = (1, 2, \ldots, 10)$.

In some subsequent time period, s, for which the model (2.22.1) still holds the value of $x_s = 10$.

(a) Calculate the best linear unbiased forecast of y_s, using the above data.

(b) Estimate the standard error of your forecast in (a).

(Adapted from University of Birmingham B Soc.Sc. examinations, 1966.)

Question 2.23

(a) Let $\hat{\beta}_1$ and $\hat{\beta}_2$ denote the estimated regression coefficients for the linear model

$$y = X_1 \beta_1 + X_2 \beta_2 + u.$$

Show that

$$b_1 = \hat{\beta}_1 + (X_1' X_1)^{-1} X_1' X_2 \hat{\beta}_2$$

where b_1 is a vector of coefficients from the regression of y on X_1.

(b) Given the following estimated regression equations

$$C_t = \text{const} + 0.92\,Y_t + \hat{u}_{1t}$$
$$C_t = \text{const} + 0.84\,C_{t-1} + \hat{u}_{2t}$$
$$C_{t-1} = \text{const} + 0.78\,Y_t + \hat{u}_{3t}$$
$$Y_t = \text{const} + 0.55\,C_{t-1} + \hat{u}_{4t}$$

Calculate the regression estimates of β_1 and β_2 for

$$C_t = \beta_0 + \beta_1\,Y_t + \beta_2\,C_{t-1} + u_t.$$

(University of Essex BA examinations, 1977.)

Question 2.24

A researcher obtained by ordinary least squares (OLS) the following model estimates: $y = a + bx + \hat{e}$. Another specification tried was: $y = a^* + b^*x + c^*z + \hat{u}$, again estimated by OLS.
Explain in detail under what circumstances the following could be true:
(a) $b^* = b$,
(b) $\Sigma \hat{u}_i^2 \leqslant \Sigma \hat{e}_i^2$,
(c) b is statistically significant at the 5% level yet b^* is not,
(d) b^* is statistically significant at the 5% level yet b is not.

(University of London M Sc.(Econ.) examinations, 1977.)

Question 2.25

The model $y_t = \beta_0 + \beta_1 x_{1t} + \beta_2 x_{2t} + \beta_3 x_{3t} + u_t$ was estimated by ordinary least squares from 26 observations yielding:

$$y_t = 2 + 3.5\,x_{1t} - 0.7\,x_{2t} + 2\,x_{3t} + e_t$$
$$\qquad\quad (1.9)\qquad (2.2)\quad (1.5)$$

with t-ratios in brackets and $R^2 = 0.982$.

The same model was estimated with the restriction $\beta_2 = \beta_1$. Estimates were:

$$y_t = 1.5 + 3(x_{1t} + x_{3t}) - 0.6\,x_{2t} + e'_t$$
$$\qquad\quad (2.7)\qquad\qquad\quad (2.4)$$

$$R^2 = 0.876.$$

(a) Test the significance of the vector $\begin{pmatrix}\beta_1\\\beta_2\\\beta_3\end{pmatrix}$ from the unrestricted estimates.

(b) Test the significance of the restriction $\beta_2 = \beta_1$. Clearly state any assumptions utilised.

(University of London M Sc.(Econ.) examinations, 1977.)

Question 2.26

The simple accelerator theory of investment behaviour says that net investment (I_t^N) increases as the *change* in output (Q_t) increases i.e.

$$I_t^N = \alpha(Q_t - Q_{t-1}) \qquad (\alpha > 0). \qquad\qquad (2.26.1)$$

In order to test this theory three more equations are used:

$$I_t = I_t^N + I_t^R \qquad\qquad\qquad (2.26.2)$$

i.e. gross investment (I_t) equals net investment plus replacement investment (I_t^R).

$$I_t^R = \delta K_{t-1} \qquad\qquad\qquad (2.26.3)$$

i.e. a constant proportion δ of last period's capital stock (K_{t-1}) is replaced each year.

$$K_t/Q_t = \alpha \qquad\qquad\qquad (2.26.4)$$

i.e. the capital output—ratio is a constant α.

Given the following estimated equation for the US 1946—59:

$$I_t = 0.245Q_t - 0.102K_{t-1} \qquad R^2 = 0.966 \qquad (2.26.5)$$
$$\quad\ (13.2)\qquad (-3.6)$$

where the figures in parentheses are the ratios of the estimate to the standard errors i.e. the t statistic:

(a) Combine equations (2.26.1—4) so that an equation like (2.26.5) is obtained.

(b) Deduce estimates of α and δ.

(c) It is believed that the capital output ratio is approximately 3. Test the hypothesis that $\alpha = 3$.

(University of Essex BA examinations, 1975.)

Question 2.27

In the model

$$y_t = \beta x_t + u_t \qquad (t = 1, \ldots, T) \tag{2.27.1}$$

y_t is endogenous, x_t is a non-random exogenous variable and the u_t are serially uncorrelated random disturbances each with zero mean and variance σ^2.

The T observations are arranged into n groups. The ith group contains T_i observations of y and x and $\Sigma_{i=1}^n T_i = T$. The means of y and x in the ith group are denoted by $\bar{y}_i$ and $\bar{x}_i$ $(i = 1, \ldots, n)$.

Suppose that only the *data on the group means* $[(\bar{y}_i, \bar{x}_i): i = 1, \ldots, n]$ is available.

(a) Write down the best linear unbiased estimator (BLUE) of β in (2.27.1).

(b) Derive an expression for the variance of your estimator in (a).

(c) Find the variance of the ordinary least squares estimator (OLS) of β and hence derive an expression for the efficiency of the OLS estimator relative to the BLUE.

(d) What is this efficiency (numerically) when $T_1 = T_2 = \ldots = T_n$?

Now suppose that the *underlying data* $[(y_t, x_t): t = 1, \ldots, T]$ is available.

(e) Write down the BLUE of β in this case and verify that the variance of this estimator is at least as small as the variance of your estimator in (a) when the available data was on group means.

(Adapted, in part, from University of Birmingham B Soc.Sc. examinations, 1966.)

Question 2.28

For the linear model

$$y = X\beta + u \tag{2.28.1}$$

where u is $N(0, \sigma^2 I_T)$ we wish to test the hypothesis that the coefficient vector β satisfies the independent linear restrictions

$$R\beta = r \tag{2.28.2}$$

where R is a known $s \times k$ matrix and r is a known $s \times 1$ vector.

(a) Derive the Lagrange multiplier statistic (LM), the likelihood ratio

statistic (LR) and the Wald statistic (W) for testing (2.28.2) against the hypothesis that β does not satisfy (2.28.2).
(b) Show that

$$LM \leqslant LR \leqslant W. \tag{2.28.3}$$

(c) Comment on the relationship between these three statistics and the appropriate finite sample statistic for performing this test.

Reference: Berndt and Savin (1977) and Breuch (1976).

Question 2.29

(a) For the model $Y_t = \beta_0 + \beta_1 X_{1t} + \beta_2 X_{2t} + \epsilon_t$ where the X's are fixed

in repeated samples, $E(\epsilon_t) = 0$, $E(\epsilon_t \epsilon_s) = \begin{cases} \sigma^2 \; (s = t) \\ 0 \; (s \neq t) \end{cases}$ and

when ϵ_t is normally distributed, derive a test statistic for the hypothesis that X_2 has no influence on Y.
(b) Discuss the validity of the following procedure for testing the same hypothesis.
(i) Use the estimated regression $Y_t = \hat{\gamma}_0 + \hat{\gamma}_1 X_{1t} + \hat{V}_t$, regress $\hat{V}_t$ on X_{2t} to give:

$$\hat{V}_t = \hat{\delta}_0 + \hat{\delta}_1 X_{2t} + \hat{w}_t$$

(ii) Test the null hypothesis $H_0 : \delta_1 = 0$.

(University of London B Sc.(Econ.) examinations, 1975.)

Question 2.30

Given a CES production function

$$V_t = A[\delta K_t^{-\rho} + (1 - \delta)L_t^{-\rho}]^{-1/\rho} \tag{2.30.1}$$

where V, K, L are output, capital and labour respectively, and given data on these variables together with the real wage rate (w), an investigator has a choice of estimating either of the following two equations:

$$\ln \left(\frac{V}{L}\right)_t = \beta_0 + \beta_1 \ln w_t + u_{1t} \tag{2.30.2}$$

$$\ln w_t = \gamma_0 + \gamma_1 \ln \left(\frac{V}{L}\right)_t + u_{2t} \tag{2.30.3}$$

(a) What assumptions about the nature of the product and factor markets are crucial to the choice between (2.30.2 and 3)?

(b) Show that β_1 is the elasticity of substitution.

(c) If $\hat{\beta}_1$ and $\hat{\gamma}_1$ are the least squares estimates of β_1 and γ_1 show that $\hat{\beta}_1 \hat{\gamma}_1 \leqslant 1$.

(University of London, M Sc.(Econ.) examinations, 1970.)

Question 2.31

The following relationship holds for OLS estimates:

$$\frac{\hat{\beta}_i^2}{\text{var}(\hat{\beta}_i)} = \frac{(T-k)r_{1i.q}^2}{1 - r_{1i.q}^2}$$

when $\hat{\beta}_i$ = OLS estimator of coefficient of $x_i (i = 2, 3, \ldots, k+1)$

$\quad x_{k+1} = 1$ for all observations (i.e. constant term)

$\quad T$ = number of observations

$\quad \text{var}(\hat{\beta}_i)$ = estimated variance of $\hat{\beta}_i$.

$\quad r_{1i.q}$ = partial correlation coefficient between the dependent variable
$\qquad x_1$ and x_i $(i \neq 1, i \neq k+1)$ in the regression including all the
$\qquad$ other x's.

Using this relationship, discuss the effect of varying degrees of collinearity among the regressors $x_2, \ldots, x_{k+1}$ on the OLS estimates $\hat{\beta}_i$.

(b) In the model $x_1 = \beta_2 x_2 + \beta_3 x_3 + \beta_4 + u$ an extraneous estimate β_2^* of β_2 is available. Discuss how this information can be used to obtain a better estimate of β_3 than the OLS estimate.

(University of London B Sc.(Econ.) examinations, 1975.)

Question 2.32

The matrix X of the linear model $y = X\beta + u$ is partitioned into sub-matrices X_1 and X_2 of rank k_1 and k_2 respectively, where $k_1 + k_2 = k$, and the vector β is partitioned conformably. Consider the following procedures for estimating β_1, some of which utilise the residuals from prior regressions of y and/or X_1 on X_2:

(a) Regress the residuals from the regression of y on X_2 on those from the regressions of X_1 on X_2.

(b) Regress y on the residuals from the regressions of X_1 on X_2.

(c) Regress y on X_2 and the residuals from the regressions of X_1 on X_2.

(d) Direct regression of y on X_1 and X_2.

Show that the estimate of β_1 is the same in all four cases, and comment on this result.

Compare the residual sum of squares and R^2 values obtained from each of the four regressions.

(University of London B Sc(Econ) examinations, 1976.)

Question 2.33

Consider the linear model

$$y_t = \beta x_t + u_t \qquad (t = 1, \ldots, T)$$

where $E(u_t) = 0$ and the covariance matrix of the u_t is known. Under what assumptions would

(a) $\quad T^{-1} \sum\limits_{t=1}^{T} (y_t/x_t), \quad$ and

(b) $\quad \sum\limits_{t=1}^{T} y_t \Big/ \sum\limits_{t=1}^{T} x_t$

be best linear unbiased estimators?

Question 2.34

For the linear model

$$Y_t = \sum_{i=1}^{k} x_{it} \beta_i + u_t \qquad (t = 1, \ldots, T)$$

$$Y_t = \sum_{i=1}^{k} x_{it} \beta_i + \delta_t + u_t \qquad (t = T+1, \ldots, T+R)$$

(a) interpret the OLS estimators of $\beta_i (i = 1, \ldots, k)$ and $\delta_t (t = T+1, \ldots, T+R)$ obtained using the complete sample $t = 1, \ldots, T+R$ and also the covariance matrix of these estimators.
(b) Interpret the multiple correlation coefficient when

$$y_t = \bar{y} \quad \text{for} \quad t = T+1, \ldots, T+R$$

Reference: D.S. Salkever (1976).

Question 2.35

In the model

$$y_t = \beta x_t + u_t \qquad (t = 1, \ldots, T)$$

the $x_t (t = 1, \ldots, T)$ are non-random positive quantities, y_t is an observable random variable and the u_t are serially uncorrelated random disturbances distributed with zero means and variances given by

$$E(u_t^2) = \sigma^2 x_t^p \qquad (p > 0)$$

It is known that the jth moment about the origin of the quantities $\{x_t : t = 1, \ldots, T\}$ is

$$T^{-1} \sum_{t=1}^{T} x_t^j = \omega^j (1 + \eta^2)^{(j^2 - j)/2} \qquad (-\infty < j < \infty)$$

where $\omega > 0$ and η is the coefficient of variation of the x_t.
(a) Find expressions as functions of p and η for the efficiencies of the following estimators of β relative to the BLUE of β:

$$b_1 = \sum_{t=1}^{T} x_t y_t \Big/ \sum_{t=1}^{T} x_t^2$$

$$b_2 = \sum_{t=1}^{T} y_t \Big/ \sum_{t=1}^{T} x_t$$

(b) Evaluate the efficiencies of b_1 and of b_2 numerically for $p = 1$ and $\eta = \frac{1}{2}$. Comment on your results.

(Adapted from University of Birmingham B Soc.Sc. examinations, 1966.)

Question 2.36

In the model:

$$y = X\beta + u$$

where y is $T \times 1$, X is a fixed $T \times k$ matrix of rank k and u is $N(0 : \sigma^2 IT)$, consider imposing the restriction $R\beta = 0$ where R is a known $r \times k$ matrix of rank r.
(a) Show that the difference between the restricted and unrestricted residual sums of squares in this model is given by

$$(R\hat{\beta})' [R(X'X)^{-1} R']^{-1} (R\beta)$$

where $\hat{\beta}$ denotes the ordinary least squares estimator of β.
(b) For the particular case:

$$y_t = a_1 x_{1t} + a_2 x_{2t} + a_3 x_{3t} + u_t, \qquad (t = 1, \ldots, T)$$

a sample of size $T = 46$ yields the following data on sums of squares and cross-products of the variables:

	y	x_1	x_2	x_3
y	8	0	$\frac{5}{2}$	1
x_1	0	2	1	2
x_2	$\frac{5}{2}$	1	3	1
x_3	1	2	1	4

Carry out a test of

$$H_0 : a_1 + a_2 - a_3 = 0 \quad \text{and} \quad a_1 - a_2 + 2a_3 = 0$$

against $H_1 : H_0$ is false.

(University of Essex MA examinations, 1977.)

Question 2.37

(a) $\{\alpha_T : T = 1, 2, \ldots\}$ is a sequence of $n \times 1$ random vectors that
converges in probability to the constant vector α^0. It is known that
$\sqrt{T}(\alpha_T - \alpha^0)$ has a limiting normal distribution with zero mean and
non-singular covariance matrix Ω. If f is a continuous (scalar) function
with continuous derivatives to the second order (at least), find the
limiting distribution of $\sqrt{T}[f(\alpha_T) - f(\alpha^0)]$.
(b) If b_1 and h_2 denote the least squares estimates of β_1 and β_2 in the
model

$$y_t = \beta_1 x_{1t} + \beta_2 x_{2t} + u_t \qquad (t = 1, \ldots, T)$$

under what conditions will

$$\sqrt{T}(b_1/b_2 - \beta_1/\beta_2)$$

have a limiting normal distribution? What is the variance of this limiting
distribution?

Question 2.38

(a) If $X_1, X_2, \ldots, X_T$ is a random sample from a population with
distribution function $F(X)$ and frequency function $f(X)$ what conditions
on this distribution are sufficient to ensure that the sample moment
$(1/T)\Sigma_{t=1}^{T} x_t^r$ tends in probability to the rth moment of the distribution
(r integer and $r > 1$) as T tends to infinity? Prove your result.
(b) Consider the linear model $y = X\beta + u$ where $E(u) = 0$ and $E(uu') = \sigma^2 I_T$. If b is the least squares estimator of β show that

$$s^2 = (y - Xb)'(y - Xb)/(T - k)$$

is a consistent estimator of σ^2,

(Adapted from University of Essex BA examinations, 1973.)

Question 2.39

In the following three models

$$y_t = \frac{\alpha}{t} + u_t \qquad (t = 1, \ldots, T) \tag{2.39.1}$$

$$y_t = \alpha g^t + u_t \qquad (t = 1, \ldots, T) \tag{2.39.2}$$

$$y_t = \alpha + \frac{\beta}{t^2} + u_t \qquad (t = 1, \ldots, T) \tag{2.39.3}$$

the $y_t (t = 1, \ldots, T)$ are observable random variables and the u_t $(t = 1, \ldots, T)$ are serially independent random disturbances with zero mean and finite variance σ^2. In (2.39.2), g is a known constant.
(a) Show that the least squares estimator of the parameter α in (2.39.1) cannot be consistent. Is the same true for (2.39.2)?
(b) Examine whether the least squares estimators of α and β are consistent in (2.39.3)

$$\left(Hint: \ \sum_{t=1}^{\infty} \frac{1}{t^2} = \frac{\pi^2}{6}, \ \sum_{t=1}^{\infty} \frac{1}{t^4} = \frac{\pi^4}{90}. \right)$$

(Adapted from University of Essex BA examinations, 1976.)

3. SOLUTIONS

Solution 2.1

Part (a). Using the notation discussed in the introduction to this chapter, equation (2.1.1) can be written more compactly as

$$y = X\beta + u \tag{2.1.2}$$

where the tth row of X is $(1, x_{1t}, x_{2t})$ and $\beta = (\alpha, \beta, \gamma)'$. We can also partition X as $(i \vdots X_1 \vdots X_2)$ where i denotes a column vector of ones and X_1 and X_2 are column vectors with tth elements x_{1t} and x_{2t}, respectively. The least squares estimator of β defined in (2.1.2) is

$$b_{OLS} = (X'X)^{-1} X'y. \tag{2.1.3}$$

Denoting the least squares estimators of α, β and γ by a, b and c, and substituting for X in (2.1.3) we obtain

$$
\begin{bmatrix} a \\ b \\ c \end{bmatrix} = [(iX_1 X_2)'(iX_1 X_2)]^{-1} (iX_1 X_2)'y
$$

$$
= \begin{bmatrix} T & T\bar{X}_1 & T\bar{X}_2 \\ T\bar{X}_1 & X_1' X_1 & X_1' X_2 \\ T\bar{X}_2 & X_2' X_1 & X_2' X_2 \end{bmatrix}^{-1} \begin{bmatrix} T\bar{y} \\ X_1' y \\ X_2' y \end{bmatrix}
$$

or

$$
\begin{bmatrix} a \\ b^* \end{bmatrix} = \begin{bmatrix} 1 & \bar{X} \\ \bar{X}' & M_{xx} \end{bmatrix}^{-1} \begin{bmatrix} \bar{y} \\ M_{xy} \end{bmatrix} \tag{2.1.4}
$$

where

$$
\bar{X} = (\bar{X}_1, \bar{X}_2), M_{xx} = \frac{1}{T} \begin{bmatrix} X_1' X_1 & X_1' X_2 \\ X_2' X_1 & X_2' X_2 \end{bmatrix}, M_{xy} = \frac{1}{T} \begin{bmatrix} x_1' y \\ x_2' y \end{bmatrix}
$$

and $b^{*\prime} = (b, c)$.

Pre-multiplying (2.1.4) by

$$
\begin{bmatrix} 1 & \bar{X} \\ \bar{X}' & M_{xx} \end{bmatrix}
$$

we find that

$$
a + \bar{X}b^* = \bar{y} \tag{2.1.5}
$$

$$
\bar{X}'a + M_{xx}b^* = M_{xy} \tag{2.1.6}
$$

Substituting (2.1.5) into (2.1.6) and simplifying we obtain

$$
a = \bar{y} - \bar{X}b^* \tag{2.1.7}
$$

$$
b^* = \bar{M}_{xx}^{-1} \bar{M}_{xy} \tag{2.1.8}
$$

where $\bar{M}_{xx} = M_{xx} - \bar{X}'\bar{X}, \bar{M}_{xy} = M_{xy} - \bar{X}'\bar{y}$, the ijth element of $\bar{M}_{xx}$ is

$$
\frac{1}{T} \sum_{t=1}^{T} (x_{it} - \bar{x}_i)(x_{jt} - \bar{x}_j) \qquad (i, j = 1, 2)
$$

and the ith element of $\bar{M}_{xy}$ is

$$
\frac{1}{T} \sum_{t=1}^{T} (x_{it} - \bar{x}_i)(y_t - \bar{y}) \qquad (i = 1, 2)
$$

We can now substitute directly into (2.1.7) and (2.1.8) to obtain the required estimates. Thus

$$\begin{bmatrix} b \\ c \end{bmatrix} = \begin{bmatrix} 10 & 5 \\ 5 & 5 \end{bmatrix}^{-1} \begin{bmatrix} 100 \\ 90 \end{bmatrix}$$

$$= \frac{1}{25} \begin{bmatrix} 5 & -5 \\ -5 & 10 \end{bmatrix} \begin{bmatrix} 100 \\ 90 \end{bmatrix}$$

$$= \begin{bmatrix} 2 \\ 16 \end{bmatrix}$$

and

$$a = 1200 - (100, 50) \begin{bmatrix} 2 \\ 16 \end{bmatrix} = 1200 - 100$$

$$= 200.$$

The estimated line is therefore

$$\hat{y} = 200 + 2x_1 + 16x_2$$

Part (b). We estimate σ^2 by $s^2 = \hat{u}'\hat{u}/(T-k)$. But

$$\hat{u}'\hat{u} = (y - Xb_{\text{OLS}})'(y - Xb_{\text{OLS}})$$

$$= \sum_{t=1}^{T} (y_t - a - bx_{1t} - cx_{2t})^2$$

or, from (2.1.7),

$$= \sum_{t=1}^{T} [y_t - \bar{y} - b(x_{1t} - \bar{x}_1) - c(x_{2t} - \bar{x}_2)]^2$$

$$= \sum_{t=1}^{T} (y_t - \bar{y})^2 - 2b \sum_{t=1}^{T} (x_{1t} - \bar{x}_1)(y_t - \bar{y})$$

$$- 2c \sum_{t=1}^{T} (x_{2t} - \bar{x}_2)(y_t - \bar{y}) + b^2 \sum_{t=1}^{T} (x_{1t} - \bar{x})^2$$

$$+ 2bc \sum_{t=1}^{T} (x_{1t} - \bar{x}_1)(x_{2t} - \bar{x}_2) + c^2 \sum_{t=1}^{T} (x_{2t} - \bar{x}_2)^2$$

$$= T(\bar{M}_{yy} - 2b^{*\prime}\bar{M}_{xy} + b^{*\prime}\bar{M}_{xx}b^{*})$$

where

$$\bar{M}_{yy} = \frac{1}{T}\sum_{t=1}^{T}(y_t - \bar{y})^2.$$

Using (2.1.8) we find that $\bar{M}_{xy} = \bar{M}_{xx}b^{*}$ and hence that

$$\hat{u}'\hat{u} = T(\bar{M}_{yy} - b^{*\prime}\bar{M}_{xx}b^{*}) \tag{2.1.9}$$

Thus

$$\hat{u}'\hat{u}/T = 2000 - (2, \quad 16)\begin{bmatrix} 10 & 5 \\ 5 & 5 \end{bmatrix}\begin{bmatrix} 2 \\ 16 \end{bmatrix}$$

$$= 2000 - 1640 = 360$$

and hence

$$s^2 = 100 \times 360/(100 - 3) = 371.134.$$

Part (c). In order to derive the covariance matrix of the estimates we shall make use of the following results on the inverse of a partitioned matrix, Theil (1971, p.18)

$$\begin{bmatrix} A & B \\ C & D \end{bmatrix}^{-1} = \begin{bmatrix} A^{-1} + A^{-1}B(D - CA^{-1}B)CA^{-1} & \vdots & -A^{-1}B(D - CA^{-1}B) \\ -(D - CA^{-1}B)^{-1}CA^{-1} & \vdots & (D - CA^{-1}B)^{-1} \end{bmatrix}$$

$$\tag{2.1.10}$$

where A is assumed to be non-singular. An important special case in econometrics is where the partitioned matrix is symmetric. Thus from (2.1.10):

$$\begin{bmatrix} X'X & X'Z \\ Z'X & Z'Z \end{bmatrix}^{-1} = \begin{bmatrix} (X'X)^{-1} + (X'X)^{-1}X'Z(Z'QZ)^{-1}Z'X(X'X)^{-1} \\ -(Z'QZ)^{-1}Z'X(X'X)^{-1} \end{bmatrix}$$

$$\begin{bmatrix} -(X'X)^{-1}X'Z(Z'QZ)^{-1} \\ (Z'QZ)^{-1} \end{bmatrix} \tag{2.1.11}$$

where $Q = I - X(X'X)^{-1}X'$.

Now the estimated covariance matrix of the estimates is

$$s^2 (X'X)^{-1} = \frac{s^2}{T} \begin{bmatrix} 1 & \bar{X} \\ \bar{X}' & M_{xx} \end{bmatrix}^{-1}$$

Using (2.1.11) this is

$$s^2 (X'X)^{-1} = \frac{s^2}{T} \begin{bmatrix} 1 + \bar{X}\bar{M}_{xx}^{-1}\bar{X}' & -\bar{X}\bar{M}_{xx}^{-1} \\ -\bar{M}_{xx}^{-1}\bar{X}' & \bar{M}_{xx}^{-1} \end{bmatrix}$$

where $\bar{M}_{xx} = Z'QZ = M_{xx} - \bar{X}'\bar{X}$.
Hence the covariance matrix of a, b and c is

$$V = \frac{371.134}{100} \left[\begin{array}{c|c} 1 + (100,\ 50)\begin{pmatrix} 10 & 5 \\ 5 & 5 \end{pmatrix}^{-1}\begin{pmatrix} 100 \\ 50 \end{pmatrix} & -(100,\ 50)\begin{pmatrix} 10 & 5 \\ 5 & 5 \end{pmatrix}^{-1} \\ \hline -\begin{pmatrix} 10 & 5 \\ 5 & 5 \end{pmatrix}^{-1}\begin{pmatrix} 100 \\ 50 \end{pmatrix} & \begin{pmatrix} 10 & 5 \\ 5 & 5 \end{pmatrix}^{-1} \end{array} \right]$$

$$= 3.71134 \left[\begin{array}{c|c} 1 + \tfrac{1}{25}(100,\ 50)\begin{pmatrix} 5 & -5 \\ -5 & 10 \end{pmatrix}\begin{pmatrix} 100 \\ 50 \end{pmatrix} & -\tfrac{1}{25}(100,\ 50)\begin{pmatrix} 5 & -5 \\ -5 & 10 \end{pmatrix} \\ \hline -\tfrac{1}{25}\begin{pmatrix} 5 & -5 \\ -5 & 10 \end{pmatrix}\begin{pmatrix} 100 \\ 50 \end{pmatrix} & \tfrac{1}{25}\begin{pmatrix} 5 & -5 \\ -5 & 10 \end{pmatrix} \end{array} \right]$$

$$= 3.71134 \left[\begin{array}{c|c} 1 + 1000 & -(10,\ 0) \\ \hline -\begin{pmatrix} 10 \\ 0 \end{pmatrix} & \begin{pmatrix} 0.2 & -0.2 \\ -0.2 & 0.4 \end{pmatrix} \end{array} \right]$$

$$= \begin{bmatrix} 3715.05 & -37.113 & 0 \\ -37.113 & 0.7423 & -0.7423 \\ 0 & -0.7423 & 1.4845 \end{bmatrix}$$

The standard errors of a, b and c are the square roots of the respective elements on the leading diagonal of the covariance matrix. We write these as

$$s_a = \sqrt{3715.05} = 60.95, \; s_b = \sqrt{0.7423} = 0.862 \text{ and } s_c = \sqrt{1.4845}$$
$$= 1.218.$$

Part (d). If uncorrected for the constant term, R^2 measures the proportion of the total sum of squares explained by the model. We distinguish this case from the coefficient of determination, R^2, by using the symbol R_u^2. Here we have

$$R_u^2 = 1 - \frac{\hat{u}'\hat{u}}{y'y}$$

$$= 1 - \frac{\hat{u}'\hat{u}/T}{\bar{M}_{yy} + \bar{y}^2}$$

$$= 1 - \frac{360}{2000 + 1200^2}$$

$$= 0.99975$$

(we retain 5 significant figures for use later).

It is more usual, however, to measure instead the proportion of the variance of y explained by the model, i.e.

$$R^2 = 1 - \frac{\hat{u}'\hat{u}}{\bar{M}_{yy}}$$

$$= 1 - 360/2000$$

$$= 0.820$$

$\bar{R}^2$, the corrected coefficient of determination, is defined as

$$\bar{R}^2 = R^2 - \frac{k-1}{T-k} \cdot (1 - R^2)$$

$$= 0.82 - \frac{2}{97} 0.18$$

$$= 0.8163$$

See Johnston (1972, pp.129–135) and Theil (1971, ch.4) for further discussion of R^2 and questions (2.10) and (2.11).

Solution 2.2

Part (a). (i) First, consider the estimated regression

$$y = Xb + \hat{u} = \hat{y} + \hat{u} \tag{2.2.1}$$

where $b = (X'X)^{-1}X'y$ is the OLS estimator of β, $\hat{u} = y - Xb = [I - X(X'X)^{-1}X']y$ is the vector of residuals and $\hat{y}$ is the fitted value of y from the regression. We introduce the idempotent (or projection) matrices $P = X(X'X)^{-1}X'$ and $Q = I - P$. As P is a symmetric idempotent matrix, $P = P^2 = P'P$ and $PQ = QP = P$. Hence, $\hat{y} = Py$ and $\hat{u} = (I - P)y = Qy$.

The total sum of squares $y'y$ can now be shown to satisfy

$$
\begin{aligned}
y'y &= y'(P + I - P)y \\
&= y'Py + y'Qy \\
&= y'P'Py + y'Q'Qy \\
&= y'\hat{y} + \hat{u}'\hat{u}
\end{aligned}
\tag{2.2.2}
$$

We have, therefore, decomposed the total sum of squares $y'y$ (or TSS) into two components: the explained sum of squares $\hat{y}'\hat{y}$ (or ESS) due to the explanatory variables X and the unexplained or residual sum of squares $\hat{u}'\hat{u}$ (or RSS). Thus (2.2.2) can be written as

$$
\text{TSS} = \text{ESS} + \text{RSS}
\tag{2.2.3}
$$

From this decomposition we can construct our test by checking whether or not ESS is significantly different from zero; a significantly large ESS implies that H_0 is incorrect and hence that $\beta \neq 0$.

We shall require the following results in order to find the distribution of ESS (see Theil, 1971, pp. 137–143).

(A) If y is $N(\mu, \Sigma)$ and Σ is non-singular then $(y - \mu)'\Sigma^{-1}(y - \mu)$ is distributed as a χ_T^2 where T is the size of y. Hence if y is $N(0, \sigma^2 I_T)$ then $y'y/\sigma^2$ is distributed as χ_T^2. Also, if A_1 and A_2 are two idempotent matrices then

(B) $y'A_i y/\sigma^2$ is a $\chi_{trA_i}^2$ ($i = 1, 2$)
Further if $A_1 A_2 = 0$ then

(C) $y'A_1 y/\sigma^2$ and $y'A_2 y/\sigma^2$ are independently distributed, and

(D) $y'(A_1 + A_2)y/\sigma^2$ is distributed as $\chi_{trA_1 + trA_2}^2$

(E) $\dfrac{y'A_1 y}{y'A_2 y} \cdot \dfrac{trA_2}{trA_1}$ is distributed as F_{trA_1, trA_2}

Now on H_0, y is $N(0, \sigma^2 I_T)$ and hence from (B) above $\text{ESS}/\sigma^2 = y'Py/\sigma^2$ is distributed as χ_k^2, since P is idempotent and $\text{tr}P = \text{tr}[X(X'X)^{-1}X'] = \text{tr}[(X'X)^{-1}X'X] = \text{tr}I_k = k$. Thus, if σ^2 is known, H_0 will be rejected in favour of H_1 if $\text{ESS}/\sigma^2 > \chi_k^2(\alpha)$, where α is the significance level of the test.

When σ^2 is unknown it can be estimated by $s^2 = \text{RSS}/(T - k)$. The above test statistic now becomes

$$\frac{\text{ESS}}{s^2} = \frac{y'Py/\sigma^2}{y'Qy/\sigma^2} \cdot (T - k)$$

$$= \frac{\chi_k^2}{\chi_{T-k}^2} \cdot (T - k)$$

since $y'Qy/\sigma^2$ is also a χ^2 with $\text{tr}\, Q = T - k$ degrees of freedom and in view of the fact that $PQ = 0$, it is distributed independently of $y'Py/\sigma^2$ (see (C) above). It follows that

$$\frac{\text{ESS}}{s^2 k} = \frac{\chi_k^2}{\chi_{T-k}^2} \cdot \frac{T - k}{k}$$

has an $F_{k, T-k}$ distribution. Thus, when σ^2 is unknown, H_0 is rejected when $\text{ESS}/s^2 k > F_{k, T-k}(\alpha)$.

Part (b). (i) From part (a) our required test statistic is ESS/σ^2, which in this case is distributed as χ_3^2. Now from question (2.1)

$$\begin{aligned}
\text{ESS} = y'y - \hat{u}'\hat{u} &= T(\bar{M}_{yy} + \bar{y}^2 - \hat{u}'\hat{u}/T) \\
&= 100(2000 + 1200^2 - 360) \\
&= 144,164,000
\end{aligned}$$

Therefore

$$\text{ESS}/\sigma^2 = 144,164,000/400 = 360,410$$

which is clearly significant. We can, therefore, reject H_0 in favour of H_1. (ii) When σ^2 is unknown we use the test statistic

$$\frac{\text{ESS}}{s^2 k} = \frac{144,164,000}{371.134 \times 3} = 129,481$$

which is distributed as an $F_{3, 97}$. But $F_{3, 97}(0.01) = 3.98$ so that we again reject H_0 in favour of H_1.

Part (c). If we have data on R_u^2, T and k, then we can use the fact that $\text{ESS} = R_u^2 \times \text{TSS}$ and $s^2 = (1 - R_u^2) \times \text{TSS}/(T - k)$. Substituting these into the test statistic $\text{ESS}/s^2 k$ we have

$$\frac{\text{ESS}}{s^2 k} = \frac{R_u^2}{1 - R_u^2} \cdot \frac{T - k}{k}$$

For question (2.1) $R_u^2 = 0.99975$. Hence

$$\frac{\text{ESS}}{s^2 k} = \frac{0.99975}{0.00025} \cdot \frac{97}{3} = 129,481$$

as before.

Solution 2.3

Part (a). On H_0 equation (2.3.1) becomes

$$y = X_1\beta_1 + u \tag{2.3.2}$$

whereas on H_1 we have

$$y = X_1\beta_1 + X_2\beta_2 + u \tag{2.3.3}$$

or, more compactly,

$$y = X\beta + u \tag{2.3.4}$$

where $X = (X_1 \vdots X_2)$ and $\beta' = (\beta_1', \beta_2')$. On H_0 the total sum of squares $y'y$ can be written as

$$y'y = y'P_1 y + y'(I - P_1)y$$

where $P_1 = X_1(X_1'X_1)^{-1}X_1'$. On H_1 we obtain

$$
\begin{aligned}
y'y &= y'Py + y'(I - P)y \\
&= y'P_1 y + y'(P - P_1)y + y'(I - P)y \tag{2.3.5}
\end{aligned}
$$

where $P = X(X'X)^{-1}X'$. The term $y'P_1 y$ represents the explained sum of squares due to X_1 and $y'(I - P)y$ is the residual sum of squares on H_1 which we denote by RSS_1. $y'(P - P_1)y$ can be interpreted either as the additional explained sum of squares due to adding X_2, given that X_1 is already included, or as the reduction in the residual sum of squares on H_0, namely $\text{RSS}_0 = y'(I - P_1)y$, due to adding X_2. That is,

$$y'(P - P_1)y = y'Py - y'P_1 y = y'(I - P_1)y - y'(I - P)y.$$

We can base a test of H_0 against H_1 on the observation that if H_0 is correct then adding the variables X_2 to equation (2.3.2) will not increase significantly the explained variation in y. In other words we would not expect $y'(P - P_1)y$ to be significantly different from zero. In order to test this we require the distribution of $y'(P - P_1)y$ on H_0.

On H_0 we know that y is distributed as $N(X_1\beta, \sigma^2 I_T)$, or equivalently, that $y - X_1\beta_1$ is distributed as $N(0, \sigma^2 I_T)$. Therefore, $(y - X_1\beta_1)'A(y - X_1\beta_1)/\sigma^2$ is distributed as χ^2_{trA} if A is an idempotent matrix. We can show that $P - P_1$ is an idempotent matrix as follows:

$$(P - P_1)(P - P_1) = P^2 - PP_1 - P_1 P + P_1^2 = P - PP_1 - P_1 P + P_1$$

as P and P_1 are idempotent. But since $X_1' = (I_{k_1} \vdots 0)X'$

$$PP_1 = X(X'X)^{-1}X'X_1(X_1'X_1)^{-1}X_1' = X(X'X)^{-1}X'X \begin{bmatrix} I \\ 0 \end{bmatrix} (X_1'X_1)^{-1}X_1'$$

$$= X \begin{bmatrix} I \\ 0 \end{bmatrix} (X_1'X_1)^{-1}X_1' = P_1$$

and similarly $PP_1 = P_1$, we find that

$$(P - P_1)(P - P_1) = P - P_1 - P_1 + P_1 = P - P_1,$$

as required. It follows that $(y - X_1\beta_1)'(P - P_1)(y - X_1\beta_1)/\sigma^2$ is distributed as $\chi^2_{k_2}$, since $\text{tr}(P - P_1) = \text{tr}\,P - \text{tr}\,P_1 = k - k_1 = k_2$. But

$$(P - P_1)X_1 = X(X'X)^{-1}X'X_1 - X_1(X_1'X_1)^{-1}X_1'X_1$$

$$= X(X'X)^{-1}X'X \begin{bmatrix} I \\ 0 \end{bmatrix} - X_1 = X \begin{bmatrix} I \\ 0 \end{bmatrix} - X_1 = 0.$$

Therefore,

$$(y - X_1\beta_1)'(P - P_1)(y - X_1\beta_1)/\sigma^2 = y'(P - P_1)y/\sigma^2.$$

Thus, if σ^2 is known, we use the statistic $y'(P - P_1)y/\sigma^2 = (\text{RSS}_0 - \text{RSS}_1)/\sigma^2$, which is distributed as $\chi^2_{k_2}$, to test H_0 against H_1. If σ^2 is unknown then, as in question (2.2), we can replace σ^2 by the estimator

$$s^2 = \text{RSS}_1/(T - k) = y'(I - P)y/(T - k),$$

to obtain

$$\frac{y'(P - P_1)y}{y'(I - P)y/(T - k)} = \frac{y'(P - P_1)y/\sigma^2}{y'(I - P)y/\sigma^2}(T - k).$$

We have shown above that on H_0, $y'(P - P_1)y/\sigma^2$ is distributed as a $\chi^2_{k_2}$. We can also show that on H_0, $(y - X_1\beta_1)'(I - P)(y - X_1\beta_1)/\sigma^2 = y'(I - P)y/\sigma^2$ is distributed as a χ^2_{T-k} and that as

$$(P - P_1)(I - P) = P - P_1 - P^2 + P_1P = P - P_1 - P + P_1 = 0$$

these two are distributed independently of each other. Hence

$$\frac{y'(P - P_1)y/\sigma^2}{y'(I - P)y/\sigma^2} \cdot \frac{T - k}{k_2} = \frac{\text{RSS}_0 - \text{RSS}_1}{\text{RSS}_1} \cdot \frac{T - k}{k_2} \tag{2.3.6}$$

is distributed as $F_{k_2, T-k}$.

Part (b). The likelihood ratio test is based upon the ratio of the likelihood function, evaluated on H_0, i.e. $L(H_0)$, to that evaluated on H_1, i.e. $L(H_1)$. Let $\lambda = L(H_0)/L(H_1)$ then, since $L(H_0)$ and $L(H_1)$ are non-negative and $L(H_0) \leqslant L(H_1)$, we have $0 \leqslant \lambda \leqslant 1$. $L(H_0) \leqslant L(H_1)$ because on H_0 we are maximising on a subset of the parameters over which we are maximising on H_1. Thus, in the present example, on H_1 we are maximising over β_1, β_2 and σ^2 whereas on H_0 we are maximising over β_1 and σ^2. $L(H_0)$ can, therefore, be viewed as a constrained maximum in which $\beta_2 = 0$.

If H_0 is correct then the data are generated by equation (2.3.2) and are, therefore, consistent with $\beta_2 = 0$. In this case, we expect a value of λ close to unity. A low value of λ on the other hand suggests that we have imposed an effective constraint on H_0 implying that H_0 is not correct. Our decision criterion is, therefore, to reject H_0 if $\lambda < C_\alpha$, where C_α is the critical level of λ for a level of significance α.

Since the OLS estimator is a maximum likelihood estimator for the general linear model (2.3.1), we obtain the following expressions in the present example:

$$L(H_0) \propto (\hat{\sigma}^2)^{-T/2} \exp\left(\frac{-(y - X_1\hat{\beta}_1)'(y - X_1\hat{\beta}_1)}{2\sigma^2}\right)$$

$$= (\hat{\sigma}^2)^{-T/2} \exp\left(-\frac{T}{2}\right)$$

and

$$L(H_1) \propto (\tilde{\sigma}^2)^{-T/2} \exp\left(\frac{-(y - X\tilde{\beta})'(y - X\tilde{\beta})}{2\tilde{\sigma}^2}\right)$$

$$= (\tilde{\sigma}^2)^{-T/2} \exp\left(-\frac{T}{2}\right)$$

where the symbol $\propto$ means 'proportional to' and we denote a maximum likelihood estimator on H_0 by $\hat{\ }$ and on H_1 by $\tilde{\ }$. It follows that

$$\lambda = (\tilde{\sigma}^2/\hat{\sigma}^2)^{T/2}$$

But $\hat{\sigma}^2 = \text{RSS}_0/T$ and $\tilde{\sigma}^2 = \text{RSS}_1/T$ hence

$$\lambda = \left(\frac{\text{RSS}_1}{\text{RSS}_0}\right)^{T/2} = 1\bigg/\left(1 + \frac{\text{RSS}_0 - \text{RSS}_1}{\text{RSS}_1}\right)^{T/2}$$

$$= 1\bigg/\left(1 + \frac{k_2}{T-k}F\right)^{T/2}$$

where F was defined in Part (a) above. λ is, therefore, a decreasing monotonic function of F implying that low values of λ correspond to high values of F. (See Figure 2.1). Thus if $\lambda < C_\alpha$ then $F > F_\alpha$, implying that we would reject H_0 for $F > F_\alpha$. We have shown, therefore, that the intuitively based test derived in Part (a) corresponds to a likelihood ratio test.

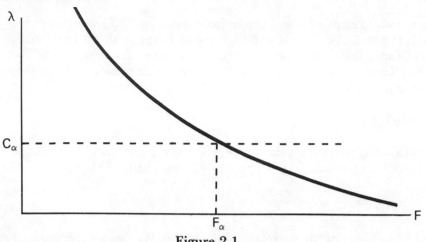

Figure 2.1

Part (c). First, we wish to test $H_0 : \alpha \neq 0, \beta = \gamma = 0$ against $H_2 : \alpha, \beta, \gamma = 0$ for the model

$$X_1 = \alpha + \beta x_{1t} + \gamma x_{2t} + u_t.$$

From Parts (a) and (b) our test statistic is

$$F = \frac{RSS_0 - RSS_2}{RSS_2} \cdot \frac{100 - 3}{2},$$

where RSS_0 is the residual sum of squares on H_0, i.e. of the regression of y on a constant which is just $\Sigma(y - \bar{y})^2$ and RSS_2 is the residual sum of squares of the regression of y on a constant, x_1 and x_2.

Now $\Sigma(y - \bar{y})^2 = 100 \times 2000$ and RSS_2 is already calculated in the answer to Question (2.1) to be 100×360. Therefore

$$F = \frac{100 \times (2000 - 360)}{100 \times 360} \times \frac{97}{2} = 221.$$

This value is highly significant at all conventional significant levels. We reject H_0, therefore, in favour of H_2.

We now want to test $H_1 : \alpha, \beta \neq 0, \gamma = 0$ against H_2. Our test becomes

$$F = \frac{RSS_1 - RSS_2}{RSS_2} \cdot \frac{100 - 3}{1},$$

where RSS_1 is the residual sum of squares of the regression of y on a constant and x_1. Instead of computing RSS_1, however, there is a simpler but equivalent way to proceed. We note that F above is distributed as $F_{1, T-k}$ and that the distribution of $F_{1, T-k}$ is identical to that of t^2_{T-k}, i.e. the square of a student's t-variate. Thus our equivalent test is to use a t-test on the coefficient γ. We recall that $t = \hat{\gamma}/SE(\hat{\gamma})$ where $SE(\hat{\gamma})$ denotes the standard error of $\hat{\gamma}$ and hence from question (2.1) we have $t = 16/1.218 = 13.14$. This is also highly significant at all conventional significance levels. We may, therefore, also reject H_1 in favour of H_2.

See Theil 1971, (pp. 137–143) for further discussion of hypothesis testing in the linear model.

Solution 2.4

Part (a). The partial correlation coefficient $r_{y1.2}$ is usually defined as follows (c.f. Johnston, 1972, pp.61–65 and Theil, 1971, pp.171–175)

$$r_{y1.2} = \frac{r_{y1} - r_{y2} r_{12}}{\sqrt{1 - r_{y2}^2}\, \sqrt{1 - r_{12}^2}} \tag{2.4.2}$$

where r_{ab} denotes the correlation of a and b. We denote the residual sum of squares of the regression of y on $x_1, x_2, x_3, \ldots$ as $\text{RSS}_{y.123\ldots}$. The question requires we show that

$$r_{y1.2}^2 = \frac{\text{RSS}_{y.2} - \text{RSS}_{y.12}}{\text{RSS}_{y.2}} \tag{2.4.3}$$

In general

$$\text{RSS}_{y.123\ldots} = y'y - y'X(X'X)^{-1}X'y$$

where $X = (x_1 \vdots x_2 \vdots x_3 \vdots \ldots)$. Thus for X consisting of the single variable x_2

$$\text{RSS}_{y.2} = y'y - y'x_2 (x_2'x_2)^{-1} x_2'y$$
$$= y'y - (y'x_2)^2 / x_2'x_2$$

If all variables are measured about their means (this is equivalent to including a constant in the regression)

$$\text{RSS}_{y.2} = y'y\{1 - (y'x_2)^2 / [(x_2'x_2)\,(y'y)]\}$$
$$= y'y(1 - r_{y2}^2) \tag{2.4.4}$$

Similarly, for $X = [x_1 \vdots x_2]$,

$$\text{RSS}_{y.12} = y'y - (y'x_1, y'x_2) \begin{bmatrix} x_1'x_1 & \vdots & x_1'x_2 \\ - - - & \vdots & - - - \\ x_2'x_1 & \vdots & x_2'x_2 \end{bmatrix}^{-1} \begin{bmatrix} y'x_1 \\ y'x_2 \end{bmatrix}$$

$$= y'y - (y'x_1, y'x_2) \begin{bmatrix} x_2'x_2 & \vdots & -x_1'x_2 \\ - - - & \vdots & - - - \\ -x_2'x_1 & \vdots & x_1'x_1 \end{bmatrix} \begin{bmatrix} y'x_1 \\ y'x_2 \end{bmatrix}$$

$$\cdot \frac{1}{(x_1'x_1)(x_2'x_2) - (x_1'x_2)^2}$$

$$= y'y - \frac{(y'x_1)^2 \cdot (x_2'x_2) - 2(y'x_1)(y'x_2)(x_1'x_2) + (y'x_2)^2 (x_1'x_1)}{(x_1'x_1)(x_2'x_2) - (x_1'x_2)^2}$$

$$= y'y \left(1 - \frac{r_{y1}^2 - 2r_{y1}r_{y2}r_{12} + r_{y2}^2}{1 - r_{12}^2} \right) \tag{2.4.5}$$

It follows that

$$\frac{\text{RSS}_{y.2} - \text{RSS}_{y.12}}{\text{RSS}_{y.2}} = \left[(1 - r_{y2}^2) - \left(1 - \frac{r_{y1}^2 - 2r_{y1}\gamma_{y2}r_{12} + r_{y2}^2}{1 - r_{12}^2} \right) \right] \bigg/ (1 - r_{y2}^2)$$

$$\tag{2.4.5}$$

$$= \frac{-r_{y2}^2(1 - r_{12}^2) + r_{y1}^2 - 2r_{y1}r_{y2}r_{12} + r_{y2}^2}{(1 - r_{y2}^2)(1 - r_{12}^2)}$$

$$= \frac{r_{y1}^2 - 2r_{y1}r_{y2}r_{12} + r_{y2}^2 r_{12}^2}{(1 - r_{y2}^2)(1 - r_{12}^2)}$$

$$= \frac{(r_{y1} - r_{y2}r_{12})^2}{(1 - r_{y2}^2)(1 - r_{12}^2)}$$

$$= r_{y1.2}^2$$

the required result.
The following more general result can be obtained in a similar way

$$r_{y1.23..k}^2 = \frac{\text{RSS}_{y.23..k} - \text{RSS}_{y.123..k}}{\text{RSS}_{y.23..k}} \tag{2.4.6}$$

Part (b). For the model

$$y = \beta_1 x_1 + \ldots + \beta_k x_k + u, \tag{2.4.7}$$

where all variables are measured as deviations about their means we define $\bar{R}^2$ for k explanatory variables as

$$\bar{R}_k^2 = R_k^2 - \frac{k}{T - k - 1}(1 - R_k^2), \tag{2.4.8}$$

with

$$R_k^2 = 1 - \frac{\text{RSS}_{y.123...k}}{y'y} \tag{2.4.9}$$

Thus

$$\bar{R}_k^2 = 1 - \frac{\text{RSS}_{y.123...k}}{y'y} - \frac{k}{T - k - 1} \cdot \frac{\text{RSS}_{y.123...k}}{y'y}$$

$$= 1 - \frac{T-1}{T-k-1} \cdot \frac{\mathrm{RSS}_{y.123...k}}{y'y}$$

or

$$\frac{\mathrm{RSS}_{y.123...k}}{y'y} = \frac{T-k-1}{T-1}(1 - \bar{R}_k^2) \qquad (2.4.10)$$

Similarly,

$$\frac{\mathrm{RSS}_{y.123...(k-1)}}{y'y} = \frac{T-k}{T-1}(1 - \bar{R}_{k-1}^2) \qquad (2.4.11)$$

Hence, taking the ratio of (2.4.11) to (2.4.10),

$$\frac{\mathrm{RSS}_{y.123...(k-1)}}{\mathrm{RSS}_{y.123...k}} = \frac{T-k}{T-k-1} \cdot \frac{1 - \bar{R}_{k-1}^2}{1 - \bar{R}_k^2} . \qquad (2.4.12)$$

But from question (2.3),

$$t_{T-k-1}^2 = \frac{\mathrm{RSS}_{y.123...(k-1)} - \mathrm{RSS}_{y.123...k}}{\mathrm{RSS}_{y.123...k}}(T-k-1)$$

or, rearranging,

$$\frac{\mathrm{RSS}_{y.123...(k-1)}}{\mathrm{RSS}_{y.123...k}} = 1 + \frac{t^2}{T-k-1} . \qquad (2.4.13)$$

Combining (2.4.12) and (2.4.13) we obtain

$$\frac{T-k}{T-k-1} \cdot \frac{1 - \bar{R}_{k-1}^2}{1 - \bar{R}_k^2} = 1 + \frac{t^2}{T-k-1}$$

or

$$\frac{1 - \bar{R}_{k-1}^2}{1 - \bar{R}_k^2} = \frac{T-k-1+t^2}{T-k}$$

$$= 1 + \frac{t^2-1}{T-k} \qquad (2.4.14)$$

Now $\bar{R}_k^2 \gtrless \bar{R}_{k-1}^2$ implies $[(1 - \bar{R}_{k-1}^2)/(1 - \bar{R}_k^2)] \gtrless 1$; but $[1 + (t^2 - 1)/(T-k)] \gtrless 1$ if and only if $t^2 \gtrless 1$, since $T - k > 0$. We have shown, therefore, that R^2 increases as a result of adding a regressor if that regressor has a t-statistic greater than unity. A further implication of this result is that in order to maximise $\bar{R}^2$ we must exclude all variables with t-statistics less than unity. This follows because $\bar{R}_k^2 < \bar{R}_{k-1}^2$ if $t^2 < 1$ for the kth variable.

Part (c). From (2.4.6) the squared partial correlation coefficient of y and x_2 given x_1 (and a constant) is

$$r_{y2.1}^2 = \frac{RSS_{y.1} - RSS_{y.12}}{RSS_{y.1}} \qquad (2.4.15)$$

We shall now show how it is possible to calculate $r_{y2.1}^2$ from the results of question (2.3), i.e. given the t-statistic for the coefficient of x_2.

In question (2.3), $RSS_{y.1}$ and $RSS_{y.12}$ were denoted by RSS_1 and RSS_2, respectively. It was also shown that

$$t^2 = F = \frac{RSS_1 - RSS_2}{RSS_2}(T-3) \qquad (2.4.16)$$

From (2.4.16) it follows that

$$\frac{RSS_1}{RSS_2} = 1 + \frac{t^2}{T-3}$$

Consequently,

$$\begin{aligned}
r_{y2.1}^2 &= \frac{RSS_1 - RSS_2}{RSS_1} \\
&= 1 - \frac{RSS_2}{RSS_1} \\
&= 1 - \left(1 + \frac{t^2}{T-3}\right)^{-1} \\
&= 1 - \left(1 + \frac{13.14^2}{97}\right)^{-1} \\
&= 0.640.
\end{aligned}$$

Hence $r_{y2.1} = 0.800$ our required result. We can interpret this as implying that there is a 64% reduction in the unexplained variance of the model as a consequence of introducing x_2 in addition to x_1 and a constant.

Finally, since we already know that the t-statistic of x_2 is greater than unity, we are required to show that $\bar{R}^2$ increases through adding x_2. For a regression of y on x_1 and a constant, equation (2.4.8) yields

$$\bar{R}^2 = R^2 - \frac{1}{T-2}(1-R^2)$$

But for the bivariate model

$$R^2 = r_{y1}^2 = m_{1y}^2/m_{yy}m_{11}$$

where $M_{1y} = \Sigma x_{1t}y_t/T$ etc. Thus

$$R^2 = \frac{100^2}{2000 \times 10} = 0.5$$

and hence

$$R^2 = 0.5 - \tfrac{1}{98}(1 - 0.5) = 0.495.$$

In question (2.1) it was shown that $\bar{R}^2$ for the regression of y on x_1, x_2 and a constant equals 0.816. As expected, therefore, $\bar{R}^2$ has increased through adding x_2.

Solution 2.5

Part (a). We require a constrained least squares estimator instead of an unconstrained least squares estimator. To minimise $u'u$ with respect to β subject to the linear constraint $R\beta = r$ we set up the Lagrangean (see Johnston, 1972, 157–159 and Theil, 1971, 143–145).

$$\mathscr{L} = u'u + 2\lambda'(R\beta - r) \tag{2.5.1}$$

Differentiating with respect to β and λ and putting the result equal to zero we have

$$\frac{\partial \mathscr{L}}{\partial \beta} = -2X'y + 2X'X\hat{\beta} + 2R'\hat{\lambda} = 0 \tag{2.5.2}$$

$$\frac{\partial \mathscr{L}}{\partial \lambda} = 2(R\hat{\beta} - r) = 0 \tag{2.5.3}$$

or, more compactly,

$$\begin{bmatrix} X'X & R' \\ R & 0 \end{bmatrix} \begin{bmatrix} \hat{\beta} \\ \hat{\lambda} \end{bmatrix} = \begin{bmatrix} X'y \\ r \end{bmatrix}$$

Hence

$$\begin{bmatrix} \hat{\beta} \\ \hat{\lambda} \end{bmatrix} = \begin{bmatrix} X'X & R' \\ R & 0 \end{bmatrix}^{-1} \begin{bmatrix} X'y \\ r \end{bmatrix} \tag{2.5.4}$$

$$= \begin{bmatrix} (X'X)^{-1} - (X'X)^{-1}R'AR(X'X)^{-1} & (X'X)^{-1}R'A \\ \hline AR(X'X)^{-1} & -A \end{bmatrix} \begin{bmatrix} X'y \\ r \end{bmatrix}$$

$$\tag{2.5.5}$$

where $A = [R(X'X)^{-1}R']^{-1}$. It follows that

$$\hat{\beta} = [I - (X'X)^{-1}R'AR](X'X)^{-1}X'y + (X'X)^{-1}R'Ar$$
$$= b + W(r - Rb),\tag{2.5.6}$$

where $W = (X'X)^{-1}R'A$. Equation (2.5.6) shows how it is possible to use b to obtain an alternative estimator of β. To prove that $\hat{\beta}$ is more efficient than b first we note that

$$E(\hat{\beta}) = E(b) + W(r - E(b)) = \beta + W(r - R\beta) = \beta$$

and second that

$$\hat{\beta} - \beta = b - \beta + W(r - Rb) - W(r - R\beta)$$
$$= (I - WR)(b - \beta)$$

Setting the covariance matrix of b equal to $V = \sigma^2(X'X)^{-1}$, the covariance matrix of $\hat{\beta}$ is given by

$$V_{\hat{\beta}} = (I - WR)V(I - WR)'$$
$$= V - WRV - VR'W' + WRVR'W'$$

But from the definition of W and V it follows that

$$WRV = VR'W' = WRVR'W'$$
$$= \sigma^2(X'X)^{-1}R'[R(X'X)^{-1}R']^{-1}R(X'X)^{-1}$$
$$= VR'(RVR')^{-1}RV,$$

which is non-negative definite. Thus

$$V_{\hat{\beta}} = V - VR'(RVR')^{-1}RV$$

and so $\hat{\beta}$ is more efficient than b because V exceeds $V_{\hat{\beta}}$ by a non-negative definite matrix.

Part (b). The null hypothesis H_0 is a special case of the more general hypothesis $R\beta = r$ or, equivalently, $R\beta - r = 0$. In this case, if all variables are measured about their means, α is eliminated and H_0 becomes

$$(5, -1)\begin{bmatrix} \beta^* \\ \gamma \end{bmatrix} = 0$$

where, to avoid confusion we have re-defined the scalar β of equation (2.1.1) as β^*. The alternative hypothesis is $R\beta \neq r$ or $R\beta - r \neq 0$, implying that β is unrestricted. The Wald test of $H_0: R\beta - r = 0$ against $H_1: R\beta - r \neq 0$ consists first of obtaining an estimator b of β on H_1 and then using the distribution of $Rb - r$ as the basis of the test. On H_1, b is just the unrestricted OLS estimator and hence $Rb - r$ is distributed as a

$N[R\beta - r, \quad R(X'X)^{-1}R']$ variable. This follows from the fact that
$E(b) = \beta$ and hence

$$E(Rb - r) = R\beta - r$$

and the covariance matrix of $Rb - r$ is

$$E[(Rb - r) - (R\beta - r)] \, [(Rb - r) - (R\beta - r)]'$$
$$= E[R(b - \beta)(b - \beta)'R']$$
$$= RE(b - \beta)(b - \beta)'R' = \sigma^2 R(X'X)^{-1}R'.$$

For σ^2 known, therefore, the test statistic for H_0 against H_1 is

$$K_1 = (Rb - r)'[R(X'X)^{-1}R']^{-1}(Rb - r)/\sigma^2 \qquad (2.5.7)$$

which is distributed as χ_m^2, where m is the number of restrictions. For σ^2
unknown we can replace σ^2 by the estimator $s^2 = \hat{u}'\hat{u}/(T - k)$ where $\hat{u}$ is
the vector of residuals from a least squares regression with no restrictions
on the coefficients. The statistic

$$K_2 = (Rb - r)'[R(X'X)^{-1}R']^{-1}(Rb - r)/s^2 \qquad (2.5.8)$$

is asymptotically distributed as χ_m^2 (see question 2.16 for further details
on asymptotic distribution theory). Alternatively, we can use the fact that
$F = K_2/m$ is distributed as $F_{m,T-k}$ in finite samples (Dhrymes et al,
1972).

For the present problem $m = 1$, hence

$$F = T(Rb - r)'[R\bar{M}_{xx}^{-1}R']^{-1}(Rb - r)/s^2$$

where we have used the result from question (2.1) that the ijth element of
$\bar{M}_{xx}$ is $\Sigma(x_{it} - \bar{x}_i)(x_{jt} - \bar{x}_j)/T$ for $i, j = 1, 2$. Thus

$$F = \frac{100}{371.134} (2, \quad 16) \begin{bmatrix} 5 \\ -1 \end{bmatrix} \left\{ (5, \quad -1)\tfrac{1}{25} \begin{bmatrix} 5 & -5 \\ -5 & 10 \end{bmatrix} \begin{bmatrix} 5 \\ -1 \end{bmatrix} \right\}^{-1}$$

$$(5, \quad -1) \begin{bmatrix} 2 \\ 16 \end{bmatrix}$$

$$= \frac{100}{371.34}(-6)\{185/25\}^{-1}(-6) = 1.31.$$

But $F_{1,97}(0.05) = 3.94$, hence $F < F_{1,94}(0.05)$ and so we cannot reject
$H_0 : 5\beta^* = \gamma$ at the 5% level of significance.

Remark. There are two alternative tests to the Wald test used above.
These are the Aitchison—Silvey (or Lagrange multiplier test) and the
likelihood ratio test which was explained in question (2.3). The Lagrange

multiplier test involves testing $H_0 : \lambda = 0$ against $H_1 : \lambda \neq 0$, where λ is the vector of Lagrange multipliers defined in part (a). The rationale behind this test is as follows. If the coefficients satisfy the restrictions $R\beta = r$, then imposing this constraint during estimation is unnecessary. The Lagrange multipliers measure the sensitivity of the minimised sum of squared errors to small changes in the constraint. If the constraint is already satisfied by the model, then small changes in the constraint would not affect the value of the residual sum of squares and hence the Lagrange multipliers would be zero. If the residual sum of squares is sensitive to the constraint then the Lagrange multipliers would be non-zero. In this case the model does not already satisfy the restrictions.

An estimate of λ can be obtained from equation (2.5.5) as

$$\hat{\lambda} = A(Rb - r)$$
$$= AR(b - \beta) + A(R\beta - r)$$

On $H_0 : R\beta - r = 0$ hence

$$\hat{\lambda} = AR(b - \beta)$$

Since $E(b) = \beta$ we find that $E(\hat{\lambda}) = 0$ and the covariance matrix of $\hat{\lambda}$ is

$$V_\lambda = ARVR'A'$$

But $V = \sigma^2 (X'X)^{-1}$ and $A = [R(X'X)^{-1}R']^{-1}$, thus

$$V_\lambda = \sigma^2 A = \sigma^2 [R(X'X)^{-1}R']^{-1}.$$

On H_0, therefore, $\hat{\lambda}$ is distributed as a $N(0, V_\lambda)$ variable.

For σ^2 known, to test $H_0 : \lambda = 0$ against $H_1 : \lambda \neq 0$ we can use the test statistic

$$\hat{\lambda}'V^{-1}\hat{\lambda} = (Rb - r)'[R(X'X)^{-1}R']^{-1}(Rb - r)/\sigma^2,$$

which is identical to K_1 defined by equation (2.5.7). If σ^2 is unknown and we estimate it by $s^2 = \hat{u}'\hat{u}/(T - k)$ as above, then clearly we obtain K_2 once more. On the other hand, if we estimate σ^2 by $\hat{\sigma}^2 = \tilde{u}'\tilde{u}/(T-k)$ where $\tilde{u}$ are the residuals from the restricted regression, then

$$K_3 = (Rb - r)'[R(X'X)^{-1}R']^{-1}(Rb - r)/\hat{\sigma}^2$$

is asymptotically distributed as χ_m^2. However, whereas K_2/m has an F distribution in finite samples K_3/m does not.

The likelihood ratio test statistic can be shown to be $l = \tilde{u}'\tilde{u}/\hat{u}'\hat{u}$. On H_0, the asymptotic distribution of $-2 \ln l$ is χ_m^2.

The reader may wish to attempt question (2.28) which involves an inequality between the three test statistics, the Lagrange multiplier, the likelihood ratio and the Wald test statistics.

Solution 2.6

Part (a). Consider the linear model

$$y_t = x_t'\beta + u_t \qquad (t = 1, \ldots, T) \tag{2.6.1}$$

where β is $k \times 1$ and the u_t are independent $N(0, \sigma^2)$. A structural change is said to have occurred if the model (2.6.1) is correct for a certain time period, say $t = 1, \ldots, T_1$ but not for another, say $t = T_1 + 1, \ldots, T$. We shall assume that in each time period the distribution of the u_t remains unchanged. It follows that the structural change is due to a change in β from β_1, say, to $\beta_1 + \gamma$. If we wish to test for the occurrence of structural change then we can test the null hypothesis $H_1 : \gamma \neq 0$. On H_0 we have

$$y_t = x_t'\beta_1 + u_t \qquad (t = 1, \ldots, T) \tag{2.6.2}$$

or

$$y = X\beta_1 + u \tag{2.6.3}$$

and on H_1 :

$$y_t = x_t'\beta_1 + u_t \qquad (t = 1, \ldots, T_1) \tag{2.6.4a}$$

$$y_t = x_t'\beta_1 + x_t'\gamma + u_t \qquad (t = T_1 + 1, \ldots, T) \tag{2.6.4b}$$

or

$$y_1 = X_1\beta_1 + u_1 \tag{2.6.5a}$$

$$y_2 = X_2\beta_1 + X_2\gamma + u_2 \tag{2.6.5b}$$

respectively, which can be written more compactly as

$$\begin{bmatrix} y_1 \\ y_2 \end{bmatrix} = \begin{bmatrix} X_1 & 0 \\ X_2 & X_2 \end{bmatrix} \begin{bmatrix} \beta_1 \\ \gamma \end{bmatrix} + \begin{bmatrix} u_1 \\ u_2 \end{bmatrix} \tag{2.6.6}$$

or

$$y = X\beta_1 + X^*\gamma + u \tag{2.6.7}$$

where $X^* = [0 \vdots X_2']'$. Thus testing for structural change is equivalent to testing for the significance of the additional variables X^*. The details of this test are given in question (2.3). For σ^2 unknown, the test statistic $F = \text{AESS}_2 / s^2 k$ has an $F_{k, T-2k}$ distribution with $s^2 = \text{RSS}/(T - 2k)$.

Part (b). The above test for structural change is not of use if the number of observations in the second time period $T - T_1$ is less than k; an alternative test is required in this case. To see this we can rewrite equation (2.6.6) as

$$\begin{bmatrix} y_1 \\ y_2 \end{bmatrix} = \begin{bmatrix} X_1 & 0 \\ 0 & X_2 \end{bmatrix} \begin{bmatrix} \beta_1 \\ \beta_2 \end{bmatrix} + \begin{bmatrix} u_1 \\ u_2 \end{bmatrix} \tag{2.6.8}$$

or, more compactly, as

$$y = \tilde{X}\beta + u \tag{2.6.9}$$

where $\beta_2 = \beta_1 + \gamma$.

If $T_1 > k$ and $T - T_1 > k$ then X_1, X_2, X^* and $\tilde{X}$ are all of full column rank. In this case the residual sum of squares of (2.6.9) or, equivalently, of (2.6.7), can be shown to be the sum of the residual sum of squares of a regression of y_1 on X_1 (say RSS_1) and the residual sum of squares of y_2 on X_2 (say RSS_2). But if $T - T_1 < k$ then X_2, X^* and $\tilde{X}$ are not of full column rank; in other words they are singular matrices. The regressions (2.6.7), (2.6.9) and y_2 on X_2 are now no longer defined. Since there are more explanatory variables than there are observations, y_2 can be explained perfectly by X_2 and hence $RSS_2 = 0$. It follows that RSS, the residual sum of squares of (2.6.9), reduces to just RSS_1, the residual sum of squares of a regression of y_1 on X_1. This must now be used to estimate σ^2. Our new estimator is $s_1^2 = RSS_1/(T_1 - k)$.

For σ^2 known, to test for structural change, we use the test statistic $(T_1 - k)s_1^2/\sigma^2$ which is distributed $\chi^2_{T_1 - k}$. For σ^2 unknown and with $T_1 \geqslant k$ and $T - T_1 \geqslant k$, our test statistic was based on the proportionate increase in the residual sum of squares due to omitting X^* from (2.6.7). That is

$$F = \frac{AESS_2}{s^2 k} = \frac{RSS_0 - RSS}{RSS} \cdot \frac{T - 2k}{k}$$

where RSS_0 is the residual sum of squares from the regression of y on X. When $T - T_1 < k$, $RSS = RSS_1$ and our test statistic becomes

$$F = \frac{RSS_0 - RSS_1}{RSS_1} \cdot \frac{T_1 - k}{T - T_1}$$

which is distributed as F_{T-T_1, T_1-k}. The proof of this result is left as an exercise for the reader. The test statistics derived above were first obtained by Chow (1960) and are sometimes known as the Chow test for structural change. See Fisher (1970) for further discussion of F tests for structural change.

Solution 2.7

Part (a). X_1^*, the residuals of the regression of X_1 on X_2, are defined by $X_1^* = Q_2 X_1$ where $Q_2 = I - X_2(X_2' X_2)^{-1} X_2'$. It follows that $X_1^{*\prime} X_2 = 0$, i.e. X_1^* is orthogonal to X_2. As a result, the estimates of β_1 and β_2 obtained from (2.7.2) are identically equal to the regression coefficients of y on X_1^* and y on X_2, respectively. To see this consider

$$\begin{bmatrix} \hat{\beta}_1 \\ \hat{\beta}_2 \end{bmatrix} = \begin{bmatrix} X_1^{*\prime} X_1^* & X_1^{*\prime} X_2 \\ X_2' X_1^* & X_2' X_2 \end{bmatrix}^{-1} \begin{bmatrix} X_1^{*\prime} y \\ X_2' y \end{bmatrix}$$

$$= \begin{bmatrix} X_1^{*\prime}X_1^* & 0 \\ 0 & X_2^{\prime}X_2 \end{bmatrix}^{-1} \begin{bmatrix} X_1^{*\prime}y \\ X_2^{\prime}y \end{bmatrix}$$

$$= \begin{bmatrix} (X_1^{*\prime}X_1^*)^{-1}X_1^{*\prime}y \\ (X_2^{\prime}X_2)^{-1}X_2^{\prime}y \end{bmatrix} \tag{2.7.3}$$

which is the required result.

Part (b). In order to obtain the expected value of $\hat{\beta}_2$, substitute (2.7.1) into the expression for $\hat{\beta}_2$ in (2.7.3):

$$\begin{aligned} \hat{\beta}_2 &= (X_2^{\prime}X_2)^{-1}X_2^{\prime}y \\ &= (X_2^{\prime}X_2)^{-1}X_2^{\prime}(X_1\beta_1 + X_2\beta_2 + u) \\ &= \beta_2 + (X_2^{\prime}X_2)^{-1}X_2^{\prime}(X_1\beta_1 + u) \end{aligned}$$

Hence, $E(\hat{\beta}_2) = \beta_2 + (X_2^{\prime}X_2)^{-1}X_2^{\prime}X_1\beta_1$ and the bias expression required is $(X_2^{\prime}X_2)^{-1}X_2^{\prime}X_1\beta_1$.

Part (c). Writing equation (2.7.1) more compactly we obtain

$$y = X\beta + u, \tag{2.7.4}$$

where $X = (X_1 \vdots X_2)$ and $\beta^{\prime} = (\beta_1^{\prime}, \beta_2^{\prime})$. The OLS estimator of β is

$$b = (X^{\prime}X)^{-1}X^{\prime}y$$

or

$$\begin{bmatrix} b_1 \\ b_2 \end{bmatrix} = \begin{bmatrix} X_1^{\prime}X_1 & X_1^{\prime}X_2 \\ X_2^{\prime}X_1 & X_2^{\prime}X_2 \end{bmatrix}^{-1} \begin{bmatrix} X_1^{\prime}y \\ X_2^{\prime}y \end{bmatrix} \tag{2.7.5}$$

where b_1 and b_2 are the OLS estimators of β_1 and β_2, respectively. Using the expression for the inverse of a partitioned matrix given in question (2.1) we obtain

$$\begin{bmatrix} b_1 \\ b_2 \end{bmatrix} = \left[\begin{array}{c} (X_1^{\prime}Q_2X_1)^{-1} \\ \hline -(X_2^{\prime}X_2)^{-1}X_2^{\prime}X_1(X_1^{\prime}Q_2X_1)^{-1} \end{array} \right.$$

$$\left. \begin{array}{c} -(X_1^{\prime}Q_2X_1)^{-1}X_1^{\prime}X_2(X_2^{\prime}X_2^{-1})^{-1} \\ \hline (X_2^{\prime}X_2)^{-1} + (X_2^{\prime}X_2)^{-1}X_2^{\prime}X_1(X_1^{\prime}Q_2X_1)^{-1}X_1^{\prime}X_2(X_2^{\prime}X_2)^{-1} \end{array} \right] \begin{bmatrix} X_1^{\prime}y \\ X_2^{\prime}y \end{bmatrix}$$

$$\tag{2.7.6}$$

Solving (2.7.6) for b_1 where Q_2 is defined in part (a), we find that

$$b_1 = (X_1' Q_2 X_1)^{-1} X_1' Q_2 y \tag{2.7.7}$$

But since Q_2 is idempotent, (2.7.7) can be written as

$$\begin{aligned} b_1 &= (X_1' Q_2' Q_2 X_1)^{-1} X_1' Q_2 y \\ &= (X_1^{*'} X_1^*)^{-1} X_1^{*'} y \end{aligned} \tag{2.7.8}$$

Equation (2.7.8) is the same as the expression for $\hat{\beta}_1$ in (2.7.3) where $X_1^* = Q_2 X_1$. Comparing b_1 defined by equation (2.7.8) with $\hat{\beta}_1$ defined in equation (2.7.3) we see that the two expressions are identical. Hence b_1, the OLS estimator of β_1 obtained from (2.7.1), is identical to $\hat{\beta}_1$, the OLS estimator of β_1 obtained from (2.7.2).

Solution 2.8

Part (a). The Gauss–Doolittle pivotal condensation method for inverting a matrix operates as follows. Consider the $n \times n$ matrix A with elements a_{ij}. An iterative scheme is performed in which in each iteration a new matrix is formed from the matrix obtained in the previous iteration. For the first iteration we form the new matrix B from the matrix A as follows.

1. Choose an element on the leading diagonal of A. Let this be a_{kk}. This acts as a pivot.

2. In forming the elements of the matrix B from the elements of A we must distinguish between four types of elements
   (i) the pivotal element of B is formed as

   $$b_{kk} = 1/a_{kk}$$

   (ii) elements in the same row as the pivot are

   $$b_{ki} = a_{ki}/a_{kk} \qquad (i \neq k)$$

   (iii) elements in the same column as the pivot are

   $$b_{jk} = -a_{jk}/a_{kk} \qquad (j \neq k)$$

   (iv) the remaining elements are

   $$b_{ij} = a_{ij} - a_{ki} a_{jk}/a_{kk} \qquad (i, j \neq k)$$

For the second iteration we construct a new matrix by performing steps 1 and 2 on the matrix B obtained in the first iteration. Iteration is continued until every element on the leading diagonal has been used once as the pivotal element. Thus there are in all n iterations. It is best to choose the largest unused diagonal element as the pivot. It is not necessary to work in sequence from 1 to n. At the completion of the nth iteration the resulting matrix is A^{-1}.

To illustrate the use of this method in computing OLS estimates of the model $y = X\beta + u$, first we set up the cross product matrix of all the variables. Denote this by A. Thus

$$A = \begin{bmatrix} X'X & X'y \\ y'X & y'y \end{bmatrix} \tag{2.8.1}$$

Next we perform one iteration of the pivotal condensation method with $X'X$ as the pivot. Note this is a matrix and so the operations 2(i)–2(iv) above must be adapted to matrix notation accordingly. The result is the matrix B:

$$B = \begin{bmatrix} (X'X)^{-1} & (X'X)^{-1}X'y \\ -y'X(X'X)^{-1} & y'y - y'X(X'X)^{-1}X'y \end{bmatrix}$$

$$= \begin{bmatrix} B_{11} & B_{12} \\ B_{21} & B_{22} \end{bmatrix} \tag{2.8.2}$$

Now B_{12} is a column of regression coefficients; it is the OLS estimator of β. B_{22} is a scalar and is the residual sum of squares from the regression and B_{11}, when multiplied by $B_{22}/(T-k)$, is the estimated covariance matrix of the OLS estimates, i.e.

$$B = \begin{bmatrix} V/s^2 & b \\ -b' & (T-k)s^2 \end{bmatrix}$$

where b is the OLS estimator, V is the covariance matrix of b and $s^2 = B_{22}/(T-k)$.

Part (b). It is possible to introduce a subset of variables instead of all the variables in X by partitioning X appropriately and using as the pivotal matrix the cross-products of the chosen variables. Additional variables, or blocks of variables, can be introduced by pivoting on these variables subsequently. The advantage of this computational design for stepwise regression is that it is possible to calculate the reduction in the residual sum of squares due to adding the extra variable(s), and test to see whether or not this is significant without having to compute a complete set of estimates and the corresponding covariance matrix of estimates. Thus initially only one number has to be calculated at each step. If that variable is found to be significant then the remaining elements in the tableau are calculated.

In effect, therefore, a variable is introduced into a regression by pivoting on the corresponding element in the leading diagonal of the cross-product matrix A. It is useful to note that it is also removed from the regression by pivoting again on that element.

Part (c). For the model given, the matrix A corresponding to (2.8.1) is

$$A = \begin{bmatrix} X_1'X_1 & X_1'X_2 & X_1'y \\ X_2'X_1 & X_2'X_2 & X_2'y \\ y'X_1 & y'X_2 & y'y \end{bmatrix} \tag{2.8.3}$$

Introducing first X_1 we pivot on $X_1'X_1$ giving

$$B = \left[\begin{array}{c|c|c} (X_1'X_1)^{-1} & (X_1'X_1)^{-1}X_1'X_2 & (X_1'X_1)^{-1}X_1'y \\ \hline -X_2'X_1(X_1'X_1)^{-1} & X_2'X_2 - X_2'X_1(X_1'X_1)^{-1}X_1'X_2 & X_2'y - X_2'X_1(X_1'X_1)^{-1}X_1'y \\ \hline -y'X_1(X_1'X_1)^{-1} & y'X_2 - y'X_1(X_1'X_1)^{-1}X_1'X_2 & y'y - y'X_1(X_1'X_1)^{-1}X_1'y \end{array} \right]$$

$$= \left[\begin{array}{c|c|c} (X_1'X_1)^{-1} & (X_1'X_1)^{-1}X_1'X_2 & (X_1'X_1)^{-1}X_1'y \\ \hline -X_2'X_1(X_1'X_1)^{-1} & X_2'Q_1X_2 & X_2'Q_1y \\ \hline -y'X_1(X_1'X_1)^{-1} & y'Q_1X_2 & y'Q_1y \end{array} \right] \tag{2.8.4}$$

where $Q_1 = I - X_1(X_1'X_1)^{-1}X_1'$. Denoting the ijth elements of A and B by A_{ij} and B_{ij} respectively, where A is given by (2.8.3) and B by (2.8.4), we find that $B_{13} = (X_1'X_1)^{-1}X_1'y$ is the regression coefficient of y on X_1 and B_{33} is the corresponding residual sum of squares. The difference $A_{33} - B_{33}$ is the explained sum of squres due to X_1.

Next we introduce X_2 by pivoting on B_{22}, obtaining

$$C = \left[\begin{array}{c} (X_1'X_1)^{-1} + (X_1'X_1)^{-1}X_1'X_2(X_2'Q_1X_2)^{-1}X_2'X_1(X_1'X_1)^{-1} \\ \hline -(X_2'Q_1X_2)^{-1}X_2'X_1(X_1'X_1)^{-1} \\ \hline -y'X_1(X_1'X_1)^{-1} + y'Q_1X_2(X_2'Q_1X_2)^{-1}X_2'X_1(X_1'X_1)^{-1} \end{array} \right.$$

$$\left. \begin{array}{c|c} -(X_1'X_1)^{-1}X_1'X_2(X_2'Q_1X_2)^{-1} & (X_1'X_1)^{-1}X_1'y - (X_1'X_1)^{-1}X_1'X_2(X_2'Q_1X_2)^{-1}X_2'Q_1y \\ \hline (X_2'Q_1X_2)^{-1} & (X_2'Q_1X_2)^{-1}X_2'Q_1y \\ \hline -y'Q_1X_2(X_2'Q_1X_2)^{-1} & y'Q_1y - y'Q_1X_2(X_2'Q_1X_2)^{-1}X_2'Q_1y \end{array} \right]$$

$$\tag{2.8.5}$$

$$= \begin{bmatrix} (X'X)^{-1} & \vdots & (X'X)^{-1} X'y \\ \overline{-y'X(X'X)^{-1}} & \vdots & \overline{y'y - y'X(X'X)^{-1} X'y} \end{bmatrix} \qquad (2.8.6)$$

where $X = (X_1 \vdots X_2)$. Equation (2.8.5) is identical to (2.8.2) since all of the explanatory variables have now been included in the regression. The expression $y'Q_1 X_2 (X_2' Q_1 X_2)^{-1} X_2' Q_1 y$ is the additional explained sum of squares due to X_2. Clearly, it can be calculated before we calculate the other elements in the matrix C.

Part (d). First we introduce x_1 by 'pivoting' on the first element of the moment matrix. We obtain

$$\begin{bmatrix} 1 & 1 & 2 \\ -1 & 3 & 3 \\ -2 & 3 & 6 \end{bmatrix}$$

Next we can introduce x_2 by pivoting on the second element in the leading diagonal. However, since we only want the reduction in the sum of squares due to introducing x_2 we need only calculate one element of the new matrix, namely the last. It is $6 - (3 \times 3)/3 = 3$. The F test appropriate for testing $H_0 : \alpha, \beta_1 \neq 0, \beta_2 = 0$ against $H_1 : \alpha, \beta_1, \beta_2 \neq 0$ is given by equation (2.3.5). It is

$$F = \frac{\text{RSS}_0 - \text{RSS}_1}{\text{RSS}_1} \cdot \frac{T - m - n}{n}$$

$$= \frac{6 - 3}{3} \cdot \frac{12 - 2 - 1}{1}$$

$$= 9$$

Since F is distributed as $F_{1,9}$ we can use the t-distribution with 9 degrees of freedom. The t-statistic is $\sqrt{F} = 3$. This is significant at the 2% level. To test the significance of the coefficient of x_1 we first introduce x_2 to obtain

$$\begin{bmatrix} 0.75 & -0.25 & 0.75 \\ 0.25 & 0.25 & 1.25 \\ 0.75 & -1.25 & 3.75 \end{bmatrix}$$

Next we introduce x_1 using the first element as pivot. The new last element is $3.75 - (0.75^2)/(0.75) = 3$. The t-statistic we require is, therefore,

$$t = \left(\frac{3.75 - 3}{3} \times 9 \right)^{1/2}$$

$$= 1.5$$

This is significant at the 10% level.

Solution 2.9

Part (a). First we rewrite equations (2.9.1) and (2.9.2) more compactly as

$$y = X_1 \beta_1 + X_2 \beta_2 + u \qquad\qquad (2.9.5)$$

and

$$y = X_1^* \beta_1 + u^*, \qquad\qquad (2.9.6)$$

respectively, where

$$y = \begin{bmatrix} y_1 \\ \cdot \\ \cdot \\ \cdot \\ y_T \end{bmatrix}, \quad y^* = \begin{bmatrix} y_1^* \\ \cdot \\ \cdot \\ \cdot \\ y_T^* \end{bmatrix}, \quad X_1 = \begin{bmatrix} x_1 \\ \cdot \\ \cdot \\ \cdot \\ x_T \end{bmatrix}, \quad X_2 = \begin{bmatrix} 1 \\ \cdot \\ \cdot \\ \cdot \\ T \end{bmatrix}, \quad X_1^* = \begin{bmatrix} x_1^* \\ \cdot \\ \cdot \\ \cdot \\ x_T^* \end{bmatrix},$$

$$u = \begin{bmatrix} u_1 \\ \cdot \\ \cdot \\ \cdot \\ u_T \end{bmatrix} \quad \text{and} \quad u^* = \begin{bmatrix} u_1^* \\ \cdot \\ \cdot \\ \cdot \\ u_T^* \end{bmatrix}$$

y^* and X_1^* are now the residuals of the regression of y on X_2 and X_1 on X_2, respectively. Thus $y^* = Q_2 y$ and $X_1^* = Q_2 X_1$ where $Q_2 = I_T - X_2 (X_2' X_2)^{-1} X_2'$.

The least squares estimators of β_1 and β_2 from (2.9.3) are

$$\begin{bmatrix} b_1 \\ b_2 \end{bmatrix} = \begin{bmatrix} X_1' X_1 & X_1' X_2 \\ X_2' X_1 & X_2' X_2 \end{bmatrix}^{-1} \begin{bmatrix} X_1' y \\ X_2' y \end{bmatrix}$$

Using the results of question (2.7) we find that

$$b_1 = (X_1' Q_2 X_1)^{-1} X_1' Q_2 y$$

$$= (X_1' Q_2' Q_2 X_1)^{-1} X_1' Q_2' Q_2 y$$
$$= (X_1^{*'} X_1^*)^{-1} X_1^{*'} y^* \tag{2.9.7}$$

But (2.9.7) is the expression for the regression coefficients in the regression of y^* on X_1^*. We have shown, therefore, that the OLS estimator of β_1 obtained from (2.9.1) is identical to that obtained from (2.9.2).

Part (b). In general we can obtain an equation like (2.9.4) from (2.9.3) by eliminating a set of variables through projecting the variables in the original linear model onto the space orthogonal to the range space of the variables to be eliminated. This is accomplished by pre-multiplying the original model by the appropriate projection matrix. Equations (2.9.3) and (2.9.4) can be written in matrix form as (2.9.5) and (2.9.6), respectively. To reduce (2.9.5) to (2.9.6) we pre-multiply (2.9.5) by $Q_2 = I - X_2 (X_2' X_2)^{-1} X_2'$ to get

$$Q_2 y = Q_2 X_1 \beta_1 + Q_2 X_2 \beta_2 + Q_2 u \tag{2.9.8}$$

Now $Q_2 X_2 = 0$, therefore (2.9.8) becomes

$$y^* = X_1^* \beta_1 + u^* \tag{2.9.9}$$

where y^*, X_1^* and u^* are defined as part (a) above; we note that y^* and X_1^*, residuals from the regressions on X_2, can also be interpreted as detrended series.

Part (c). The test statistic for $H_0: \beta_1 = 0$ from (2.9.7) is a special case of a test for the significance of a subset of regression coefficients. If in equation (2.9.5) X_1 is a $T \times k_1$ matrix and X_2 is a $T \times k_2$ matrix, then the required test statistic for $H_0: \beta_1 = 0$, $\beta_2 \neq 0$ against $H_1: \beta_1, \beta_2 \neq 0$ is given by equation (2.3.5) as

$$F = \frac{RSS_0 - RSS_1}{RSS_1} \cdot \frac{T - k_1 - k_2}{k_1} \tag{2.9.10}$$

where RSS_0 is the residual sum of squares on H_0 and is obtained from the regression of y on X_2, and RSS_1 is the residual sum of squares on H_1 and is obtained from a regression of y on X_1 and X_2. Thus $RSS_0 = y' Q_2 y$ and $RSS_1 = y' [I - X(X'X)^{-1} X'] y$, where $X = (X_1 : X_2)$. F is distributed as $F_{k_1, T-k_1-k_2}$. In the present case, equation (2.9.1), $k_1 = k_2 = 1$.

The test statistic for $H_0: \beta_1 = 0$ against $H_1: \beta_1 \neq 0$ from (2.9.2) is a special case of the test of significance of all of the regression coefficients. From question (2.2) the required test statistic in the present case is

$$F = ESS/(s^2 k_1) \tag{2.9.11}$$

where ESS is the explained sum of squares in the regression of y on X_1; s^2 is an estimate of σ^2 obtained on H_1 and X_1 is assumed to be a $T \times k_1$ matrix. Thus

$$\text{ESS} = y^{*\prime}X_1^*(X_1^{*\prime}X_1^*)^{-1}X_1^{*\prime}y^*$$
$$= y'Q_2X_1(X_1'Q_2X_1)^{-1}X_1'Q_2y \qquad (2.9.12)$$

and

$$s^2 = \text{RSS}_1^*/(T^* - k_1)$$
$$= (y^{*\prime}y^* - \text{ESS})/(T^* - k_1)$$
$$= (y'Q_2y - y'Q_2X_1(X_1'Q_2X_1)^{-1}X_1'Q_2y)/(T^* - k_1) \qquad (2.9.13)$$

where RSS_1^* is the residual sum of squares from the regression of y^* on X_1^* and T^* is chosen to equal $T - k_2$ because $y^{*\prime}y^*/\sigma^2$ is distributed $\chi^2_{T-k_2}$ and not χ^2_T. F, defined in equation (2.9.11), is distributed as F_{k_1, T^*-k_1}. In the case of equation (2.9.2), $k_1 = 1$.

Comparing the bottom right-hand element of equation (2.8.5) with that of equation (2.8.6) we can see that the residual sum of squares from the regression of y on X_1 and X_2 is

$$y'[I - X(X'X)^{-1}X']y = y'Q_2y - y'Q_2X_1(X_1'Q_2X_1)^{-1}X_1'Q_2y \qquad (2.9.14)$$

Hence, from (2.9.14),

$$\text{RSS}_0 - \text{RSS}_1 = y'Q_2y - y'[I - X(X'X)^{-1}X']y$$
$$= y'Q_2X_1(X_1'Q_2X_1)^{-1}X_1'Q_2y$$

and so (2.9.10), the test statistic using (2.9.1), becomes

$$F = \frac{y'Q_2X_1(X_1'Q_2X_1)^{-1}X_1'Q_2y}{y'Q_2y - y'Q_2X_1(X_1'Q_2X)^{-1}X_1'Q_2y} \cdot \frac{T - k_1 - k_2}{k_1} \qquad (2.9.15)$$

If we substitute (2.9.12) and (2.9.13) into (2.9.11), the test statistic using (2.9.2), we obtain once more equation (2.9.15). The two test statistics are clearly identical.

Solution 2.10

Part (a). The coefficient of determination from the first regression is given by

$$R_1^2 = 1 - \sum_{t=1}^{T} \hat{u}_t^2 \Big/ \sum_{t=1}^{T} (y_t - \bar{y})^2$$

where $\bar{y}$ is the sample mean of $y_1, \ldots, y_T$

$$\hat{u}_t = y_t - \hat{\beta}_0 - \hat{\beta}_1 x_{1t} - \ldots - \hat{\beta}_{k+1,t}$$

and the $\hat{\beta}_i \, (i = 0, \ldots, k + 1)$ are the estimated coefficients in the regression which minimises the sum of squares

$$Q(\beta_0, \beta_1, \ldots, \beta_{k+1}) = \sum_{t=1}^{T} (y_t - \beta_0 - \beta_1 x_{1t} - \ldots - \beta_{k+1} x_{k+1,t})^2$$

Thus the inequality

$$Q(\hat{\beta}_0, \hat{\beta}_1, \ldots, \hat{\beta}_{k+1}) \leqslant Q(\beta_0, \beta_1, \ldots, \beta_{k+1}) \qquad (2.10.1)$$

is satisfied for all values of $\beta_0, \beta_1, \ldots, \beta_{k+1}$.

From the second regression we obtain

$$R_2^2 = 1 - \sum_{t=1}^{T} \hat{\hat{u}}_t^2 \sum_{t=1}^{T} (y_t - \bar{y})^2$$

where

$$\hat{\hat{u}}_t = y_t - \hat{\hat{\beta}}_0 - \hat{\hat{\beta}}_1 x_{1t} - \ldots - \hat{\hat{\beta}}_k x_{k,t}$$

However,

$$\sum_{t=1}^{T} \hat{\hat{u}}_t^2 = Q(\hat{\hat{\beta}}_0, \hat{\hat{\beta}}_1, \ldots, \hat{\hat{\beta}}_k, 0)$$

which from (2.10.1) is greater than $Q(\hat{\beta}_0, \hat{\beta}_1, \ldots, \hat{\beta}_{k+1})$. Hence

$$\sum_{t=1}^{T} \hat{\hat{u}}_t^2 \geqslant \sum_{t=1}^{T} \hat{u}_t^2$$

and, therefore, $R_1^2 \geqslant R_2^2$ as required.

Part (b). To find an exact relation between R_1^2 and R_2^2 we must examine the residual sums of squares $\sum_{t=1}^{T} \hat{u}_t^2$ and $\sum_{t=1}^{T} \hat{\hat{u}}_t^2$ more closely. First we introduce the notation

$$X = \begin{bmatrix} 1 & x_{11} & x_{k1} \\ \vdots & \vdots & \vdots \\ 1 & x_{1T} & x_{kT} \end{bmatrix}, \quad x = \begin{bmatrix} x_{k+1,1} \\ \vdots \\ x_{k+1,T} \end{bmatrix}, \quad y = \begin{bmatrix} y_1 \\ \vdots \\ y_T \end{bmatrix}$$

and

$$Z = [X \vdots x]$$

Then

$$\sum_{t=1}^{T} \hat{u}_t^2 = y'(I - P_1)y \quad \text{and} \quad \sum_{t=1}^{T} \hat{\hat{u}}_t^2 = y'(I - P_2)y$$

where

$$P_1 = Z(Z'Z)^{-1}Z' \quad \text{and} \quad P_2 = X(X'X)^{-1}X'$$

But

$$P_1 = [X \vdots x] \begin{bmatrix} X'X & X'x \\ x'X & x'x \end{bmatrix}^{-1} \begin{bmatrix} X' \\ x' \end{bmatrix}$$

which, from the inverse of a partitioned matrix (see the solution to 2.1 above), is

$$[X \vdots x] \begin{bmatrix} (X'X)^{-1} + (X'X)^{-1} X'xBx'X(X'X)^{-1} & \vdots & -(X'X)^{-1} X'xB \\ \cdots\cdots\cdots\cdots\cdots\cdots\cdots\cdots\cdots\cdots\cdots\cdots\cdots\cdots\cdots\cdots\cdots\cdots \\ -Bx'X(X'X)^{-1} & \vdots & B \end{bmatrix}$$

$$\begin{bmatrix} X' \\ x' \end{bmatrix} \qquad (2.10.2)$$

where B is the scalar

$$B = \{x'[I - X(X'X)^{-1} X'] x\}^{-1}. \qquad (2.10.3)$$

Thus, expanding (2.10.2), we obtain

$$P_1 = X(X'X)^{-1} X' + [I - X(X'X)^{-1} X'] xBx'[I - X(X'X)^{-1} X']$$
$$= P_2 + W, \text{ say.}$$

Now, setting $Q = I - X(X'X)^{-1} X'$, we have

$$W = QxBx'Q = \frac{1}{x'Qx} Qxx'Q$$

in view of (2.10.3). We note that $x'Qx > 0$. For, if this were not so, Qx would equal zero and we could write x as a linear combination of the columns of X in which case $Z'Z$ would be a singular matrix and the first regression would be impossible.

Writing $\bar{m}_{yy} = \Sigma_{t=1}^T (y_t - \bar{y})^2$, we now have

$$R_1^2 = 1 - \frac{y'(I - P_1)y}{\bar{m}_{yy}}$$

$$= 1 - \frac{y'(I - P_2)y}{\bar{m}_{yy}} + \frac{y'Wy}{\bar{m}_{yy}}$$

$$= R_2^2 + \frac{y'Wy}{\bar{m}_{yy}}$$

But

$$y'Wy = \left(\frac{1}{x'Qx}\right) y'Qxx'Qy = \frac{(y'Qx)^2}{x'Qx} \geqslant 0$$

so that $R_1^2 \geqslant R_2^2$ as shown above. However, we now see that equality occurs only when $y'Wy = 0$. That is, when $y'Qx = 0$ or when y is orthogonal to the residuals from the regression of x on X.

Solution 2.11

Part (a). From $y = Zb + u^*$ and $b = (Z'Z)^{-1}Z'y$, we have

$$u^* = y - Zb = y - Z(Z'Z)^{-1}Z'y = [I - Z(Z'Z)^{-1}Z']y$$

so that

$$Z'u^* = Z'[I - Z(Z'Z)^{-1}Z']y = 0 \qquad (2.11.2)$$

Thus

$$y'y = (Zb + u^*)'(Zb + u^*) = b'Z'Zb + b'Z'u^* + u^{*'}Zb + u^{*'}u^*$$
$$= b'Z'Zb + u^{*'}u^* \qquad (2.11.3)$$

Part (b). We take as an example the case where Z has a single column and there are three observations

t	y_t	Z_t
1	2	0
2	1	1
3	0	2

Then

$$b = \sum_{t=1}^{T} y_t Z_t \bigg/ \sum_{t=1}^{T} Z_t^2 = 1/5$$

From (2.11.3) we see that

$$\sum_{t=1}^{T} \hat{y}_t^2 = b'Z'Zb$$

where $\hat{y}_t$ is the estimated or calculated value of y_t from the regression. Now in the usual case where there is a constant term in the regression (and hence one column of Z is the sum vector i) the orthogonality condition (2.11.2) implies that

$$Z'y = Z'\hat{y}$$

where $\hat{y} = Zb$, and hence (taking that row of Z' which is the sum vector)

$$\sum_{t=1}^{T} y_t = \sum_{t=1}^{T} \hat{y}_t \qquad (2.11.5)$$

Then, in the numerator of (2.11.4) we would have

$$\sum_{t=1}^{T} \hat{y}_t^2 - \left(\sum_{t=1}^{T} y_t\right)^2 \Big/ T = \sum_{t=1}^{T} \hat{y}_t^2 - \left(\sum_{t=1}^{T} \hat{y}_t\right)^2 \Big/ T = \sum_{t=1}^{T} (\hat{y}_t - \bar{y})^2 \geqslant 0$$

But in the present case, where there is no constant term in the regression, (2.11.5) does not necessarily hold and consequently the numerator of (2.11.4) cannot be written as a sum of squares and is, therefore, not necessarily non-negative. In fact

$$R^2 = 1 - \frac{\Sigma_{t=1}^{T} \hat{u}_t^2}{\Sigma_{t=1}^{T} (y_t - \bar{y})^2} = 1 - \frac{4\frac{4}{5}}{2} = -\frac{14}{10} < 0$$

The observations and the regression line in this case are given in figure 2.2.

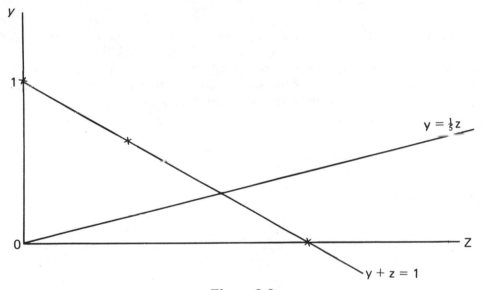

Figure 2.2

The observations all lie on the line $y + z = 1$ and forcing the regression line through the origin gives a very poor fit. To see why R^2 as defined by (2.11.1) can be negative in such cases we write it in the form

$$R^2 = \frac{\Sigma_{t=1}^{T} (y_t - \bar{y})^2 - \Sigma_{t=1}^{T} \hat{u}_t^2}{\Sigma_{t=1}^{T} (y_t - \bar{y})^2} = \frac{\Sigma_{t=1}^{T} y_t^2 - (\Sigma_{t=1}^{T} y_t)^2 / T - \Sigma_{t=1}^{T} \hat{u}_t^2}{\Sigma_{t=1}^{T} (y_t - \bar{y})^2}$$

$$= \frac{\Sigma_{t=1}^{T} \hat{y}_t^2 - (\Sigma_{t=1}^{T} y_t)^2 / T}{\Sigma_{t=1}^{T} (y_t - \bar{y})^2} \qquad (2.11.4)$$

Part (c). An alternative to R^2 in this case is the R_u^2 defined in statistic question 2.1. Thus

$$R_m^2 = R_u^2 = 1 - \frac{\sum_{t=1}^{T} \hat{u}_t^2}{\sum_{t=1}^{T} y_t^2}$$

Now

$$R_m^2 = \frac{y'y - \hat{u}'\hat{u}}{y'y} = \frac{\hat{y}'\hat{y}}{y'y} \geqslant 0$$

so that

$$0 \leqslant R_m^2 \leqslant 1$$

For the data in part (b) we have

$$R_m^2 = 1 - \frac{4\frac{4}{5}}{5} = \frac{1}{25}.$$

Part (d). The fact that R^2 can be negative when the constant term is suppressed in a regression holds even if the true model itself does not involve a constant. For example, if $y = Z\beta_Z + u$ were the true model in the example of part (b), the observations given in that example could still have been generated, viz from the disturbance sequence

t	1	2	3
u_t	2	0	-2

Solution 2.12

Part (a). The GLS estimator can be derived by first transforming the model (2.12.1) to produce a linear model with a scalar diagonal error covariance matrix. Then we apply the Gauss–Markov theorem to the new model. The resulting estimator written in terms of the original variables is the GLS estimator.

Consider a $T \times T$ non-singular matrix R which satisfies $R'R = \Sigma^{-1}$. One such matrix is obtained by writing $\Sigma = Q\Lambda Q'$ where Q is a $T \times T$ matrix of the eigenvectors of Σ, Λ is a diagonal matrix of non-negative eigenvalues of Σ and $Q'Q = I$. Hence $\Sigma^{-1} = Q\Lambda^{-1}Q' = Q\Lambda^{-1/2}\Lambda^{-1/2}Q'$. If we define $R = \Lambda^{-1/2}Q'$, then $R'R = \Sigma^{-1}$ as required.

Pre-multiplying (2.12.1) by R we obtain

$$Ry = RX\beta + Ru$$

or

$$y^* = X^*\beta + u^* \tag{2.12.3}$$

where $y^* = Ry$, $X^* = RX$, $u^* = Ru$, $E(u^*) = 0$ and $E(u^*u^*) = RE(uu')R'$
$= R\Sigma R' = R(R'R)^{-1}R' = I$. Thus (2.12.3) is a linear model whose error

term has mean zero and a scalar diagonal covariance matrix.

From the Gauss—Markov theorem, (Theil, 1971, pp.119—121), the BLUE estimator of β in (2.12.3) is the OLS estimator

$$\hat{\beta} = (X^{*\prime}X^*)^{-1}X^{*\prime}y^* = (X'R'RX)^{-1}X'R'Ry$$
$$= (X'\Sigma^{-1}X)^{-1}X'\Sigma^{-1}y \qquad (2.12.4)$$

which has a covariance matrix

$$V = (X^{*\prime}X^*)^{-1} = (X'R'RX)^{-1} = (X'\Sigma^{-1}X)^{-1}. \qquad (2.12.5)$$

To see that (2.12.4) is a BLUE estimator of β consider another linear estimator

$$b^* = [(X'\Sigma^{-1}X)^{-1}X'\Sigma^{-1} + D]y = \beta + DX\beta + [(X'\Sigma^{-1}X)^{-1}X'\Sigma^{-1} + D]u.$$

For b^* to be an unbiased linear estimator we require that

$$E(b^*) = \beta + DX\beta = \beta$$

implying that $DX = 0$. The covariance matrix of b^* is

$$V^* = E(b^* - \beta)(b^* - \beta)'$$
$$= [(X'\Sigma^{-1}X)^{-1}X'\Sigma^{-1} + D]E(uu')[(X'\Sigma^{-1}X)^{-1}X'\Sigma^{-1} + D]'$$
$$= (X'\Sigma^{-1}X)^{-1} + D\Sigma D',$$

since the cross product terms $(X'\Sigma^{-1}X)^{-1}X'\Sigma^{-1}\Sigma D = 0$. As $D\Sigma D'$ is a positive semi-definite matrix, it follows that choosing $D = 0$ minimises V^* and makes $b^* = \hat{\beta}$. See Theil (1971, pp.237—241).

Part (b). The OLS estimator of β is

$$b = (X'X)^{-1}X'y = \beta + (X'X)^{-1}X'u.$$

Therefore, $E(b) = \beta$ and the covariance matrix of b is

$$\bar{V} = E(b - \beta)(b - \beta)' = E[(X'X)^{-1}X'uu'X(X'X)^{-1}]$$
$$= (X'X)^{-1}X'\Sigma X(X'X)^{-1}. \qquad (2.12.6)$$

Let x_j denote the jth column of X, $(j = 1, \ldots, k)$, then if x_j is an eigenvector of Σ we have $\Sigma x_j = \lambda_j x_j$, where λ_j is the jth eigenvalue of Σ, or $\Sigma X = X\Lambda_1$ where Λ_1 is a diagonal matrix whose jjth element is λ_j. From part (a)

$$\Sigma = Q\Lambda Q' = (X \vdots Z)\begin{bmatrix} \Lambda_1 & 0 \\ 0 & \Lambda_2 \end{bmatrix}\begin{bmatrix} X' \\ Z' \end{bmatrix} \qquad (2.12.7)$$

where the columns of Z are the remaining $T - k$ eigenvectors of Σ and the diagonal elements of Λ_2 are the corresponding eigenvalues. Moreover,

$$\Sigma^{-1} = Q\Lambda^{-1}Q' = (X \vdots Z) \begin{bmatrix} \Lambda_1^{-1} & 0 \\ 0 & \Lambda_2^{-1} \end{bmatrix} \begin{bmatrix} X' \\ Z' \end{bmatrix} \qquad (2.12.8)$$

and

$$Q'Q = \begin{bmatrix} X'X & X'Z \\ Z'X & Z'Z \end{bmatrix} = I. \qquad (2.12.9)$$

Consider now the covariance matrix of the GLS estimator, equation (2.12.5). Using (2.12.8) and (2.12.9) we have

$$V = (X'\Sigma^{-1}X)^{-1} = \left\{ X'(X \vdots Z) \begin{bmatrix} \Lambda_1^{-1} & 0 \\ 0 & \Lambda_2^{-1} \end{bmatrix} \begin{bmatrix} X' \\ Z' \end{bmatrix} X \right\}^{-1}$$

$$= \left\{ (X'X \vdots X'Z) \begin{bmatrix} \Lambda_1^{-1} & 0 \\ 0 & \Lambda_2^{-1} \end{bmatrix} \begin{bmatrix} X'X \\ X'Z \end{bmatrix} \right\}^{-1}$$

$$= \left\{ (I \vdots 0) \begin{bmatrix} \Lambda_1^{-1} & 0 \\ 0 & \Lambda_2^{-1} \end{bmatrix} \begin{bmatrix} I \\ 0 \end{bmatrix} \right\}^{-1} = \Lambda_1 . \qquad (2.12.10)$$

Using (2.12.7) and (2.12.9), the covariance matrix of the OLS estimator, equation (2.12.6) can be shown to be

$$\bar{V} = (X'X)^{-1} X'\Sigma X(X'X)^{-1} = X'\Sigma X$$

$$= X'(X \vdots Z) \begin{bmatrix} \Lambda_1 & 0 \\ 0 & \Lambda_2 \end{bmatrix} \begin{bmatrix} X' \\ Z' \end{bmatrix} X$$

$$= (I \vdots 0) \begin{bmatrix} \Lambda_1 & 0 \\ 0 & \Lambda_2 \end{bmatrix} \begin{bmatrix} I \\ 0 \end{bmatrix} = \Lambda_1 . \qquad (2.12.11)$$

Thus $V = \bar{V}$ and hence the OLS estimator is as efficient as the GLS estimator. See also Anderson (1971, pp.18–20).

Part (c). From the results of part (b), OLS will be efficient if the columns of X are eigenvectors of Σ and x is an eigenvector of Σ with elements $x_1, \ldots, x_T$ and λ is the corresponding eigenvalue i.e. if $\Sigma x = \lambda x$. The following results are similar to those of Anderson (1971, pp.276–293). From $\Sigma x = \lambda x$ we have

$$\sigma^2 (x_1 - x_2) = \lambda x_1 \qquad (2.12.12)$$

$$\sigma^2 (-x_{t-1} + 2x_t - x_{t+1}) = \lambda x_t \qquad (t = 2, \ldots, T-1) \quad (2.12.13)$$

$$\sigma^2(-x_{T-1} + x_T) = \lambda x_T. \tag{2.12.14}$$

Equation (2.12.13) can also be written

$$x_{t+1} + (\lambda\sigma^{-2} - 2)x_t + x_{t-1} = 0 \qquad (t = 2, \ldots, T-1) \tag{2.12.15}$$

which is a second-order difference equation. The solution is

$$x_t = c_1\alpha_1^t + c_2\alpha_2^t \tag{2.12.16}$$

where α_1 and α_2 are the roots of the characteristic polynomial equation

$$x^2 - 2\theta x + 1 = 0 \tag{2.12.17}$$

for $\theta = 1 - \lambda\sigma^{-2}/2$. The roots of (2.12.17) are $\theta \pm \sqrt{\theta^2 - 1}$; hence $\alpha_1\alpha_2 = [\theta + (\theta^2 - 1)^{1/2}][\theta - (\theta^2 - 1)^{1/2}] = 1$ and $\alpha_1 + \alpha_2 = 2\theta$.

It follows that we can write (2.12.16) as

$$x_t = c_1\alpha^t + c_2\alpha^{-t} \tag{2.12.18}$$

where $\alpha_1 = \alpha_2 = \alpha$ and $2\theta = \alpha + \alpha^{-1}$. Substituting (2.12.18) into (2.12.12) we obtain

$$
\begin{aligned}
0 &= (1 - \lambda\sigma^{-2})x_1 - x_2 = (2\theta - 1)x_1 - x_2 \\
&= (\alpha + \alpha^{-1} - 1)(c_1\alpha + c_2\alpha^{-1}) - c_1\alpha^2 - c_2\alpha^{-2} \\
&= c_1\alpha^2 + c_1 - c_1\alpha + c_2 + c_2\alpha^{-2} - c_2\alpha^{-1} - c_1\alpha^2 - c_2\alpha^{-2} \\
&= c_1(1 - \alpha) + c_2(1 - \alpha^{-1})
\end{aligned}
$$

Therefore $c_2 = -(1 - \alpha)c_1/(1 - \alpha^{-1}) = \alpha c_1$ and hence if we take $c_1 = \alpha^{-1/2}$ we find that $c_2 = \alpha^{1/2}$ and

$$x_t = \alpha^{t-1/2} + \alpha^{-t+1/2}. \tag{2.12.19}$$

From (2.12.14)

$$
\begin{aligned}
0 &= -x_{T-1} + (2 - \lambda\sigma^{-2})x_T = -x_{T-1} + (2\theta - 1)x_T \\
&= -(\alpha^{T-3/2} + \alpha^{-(T-3/2)}) + (\alpha + \alpha^{-1} - 1)(\alpha^{T-1/2} + \alpha^{-(T-1/2)}) \\
&= -\alpha^{T-3/2} - \alpha^{-T+3/2} + \alpha^{T+1/2} + \alpha^{-T+3/2} + \alpha^{T-3/2} + \alpha^{T-1/2} + \alpha^{-T+1/2} \\
&= (\alpha^T - \alpha^{-T})(\alpha^{1/2} - \alpha^{-1/2}).
\end{aligned}
$$

Thus either $\alpha = 1$ or $\alpha^{2T} = 1$. The roots of $\alpha^{2T} = 1$ are $e^{i2\pi s/2T} = e^{i\pi s/T}$ for $s = 0, 1, \ldots, 2T - 1$. It follows that

$$\theta = (e^{i\pi s/T} + e^{-i\pi s/T})/2 = \cos(\pi s/T)$$

and hence

$$\lambda = 2\sigma^2[1 - \cos(\pi 2/T)] \tag{2.12.20}$$

But as $\cos(\pi s/T) = \cos(2\pi + \pi s/T)$, there are $T + 1$ different roots of λ for which (2.12.20) holds. However, we can rule out one of the roots since if $s = T$ then $\theta = -1, \alpha = -1$ and $x_t = 0$ which is inadmissable. The remaining λ's are the required T eigenvalues of Σ. The corresponding eigenvectors are obtained from (2.12.19). Thus for $t = 1, \ldots, T$ and $s = 0, \ldots, T-1$

$$x_t = \alpha^{t-1/2} + \alpha^{-(t-1/2)} = e^{i(2t-1)\pi s/2T} + e^{-i(2t-1)\pi s/2T}$$

$$= \cos[(2t-1)\pi s/2T]$$

The sth eigenvector is, therefore,

$$\mathbf{x}' = \{\cos(\pi s/2T), \cos(3\pi s/2T), \ldots, \cos[(2T-1)\pi s/2T]\}.$$

Thus, to form X we must choose k of these T eigenvectors.

Σ as defined in (2.12.2) can be obtained if the errors $u_t (t = 1, \ldots, T)$ are generated by the moving average process $u_t = e_t - e_{t-1}$ where $E(e_t) = 0, E(e_t^2) = \sigma^2, E(e_t e_s) = 0$ for $s = t$ and $e_0 = e_T = 0$. For $t = 2, \ldots, T-1$

$$E(u_t^2) = E(e_t - e_{t-1})^2 = E(e_t^2) - 2E(e_t e_{t-1}) + E(e_{t-1}^2) = 2\sigma^2$$

For $t = 1, \ldots, T$

$$E(u_t u_{t-1}) = E(e_t - e_{t-1})(e_{t-1} - e_{t-2})$$

$$= E(e_t e_{t-1}) - E(e_{t-1}^2) - E(e_t e_{t-2}) + E(e_{t-1} e_{t-2}) = \sigma^2$$

For $s > 2, E(u_t u_{t-s}) = 0$. Further, $E(u_1^2) = E(e_1^2) = \sigma^2$ and $E(u_T^2) = E(e_{T-1}^2) = \sigma^2$. Combining these results we obtain Σ as defined in (2.12.2).

It should be noted, however, that Σ is a singular matrix (the columns and rows sum to zero) and hence the GLS estimator cannot be computed from (2.12.4). A generalised inverse of Σ must be used in place of Σ^{-1}. But since OLS is fully efficient and presents no computational problems we can use this estimator instead.

Solution 2.13

Part (a). Let the model be written in the sample period as

$$y = X\beta + u \tag{2.13.1}$$

and in the forecast period as

$$y_F = X_F\beta + u_F \tag{2.13.2}$$

If $\hat{y}_F$ is a linear predictor of y_F then $\hat{y}_F = Cy$. It is an unbiased predictor if $E(\hat{y}_F) = y_F$. Now

$$E(\hat{y}_F - y_F) = E(Cy - y_F)$$

$$= E(CX\beta + Cu - X_F\beta - u_F)$$

$$= (CX - X_F)\beta + E(Cu - u_F)$$

$$= (CX - X_F)\beta$$

Thus $\hat{y}_F$ is unbiased for y_F if $CX = X_F$. The covariance matrix of the forecast error is

$$E(\hat{y}_F - y_F)(\hat{y}_F - y_F)' = E(Cu - u_F)(Cu - u_F)'$$
$$= \sigma^2(CC' + I_R) \qquad (2.13.3)$$

if $E(uu'_F) = 0$, i.e. if the errors are serially uncorrelated. If we estimate β using b, the OLS estimator of β from (2.13.1), then an estimator of y_F is given by

$$\hat{y}_F = X_F b$$
$$= X_F(X'X)^{-1}X'y$$
$$= Cy$$

where $C = X_F(X'X)^{-1}X'$. Thus $\hat{y}_F$ is a linear estimator. Moreover, since $CX = X_F(X'X)^{-1}X'X = X_F$, y_F is also an unbiased predictor of y_F. The covariance matrix of the forecast error is, therefore, given by (2.13.3).

Consider now another linear estimator

$$\tilde{y}_F = (C + D)y$$

where $C = X_F(X'X)^{-1}X'$. The expected forecast error of $\tilde{y}_F$ is

$$E(\tilde{y}_F - y_F) = (CX + DX - X_F)\beta = DX\beta$$

which is zero for all values of β if and only if $DX = 0$.

When $\tilde{y}_F$ is an unbiased predictor, the covariance matrix of the forecast error of $\tilde{y}_F$ is (using the fact that $CX = X_F$ and $DX = 0$)

$$E(\tilde{y}_F - y_F)(\tilde{y}_F - y)' = E[(C + D)u - u_F][(C + D)u - u_F]'$$
$$= \sigma^2(CC' + DD' + I_R)$$

In order to minimise this covariance matrix we must choose $D = 0$. Thus $\hat{y}_F = X_F(X'X)^{-1}X'y$ is a best linear unbiased predictor of y_F.

Part (b). Substituting $C = X_F(X'X)^{-1}X'$ we find in (2.13.3) that the covariance matrix of the forecast error of $\hat{y}_F$ is

$$\sigma^2[X_F(X'X)^{-1}X'_F + I_R] = X_F \text{var}(b_{\text{OLS}})X'_F + \sigma^2 I_R \qquad (2.13.4)$$

Part (c). A one period ahead 95% confidence interval (C_1, C_2) will satisfy $\text{Prob}[C_1 \leqslant \hat{y}_{T+1} - y_{T+1} \leqslant C_2] = 0.95$ and will lead to the interval

$$\hat{y}_{T+1} - C_2 \leqslant y_{T+1} \leqslant \hat{y}_{T+1} - C_1$$

In the present case the forecast error $\hat{y}_{T+1} - y_{T+1}$ is distributed as t_7 so that we obtain $C_1 = -t_7(0.025)s_F$ and $C_2 = t_7(0.025)s_F$, where s_F is the standard error of the forecast error. The required confidence interval is, therefore,

$$\hat{y}_{T+1} - t_7(0.025)s_F < y_{T+1} < \hat{y}_{T+1} + t_7(0.025)s_F$$

For the given estimated model

$$\hat{y}_{T+1} = 100 + 5(1) - 2(2) = 101$$

and

$$s_F = s[X_{T+1}(X'X)^{-1}X'_{T+1} + 1]^{1/2}$$

$$= 3\left[(1, 1, 2)\begin{bmatrix} 10 & 10 & 20 \\ 10 & 20 & 0 \\ 20 & 0 & 90 \end{bmatrix}^{-1}\begin{bmatrix} 1 \\ 1 \\ 2 \end{bmatrix} + 1\right]^{1/2}$$

$$= 3\left[(1, 1, 2)\begin{bmatrix} 1.8 & -0.9 & -0.4 \\ -0.9 & 0.5 & 0.2 \\ -0.4 & 0.2 & 0.1 \end{bmatrix}\begin{bmatrix} 1 \\ 1 \\ 2 \end{bmatrix} + 1\right]^{1/2}$$

$$= 3[0.1 + 1]^{1/2}$$

$$= 3.146$$

A simpler way of obtaining the expression in this example is to use the fact that $10\,X_{T+1}$ is a row of $X'X$ and hence $X_{T+1}(X'X)^{-1} = (0.1, 0, 0)$. Finally the required confidence interval is

$$101 - 2.365 \times 3.146 \leqslant y_{T+1} \leqslant 101 + 2.365 \times 3.146$$

or

$$93.56 \leqslant y_{T+1} \leqslant 108.44$$

See Theil (1971, pp.119–124) for further details on forecasting.

Solution 2.14

Part (a). If σ^2 is known then from question (2.13) $\hat{y}_F - y_F$ is distributed $N[0, \sigma^2(I_r + X_F(X'X)^{-1}X'_F)]$. The appropriate test statistic is then

$$K = (\hat{y}_F - y_F)'[I_r + X_F(X'X)^{-1}X'_F]^{-1}(\hat{y}_F - y_F)/\sigma^2$$

which is distributed as χ_r^2. If σ^2 is unknown we use instead

$$F = \frac{K/r}{s^2/\sigma^2}$$

which can be shown to be distributed as $F_{r, T-k}$. To prove these results we note that $\hat{y}_F = X_F (X'X)^{-1} X'y = A'y$ and hence that $\hat{y}_F - y_F = B'y_*$, where $B' = [A' \vdots -I_r]$ and $y'_* = (y', y'_F)$. It follows that

$$K = \sigma^{-2} y'_* B (I_r + A'A)^{-1} B' y_*$$
$$= \sigma^{-2} y'_* B (B'B)^{-1} B' y_*$$

which is distributed as χ_r^2 and $B(B'B)^{-1} B'$ is an idempotent matrix of rank r. See question 2.2 for further details of the distribution of quadratic forms.

It has already been shown (question 2.3) that $(T-k)s^2/\sigma^2$ is distributed as χ_{T-k}^2. But

$$(T-k)s/\sigma^2 = \sigma^{-2} y'_* \left[\begin{array}{c|c} I_T - X(X'X)^{-1} X' & 0 \\ \hline 0 & 0 \end{array} \right] y_* = \sigma^{-2} y'_* C y_*$$

where C is idempotent with rank $T-k$. It follows that

$$F = \frac{y'_* B (B'B)^{-1} B' y_*}{y'_* C y_*} \cdot \frac{T-k}{r}$$

which has an F distribution if $B(B'B)^{-1} B'C = 0$. Now

$$B'C = \left[\begin{array}{c|c} A' - A'X(X'X)^{-1} X' & 0 \\ \hline 0 & 0 \end{array} \right]$$

and $A'X(X'X)^{-1} X' = X_F (X'X)^{-1} X'X(X'X)^{-1} X' = X_F (X'X)^{-1} X' = A'$. Therefore $B'C = 0$ as required.

Part (b). In testing for structural change (see question 2.6) we wish to know if the model in a certain time period applies in another time period. Consider the null hypothesis

$$H_0: y_t = x'_t \beta + u_t, \quad u_t \text{ are independent } N(0, \sigma^2) \quad (t=1,\ldots, T+r)$$

and the two alternative hypotheses

$$H_1: \begin{cases} y_t = x'_t \beta_1 + u_t, & u_t \text{ are independent } N(0, \sigma_1^2) \quad (t = 1, \ldots, T) \\ y_t = x'_t \beta_2 + u_t, & u_t \text{ are independent } N(0, \sigma_2^2) \quad (t = T+1, \ldots, T+r) \end{cases}$$

and

$$H_2: \begin{cases} y_t = x'_t \beta_1 + u_t & (t = 1, \ldots, T) \\ y_t = x'_t \beta_2 + u_t & (t = T+1, \ldots, T+r) \end{cases}$$

with u_t independent $N(0, \sigma^2)$, $t = 1, \ldots, T+r$. On H_1, structural change is due both to a change in the coefficient vector and in the variance of u_t; whereas, on H_2, only the coefficient vector has changed.

Turning now to the question, the test statistic derived in part (a) which is based on forecast errors, is suitable for H_0 against H_1 as it makes no assumptions about the alternative hypothesis. On the other hand, the Chow test for structural change is concerned with whether or not the coefficient vector has changed. Thus, the Chow test is preferred for H_0 against H_2. The test based on forecast errors could also be used for H_0 against H_2 but if in fact $\sigma_1^2 = \sigma_2^2 = \sigma^2$, then this test is less powerful than the Chow test (see Jorgensen *et al.* 1970).

Solution 2.15

Part (a). Consider the sequence of observations $\{x_1, x_2, \ldots, x_T\}$ of the random variable X which has a distribution function $F(X; \theta)$ depending on an unknown parameter θ. An estimator $\hat{\theta}_T$ of θ is constructed as a function of the observations $\{x_t : t = 1, \ldots, T\}$. $\hat{\theta}_T$ is said to be a consistent estimator for θ if for all $\epsilon > 0$,

$$\lim_{T \to \infty} P(|\hat{\theta}_T - \theta| > \epsilon) = 0 \qquad (2.15.3)$$

We then write $\text{plim}_{T \to \infty} \hat{\theta}_T = 0$.

Part (b). We first state a useful theorem given in Cramér (1946, p.182):

Tchebycheff's theorem *If $g(\xi)$ is a non-negative and integrable function of the random variable ξ then for every $K > 0$ we have*

$$P[g(\xi) \geqslant K] \leqslant E[g(\xi)]/K \qquad (2.15.4)$$

In particular, if $g(\xi) = (\xi - \mu)^2$ and $K = k^2 \sigma^2$, where μ and σ^2 denote the mean and variance of ξ, then for every $k > 0$ we obtain the Bienaymé–Tchebycheff inequality

$$P(|\xi - \mu| \geqslant k\sigma) \leqslant 1/k^2$$

which may also be written as

$$P(|\xi - \mu| \geqslant k) \leqslant \sigma^2/k^2 \qquad (2.15.5)$$

It follows that

$$\lim_{T \to \infty} P(|\xi - \mu| \geqslant k) = 0 \qquad (2.15.6)$$

if $\lim_{T \to \infty} \sigma^2 = 0$. Thus, if the estimator $\hat{\theta}_T$ is a random variable with $E(\hat{\theta}_T) = 0$ and $\lim_{T \to \infty} \text{var}(\hat{\theta}_T) = 0$ then these conditions are sufficient (but not necessary) to ensure that $\hat{\theta}_T$ is a consistent estimator of θ.

For the linear model (2.15.1), $E(b) = \beta$ and the covariance matrix of b is $V = \sigma^2 (X'X)^{-1}$. If, therefore, $\lim_{T \to \infty} V = 0$, then we have conditions sufficient to ensure that b is a consistent estimator of β. But

$$\lim_{T \to \infty} V = \lim_{T \to \infty} \sigma^2 (X'X)^{-1}$$

$$= \sigma^2 \lim_{T \to \infty} T^{-1} (X'X/T)^{-1}$$

By assumption $\lim_{T \to \infty} X'X/T = M$ is finite, non-singular, hence

$$\lim_{T \to \infty} V = \sigma^2 \lim_{T \to \infty} T^{-1} M = 0$$

Thus b is a consistent estimator of β.

Part (c) We note that b, the OLS estimator of β in (2.15.2), has $E(b) = \beta$ and $\text{var}(b) = \sigma^2 / \Sigma_1^T (t - \bar{t})^2$, where $\bar{t} = T^{-1} \Sigma_1^T t$. For b to be consistent for β it will be sufficient to prove that $\lim_{T \to \infty} \text{var}(b) = 0$. Now

$$\frac{\sigma^2}{\Sigma_1^T (t - \bar{t})^2} = \frac{\sigma^2}{\Sigma t^2 - T\bar{t}^2}$$

$$= \sigma^2 \Big/ \left[\frac{T(T+1)(2T+1)}{6} - \frac{T(T+1)^2}{4} \right]$$

$$= \frac{12\sigma^2}{T(T^2 - 1)}$$

Hence

$$\lim_{T \to \infty} \text{var}(b) = 0$$

It is interesting to note that for this model

$$\frac{X'X}{T} = \frac{1}{T} \begin{bmatrix} 1 & 1 & \cdots & 1 \\ 1 & 2 & \cdots & T \end{bmatrix} \begin{bmatrix} 1 & 1 \\ 1 & 2 \\ \vdots & \vdots \\ \vdots & \vdots \\ 1 & T \end{bmatrix}$$

$$= \begin{bmatrix} 1 & \dfrac{1}{T} \Sigma t \\ \dfrac{1}{T} \Sigma t & \dfrac{1}{T} \Sigma t^2 \end{bmatrix}$$

$$= \begin{bmatrix} 1 & \frac{1}{2}(T+1) \\ \frac{1}{2}(T+1) & \frac{1}{6}(T+1)(2T+1) \end{bmatrix}.$$

It follows that not all elements of $X'X/T$ have finite limits as $T \to \infty$. Consequently, we have used Tchebycheff's theorem directly to prove that b is a consistent estimator of β in (2.15.2).

Remark 1 The following results are useful in evaluating probability limits (see Dhrymes, 1970, ch3):

(i) *If x_T is a random variable with probability limit θ and a_T is a sequence of numbers with $\lim_{T \to \infty} a_T = a$ then*

$$\plim_{T \to \infty} (a_T x_T) = a\theta$$

(ii) *If y_T is another random variable with probability limit μ and $f(y_T, x_T)$ is a real function continuous at $f(\mu, \theta)$ then*

$$\plim_{T \to \infty} f(y_T, x_T) = f(\mu, \theta)$$

This result is known as Slutsky's Theorem. Important special cases of Slutsky's Theorem are

$$\plim_{T \to \infty} (y_T + x_T) = \mu + \theta, \quad \plim_{T \to \infty} (y_T x_T) = \mu\theta$$

and

$$\plim_{T \to \infty} (y_T / x_T) = \mu/\theta, \quad \text{for} \quad \theta \neq 0.$$

Remark 2 Frequently the probability limit of a random variable is equal to its expectation or to the limit as $T \to \infty$ of its expectation (assuming these expectations exist). Sufficient conditions for evaluating the probability limit of the random variable x_T by its expectation are derived from the Bienaymé–Tchebycheff inequality. If, for all T, $E(x_T) = \mu$, $E(x_T - \mu)^2 = \sigma^2$ and $\lim_{T \to \infty} \sigma^2 = 0$ then from (2.15.5) and (2.15.6) $\plim_{T \to \infty} x_T = E(x_T) = \mu$.

Sufficient conditions for evaluating $\plim_{T \to \infty} x_T$ by $\lim_{T \to \infty} E(x_T)$ are obtained from Tchebycheff's theorem (2.15.4). If $g(x_T) = [x_T - \lim_{T \to \infty} E(x_T)]^2$,

$$E[x_T - \lim_{T \to \infty} E(x_T)]^2 = \sigma_T^2, \quad \lim_{T \to \infty} \sigma_T^2 = 0$$

and $K = k^2 \sigma_T^2$, then for every $k > 0$, (2.15.4) implies that

$$P(|x_T - \lim_{T \to \infty} E(x_T)| \geq k) \leq \sigma_T^2 / k^2$$

and hence that

$$\lim_{T \to \infty} P(|x_T - \lim_{T \to \infty} E(x_T)| \geq k) = 0$$

Thus, from (2.15.3), $\plim_{T \to \infty} x_T = \lim_{T \to \infty} E(x_T)$.

Example The set of T observations $x_1, x_2, \ldots, x_T$ are an independent random sample from a distribution with finite moments up to the fourth order denoted by $\{\mu_i: i = 1, \ldots, 4\}$. Show that $s^2 = T^{-1} \Sigma_{t=1}^T (x_t - \bar{x})^2$ is a consistent estimator of the variance $\mu_2 (= \sigma^2)$, where $\bar{x}$ is the sample mean.

Cramér (1946, pp.345–349) has shown that $E(s^2) = \mu_2 (1 - T^{-1})$ and $E(s^4) = \mu_2^2 + (\mu_4 - 3\mu_2^2)/T - (2\mu_4 - 5\mu_2^2)/T^2 + (\mu_4 - 3\mu_2^2)/T^3$. Hence $E(s^2) \neq \sigma^2$ but $\lim_{T \to \infty} E(s^2) = \sigma^2$.

Furthermore,

$$E[s^2 - \lim_{T \to \infty} E(s^2)]^2 = E(s^2 - \sigma^2)^2 = E(s^4) - 2\sigma^2 E(s^2) + \sigma^4$$
$$= \sigma^4 + (\mu_4 - 3\sigma^4) T^{-1} - 2\sigma^4 (1 - T^{-1})$$
$$+ \sigma^4 + 0(T^{-2})$$
$$= (\mu_4 - \sigma^4) T^{-1} + 0(T^{-2})$$

where $0(T^{-2})$ denotes terms of order T^{-2} and smaller. Hence $\lim_{T \to \infty} E[s^2 - \lim_{T \to \infty} E(s^2)]^2 = 0$ and so s^2 is a consistent estimator of σ^2.

Solution 2.16

Part (a) Although we would like to know the exact distribution of an estimator for the sample size T with which we are working, very often the derivation of this distribution presents mathematical difficulties and is, therefore, not usually available. However, as T tends to infinity, we are often able to obtain the limiting distribution of the estimator in suitably standardised form. This limiting distribution of the suitably standardised estimator gives us what we call the asymptotic distribution of the estimator itself; we will explain this distinction more fully below when we consider which function of the estimator is required to achieve a suitable standardisation. Frequently, the exact sampling distribution of an estimator can be closely approximated by the asymptotic distribution of the estimator even for moderate values of T. This approximation is commonly used when conducting statistical tests in econometrics; and it also helps us to analyse and compare the properties of different estimators of the same parameters.

In order to derive the asymptotic distribution of the OLS estimator for (2.16.1) we shall use the following central limit theorem.

Result 1: A Central Limit Theorem (Malinvaud 1970, p.251)

Suppose $\{u_t; t = 1, 2, \ldots, T\}$ are independent identically distributed m-vector random variables with zero means and finite covariance matrix Ω. We define

$$x_T = \sum_{1}^{T} \frac{A_t}{\sqrt{T}} u_t \qquad\qquad (2.16.4)$$

where A_t is an $n \times m$ matrix of non-random variables that are uniformly bounded (i.e. $|A_t| < R$ for all t and some finite R), such that $\lim_{T\to\infty} T^{-1} \sum_1^T A_t \,\Omega\, A_t' = V$ is finite. Then the limiting distribution of x_T is $N(0, V)$.

We shall also make use of the following result:

Result 2: (Cramér, 1946, p.254, Dhrymes, 1970, pp.112–114) *Suppose that the sequence $\{x_T, y_T; T = 1, 2, \ldots\}$ is such that x_t has a limiting distribution represented by the distribution function $F(x)$ and y_T converges in probability to the constant c (i.e. $\mathrm{plim}_{T\to\infty} y_T = c$) then $x_T y_T$ has the same limiting distribution as $c x_T$, namely, $F(cx)$.* We now make the following assumptions:

Assumption 2.16.A *The vector of disturbances u in (2.16.1) has elements u_t $(t = 1, \ldots, T)$ which are independently and identically distributed with zero mean and constant variance σ^2 for all values of t.*

Assumption 2.16.B *The elements x_{it} of x are uniformly bounded (i.e. $|x_{it}| < R$ for all t, all i and some finite R) and $\lim_{T\to\infty} T^{-1} X'X = M$ is finite and non-singular.*

Under the assumptions (2.16.A-B) and using Results 1 and 2 we can derive the asymptotic distribution of b, the OLS estimator of β. We note that

$$b = (X'X)^{-1} X'y$$
$$= \beta + (X'X)^{-1} X'u \qquad\qquad (2.16.5)$$

which can be written alternatively as

$$\sqrt{T}\,(b - \beta) = \left(\frac{X'X}{T}\right)^{-1} \frac{X'u}{\sqrt{T}} \qquad\qquad (2.16.6)$$

It follows that $\sqrt{T}\,(b - \beta)$ has the same limiting distribution, if it exists, as $(X'X/T)^{-1}\,(T^{-1/2}\,X'u)$. The limiting distribution of $(X'u/\sqrt{T})$ can be obtained by noting, in the notation of Result 1, that

$$\frac{X'u}{\sqrt{T}} = \sum_{1}^{T} \frac{A_t}{\sqrt{T}} u_t$$

where $A_t' = x_t$, the tth row of X. Since u_t is a scalar random variable with variance σ^2 we have $\Omega = \sigma^2$. Thus

$$\lim_{T\to\infty} \frac{1}{T} \sum_1^T A_t \Omega A_t' = \sigma^2 \lim_{T\to\infty} \sum \frac{x_t' x_t}{T}$$

$$= \sigma^2 \lim_{T\to\infty} \frac{X'X}{T} = \sigma^2 M$$

which is finite. It now follows from Result 1 that the limiting distribution of $X'u/\sqrt{T}$ is $N(0, \sigma^2 M)$. By virtue of Result 2 above, and $\lim_{T\to\infty}(X'X/T)^{-1} = M^{-1}$, the limiting distribution of $(X'X/T)^{-1}(T^{-1/2}X'u)$ is the same as that of $M^{-1}(T^{-1/2}X'u)$, namely $N(0, \sigma^2 M^{-1}MM^{-1}) = N(0, \sigma^2 M^{-1})$. Thus, the limiting distribution of $\sqrt{T}(b-\beta)$ is normal with mean vector zero and covariance matrix $\sigma^2 M^{-1}$.

Alternatively, we say that the asymptotic distribution of b is $N[\beta, \sigma^2 (X'X)^{-1}]$. This is the terminology used by Cramér (1946, pp. 213–214). Recall that in question 2.15 we showed that the covariance matrix of b tends to zero as $T\to\infty$. Since $\text{plim}_{T\to\infty} b = \beta$, it follows from the very definition of a probability limit that the distribution of b collapses on to the point β as $T\to\infty$; and we say that b has a degenerate limiting distribution, i.e. a distribution which assigns the probability 1 to the value β. In general, in finite samples, b will have a non-degenerate sampling distribution which we often wish to characterise or approximate. We can use the fact that the standardised statistic $\sqrt{T}(b-\beta)$ has a non-degenerate limiting distribution to construct an approximate distribution for b. In fact, the limiting distribution of $\sqrt{T}(b-\beta)$ is normal with zero mean and covariance matrix which is the limit as $T\to\infty$ of $\sigma^2 (X'X/T)^{-1}$; so an approximation to the distribution of b based on this asymptotic result is just the normal distribution with mean β and covariance matrix $\sigma^2 (X'X)^{-1}$. We call this the asymptotic distribution of b.

Part (b) We are given that

$$\lim_{T\to\infty} \frac{X'X}{T} = M$$

$$= \begin{bmatrix} 1 & 1 \\ 1 & 2 \end{bmatrix}$$

Thus

$$M^{-1} = \begin{bmatrix} 2 & -1 \\ -1 & 1 \end{bmatrix}$$

and so, using Result 1 above, the limiting distribution of $\sqrt{T}(b-\beta)$ is

$$N\left(0, \sigma^2 \begin{bmatrix} 2 & -1 \\ -1 & 1 \end{bmatrix}\right)$$

Part (c) We note that Assumption (2.16.B) no longer applies as we have shown in question (2.15) that not all of the elements of $X'X/T$ have finite limits. We shall, therefore, adopt an alternative approach: instead of considering the limiting distribution of the function $\sqrt{T}(b - \beta)$, we shall consider that of the function $(b - \beta)/\sqrt{\text{var}(b)}$. Now we know that

$$b - \beta = \frac{\Sigma_1^T (t - \bar{t})u_t}{\Sigma_1^T (t - \bar{t})^2} \quad \text{and} \quad \text{var}(b) = \frac{\sigma^2}{\Sigma_1^T (t - \bar{t})^2}.$$

Hence

$$\frac{b - \beta}{[\text{var}(b)]^{1/2}} = \frac{\Sigma_1^T (t - \bar{t})u_t}{[\sigma^2 \Sigma (t - \bar{t})^2]^{1/2}}$$

$$= \frac{\Sigma_1^T A_t u_t}{\sqrt{T}}$$

where

$$A_t = \frac{\sqrt{T}(t - \bar{t})}{[\sigma^2 \Sigma_1^T (t - t)^2]^{1/2}}$$

Thus, with $\Omega = \sigma^2$ we have

$$\lim_{T \to \infty} \frac{1}{T} \sum_1^T A_t \Omega A_t' = \lim_{T \to \infty} \frac{\sigma^2}{T} \sum_1^T \frac{(\sqrt{T}(t-t))^2}{\sigma^2 \Sigma_1^T (t - \bar{t})^2} = 1.$$

It follows from Result 1 that the limiting distribution of $(b - \beta)/\sqrt{\text{var}(b)}$ is $N(0, 1)$.

It might be helpful to supplement the answer to this question with a few additional remarks on limiting distributions and, in particular, on the appropriate choice of the function we use to standardise the estimator.

Remark 1: If x_T defined in equation (2.16.4) fails to satisfy the condition $\lim_{T \to \infty} T^{-1} \Sigma_1^T A_t \Omega A_t' = V$ due to the unboundedness of A_t, it may be possible to obtain the appropriate limiting distribution by considering instead the limiting distribution of the function of x_T given by $y_T = \theta(T)x_T$ where $\theta(T)$ is a matrix with elements dependent on T. It follows that

$$y_t = \sum_1^T \frac{A_t^*}{\sqrt{T}} u_t$$

where $A_t^* = \theta(T)A_t$. We may now appeal to Result 1 if A_t^* is bounded uniformly in t and $\lim_{T\to\infty} T^{-1}\Sigma_1^T A_t^* \Omega A_t^{*\prime} = V^*$ is finite, Given these conditions, the limiting distribution of y_t is $N(0, V^*)$. We must, therefore, choose $\theta(T)$ to satisfy these conditions.

Applying this result to part (c) we can show that whilst $\sqrt{T}(b - \beta)$ has a degenerate limiting distribution, the function $T^{3/2}(b - \beta)$ has a non-degenerate limiting distribution. This implies that we must choose $\theta(T) = T$. To see this, consider

$$\sqrt{T}(b - \beta) = \frac{\sqrt{T}\,\Sigma_1^T (t - \bar{t})u_t}{\Sigma_1^T (t - \bar{t})^2}$$

$$= \sum_1^T \frac{A_t}{\sqrt{T}} u_t$$

where

$$A_t = T(t - \bar{t})/\Sigma_1^T (t - \bar{t})^2$$

and

$$\lim_{T\to\infty} \operatorname{var}(\sqrt{T}(b - \beta)) = \lim_{T\to\infty} \frac{1}{T} \sum_1^T A_t \Omega A_t'$$

$$= \lim_{T\to\infty} \frac{T\upsilon^2}{\Sigma_1^T (t - \bar{t})^2}$$

$$= \lim_{T\to\infty} \frac{12\sigma^2}{T^2 - 1}$$

$$= 0$$

Hence, $\sqrt{T}(b - \beta)$ has a degenerate limiting distribution.

Consider now

$$T^{3/2}(b - \beta) = \sum_1^T \frac{A_t^*}{\sqrt{T}} u_t$$

where $A_t^* = T^2(t - \bar{t})/\Sigma(t - \bar{t})^2$ and,

$$\lim_{T\to\infty} \operatorname{var}(T^{3/2}(b - \beta)) = \lim_{T\to\infty} \frac{1}{T} \sum_1^T A_t^* \Omega A_t^{*\prime}$$

$$= \lim_{T\to\infty} T^2 \cdot \frac{1}{T} \sum_1^T A_t \Omega A_t'$$

$$= \lim_{T\to\infty} \frac{12\sigma^2}{1 - T^{-2}}$$

$$= 12\sigma^2$$

It follows that the limiting distribution of $T^{3/2}(b-\beta)$ is $N(0, 12\sigma^2)$.

Remark 2 In the multivariate case the matrix $\theta(T)$ is usually a diagonal matrix but the elements on the diagonal need not be identical. Consider once more the example in part (c). Suppose we want to obtain the limiting distributions associated with a and b, the OLS estimators of α and β. We can show that when we choose the matrix $\theta(T)$ to be

$$\theta(T) = \begin{bmatrix} 1 & 0 \\ 0 & T \end{bmatrix}$$

the limiting distribution of $\sqrt{T}\,\theta(T)(a-\alpha, b-\beta)'$ is non-degenerate. Now

$$\begin{bmatrix} a-\alpha \\ b-\beta \end{bmatrix} = \begin{bmatrix} T & T\bar{t} \\ T\bar{t} & \Sigma t^2 \end{bmatrix}^{-1} \begin{bmatrix} \Sigma_1^T u_t \\ \Sigma t u_t \end{bmatrix}$$

$$= \begin{bmatrix} \{(T^{-1}\Sigma t^2)(\Sigma u_t - \bar{t}\Sigma t u_t)\}/\Sigma(t-\bar{t})^2 \\ \Sigma(t-\bar{t})u_t/\Sigma(t-\bar{t})^2 \end{bmatrix}$$

$$= \sum_1^T \begin{bmatrix} (T^{-1}\Sigma t^2 - \bar{t})t/\Sigma(t-\bar{t})^2 \\ (t-\bar{t})/\Sigma(t-\bar{t})^2 \end{bmatrix} u_t$$

Hence,

$$\sqrt{T} \begin{bmatrix} a-\alpha \\ b-\beta \end{bmatrix} = \sum_1^T \frac{A_t}{\sqrt{T}} u_t$$

where,

$$A_t = \frac{1}{\Sigma_1^T(t-\bar{t})^2} \begin{bmatrix} \Sigma_1^T t^2 - T\bar{t}.t \\ T(t-\bar{t}) \end{bmatrix}$$

Now we introduce $\theta(T)$ as defined above, so that

$$\sqrt{T}\,\theta(T) \begin{bmatrix} a-\alpha \\ b-\beta \end{bmatrix} = \sum_1^T \frac{A_t^*}{\sqrt{T}} u_t$$

and

$$\frac{1}{T}\sum_1^T A_t^* \Omega A_t^{*\prime} = \frac{\sigma^2}{T[\Sigma(t-\bar{t})^2]^2}$$

$$\times \begin{bmatrix} \sum_{1}^{T}\left(\sum_{1}^{T} t^2 - T\bar{t}.t\right)^2 & T^2 \sum_{1}^{T}\left(\sum_{1}^{T} t^2 - T\bar{t}.t\right)(t-\bar{t}) \\ \\ T^2 \sum (\Sigma t^2 - T\bar{t}.t)(t-\bar{t}) & T^4 \Sigma(t-\bar{t})^2 \end{bmatrix}$$

$$= \frac{\sigma^2}{T[\Sigma(t-\bar{t})]^2}\begin{bmatrix} T\Sigma t^2.\Sigma(t-\bar{t})^2 & -T^3\bar{t}\Sigma(t-\bar{t})^2 \\ -T^3\bar{t}\Sigma(t-\bar{t})^2 & T^4\Sigma(t-\bar{t})^2 \end{bmatrix}$$

$$= \frac{\sigma^2}{\Sigma(t-\bar{t})^2}\begin{bmatrix} \Sigma t^2 & -T^2\bar{t} \\ -T^2\bar{t} & T^3 \end{bmatrix}$$

$$= \frac{12\sigma^2}{T(T^2-1)}\begin{bmatrix} \dfrac{T(T+1)(2T+1)}{12} & \dfrac{-T^2(T+1)}{2} \\ \dfrac{-T^2(T+1)}{2} & T^3 \end{bmatrix}$$

Hence,

$$\lim_{T\to\infty} \frac{1}{T}\sum_{1}^{T} A_t^* \Omega A_t^{*\prime} = 2\sigma^2\begin{bmatrix} 1 & -3 \\ -3 & 6 \end{bmatrix}$$

which, as required, is clearly finite. It follows that the limiting distribution of the vector $(\sqrt{T}(a-\alpha), T^{3/2}(b-\beta))$ is normal with mean vector zero and covariance matrix

$$2\sigma^2\begin{bmatrix} 1 & -3 \\ -3 & 6 \end{bmatrix}.$$

Remark 3 We have seen how the choice of an appropriate standardisation of an estimator is crucial in obtaining its asymptotic distribution. We now introduce the concept of a probability order operation and we show how this is useful in determining an appropriate standardisation.

Suppose that z_T is a random variable which does not possess a limiting distribution, but there exists a function $\phi(T)$ such that $z_T/\phi(T)$ does have a limiting distribution, then z_T will be of order $\phi(T)$ in probability. We write this as $0[\phi(T)]$ in probability, or, $0_p[\phi(T)]$. Formally we define this concept as follows: $z_T = 0_p[\phi(T)]$ if for all $\epsilon > 0$ there exists $R > 0$ such that $P[|z_T| > R\phi(T)] < \epsilon$ for all values of T.

To illustrate, consider finding the order in probability of the mean $\bar{x}$ of a random sample of T observations $\{x_t; t = 1, \ldots, T\}$ drawn independently from a population with mean μ and variance σ^2. We know that the limiting distribution of $\sqrt{T}(\bar{x} - \mu)$ is $N(0, \sigma^2)$.

From Tchebycheff's theorem and, in particular, (2.15.4),

$$P[(\bar{x} - \mu)^2 > K^2] < \frac{E(\bar{x} - \mu)^2}{K^2} = \frac{\sigma^2}{TK^2},$$

which implies that

$$P(|\bar{x} - \mu| > K) < \frac{\sigma^2}{TK^2} \tag{2.16.7}$$

We now let $\epsilon = \sigma^2/(TK^2)$ and $R = R(\epsilon) = \sigma/\sqrt{\epsilon}$ and then (2.16.7) becomes

$$P(|\bar{x} - \mu| > RT^{-1/2}) < \epsilon \tag{2.17.8}$$

It follows from our definition that $(\bar{x} - \mu) = 0_p(T^{-1/2})$, or since (2.16.8) can be rewritten as

$$P(|\sqrt{T}(\bar{x} - \mu)| > R) < \epsilon$$

$\sqrt{T}(\bar{x} - \mu) = 0_p(1)$ as $T \to \infty$. Similarly, for the OLS estimator b of part (a) defined in (2.16.6), we can deduce that $b - \beta = 0_p(T^{-1/2})$, whilst for that obtained in part (c) $b - \beta = 0_p(T^{-3/2})$.

We also state the following useful result (see Mann and Wald, 1943). If y_T is $0_p[\phi_1(T)]$, z_T is $0_p[\phi_2(T)]$ and $\lim_{T \to \infty} \phi_2(T)/\phi_1(T) = 0$, then $x_T = y_T + z_T$ is $0_p[\phi_1(T)]$. In other words, as the term z_T is of lower order in probability than y_T, it is y_T that determines the order in probability of x_T. We can, therefore, neglect z_T when finding the asymptotic distribution of x_T. To see this we can write

$$\frac{x_T}{\phi_1(T)} = \frac{y_T}{\phi_1(T)} + \frac{z_T}{\phi_1(T)}$$

and we need only verify that $z_T/\phi_1(T) \to 0$ in probability as $T \to \infty$. In fact,

$$\frac{z_T}{\phi_1(T)} = \left(\frac{z_T}{\phi_2(T)}\right)\left(\frac{\phi_2(T)}{\phi_1(T)}\right)$$

and since $z_T = 0_p[\phi_2(T)]$ we have $z_T/\phi_2(T) = 0_p(1)$ (i.e. it is bounded in probability) whereas $\phi_2(T)/\phi_1(T) \to 0$ as $T \to \infty$.

Solution 2.17

Part (a) Equation (2.17.3) is estimated on H_0 and equation (2.17.2) is estimated on H_1. We base our test of H_0 against H_1 upon whether there is a significant increase in the residual sum of squares as a result of imposing the restrictions of H_0. If this increase is significant then we shall conclude that these restrictions provide an effective constraint on the parameter space $\{\beta_i\}$ and hence we shall reject H_0. If the increase is not significant then the restrictions appear to impose no constraint and H_0 is not rejected.

From question (2.3) our test statistic is

$$F = \frac{\text{RSS}_0 - \text{RSS}_1}{\text{RSS}_1} \cdot \frac{T-5}{2}$$

which, since $T = 22$, is distributed as $F_{2,17}$. Thus

$$F = \frac{0.6788 - 0.4277}{0.4277} \cdot \frac{17}{2} = 4.99$$

As $F_{2,17}(0.05) = 3.59$ and $F_{2,17}(0.01) = 6.11$ this is significant at the 5% level but not at the 1% level.

It is interesting to compare this result with individual tests of $\beta_1 = -1$, $\beta_2 = 0$. The t-statistics are -0.49 and 1.71 respectively which are *not* significant at the 5% level [$t_{17}(0.05) = 2.11$]. In other words, whereas we would accept either hypothesis individually, as a joint hypothesis we would reject these values for β_1 and β_2 at the 5% level of significance. The probable reason for this is that $\log P_C$ and $\log P_I$ are fairly highly correlated with each other but not with $\log P_B$ and $\log Y$. Furthermore, jointly they explain a significant amount of variation in $\log Q$ but the data do not enable us to measure their separate influences sufficiently precisely.

Part (b) With this in mind we should refer to equation (2.17.2) when we interpret the equation further. First we should notice that neither β_3 nor β_4 is significantly different from zero even at the 10% level against a two-sided alternative; the t-statistics are 1.39 and 0.69, respectively. However, without information on var$(\log Q + \log P_C)$ or R^2 on H_0 we cannot infer anything about the joint significance of β_3 and β_4.

All the coefficients are elasticities and they have the expected sign; the own-price elasticity is negative, the price elasticities of Indian tea and Brazilian coffee are positive indicating that they are substitutes for Ceylon tea. From the greater significance of Indian tea it appears to be the stronger substitute, indeed given that they are expected to be substitutes it is probably sensible to use one-sided alternative hypotheses. Indian tea is now significant at the 5% level but Brazilian coffee is not. The income elasticity is positive, indicating that Ceylon tea is a normal good, but is less than unity and is not significant, suggesting that Ceylon tea is also a necessity.

Whether or not equation (2.17.1) is a satisfactory demand function for Ceylon tea is more problematical — assuming, that is, that an import function can be interpreted in this way. We know from demand analysis that log-linear demand functions cannot be derived from a reasonable utility function except in the special case of unitary income and own-price elasticities and zero cross-price elasticities (see H. A. John Green, 1971).

The present results do not appear to satisfy these constraints. Another restriction from demand theory is the homogeneity condition which requires that the sum of the price elasticities and the income elasticity be zero. In equation (2.17.2) the sum is 0.143 which is small and probably not significantly different from zero. But without the standard error of this sum, for which we require the full covariance matrix of the estimates, we cannot perform a formal test of the homogeneity condition. Also in the absence of the demand functions for other goods we cannot test the other restrictions derived from demand theory. In conclusion, therefore, we may say that (2.17.1) is at best a useful empirical relationship which is not very well determined with the present data; it would be desirable to obtain a more precise set of estimates by using further data.

Solution 2.18

Part (a) If labour is paid its marginal product then

$$\frac{\partial Q}{\partial L} = \alpha v A^{-\rho/v} \left(\frac{Q}{L}\right)^{1+\rho} Q^{\rho(1-v)/v} = W$$

or, rearranging,

$$\ln \frac{Q}{L} = \text{constant} + \sigma \ln W - \frac{(1-\sigma)(1-v)}{v} \ln Q \qquad (2.18.3)$$

where $\sigma = 1/(1 + \rho)$. Comparing (2.18.2) and (2.18.3) we can see immediately that $\hat{\sigma} = 0.654$. Let the coefficient of $\ln Q$ be θ then $\theta = -(1-\sigma)(1-v)/v$ implies that $v = 1/[1 - \theta/(1 - \sigma)]$ and hence that $\hat{v} = 0.924$.

Part (b) (i) The statistic appropriate for testing H_0 against H_1 is $Z = (0.654 - 1)/0.266 = -1.30$. Assuming that this is normally distributed, for we have no information on the number of observations to enable us to judge how good the normal approximation is, this is not significant at the 5% level. We may conclude, therefore, that on this evidence $\sigma = 1$ cannot be rejected and hence we cannot reject the hypothesis that the production function is Cobb–Douglas.

(ii) In order to test H_0^* against H_1^* we must first derive the limiting distribution of $\sqrt{T}(\hat{\nu} - \nu)$. We can then estimate this distribution and perform a test using asymptotic theory.

In deriving this limiting distribution we shall need to use an extension of a theorem due to Cramér (1946, pp.213–218). Consider the scalar function $g(\phi_1, \phi_2, \ldots, \phi_n)'$ with continuous derivatives of first and second order. Suppose that $\hat{\theta}$ is an estimator of $\theta' = (\theta_1, \theta_2, \ldots, \theta_n)'$ and the limiting distribution of $\sqrt{T}(\hat{\theta} - \theta)$ is $N(0, \Sigma)$. Let ϕ denote the $n \times 1$ vector of first-order derivatives $\partial g / \partial \theta$, then the limiting distribution of $\sqrt{T}[g(\hat{\theta}_1, \ldots, \hat{\theta}_n) - g(\theta_1, \ldots, \theta_n)]$ is $N(0, \phi'\Sigma\phi)$. (See Theil, 1971, pp.373–375 for a further discussion of Cramér's Theorem.)

From part (a),

$$\nu = 1/[1 - \theta/(1 - \sigma)] = g(\sigma, \theta)$$

Let the limiting distribution of $\sqrt{T}(\hat{\sigma} - \sigma, \hat{\theta} - \theta)$ be $N(0, V)$. Then from the results of (2.18.1) and the assumed zero covariance between $\hat{\sigma}$ and $\hat{\theta}$, our estimate of V is

$$T \begin{bmatrix} 0.266^2 & 0 \\ 0 & 0.0403^2 \end{bmatrix}$$

It follows from Cramér's Theorem that the limiting distribution of

$$\sqrt{T}(\hat{\nu} - \nu) - \sqrt{T}[g(\hat{\sigma}, \theta) - g(\sigma, \theta)] \text{ is } N(0, \phi'V\phi)$$

where

$$\phi = \left(\frac{\partial g}{\partial \sigma}, \frac{\partial g}{\partial \theta} \right) = \left(\frac{-\nu^2 \theta}{(1 - \sigma)^2}, \frac{-\nu^2}{1 - \sigma} \right)$$

Replacing the unknowns ν, σ and θ by their estimates we obtain an estimate of ϕ, $\hat{\phi}' = (-0.204, -2.468)$. It follows that our estimate of $\phi'V\phi$ is $0.0128T$. Thus $\hat{\nu}$ is approximately distributed as $N(\nu, 0.0128T)$ and hence the required test statistic for H_0^* against H_1^* is

$$Z = \frac{\hat{\nu} - 1}{0.1133} = -0.67$$

which is not significant even at the 10% level. We may conclude, therefore, that we cannot reject the hypothesis of constant returns to scale, i.e. that $\nu = 1$.

Solution 2.19

Part (a) Equation (2.19.3) seems to imply that investment realisations are greater the greater are investment intentions but that these plans can be adversely affected by a fall in the current year's level of capacity utilisation. Both of these effects are highly significant and together explain 90% of the variance of I. The coefficient of A is not significantly different from unity implying that we cannot reject the hypothesis that the discrepancy between realisations and plans is explained by the change in capacity utilisation. Equation (2.19.2) is estimated on the assumption that this hypothesis is true. We should note that the lower R^2 value for (2.19.2) cannot be compared directly with that for equation (2.19.3) as they refer to different variances; the former to the variance in the discrepancy and the latter to the variance of realisations.

Having attributed the failure of anticipations to explain realisations exactly to short-run conditions in capacity utilisation, we turn now to the question of how to explain anticipations. Equation (2.19.1) suggests that planned investment is explained solely by the average level of capacity utilisation in the previous year; the greater is capacity utilisation the higher is the level of planned investment. The fit is remarkably good. Thus it would appear that firms invest to relieve the pressure on capacity.

An implication of this result is that we can explain investment realisations without direct recourse to anticipations at all. Combining equations (2.19.1) and (2.19.2) we obtain (the reduced form) equation (2.19.4). The reported estimates of (2.19.4) are direct estimates, they are not solved from (2.19.1) and (2.19.3) and do not impose the restriction that the coefficient of A_t is unity. We notice that the estimates of (2.19.4) are very similar to the solved reduced form which is

$$I_t = \text{const} - 54.60C_{t-1} - 19.96(C_t - C_{t-1}) \qquad (2.19.5)$$

The coefficients of (2.19.4) are not significantly different from those of (2.19.5).

In conclusion we may say that whilst anticipations can be helpful in explaining realisations they are neither necessary nor sufficient. They are not sufficient because plans are revised if there are changes in the level of economic activity from that prevailing when they were first drawn up. They are not necessary because we can explain anticipations fairly well by the level of capacity utilisation in the previous period.

Part (b) There is a very simple policy implication arising from these results: to raise the level of investment and to keep it from falling, maintain a high and steady level of capacity utilisation. Failure to do so will cause a loss of investment.

Solution 2.20

Part (a) Marginal cost pricing predicts that firms select a level of output that equates marginal revenue with marginal cost. It is usually assumed that these firms are maximising short-run profits π. Suppose that

$$\pi = PQ - C(Q) \tag{2.20.3}$$

where P is price, Q is output and $C(Q)$ is total cost, then the first-order condition for profit maximisation is

$$P = \frac{\eta}{1+\eta} \frac{\partial C}{\partial Q} \tag{2.20.4}$$

where

$$\eta = -\frac{\partial Q}{\partial P} \cdot \frac{P}{Q}$$

is the price elasticity of demand. It follows that a change in price can be expressed as

$$\Delta P = \Delta \frac{\eta}{1+\eta} \cdot \frac{\partial C}{\partial Q} + \left(\frac{\eta}{1+\eta}\right) \cdot \Delta \frac{\partial C}{\partial Q} \tag{2.20.5}$$

In other words, a change in price is due to both demand and cost factors. We consider these in turn.

Suppose that total cost consists of labour costs and material costs such that

$$C(Q) = [\text{ULC}(Q) + \text{UMC}(Q)]\,Q. \tag{2.20.6}$$

Then,

$$\frac{\partial C}{\partial Q} = \text{ULC} + \text{UMC} + \frac{\partial}{\partial Q}[\text{ULC}(Q) + \text{UMC}(Q)] \cdot Q \tag{2.20.7}$$

and so

$$\Delta \frac{\partial C}{\partial Q} = \Delta \text{ULC} + \Delta \text{UMC} + \Delta \left\{ \frac{\partial}{\partial Q}[\text{ULC}(Q) + \text{UMC}(Q)] \cdot Q \right\} \tag{2.20.8}$$

In part, the last term reflects changes in costs due to the level of output. Let this be proxied by the level of capacity utilisation.

The influence of the demand factors operates through their effect on the sensitivity of demand to changes in price. One of the most important of these is the willingness of consumers to maintain an unfilled order in the face of a price rise. We postulate that an increase in the ratio of unfilled orders to sales will cause consumers to be less prepared to abandon their orders as prices rise. Thus ΔP is greater the greater is $\Delta(O/S)$. Our final equation for price change under marginal cost pricing may, therefore, closely resemble (2.20.1).

Theories B and C are often thought to be more appropriate for oligopolistic firms for whom long-run costs exert a stronger influence than short-run costs and demand. These theories can be treated together as full cost pricing is a variant of target return pricing. Target return pricing implies that firms cover normal or standard unit costs plus a markup to achieve a target rate of return at normal output levels. Thus

$$P = \frac{\bar{\pi}K}{Q^N} + \text{ULC}^N + \text{UMC}^N \tag{2.20.9}$$

where $\bar{\pi}$ is the target rate of return on capital K; N denotes a normal level. The full cost pricing method multiplies standard unit costs by a markup factor λ. Thus

$$P = (1 + \lambda)(\text{ULC}^N + \text{UMC}^N) \tag{2.20.10}$$

Consequently theory B implies

$$\Delta P = \left(\frac{K}{Q^N}\right)\Delta\bar{\pi} + \bar{\pi}\Delta\left(\frac{K}{Q^N}\right) + \Delta\text{ULC}^N + \Delta\text{UMC}^N \tag{2.20.11}$$

and C implies

$$\Delta P = (1 + \lambda)(\Delta\text{ULC}^N + \Delta\text{UMC}^N) + \Delta\lambda(\text{ULC}^N + \Delta\text{UMC}^N) \tag{2.20.12}$$

Equation (2.20.2) corresponds to (2.20.11) with $\Delta\bar{\pi} = 0$ and K/Q^N measured by capacity utilisation whilst (2.20.2) corresponds to (2.20.12) with $\Delta\lambda = 0$.

Part (b) According to theory A, all the coefficients of equation (2.20.1) should be positive, with the coefficients of ΔULC and ΔUMC equal but, given the way the variables are measured, not necessarily equal to unity. We notice that all are positive and significant at the 5% level against one-sided alternatives. Moreover, the coefficients of ΔULC and ΔUMC are very similar in size. As we do not have an estimate of the covariance between the estimates of these coefficients or an estimate of (2.20.12) with the restriction imposed, we do not have sufficient information to perform a test of their equality, but even assuming that the two estimates are highly negatively correlated, thereby minimising the standard error of the sum, since $\text{var}(a_1 + a_2) = \text{var}(a_1) + \text{var}(a_2) + 2\,\text{cov}(a_1 a_2)$, it seems unlikely that we can reject the null hypothesis of equality. The evidence so far, therefore, strongly supports theory A.

Theories B and C predict that the coefficients of $\Delta(\text{ULC} - \text{ULC}^N)$, ΔULC^N_{-1} and $\Delta(O/S)_{-1}$ are zero. In addition theory C predicts that the coefficient of CU is zero. Clearly none of these predictions is supported by this evidence.

Equation (2.20.2) also has some adverse implications for theory A which predicts that the coefficient of ΔULC^N_{-1} should be zero and, in order that ULC^N drops out, the coefficient of ΔULC^N should be minus that of $\Delta(ULC - ULC^N)$. We see that neither of these occurs. The fact that ΔULC^N is significant suggests either that none of these theories is correct or that some firms are oligopolistic and some are not, the results presented being an aggregate of these firms. The significance of ΔULC^N_{-1} could be due to mis-specification, either of the explanatory part of the equation or of the error term.

In conclusion, whilst theory A has some support from this evidence and theories B and C have none, we cannot accept that theory A is an adequate description of pricing. It does seem, however, that both cost and demand factors are required to explain prices.

An additional useful reference for this question is: de Menil (1974).

CHAPTER 3

The multivariate linear model

0. INTRODUCTION

Econometric models typically involve a system of several equations designed to explain movements in more than one economic variable. One important special case of such a system is that in which the explanatory variables are all exogenous and non-random. In the present chapter, our questions will deal with various aspects of the problem of statistical inference in such models. Our notation will be similar to that in earlier chapters where we have used y and x (or X) to represent endogenous and exogenous variables respectively. But we will not be able to maintain a uniform notation throughout the chapter. For there is no single notation in the multivariate model which is suitable for all problems. We will employ here three different representations of the multivariate linear model each of which is in regular use in the literature.

Our first representation of the multivariate model is

$$y_t = Ax_t + u_t \qquad (t = 1, \ldots, T) \qquad (3.0.1)$$

where y_t is a vector of n endogenous variables ($y_{it}: i = 1, \ldots, n$) observed at time t, x_t is a vector of m non-random exogenous variables ($x_{jt}: j = 1, \ldots, m$), A is an $n \times m$ matrix of unknown parameters and u is a vector of random disturbances. The representation (3.0.1) corresponds with that in Malinvaud (1970b, Ch. 6). It is also commonly used for the reduced form of a system of simultaneous equations (see Chapter 6).

Often there are restrictions on the parameter matrix A which we wish to utilise in the statistical treatment of (3.0.1); our two alternative representations of the model enable us to do so in a convenient way. Thus our second representation is the system of equations which is popularly known as Zellner's seemingly unrelated regression model:

$$y_m = X_m \beta_m + u_m \qquad (m = 1, \ldots, M). \qquad (3.0.2)$$

(Zellner, 1962, Goldberger, 1964, pp. 262–265, Theil, 1971, Ch. 7) where y_m is a vector of T observations on the mth endogeneous variable, X_m is a $T \times k_m$ matrix of observations of k_m exogenous variables, β_m is a vector of k_m parameters and u_m is the T-vector of unobservable random disturbances on the mth equation. We see that the specification (3.0.2) allows us to incorporate directly any restrictions on the elements of the matrix A in (3.0.1) that arise from the exclusion of exogenous variables from certain equations. However, the specification (3.0.2) does not allow us to take account directly of simple linear parameter restrictions across equations.

A convenient way of incorporating this latter type of parameter restriction is used in our third representation:

$$y_t = X_t \delta + u_t \qquad (t = 1, \ldots, T) \tag{3.0.3}$$

where y_t and u_t are defined as in (3.0.1), X_t is a matrix of exogeneous variables observed at time t and δ is a vector of unknown parameters. The same exogenous variables may well occur in different positions of the array X_t and some elements of X_t may well be zero. The fact that the same elements of δ may occur in different equations of (3.0.3) means that the specification allows in a simple way for across-equation parameter restrictions.

To illustrate these different representations we may consider the following two-equation system:

$$\begin{bmatrix} y_{1t} \\ y_{2t} \end{bmatrix} = \begin{bmatrix} a_{11} & a_{12} \\ a_{21} & a_{22} \end{bmatrix} \begin{bmatrix} x_{1t} \\ x_{2t} \end{bmatrix} + \begin{bmatrix} u_{1t} \\ u_{2t} \end{bmatrix} \tag{3.0.4}$$

which is already in the form (3.0.1). To rewrite (3.0.4) in the form of (3.0.2) we would define

$$y_1 = \begin{bmatrix} y_{11} \\ \cdot \\ \cdot \\ \cdot \\ y_{1T} \end{bmatrix}, y_2 = \begin{bmatrix} y_{21} \\ \cdot \\ \cdot \\ \cdot \\ y_{2T} \end{bmatrix}, \beta_1 = \begin{bmatrix} a_{11} \\ a_{12} \end{bmatrix}, \beta_2 = \begin{bmatrix} a_{21} \\ a_{22} \end{bmatrix},$$

$$X_1 = \begin{bmatrix} x_{11} & x_{21} \\ \cdot & \cdot \\ \cdot & \cdot \\ \cdot & \cdot \\ x_{1T} & x_{2T} \end{bmatrix}, X_2 = \begin{bmatrix} x_{11} & x_{21} \\ \cdot & \cdot \\ \cdot & \cdot \\ \cdot & \cdot \\ x_{1T} & x_{2T} \end{bmatrix}, u_1 = \begin{bmatrix} u_{11} \\ \cdot \\ \cdot \\ \cdot \\ u_{1T} \end{bmatrix}, u_2 = \begin{bmatrix} u_{21} \\ \cdot \\ \cdot \\ \cdot \\ u_{2T} \end{bmatrix}.$$

To write (3.0.4) in the form of (3.0.3) we would define

$$X_t = \begin{bmatrix} x_{1t} & x_{2t} & 0 & 0 \\ 0 & 0 & x_{1t} & x_{2t} \end{bmatrix}$$

and

$$\delta' = [a_{11} \quad a_{12} \quad a_{21} \quad a_{22}].$$

1. QUESTIONS

Question 3.1

In the following model

$$y_{1t} = \alpha_{10} + \alpha_{11}x_{1t} + \alpha_{12}x_{2t} + u_{1t}$$

$$y_{2t} = \alpha_{20} + \alpha_{21}x_{1t} + \alpha_{22}x_{2t} + u_{2t}$$

the x_{it} are non-random and the u_{it} are random disturbances with $E(u_{1t}) = E(u_{2t}) = 0$, $E(u_{1t}^2) = \sigma_1^2$, $E(u_{2t}^2) = \sigma_2^2$ and $E(u_{1t}u_{2t}) = \sigma_{12}$ for all t, while $E(u_{1t}u_{1s}) = E(u_{1t}u_{2s}) = E(u_{2t}u_{2s}) = 0$ for $s \neq t$. The sample second moment matrix below, in terms of deviations from means, was calculated from 100 sample observations:

	y_1	y_2	x_1	x_2
y_1	20	5	3	3
y_2	5	50	2	4
x_1	3	2	9	1
x_2	3	4	1	9

(a) Find the best linear unbiased estimates of the parameters $\alpha_{11}, \alpha_{12}, \alpha_{21}$, and α_{22} in the above model.
(b) How would you estimate σ_1^2, σ_2^2 and σ_{12}?
(c) If it were known that $\sigma_{12} = 0$ how would this affect your estimates in part (a)?

Question 3.2

The observable random vectors $y_1, \ldots, y_T$ and the non-random vectors $x_1, \ldots, x_T$ satisfy the system

$$y_t = Ax_t + u_t \qquad (t = 1, \ldots, T) \tag{3.2.1}$$

where A is an $n \times m$ matrix of unknown parameters and the u_t are mutually independent random vectors with zero mean and positive definite covariance matrix Ω. It is assumed that $T > m$ and that the matrix $X' = [x_1, \ldots, x_T]$ has full rank m.
(a) If we consider (3.2.1) as an instance of the linear model

$$y = \theta + u \tag{3.2.2}$$

where $y' = (y'_1, \ldots, y'_T)$, $u' = (u'_1, \ldots, u'_T)$ and $\theta = E(y)$, show that (3.2.1) implies that θ lies in the sub-space of nT dimensional Euclidean space spanned by the columns of the matrix

$$W = \begin{bmatrix} I \otimes x'_1 \\ \cdot \\ \cdot \\ \cdot \\ I \otimes x'_T \end{bmatrix}$$

(b) If A^* is the least squares estimate of A and x_{T+1} is known, find the covariance matrix of the forecast error $y_{T+1} - A^* x_{T+1}$.

Question 3.3

In the following model

$$y_{1t} = \alpha_{11} x_{1t} + \alpha_{12} x_{2t} + u_{1t}$$

$$y_{2t} = \alpha_{21} x_{1t} + \alpha_{22} x_{2t} + u_{2t}$$

the x_{it} are non-random and the u_{it} are random disturbances with $E(u_{1t}) = E(u_{2t}) = 0$, $E(u_{1t}^2) = \sigma_1^2$, $E(u_{2t}^2) = \sigma_2^2$ and $E(u_{1t} u_{2t}) = \sigma_{12}$ for all t, while $E(u_{1s} u_{1t}) = E(u_{2s} u_{2t}) = E(u_{1s} u_{2t}) = 0$ for $s \neq t$. The following sample second moment matrix was obtained from a sample of 100 observations:

	y_1	y_2	x_1	x_2
y_1	5	2	2	2
y_2	2	10	1	3
x_1	2	1	1	1
x_2	2	3	1	2

(a) Obtain the best linear unbiased estimates of α_{11}, α_{12}, α_{21} and α_{22}.
(b) Obtain an estimate of the variance of $\alpha_{12}^* - \alpha^*_{21}$, where α_{12}^* and α_{21}^* are your estimates of α_{12} and α_{21} respectively.
(c) If σ_1^2, σ_2^2 and σ_{12} were known, would it be possible to obtain any better estimates of the α_{ij} or any better estimates of the variance of $\alpha_{12}^* - \alpha_{21}^*$?
(d) How would you test the hypothesis $H_0: \alpha_{12} = \alpha_{21}$ if it were known that the disturbances u_{it} are normally distributed?

(Adapted from University of Essex MA examinations, 1971.)

Question 3.4

In the following model

$$y_{1t} = \alpha_{11}x_{1t} + \alpha_{12}x_{2t} + u_{1t}$$
$$y_{2t} = \alpha_{21}x_{3t} + \alpha_{22}x_{4t} + u_{2t}$$

the y_{it} $(i = 1, 2)$ are endogenous variables and the x_{jt} $(j = 1, 2)$ are exogenous variables which we assume to be non-random. The u_{it} are serially independent random disturbances with zero means and second moments given by

$$E(u_{1t}^2) = \sigma^2, E(u_{2t}^2) = 2\sigma^2 \quad \text{and} \quad E(u_{1t}u_{2t}) = \sigma^2 \text{ for all } t$$

Find the best linear unbiased estimates of $\alpha_{11}, \alpha_{12}, \alpha_{21}$ and α_{22} given the following sample second moment matrix:

	y_1	y_2	x_1	x_2	x_3	x_4
y_1	2000	500	-200	400	200	100
y_2	500	1000	150	-200	30	-20
x_1	-200	150	100	0	0	0
x_2	400	-200	0	300	0	0
x_3	200	30	0	0	20	10
x_4	100	-20	0	0	10	10

(University of Essex MA examination, 1973.)

Question 3.5

In the following two-equation regression model

$$\begin{bmatrix} y_1 \\ y_2 \end{bmatrix} = \begin{bmatrix} X_1 & 0 \\ 0 & X_2 \end{bmatrix} \begin{bmatrix} \beta_1 \\ \beta_2 \end{bmatrix} + \begin{bmatrix} u_1 \\ u_2 \end{bmatrix}$$

$y_i (i = 1, 2)$ is a vector of T observations on the ith dependent variable, X_i is a matrix of observations on l_i non-random independent variables, the β_i are vectors of coefficients and the u_i are vectors of disturbances for which $E(u_1) = E(u_2) = 0$ and $E(u_1u_1') = \sigma_{11}I_T, E(u_2u_2') = \sigma_{22}I_T$ and $E(u_1u_2') = \sigma_{12}I_T$. It is assumed that the matrix

$$\Sigma = \begin{bmatrix} \sigma_{11} & \sigma_{12} \\ \sigma_{12} & \sigma_{22} \end{bmatrix}$$

is positive definite.

(a) Find the covariance matrix of the Aitken (or generalised least squares) estimator of β_1.

(b) In the case where $X_1'X_2 = 0$, compare the covariance matrix in (a) with the covariance matrix of the single equation least squares estimator of β_1.

Question 3.6

In the following model

$$y_{1t} = \alpha x_{1t} + \beta x_{2t} + u_{1t} \tag{3.6.1}$$

$$y_{2t} = \gamma x_{3t} + u_{2t} \tag{3.6.2}$$

the y_{it} $(i = 1, 2)$ are endogenous variables and the x_{jt} $(j = 1, 2)$ are exogenous variables which we assume to be non-random. The u_{it} are serially independent random disturbances with zero means and second moments given by $E(u_{1t}^2) = \sigma^2$, $E(u_{2t}^2) = 4\sigma^2$ and $E(u_{1t}u_{2t}) = 2\rho\sigma^2$ for all t where $|\rho| < 1$.

(a) Find the best linear unbiased estimates of α, β and γ given the following sample second moment matrix:

	y_1	y_2	x_1	x_2	x_3
y_1	100	20	4	1	0
y_2	20	150	0	0	1
x_1	4	0	10	−2	0 .
x_2	1	0	−2	5	0
x_3	0	1	0	0	5

(b) Comment on any special feature of your results.

Question 3.7

(a) What do you understand by the following terms:
    (i) an efficient estimator
    (ii) an asymptotically efficient estimator.
(b) In the following model

$$y_{1t} = \alpha x_{1t} + u_{1t}$$

$$y_{2t} = \beta x_{1t} + \gamma x_{2t} + u_{2t}$$

the y_{it} $(i = 1, 2)$ are endogenous variables and the x_{jt} $(j = 1, 2)$ are non-random exogenous variables whose second moment matrix converges as the sample size tends to infinity to the following positive definite limit:

$$\begin{array}{c|cc} & x_1 & x_2 \\ \hline x_1 & 2 & 1 \\ x_2 & 1 & 1 \end{array}$$

The u_{it} $(i = 1, 2)$ are serially independent random disturbances which have the same bivariate normal distribution for each value of t with $E(u_{1t}) = E(u_{2t}) = 0$ and covariance matrix

$$\Sigma = \begin{bmatrix} \sigma_1^2 & \rho\sigma_1\sigma_2 \\ \rho\sigma_1\sigma_2 & \sigma_2^2 \end{bmatrix} \quad \text{with} \quad |\rho| < 1.$$

Describe a procedure for obtaining asymptotically efficient estimates of the parameters α, β and γ in the above model. Find the covariance matrix of the limiting distribution of your estimates and compare the asymptotic variance of your estimates of α and γ with that of alternative estimates of these parameters derived by the application of ordinary least squares to each equation. Comment briefly on your results.

(Adapted in part from University of Essex BA/MA examinations, 1975.)

Question 3.8

In the following model

$$y_{1t} = \alpha x_{1t} + \beta x_{2t} + u_{1t}$$
$$y_{2t} = \beta x_{1t} + \gamma x_{2t} + u_{2t}$$

the y_{it} $(i = 1, 2)$ are endogenous variables, the x_{jt} $(j = 1, 2)$ are non-random exogenous variables and the u_{it} $(i = 1, 2)$ are random disturbances which satisfy the following conditions:

$$E(u_{1t}) = E(u_{2t}) = 0$$
$$E(u_{1t}^2) = E(u_{2t}^2) = \sigma^2$$
$$E(u_{1t}u_{2t}) = 0$$

for all t, and

$$E(u_{1s}u_{1t}) = E(u_{2s}u_{2t}) = E(u_{1s}u_{2t}) = 0 \qquad (\text{for } s \neq t)$$

Obtain the best linear unbiased estimates of α, β and γ from the following sample second moment matrix:

	y_1	y_2	x_1	x_2
y_1	120	80	20	45
y_2	80	90	25	30
x_1	20	25	10	5
x_2	45	20	5	20

(Adapted from University of Essex MA examinations, 1973.)

Question 3.9

It is assumed that the system

$$y_{1t} = \alpha x_{1t} + \beta x_{2t} + u_{1t}$$

$$y_{2t} = \gamma x_{3t} + u_{2t}$$

holds for all t and that:
   (i) $\alpha + \beta = \gamma$
   (ii) the x_{jt} $(j = 1, 2)$ are non-random, and
   (iii) the u_{it} are random disturbances which satisfy the following
      conditions:

$$E(u_{1t}) = E(u_{2t}) = 0$$

$$E(u_{1t}^2) = E(u_{2t}^2) = \sigma^2$$

$$E(u_{1t}u_{2t}) = 0$$

for all t, and

$$E(u_{1s}u_{1t}) = E(u_{2s}u_{2t}) = E(u_{1s}u_{2t}) = 0$$

for $s \neq t$. The following sample second moment matrix has been computed from a sample of T observations of the vector $(y_{1t}, y_{2t}, x_{1t}, x_{2t}, x_{3t})$

	y_1	y_2	x_1	x_2	x_3
y_1	10	4	3	4	2
y_2	4	20	2	2	7
x_1	3	2	2	1	1
x_2	4	2	1	3	1
x_3	2	7	1	1	4

(a) Find the best linear unbiased estimates of α, β and γ.
(b) Find the variance of your estimate of γ as a function of σ^2 and T.

(Adapted from University of Essex MA examinations, 1973.)

Question 3.10

Expenditure by households on a set of commodities is related to household income by the system of equations

$$y_h = M_h \beta + u_h \qquad (h = 1, \ldots, H) \tag{3.10.1}$$

where

$y_h' = (y_{h1}, \ldots, y_{hn})$ is a vector of expenditures by household h in a given period on n different commodities,

M_h = income of household h in the given period,

$\beta' = (\beta_1, \ldots, \beta_n)$ is a vector of unknown coefficients, and

$u_h' = (u_{h1}, \ldots, u_{hn})$ is a vector of random disturbances.

The n commodities in the above model are assumed to be exhaustive, so that, for all h, $i'y_h = M_h$ where i is the $n \times 1$ sum vector defined by $i' = (1, 1, \ldots, 1)$. The disturbances $\{u_h : h = 1, \ldots, H\}$ are assumed to be independently and identically distributed random vectors with $E(u_h) = 0$ and $E(u_h u_h') = V$.

(a) Show that the coefficient vector β satisfies $i'\beta = 1$.

(b) Show that V is a singular matrix and find a basis for the null space of V if it is assumed that V has rank $n - 1$.

(c) Since V has no inverse it is suggested that the parameter vector β be estimated by constrained generalised least squares on a sub-set of $n - 1$ equations of the model. Prove that the covariance matrix of the errors in this sub-system is non-singular and that the constrained generalised least squares estimator of β is the same whichever equation is neglected. How does this estimation procedure differ from single equation least squares applied to each equation of the system?

Question 3.11

An econometric model is given by the equation system

$$y_i = Z\delta_i + u_i \qquad (i = 1, \ldots, n)$$

where y_i is a vector of T observations on the ith endogenous variable, $Z = [i \vdots X]$ where $i' = (1, 1, \ldots, 1)$ is the $1 \times T$ sum vector and X is a $T \times m$ matrix of observations of m exogenous variables, u_i is a vector of disturbances, and δ_i a vector of unknown parameters. The y_i are known to satisfy the vector equation

$$\sum_{i=1}^{n} a_i y_i = 0 \qquad\qquad (3.11.1)$$

for known constants $a_1, \ldots, a_n$.

(a) If the δ_i are estimated by an ordinary least squares regression for each equation of the model, will the calculated values of y_i obtained from the regression satisfy (3.11.1)?

(b) Does your result hold if (3.11.1) were changed to

$$\sum_{i=1}^{n} a_i y_i = b \qquad\qquad (3.11.2)$$

for some constant vector $b \neq 0$?

(University of Essex BA/MA examinations, 1975.)

Question 3.12

The following model describes the behaviour of the ith household at time t

$$y_{it} = \sum_{j=1}^{k} \beta_{ij} x_{ijt} + u_{it} \qquad (i = 1, \ldots, n \quad \text{and} \quad t = 1, \ldots, T)$$
$$(3.12.1)$$

where x_{ijt} is non-random, the u_{it} are normally distributed with mean zero, $E(u_{it} u_{jt}) = 0$ for all i, j, and $E(u_{it} u_{js}) = 0$ for $t \neq s$.

(a) Under what conditions can the system of equations (3.12.1) be validly represented by the linear aggregate equation

$$\bar{y}_t = \sum_{j=1}^{k} \beta_j \bar{x}_{jt} + \bar{u}_t \qquad (t = 1, \ldots, T) \qquad (3.12.2)$$

where $\bar{y}_t = \Sigma_{i=1}^{n} y_{it}$, $\bar{x}_{jt} = \Sigma_{i=1}^{n} x_{ijt}$, $\bar{u}_t = \Sigma_{i=1}^{n} u_{it}$ and the β_j are constants for all j?

(b) Derive a test statistic for the hypothesis $\beta_{ij} = \beta_j$ for all i, j in each of the following cases:

(i) the σ_{ij} equal σ^2 for all i, j,

(ii) the σ_{ij} are known but not equal, and

(iii) the σ_{ij} are unknown.

2. SUPPLEMENTARY QUESTIONS

Question 3.13

In the model

$$y_{1t} = a_{11} x_{1t} + a_{12} x_{2t} + u_{1t}$$
$$y_{2t} = a_{21} x_{1t} + a_{22} x_{2t} + u_{2t}$$

it is assumed that the exogenous variables $x_{it} (i = 1, 2)$ are non-random and that

(i) $a_{11} + a_{12} = a_{21}$

$\quad\;\; a_{11} - a_{12} = a_{22}$

(ii) the $u_{it} (i = 1, 2)$ are serially independent random disturbances which are identically distributed for all t with first and second moments given by:

$$E(u_{1t}) = E(u_{2t}) = 0$$

$$E(u_{1t}^2) = 2\sigma^2, \quad E(u_{2t}^2) = \sigma^2, \quad E(u_{1t}u_{2t}) = \sigma^2$$

The following sample second moment matrix has been computed from a sample of T observations of the vector $(y_{1t}, y_{2t}, x_{1t}, x_{2t})$:

	y_1	y_2	x_1	x_2
y_1	10	-10	3	1
y_2	-10	20	1	1
x_1	3	1	1	-1
x_2	1	1	-1	2

(a) Find the best linear unbiased estimates of the coefficients a_{11}, a_{12}, a_{21} and a_{22}.

(b) Find expressions for the variances of your estimates of a_{21} and a_{22} as functions of T and σ^2.

(Adapted from University of Birmingham M Soc.Sc. examinations, 1977.)

Question 3.14

In the model:

$$y_{1t} = a_{11}x_{1t} + a_{12}x_{2t} + u_{1t}$$

$$y_{2t} = a_{21}x_{1t} + a_{22}x_{2t} + a_{23}x_{3t} + u_{2t}$$

the x_{it} are non-random, the u_{it} are normally distributed with:

$$E(u_{1t}) = E(u_{2t}) = 0$$

$$E(u_{1t}^2) = 2\sigma^2, \quad E(u_{2t}^2) = \sigma^2, \quad E(u_{1t}u_{2t}) = 0$$

and

$$E(u_{it}u_{js}) = 0 \quad \text{for} \quad i,j = 1, 2 \quad \text{and} \quad t \neq s$$

A sample size $T = 72$ gives the following data on second order moments

	x_1	x_2	x_3
y_1	4	2	0
y_2	2	2	2
x_1	6	2	0
x_2	2	4	0
x_3	0	0	8

(a) Calculate best linear unbiased estimates of the coefficients a_{ij} subject to the restriction $a_{12} = a_{23}$.

(b) If $\sigma^2 = 1$, test the hypothesis $H_0: a_{11} + a_{12} = \frac{1}{2}$ against the alternative $H_1: a_{11} + a_{12} \neq \frac{1}{2}$.

(c) If the restriction $a_{12} = a_{23}$ were not imposed, how would you estimate the coefficients?

(University of Essex MA examinations, 1977.)

Question 3.15

In the model

$$y_{1t} = \alpha x_{1t} + \beta x_{2t} + u_{1t} \tag{3.15.1}$$

$$y_{2t} = \beta x_{1t} + \gamma x_{2t} + u_{2t} \tag{3.15.2}$$

it is known that the exogenous variables $x_{jt} (j = 1, 2)$ are non-random and that

(i) $\gamma = \alpha - \beta$,

(ii) the $u_{it} (i = 1, 2)$ are serially independent, random disturbances which have the same bivariate normal distribution for all t with first and second moments given by:

$$E(u_{1t}) = E(u_{2t}) = 0$$

$$E(u_{1t}^2) = \sigma^2, \quad E(u_{2t}^2) = 2\sigma^2, \quad E(u_{1t}u_{2t}) = \sigma^2$$

It is also known that the second moment matrix of the $x_{jt} (j = 1, 2)$ converges as the sample size tends to infinity to the limit

	x_1	x_2
x_1	$2\omega^2$	ω^2
x_2	ω^2	ω^2

(a) Describe a procedure for obtaining asymptotically efficient estimates of the parameters α and β in the above model.

(b) Find the covariance matrix of the limiting distribution of your estimates in (a) and compare the asymptotic variances of your estimates of α and β with those of the two alternative sets of estimates of these parameters obtained by the application of ordinary least squares to each equation of (3.15.1–2).

Question 3.16

In the model

$$y_{1t} = \alpha x_{1t} + \beta x_{2t} + u_{1t} \tag{3.16.1}$$

$$y_{2t} = \alpha x_{2t} + u_{2t} \tag{3.16.2}$$

$$y_{3t} = \beta x_{1t} + u_{3t} \tag{3.16.3}$$

the $x_{jt} (j = 1, 2)$ are non-random exogenous variables whose second moment matrix is known to converge to the identity matrix as the sample size tends to infinity. The u_{it} ($i = 1, 2, 3$) are serially independent random disturbances which have the same multivariate normal distribution for all t with first and second moments given by

$$E(u_{1t}) = E(u_{2t}) = E(u_{3t}) = 0$$

$$E(u_{1t}^2) = E(u_{2t}^2) = \sigma^2, \quad E(u_{3t}^2) = \omega^2$$

and

$$E(u_{it}u_{jt}) = 0 \qquad (i \neq j)$$

(a) Describe a procedure for obtaining asymptotically efficient estimates of α and β.

(b) Can an asymptotically efficient estimate of α (or β) be obtained by neglecting one of the equations in (3.16.1−3)? Why?

Question 3.17

In the model

$$y_{1t} = a_{11}x_{1t} + a_{12}x_{2t} + u_{1t}$$

$$y_{2t} = a_{21}x_{1t} + a_{22}x_{2t} + u_{2t}$$

the x_{jt} ($j = 1, 2$) are non-random exogenous variables and the u_{it} ($i = 1, 2$) are serially independent random disturbances with the same bivariate normal distribution for all values of t in which the mean vector is zero and the covariance matrix is the known non-singular matrix Ω. The following tests are to be considered:

(1) test $H_0(1)$: $a_{11} = a_{12} = a_{21} = a_{22}$

   against $H_1(1)$: $H_0(1)$ is false

(2) test $H_0(2)$: $a_{11} = a_{22}$

   against $H_1(2)$: $a_{11} \neq a_{22}$

(3) test $H_0(3)$: $a_{11} = a_{12} = a_{21} = a_{22}$

   against $H_1(3)$: $a_{11} = a_{22}$

(a) Show how to construct F-statistics for testing each of the above hypotheses.

(b) If F_1, F_2 and F_3 are the F-statistics for testing hypotheses (1), (2) and (3), respectively, verify that if the sample size is 22 then

$$F_3 = \frac{41}{2} \left[\frac{3F_1 - F_2}{40 + F_2} \right] \tag{3.15.1}$$

(c) If $F_1 = 2.80$ and $F_2 = 1.60$ which of the three null hypotheses should be accepted and which rejected at the 5% level of significance. Comment on your result.

(d) Show how to construct χ^2-statistics for testing the above hypotheses. Is there any relationship among these statistics corresponding to (3.17.1) for the F-statistics?

(e) Is there any reason for preferring the tests based on the χ^2-statistics to those based on the F-statistics?

(Adapted in part from University of Essex MA examinations, 1976.)

Question 3.18

The following model describes the behaviour of the ith household at time t

$$y_{it} = \sum_{j=1}^{k} \beta_j x_{ijt} + u_{it} \qquad (i = 1, \ldots, n \quad \text{and} \quad t = 1, \ldots, T)$$

(3.18.1)

where x_{ijt} is non-random, $E(u_{it}) = 0$, $E(u_{it}u_{jt}) = \sigma_{ij}$ for all i, j, $E(u_{it}u_{js}) = 0$ for $t \neq s$. The corresponding macro-model is

$$\bar{y}_t = \sum_{j=1}^{k} \beta_j \bar{x}_{jt} + \bar{u}_t \qquad (t = 1, \ldots, T)$$

(3.18.2)

where $\bar{y}_t = \Sigma_{i=1}^n y_{it}$, $\bar{x}_{jt} = \Sigma_{i=1}^n x_{ijt}$ and $\bar{u}_t = \Sigma_{i=1}^n u_{it}$. Compare the efficiency of the generalised least squares estimators of β_j for $j = 1, \ldots, k$ obtained from the system of micro-equations (3.18.1) and the macro-equation (3.18.2) when

(a) $\sigma_{ij} = \sigma^2$ and

(b) the σ_{ij} are known but not equal.

(c) Reconsider your answers to parts (a) and (b) when $x_{ijt} = x_{jt}$ for all i, j, t.

3. SOLUTIONS

Solution 3.1

The given model is an instance of the multiple equation model (3.0.1), that is

$$y_t = Ax_t + u_t$$

(3.1.1)

Our problem is to estimate A using the sample observations $\{y_t, x_t: t = 1, \ldots, T\}$. We mention the important result that when there are *no restrictions on the elements of the parameter matrix A*, the best linear unbiased estimator of A is obtained by applying the method of least squares to each equation of the model (3.1.1) (Malinvaud, 1970, pp. 205–206).

Note that the ith equation of (3.1.1) can be written as

$$y_{it} = a_i'x_t + u_{it} = x_t'a_i + u_{it} \qquad (3.1.2)$$

where a_i' is the ith row of A; and if we now write down (3.1.2) for each of the sample observations $t = 1, \ldots, T$ we have the system

$$y_i = Xa_i + u_i \qquad (3.1.3)$$

where

$$y_i = \begin{bmatrix} y_{i1} \\ \cdot \\ \cdot \\ \cdot \\ y_{iT} \end{bmatrix}, \ u_i = \begin{bmatrix} u_{i1} \\ \cdot \\ \cdot \\ \cdot \\ u_{iT} \end{bmatrix} \quad \text{and} \quad X' = [x_1, \ldots, x_T]$$

(in this notation y_i is the vector of T observations on the ith endogenous variable). Applying ordinary least squares to (3.1.3) we obtain

$$a_i^* = (X'X)^{-1}X'y_i$$

and this formula holds good for all values of $i = 1, \ldots, n$. We note that

$$A = \begin{bmatrix} a_1' \\ \cdot \\ \cdot \\ \cdot \\ a_n' \end{bmatrix}$$

so that

$$A' = [a_1 \ldots a_n]$$

and the corresponding ordinary least squares estimator of A' is

$$A^{*'} = (X'X)^{-1}X'Y \qquad (3.1.4)$$

where $Y = [y_1, \ldots, y_n]$. Note that Y is a $T \times n$ matrix of observations on the n endogenous variables and we can write this matrix in the alternative transposed form as $Y' = [y_1, \ldots, y_T]$ where $y_t' = (y_{1t}, y_{2t}, \ldots, y_{nt})$.

It follows by transposing (3.1.4) that

$$A^* = Y'X(X'X)^{-1} = \left(\frac{Y'X}{T}\right)\left(\frac{X'X}{T}\right)^{-1}$$

Now

$$\frac{X'X}{T} = \frac{1}{T}[x_1, \ldots, x_T]\begin{bmatrix} x_1' \\ x_T' \end{bmatrix} = \frac{1}{T}\sum_{t=1}^{T} x_t x_t' = M_{xx}$$

say, and

$$\frac{Y'X}{T} = \frac{1}{T} [y_1, \ldots, y_T] \begin{bmatrix} x'_1 \\ x'_T \end{bmatrix} = \frac{1}{T} \sum_{t=1}^{T} y_t x'_t = M_{yx}$$

say, where we have used M_{xx} and M_{yx} to denote sample second moments of the data. We can then write A^* in the alternative form (c.f. Malinvaud, 1970, pp. 205–206)

$$A^* = M_{yx} M_{xx}^{-1} \tag{3.1.5}$$

and, of course,

$$A^{*'} = M_{xx}^{-1} M_{xy}$$

corresponding to (3.1.4).

When a constant term occurs in each equation of the model we can rewrite (3.1.1) more explicitly as

$$y_t = b + A x_t + u_t$$

where b is a vector of constants. Then the best linear unbiased estimator of the augmented matrix $[b \vdots A]$ is, from (3.1.5),

$$[b^* \vdots A^*] = [\bar{y} \vdots M_{yx}] \begin{bmatrix} 1 & \bar{x}' \\ \bar{x} & M_{xx} \end{bmatrix}^{-1} \tag{3.1.6}$$

where $\bar{y} = (\bar{y}_i)$ with $\bar{y}_i = (\Sigma_{t=1}^{T} y_{it})/T$ and $\bar{x} = (\bar{x}_j)$ with $\bar{x}_j = (\Sigma_{t=1}^{T} x_{jt})/T$. Inverting the partitioned matrix on the right side of (3.1.6) and solving the resulting equations for b^* and A^* as in Solution 2.1 (see also Malinvaud, 1970 pp. 211–212) we obtain

$$A^* = \bar{M}_{yx} \bar{M}_{xx}^{-1} \tag{3.1.7}$$

and

$$b^* = \bar{y} - A^* \bar{x}$$

where

$$\bar{M}_{yx} = (1/T) \Sigma_{t=1}^{T} (y_t - \bar{y})(x_t - \bar{x})'$$

and

$$\bar{M}_{xx} = (1/T) \Sigma_{t=1}^{T} (x_t - \bar{x})(x_t - \bar{x})'.$$

Part (a) Turning now to the question, we notice that there are no restrictions on the coefficients to be estimated. Hence, the best linear unbiased estimates of the coefficients of x_{1t} and x_{2t} are [using (3.1.7) and the given data] :

$$\begin{bmatrix} \alpha_{11}^* & \alpha_{12}^* \\ \alpha_{21}^* & \alpha_{22}^* \end{bmatrix} = \begin{bmatrix} 3 & 3 \\ 2 & 4 \end{bmatrix} \begin{bmatrix} 9 & 1 \\ 1 & 9 \end{bmatrix}^{-1}$$

$$= \frac{1}{80} \begin{bmatrix} 3 & 3 \\ 2 & 4 \end{bmatrix} \begin{bmatrix} 9 & -1 \\ -1 & 9 \end{bmatrix} = \begin{bmatrix} 0.3 & 0.3 \\ 0.175 & 0.425 \end{bmatrix}$$

Part (b) Estimates of σ_1^2, σ_2^2 and σ_{12} can be obtained in the usual way (c.f. Malinvaud, 1970b, pp. 209–210) from the sample moments of the residuals $\{u_{it}^* : i = 1, 2; t = 1, \dots, T\}$ from the least squares regression. Writing

$$\Omega = \begin{bmatrix} \sigma_1^2 & \sigma_{12} \\ \sigma_{12} & \sigma_2^2 \end{bmatrix}$$

we estimate Ω by

$$M_{uu}^* = \frac{1}{T} \sum_{t=1}^{T} u_t^* u_t^{*\prime} = \frac{1}{T} \begin{bmatrix} \sum_{t=1}^{T} u_{1t}^{*2} & \sum_{t=1}^{T} u_{1t}^* u_{2t}^* \\ \sum_{t=1}^{T} u_{2t}^* u_{1t}^* & \sum_{t=1}^{T} u_{2t}^{*2} \end{bmatrix}$$

using the formula (Malinvaud, 1970b, p. 210)

$$M_{uu}^* = M_{yy} - M_{yx} M_{xx}^{-1} M_{xy} = M_{yy} - A^* M_{xy}$$

where $M_{yy} = T^{-1} \sum_{t=1}^{T} y_t y_t'$. From the given data we have, in this case,

$$M_{uu}^* = \begin{bmatrix} 20 & 5 \\ 5 & 50 \end{bmatrix} - \begin{bmatrix} 0.3 & 0.3 \\ 0.175 & 0.425 \end{bmatrix} \begin{bmatrix} 3 & 2 \\ 3 & 4 \end{bmatrix}$$

$$= \begin{bmatrix} 18.2 & 3.2 \\ 3.2 & 47.95 \end{bmatrix}.$$

Remark We remark that M_{uu}^* is not an unbiased estimator of Ω. But the following rescaled matrix is an unbiased estimator of Ω (c.f. Malinvaud, 1970b, p. 210):

$$\left(\frac{T}{T-m} \right) M_{uu}^* = \left(\frac{1}{T-m} \right) \sum_{t=1}^{T} u_t^* u_t^{*\prime}$$

where m is the number of exogenous variables in the model (in this case $m = 3$).

Part (c) The estimates of the coefficients $\alpha_{ij} (i = 1, 2; j = 0, 1, 2)$ obtained in Part (a) are the best linear unbiased estimates *regardless* of the value of σ_{12} in the present model (Malinvaud, 1970, p. 206).

What this means is that there is no information contained in the specification of either equation which is useful in the estimation of the other. We may well have expected this to be the case when $\sigma_{12} = 0$ and the errors on the two equations are uncorrelated. For then the endogenous variables y_{1t} and y_{2t} are uncorrelated and the two equations are in a sense quite separate. But when $\sigma_{12} \neq 0$ the two endogenous variables are correlated and it is an interesting result that an ordinary least squares regression on the two equations separately still produces the best linear unbiased estimates.

We will see in our later examples in this chapter that an ordinary least squares regression on the two equations does *not* produce the best linear unbiased estimates of all of the unknown coefficients *when some of these coefficients satisfy known restrictions*; and, moreover, there are some cases where this is true even when $\sigma_{12} = 0$.

Solution 3.2

Part (a) We first write (3.2.1) complete with T observations as

$$\begin{bmatrix} y_1 \\ \cdot \\ \cdot \\ \cdot \\ y_T \end{bmatrix} = \begin{bmatrix} Ax_1 \\ \cdot \\ \cdot \\ \cdot \\ Ax_T \end{bmatrix} + \begin{bmatrix} u_1 \\ \cdot \\ \cdot \\ \cdot \\ u_T \end{bmatrix}$$

and note that

$$Ax_t = \text{vec}(Ax_t) = (I_n \otimes x_t')\,\text{vec}(A)$$

since Ax_t is already a vector. [In this operation we have used the vec( ) operator which we discuss fully in Appendix A and the right hand Kronecker product $\otimes$; for a discussion of the algebra of Kronecker products the reader is referred to Theil (1971, pp. 303–306) and Dhrymes (1970, pp. 155–156)]. We then have

$$\begin{bmatrix} y_1 \\ \cdot \\ \cdot \\ \cdot \\ y_T \end{bmatrix} = \begin{bmatrix} I_n \otimes x_1' \\ \cdot \\ \cdot \\ \cdot \\ I_n \otimes x_T' \end{bmatrix} \text{vec}(A) + \begin{bmatrix} u_1 \\ \cdot \\ \cdot \\ \cdot \\ u_T \end{bmatrix}$$

or

$$y = W \operatorname{vec}(A) + u. \tag{3.2.3}$$

This representation of (3.2.1) shows that if $\theta = E(y)$ as in (3.2.2) then θ can always be written as a linear combination of the columns of W. Thus, θ, which is an nT-component vector, lies in the sub-space of nT-dimensional Euclidean space spanned by the columns of W (for a definition of Euclidean space see Halmos, 1958, p. 121). Thus, θ lies in the range space of W. If we call this latter space L then the dimension of L is given by the rank of the matrix W (Halmos, 1958, p. 90). Now

$$W = \begin{bmatrix} x_1' & 0 & \ldots & 0 \\ 0 & x_1' & \ldots & 0 \\ \cdot & \cdot & \ldots & \cdot \\ 0 & 0 & \ldots & x_1' \\ x_2' & 0 & \ldots & 0 \\ 0 & x_2' & \ldots & 0 \\ \cdot & \cdot & \ldots & \cdot \\ 0 & 0 & \ldots & x_2' \\ & & \cdot & \\ & & \cdot & \\ & & \cdot & \\ x_T' & 0 & \ldots & 0 \\ 0 & x_T' & \ldots & 0 \\ \cdot & \cdot & \ldots & \cdot \\ 0 & 0 & \ldots & x_T' \end{bmatrix} \begin{matrix} (1) \ (2) \ \ \ \ (n) \end{matrix}$$

and we see that this matrix will have rank nm if each of the submatrices of W based on the column blocks $(1), (2), \ldots, (n)$ have rank m. But each of these column blocks will have rank less than m only if there exists a non-zero vector λ for which

$$x_t' \lambda = 0 \qquad (\text{for all } t = 1, \ldots, T)$$

that is, only if there exists a non-zero vector λ for which

$$X \lambda = 0$$

But X has full rank $(= m)$ by assumption, so that each of the column blocks $(1), (2), \ldots, (n)$ has rank m. Hence, W has rank nm.

Remark 1 Since W has full rank nm, we can always find the elements of A once we are given θ in the sub-space L. For we can always find a vector α such that

$$\theta = W\alpha$$

and then

$$W'\theta = W'W\alpha$$

and

$$\alpha = (W'W)^{-1}W'\theta$$

The elements of A can now be recovered by rearranging the elements of α into an $n \times m$ matrix, i.e. reversing the rule by which $\alpha = \text{vec}(A)$.

Remark 2 Note that α is obtained uniquely from θ by means of the linear transformation $(W'W)^{-1}W'$.

Remark 3 According to the geometrical interpretation of least squares (see, in particular, Seber, 1964, p. 13) we know that the least squares estimator of θ is obtained as the orthogonal projection of the observed vector y onto the sub-space L in which θ is known to lie. Since L is, in this case, the range space of W we have, for the least squares estimator of θ, the vector

$$\hat{\theta} = W(W'W)^{-1}W'y$$

(c.f. Seber, 1964, p. 14) and $W(W'W)^{-1}W'$ is the matrix which projects vectors in nT-dimensional space orthogonally onto L. It now follows from Remark 2 that the corresponding estimator of α is obtained uniquely from $\hat{\theta}$ as

$$\hat{\alpha} = (W'W)^{-1}W'\hat{\theta} = (W'W)^{-1}W'y \tag{3.2.4}$$

which corresponds to the familiar formula for the least squares estimator applied directly in (3.2.3). We leave it as an exercise for the reader to verify that $\hat{\alpha}$ as given by (3.2.4) is consistent with the formula (3.1.5) given in the last solution for the least squares estimator of A.

Part (b) We write the forecast error as

$$y_{T+1} - y^*_{T+1} = (A - A^*)x_{T+1} + u_{T+1}$$

Then, the forecast error covariance matrix is

$$E[(y_{T+1} - y^*_{T+1})(y_{T+1} - y^*_{T+1})']$$
$$= E(u_{T+1}u'_{T+1}) + E[(A - A^*)x_{t+1}x'_{T+1}(A - A^*)']$$

at least under the additional assumption that u_{T+1} is statistically independent of u_t for $t \leqslant T$. We take

$$E(u_{T+1}u'_{T+1}) = \Omega$$

and note that

$$(A - A^*)\, x_{T+1} = \text{vec}\,[(A - A^*)\, x_{T+1}]$$
$$= (I \otimes x'_{T+1})\, \text{vec}\,(A - A^*)$$

It now follows that the forecast error covariance matrix is

$$\Omega + E\{(I \otimes x'_{T+1})\, [\text{vec}\,(A - A^*)]\, [\text{vec}\,(A - A^*)]'\, (I \otimes x_{T+1})\}$$
$$= \Omega + (I \otimes x'_{T+1})\, E\{[\text{vec}\,(A - A^*)]\, [\text{vec}\,(A - A^*)]'\}\, (I \otimes x_{T+1})$$
$$= \Omega + (I \otimes x'_{T+1})\, (\Omega \otimes (X'X)^{-1})\, (I \otimes x_{T+1}) \tag{3.2.5}$$

since the covariance matrix of $\text{vec}\,(A^* - A)$ is given by (Malinvaud, 1970, p. 209; Goldberger, 1964, p. 209):

$$\frac{1}{T}\, \Omega \otimes M_{xx}^{-1} = \Omega \otimes (X'X)^{-1} \tag{3.2.6}$$

where $M_{xx} = (1/T)\, \Sigma_{t=1}^{T} x_t x'_t = (1/T)\, X'X$ and $X' = [x_1, \ldots, x_T]$.

Multiplying out the matrices on the right side of (3.2.5) above we obtain

$$\Omega + \Omega \otimes x'_{T+1}\, (X'X)^{-1} x_{T+1} = \Omega\, [1 + x'_{T+1}\, (X'X)^{-1} x_{T+1}]$$

since $x'_{T+1}(X'X)^{-1} x_{T+1}$ is a scalar.

Solution 3.3

Part (a) As in question 3.1 the best linear unbiased estimates of the coefficients are obtained by least squares on each equation. We have

$$\begin{bmatrix} \alpha_{11}^* & \alpha_{12}^* \\ \alpha_{21}^* & \alpha_{22}^* \end{bmatrix} = \begin{bmatrix} 2 & 2 \\ 1 & 3 \end{bmatrix} \begin{bmatrix} 1 & 1 \\ 1 & 2 \end{bmatrix}^{-1}$$

$$= \begin{bmatrix} 2 & 2 \\ 1 & 3 \end{bmatrix} \begin{bmatrix} 2 & -1 \\ -1 & 1 \end{bmatrix} = \begin{bmatrix} 2 & 0 \\ -1 & 2 \end{bmatrix}$$

Part (b) We introduce the long vector $\alpha' = (\alpha_{11}, \alpha_{12}, \alpha_{21}, \alpha_{22})$ so that the covariance matrix of α^*, given by (3.2.6) (Goldberger, 1964, p. 209; Malinvaud, 1970, p. 209), is

$$E(\alpha^* - \alpha)\, (\alpha^* - \alpha)' = \frac{1}{100} \begin{bmatrix} \sigma_1^2 & \sigma_{12} \\ \sigma_{12} & \sigma_2^2 \end{bmatrix} \otimes \begin{bmatrix} 1 & 1 \\ 1 & 2 \end{bmatrix}^{-1}$$

$$= \frac{1}{100} \left[\begin{array}{c|c} \sigma_1^2 \begin{pmatrix} 2 & -1 \\ -1 & 1 \end{pmatrix} & \sigma_{12} \begin{pmatrix} 2 & -1 \\ -1 & 1 \end{pmatrix} \\ \hline \sigma_{12} \begin{pmatrix} 2 & -1 \\ -1 & 1 \end{pmatrix} & \sigma_2^2 \begin{pmatrix} 2 & -1 \\ -1 & 1 \end{pmatrix} \end{array} \right]$$

Hence, using the fact that if $c'\alpha^*$ is a linear combination of the elements of α^* then $\mathrm{var}(c'\alpha^*) = c'V(\alpha^*)\,c$, where $V(\alpha^*)$ is the covariance matrix of α^*, we have

$$\mathrm{var}(\alpha_{12}^* - \alpha_{21}^*) = [0, 1, -1, 0] \; [E(\alpha^* - \alpha)(\alpha^* - \alpha)'] \begin{bmatrix} 0 \\ 1 \\ -1 \\ 0 \end{bmatrix}$$

$$= \frac{1}{100} [-\sigma_1^2 - 2\sigma_{12}, \; \sigma_1^2 + \sigma_{12}, \; -\sigma_{12} - 2\sigma_2^2, \; \sigma_{12} + \sigma_2^2]$$

$$\begin{bmatrix} 0 \\ 1 \\ -1 \\ 0 \end{bmatrix}$$

$$= [(\sigma_1^2 + \sigma_{12}) + (\sigma_{12} + 2\sigma_2^2)]/100$$

$$= (\sigma_1^2 + 2\sigma_2^2 + 2\sigma_{12})/100 \tag{3.3.1}$$

We now estimate the parameters σ_1^2, σ_2^2 and σ_{12} using the sample moment matrix of residuals

$$M_{uu}^* = \frac{1}{T} \sum_{t=1}^{T} u_t^* u_t^{*\prime}$$

where $u_t^{*\prime} = (u_{1t}^*, u_{2t}^*)$ is the vector of residuals on each equation. We calculate this matrix from the formula (c.f. solution 3.1 and Malinvaud, 1970, p. 210)

$$M_{uu}^* = M_{yy} - A^* M_{xy}$$

$$= \begin{bmatrix} 5 & 2 \\ 2 & 10 \end{bmatrix} - \begin{bmatrix} 2 & 0 \\ -1 & 2 \end{bmatrix} \begin{bmatrix} 2 & 1 \\ 2 & 3 \end{bmatrix}$$

$$= \begin{bmatrix} 5 & 2 \\ 2 & 10 \end{bmatrix} \begin{bmatrix} 4 & 2 \\ 2 & 5 \end{bmatrix} = \begin{bmatrix} 1 & 0 \\ 0 & 5 \end{bmatrix}$$

Hence, our estimate of $\mathrm{var}(\alpha_{12}^* - \alpha_{21}^*)$ is

$$[1 + 2(5)]/100 = 11/100 = 0.11$$

Part (c) As in Part (c) of Solution 3.1, since there are no prior restrictions on the coefficients of the model, the knowledge of σ_1^2, σ_2^2 and σ_{12} does not enable us to obtain more efficient linear unbiased estimates of the α_{ij}. On the other hand, knowledge of σ_1^2, σ_2^2 and σ_{12} does enable us to state the variance of $\alpha_{12}^* - \alpha_{21}^*$ *precisely* as (3.3.1); whereas without this knowledge we must *estimate* this variance; and the variance of an estimate of (3.3.1) is always at least as great as the variance of the non-random true value of (3.3.1) which is, of course, zero.

Part (d) When the disturbances u_{it} are normally distributed the estimates α_{ij}^* are also normally distributed and so too is the linear combination $\alpha_{12}^* - \alpha_{21}^*$. Thus

$$[(\alpha_{12}^* - \alpha_{21}^*) - (\alpha_{12} - \alpha_{21})]^2 / \mathrm{var}(\alpha_{12}^* - \alpha_{21}^*)$$

is distributed as χ^2 with one degree of freedom. If σ_1^2, σ_2^2 and σ_{12} were known, then to test H_0 we would compute the statistic

$$\chi^2 = \frac{(\alpha_{12}^* - \alpha_{21}^*)^2}{(\sigma_1^2 + 2\sigma_2^2 + 2\sigma_{12})/100}$$

and reject H_0 if $\chi^2 > \chi_1^2(\alpha)$, where α is the level of significance and $\chi_1^2(\alpha)$ is the tabulated percentage point of the distribution.

If σ_1^2, σ_2^2 and σ_{12} are unknown then there is no exact test (Malinvaud, 1970, pp. 235–236). We can instead use the same test but replace χ^2 above with the statistic

$$\frac{(\alpha_{12}^* - \alpha_{21}^*)^2}{(\sigma_1^{*2} + 2\sigma_2^{*2} + 2\sigma_{12}^{*2})/100} \tag{3.3.2}$$

where

$$\begin{bmatrix} \sigma_1^{*2} & \sigma_{12}^* \\ \sigma_{12}^* & \sigma_2^{*2} \end{bmatrix} = M_{uu}^*$$

This test is justified asymptotically because if the second moment matrix M_{zz} of the exogenous variables converges to a positive definite limit as the sample size $T \to \infty$, then M_{uu}^* is a consistent estimator of

$$\Omega = \begin{bmatrix} \sigma_1^2 & \sigma_{12} \\ \sigma_{12} & \sigma_2^2 \end{bmatrix}$$

and the limiting distribution of (3.3.2) is χ_1^2 (c.f. Malinvaud, 1970, p. 235). In the present case (3.3.2) is

$$\frac{1}{0.11} = 9.09 > \chi_1^2(0.01) = 6.635.$$

Hence, we reject H_0 at the 1% level of significance.

Remark We note that in Part (c) the hypothesis concerned the coefficients of different exogenous variables in the two equations. In this case there is no exact test. But, when the hypothesis concerns coefficients of the *same* exogenous variable in the different equations there is an exact test based on the F-distribution and called Hotelling's T^2-test (see Malinvaud, 1970b, pp. 236–237).

Solution 3.4

The given model is a linear multiple equation model similar in form to (3.0.1) but in which there are restrictions on the coefficients. In fact, the model is a special case of Zellner's seemingly unrelated regression model (3.0.2) and, therefore, can be represented by

$$y_m = X_m \beta_m + u_m \qquad (m = 1, \ldots, M) \tag{3.4.1}$$

where the u_m satisfy $E(u_m) = 0$ and $E(u_m u_n') = \sigma_{mn} I_T$ and the matrix $\Sigma = [(\sigma_{mn})]$ is assumed to be positive definite.

Writing (3.4.1) as the system

$$y = X\beta + u$$

where

$$y = \begin{bmatrix} y_1 \\ y_2 \\ \cdot \\ \cdot \\ \cdot \\ y_M \end{bmatrix}, X = \begin{bmatrix} X_1 & 0 & \cdots & 0 \\ 0 & X_2 & \cdots & 0 \\ \cdot & \cdot & \cdots & \cdot \\ 0 & 0 & \cdots & X_M \end{bmatrix}, \beta = \begin{bmatrix} \beta_1 \\ \beta_2 \\ \cdot \\ \cdot \\ \cdot \\ \beta_M \end{bmatrix} \text{ and } u = \begin{bmatrix} u_1 \\ u_2 \\ \cdot \\ \cdot \\ \cdot \\ u_M \end{bmatrix}$$

and noting that $E(uu') = \Sigma \otimes I_T$ we see that the best linear unbiased estimator of β is obtained by generalised least squares and is given by

$$\hat{\beta} = [X'(\Sigma^{-1} \otimes I_T) X]^{-1} [X'(\Sigma^{-1} \otimes I_T)y] \tag{3.4.2}$$

In the given question we have $M = 2$ and

$$\Sigma \otimes I_T = \begin{bmatrix} \sigma^2 & \sigma^2 \\ \sigma^2 & 2\sigma^2 \end{bmatrix} \otimes I_T = \begin{bmatrix} \sigma^2 I_T & \sigma^2 I_T \\ \sigma^2 I_T & 2\sigma^2 I_T \end{bmatrix},$$

$$X_1' = \begin{bmatrix} x_{11} & \cdots & x_{1T} \\ x_{21} & \cdots & x_{2T} \end{bmatrix} \quad \text{and} \quad X_2' = \begin{bmatrix} x_{31} & \cdots & x_{3T} \\ x_{41} & \cdots & x_{4T} \end{bmatrix}$$

Hence, using (3.4.2) we obtain

$$\begin{bmatrix} \hat{\alpha}_{11} \\ \hat{\alpha}_{12} \\ \hat{\alpha}_{21} \\ \hat{\alpha}_{22} \end{bmatrix} = \left\{ \frac{1}{T} \begin{bmatrix} X_1' & 0 \\ 0 & X_2' \end{bmatrix} \left(\begin{bmatrix} \sigma^2 & \sigma^2 \\ \sigma^2 & 2\sigma^2 \end{bmatrix}^{-1} \otimes I_T \right) \begin{bmatrix} X_1 & 0 \\ 0 & X_2 \end{bmatrix} \right\}^{-1} \tag{3.4.3}$$

$$\times \left\{ \frac{1}{T} \begin{bmatrix} X_1' & 0 \\ 0 & X_2' \end{bmatrix} \left(\begin{bmatrix} \sigma^2 & \sigma^2 \\ \sigma^2 & 2\sigma^2 \end{bmatrix}^{-1} \otimes I_T \right) \begin{bmatrix} y_1 \\ y_2 \end{bmatrix} \right\}$$

$$= \left\{ \frac{1}{T\sigma^2} \begin{bmatrix} X_1' & 0 \\ 0 & X_2' \end{bmatrix} \begin{bmatrix} 2I_T & -I_T \\ -I_T & I_T \end{bmatrix} \begin{bmatrix} X_1 & 0 \\ 0 & X_2 \end{bmatrix} \right\}^{-1} \tag{3.4.4}$$

$$\times \left\{ \frac{1}{T\sigma^2} \begin{bmatrix} X_1' & 0 \\ 0 & X_2' \end{bmatrix} \begin{bmatrix} 2I_T & -I_T \\ -I_T & I_T \end{bmatrix} \begin{bmatrix} y_1 \\ y_2 \end{bmatrix} \right\}$$

$$= \left\{ \frac{1}{T} \begin{bmatrix} 2X_1'X_1 & -X_1'X_2 \\ -X_2'X_1 & X_2'X_2 \end{bmatrix} \right\}^{-1} \left\{ \frac{1}{T} \begin{bmatrix} 2X_1'y_1 - X_1'y_2 \\ -X_2'y_1 + X_2'y_2 \end{bmatrix} \right\} \tag{3.4.5}$$

$$= \begin{bmatrix} 200 & 0 & 0 & 0 \\ 0 & 600 & 0 & 0 \\ 0 & 0 & 20 & 10 \\ 0 & 0 & 10 & 10 \end{bmatrix}^{-1} \begin{bmatrix} 2\begin{pmatrix} -200 \\ 400 \end{pmatrix} - \begin{pmatrix} 150 \\ -200 \end{pmatrix} \\ -\begin{pmatrix} 200 \\ 100 \end{pmatrix} + \begin{pmatrix} 30 \\ -20 \end{pmatrix} \end{bmatrix}$$

$$= \begin{bmatrix} 1/200 & 0 & 0 & 0 \\ 0 & 1/600 & 0 & 0 \\ 0 & 0 & 0.1 & -0.1 \\ 0 & 0 & -0.1 & 0.2 \end{bmatrix} \begin{bmatrix} -550 \\ 1000 \\ -170 \\ -120 \end{bmatrix} = \begin{bmatrix} -11/4 \\ -5/3 \\ -5 \\ 5 \end{bmatrix}.$$

Notice that we have introduced the factor $1/T$ inside each of the braces in (3.4.3) and we have cancelled the factor σ^2 (which comes outside the matrix Σ as a common factor) in passing from (3.4.4) to (3.4.5).

Solution 3.5

Part (a) From Solution 3.4 and, in particular, (3.4.2), the Aitken estimator of (β_1', β_2') is given by

$$\begin{bmatrix} \hat{\beta}_1 \\ \hat{\beta}_2 \end{bmatrix} = \begin{bmatrix} \sigma^{11}X_1'X_1 & \sigma^{12}X_1'X_2 \\ \sigma^{21}X_2'X_1 & \sigma^{22}X_2'X_2 \end{bmatrix}^{-1} \begin{bmatrix} \sigma^{11}X_1'y_1 + \sigma^{12}X_1'y_2 \\ \sigma^{21}X_2'y_1 + \sigma^{22}X_2'y_2 \end{bmatrix}$$

where

$$\Sigma^{-1} = \begin{bmatrix} \sigma^{11} & \sigma^{12} \\ \sigma^{21} & \sigma^{22} \end{bmatrix} = \frac{1}{\sigma_{11}\sigma_{22} - \sigma_{12}^2} \begin{bmatrix} \sigma_{22} & -\sigma_{12} \\ -\sigma_{12} & \sigma_{11} \end{bmatrix}$$

and, introducing $\rho = \sigma_{12}/(\sigma_{11}\sigma_{22})^{1/2}$, this matrix becomes

$$\frac{1}{\sigma_{11}\sigma_{22}(1 - \rho^2)} \begin{bmatrix} \sigma_{22} & -\rho(\sigma_{11}\sigma_{22})^{1/2} \\ -\rho(\sigma_{11}\sigma_{22})^{1/2} & \sigma_{11} \end{bmatrix}$$

The covariance matrix of $(\hat{\beta}_1, \hat{\beta}_2)$ is

$$\begin{bmatrix} \sigma^{11}X_1'X_1 & \sigma^{12}X_1'X_2 \\ \sigma^{21}X_2'X_1 & \sigma^{22}X_2'X_2 \end{bmatrix}^{-1}$$

(c.f. Zellner, 1962, p. 351) and inverting this partitioned matrix we find that the top left hand block is

$$\left\{ \sigma^{11}X_1'X_1 - \frac{(\sigma^{12})^2}{\sigma^{22}} X_1'X_2(X_2'X_2)^{-1}X_2'X_1 \right\}^{-1} \tag{3.5.1}$$

[see (2.1.10) for the formula for a partitioned inversion]. This matrix is then the covariance matrix of $\hat{\beta}_1$.

Part (b) When $X_1'X_2 = 0$, (3.5.1) reduces to

$$(\sigma^{11}X_1'X_1)^{-1} = \frac{1}{\sigma^{11}}(X_1'X_1)^{-1} = \sigma_{11}(1 - \rho^2)(X_1'X_1)^{-1} \tag{3.5.2}$$

The single equation least squares estimator of β_1 is $\hat{\beta}_1 = (X_1'X_1)^{-1}X_1'y_1$ and has covariance matrix

$$\sigma_{11}(X_1'X_1)^{-1} \qquad\qquad\qquad\qquad\qquad\qquad (3.5.3)$$

When we subtract (3.5.2) from (3.5.3) we are left with the positive definite matrix $\rho^2(X_1'X_1)^{-1}$. It follows that when $\rho \neq 0$ the use of the Aitken (or generalised least squares) procedure leads to an efficiency gain. When $\rho = 0$, the two procedures are in fact equivalent. Finally, we may note that when $X_1 = X_2$ the GLS estimator is identical to the OLS estimator (see Question 3.1).

Solution 3.6

Part (a) The given model (3.6.1–2) is, once again, an instance of (3.4.1). The best linear unbiased estimates of α, β and γ are given by

$$\begin{bmatrix} \hat{\alpha} \\ \hat{\beta} \\ \hat{\gamma} \end{bmatrix} = \left\{ \frac{1}{T} \begin{bmatrix} X_1' & 0 \\ 0 & X_2' \end{bmatrix} \left(\begin{bmatrix} \sigma^2 & 2\rho\sigma^2 \\ 2\rho\sigma^2 & 4\sigma^2 \end{bmatrix}^{-1} \otimes I_T \right) \begin{bmatrix} X_1 & 0 \\ 0 & X_2 \end{bmatrix} \right\}^{-1}$$

$$\times \left\{ \frac{1}{T} \begin{bmatrix} X_1' & 0 \\ 0 & X_2' \end{bmatrix} \left(\begin{bmatrix} \sigma^2 & 2\rho\sigma^2 \\ 2\rho\sigma^2 & 4\sigma^2 \end{bmatrix}^{-1} \otimes I_T \right) \begin{bmatrix} y_1 \\ y_2 \end{bmatrix} \right\}$$

$$= \left\{ \frac{1}{T4\sigma^4(1-\rho^2)} \begin{bmatrix} X_1' & 0 \\ 0 & X_2' \end{bmatrix} \begin{bmatrix} 4\sigma^2 I_T & -2\rho\sigma^2 I_T \\ -2\rho\sigma^2 I_T & \sigma^2 I_T \end{bmatrix} \begin{bmatrix} X_1 & 0 \\ 0 & X_2 \end{bmatrix} \right\}^{-1}$$

$$\times \left\{ \frac{1}{T4\sigma^4(1-\rho^2)} \begin{bmatrix} X_1' & 0 \\ 0 & X_2' \end{bmatrix} \begin{bmatrix} 4\sigma^2 I_T & -2\rho\sigma^2 I \\ -2\rho\sigma^2 I_T & \sigma^2 I_T \end{bmatrix} \begin{bmatrix} y_1 \\ y_2 \end{bmatrix} \right\}$$

$$= \left\{ \frac{1}{T} \begin{bmatrix} 4\sigma^2 X_1'X_1 & -2\rho\sigma^2 X_1'X_2 \\ -2\rho\sigma^2 X_2'X_1 & \sigma^2 X_2'X_2 \end{bmatrix} \right\}^{-1}$$

$$\times \left\{ \frac{1}{T} \begin{bmatrix} 4\sigma^2 X_1'y_1 & -2\rho\sigma^2 X_1'y_2 \\ -2\rho^2 X_2'y_1 & +\sigma^2 X_2'y_2 \end{bmatrix} \right\} \qquad (3.6.3)$$

$$= \left\{ \frac{1}{T} \begin{bmatrix} 4X_1'X_1 & -2\rho X_1'X_2 \\ -2\rho X_2'X_1 & X_2'X_2 \end{bmatrix} \right\}^{-1} \left\{ \frac{1}{T} \begin{bmatrix} 4X_1'y_1 & -2\rho X_1'y_2 \\ -2\rho X_2'y_1 + & X_2'y_2 \end{bmatrix} \right\}$$

$$\qquad\qquad\qquad\qquad\qquad\qquad\qquad\qquad\qquad (3.6.4)$$

$$= \begin{bmatrix} 4\begin{pmatrix} 10 & -2 \\ -2 & 5 \end{pmatrix} & \vdots & 0 \\ & & \vdots & 0 \\ \hline 0 & 0 & \vdots & 5 \end{bmatrix}^{-1} \begin{bmatrix} 4\begin{pmatrix} 4 \\ 1 \end{pmatrix} \\ \hline 1 \end{bmatrix}$$

$$= \begin{bmatrix} \dfrac{1}{4 \times 46}\begin{pmatrix} 5 & 2 \\ 2 & 10 \end{pmatrix} & \begin{matrix} 0 \\ 0 \end{matrix} \\ 0 \quad 0 & \frac{1}{5} \end{bmatrix} \begin{bmatrix} 16 \\ 4 \\ 1 \end{bmatrix}$$

$$= \begin{bmatrix} 88/184 \\ 72/184 \\ 1/5 \end{bmatrix} = \begin{bmatrix} 11/23 \\ 9/23 \\ 1/5 \end{bmatrix}$$

Part (b) We notice that σ^2 comes out as a common factor of the elements in the covariance matrix of the disturbances, viz

$$\begin{bmatrix} \sigma^2 & 2\rho\sigma^2 \\ 2\rho\sigma^2 & 4\sigma^2 \end{bmatrix} = \sigma^2 \begin{bmatrix} 1 & 2\rho \\ 2\rho & 4 \end{bmatrix}$$

and, as a result, σ^2 cancels in passing from (3.6.3) to (3.6.4). But, we cannot, in general, calculate the best linear unbiased estimates from (3.6.4) because ρ is an unknown parameter. However, in the special case of the data given in this problem, we find that

$$X_1'X_2 = 0, \quad X_1'y_2 = 0 \quad \text{and} \quad X_2'y_1 = 0 \tag{3.6.5}$$

so that the exogenous variables in each equation are orthogonal to *all the variables* in the other equation. This means that the terms involving the unknown parameter ρ in (3.6.4) are all zero and we can, therefore, proceed to calculate (3.6.4) in the present case without the knowledge of ρ.

In fact, the estimates obtained in Part (a) are identical to the estimates we would obtain by applying ordinary least squares to each equation. To see this we need only observe that when (3.6.5)˙holds, (3.6.4) becomes

$$\left\{ \frac{1}{T}\begin{bmatrix} 4X_1'X_1 & 0 \\ 0 & X_2'X_2 \end{bmatrix} \right\}^{-1} \left\{ \frac{1}{T}\begin{bmatrix} 4X_1'y_1 \\ X_2'y_2 \end{bmatrix} \right\}$$

which reduces to

$$\begin{bmatrix} (X_1'X_1)^{-1}X_1'y_1 \\ (X_2'X_2)^{-1}X_2'y_2 \end{bmatrix}$$

Remark We should emphasise that data for which (3.6.5) holds are very special indeed. For the variables y_{1t} and y_{2t} are endogenous variables and the two sets of equations

$$X_1' y_2 = 0 \quad \text{and} \quad X_2' y_1 = 0 \tag{3.6.6}$$

can be viewed as restrictions on the space of possible realisations of these endogenous variables. In general, of course, (3.6.6) will not hold.

Solution 3.7

Part (a) When we use the words "efficient" and "asymptotically efficient" in the context of an estimator (or estimation procedure) we mean that this estimator has a particular property or set of properties (relating to the degree of concentration its distribution — or asymptotic distribution — displays about the true value) which distinguishes it from all other members of a certain class. We must, therefore, be specific not only about the property (or properties) which distinguish such an estimator but also the class of estimators that we are considering.

In the case of an efficient estimator, we consider the particular class of estimators which are unbiased and regular in the sense that the probability density of the sample observations satisfies certain regularity conditions (Dhrymes, 1970, p. 115 and Cramér, 1946, p. 479). Then, within this class an efficient estimator is an estimator whose variance (or covariance matrix in the case of a parameter *vector*) attains the Cramér–Rao lower bound (Dhrymes, 1970, p. 124; Theil, 1971, p. 386; and Cramér, 1946, p. 480).

Consider, for instance, the case where the sample observations are independent and identically distributed with probability density $f(x; \theta)$ depending on the scalar parameter θ. The joint probability density of the sample of T observations $\{x_t : t = 1, \ldots, T\}$ is then

$$\prod_{t=1}^{T} f(x_t; \theta) = L(x_1, \ldots, x_T; \theta) \tag{3.7.3}$$

say. [Note that when we treat $L(\ )$ as a function of θ for the given values of the sample $x_1, \ldots, x_T$ we call it the likelihood function.] If $\hat{\theta} = \theta(x_1, \ldots, x_T)$ is a regular, unbiased estimator of θ then we say that the $\hat{\theta}$ is an efficient estimator if the variance of $\hat{\theta}$ satisfies the equality

$$\text{var}(\hat{\theta}) = \frac{1}{-E\left(\dfrac{\partial^2 \ln L(x_1, \ldots, x_T; \theta)}{\partial \theta^2}\right)}; \tag{3.7.4}$$

and the right hand side of (3.7.4) is known as the Cramér–Rao lower bound since all regular, unbiased estimators of θ have variance which is at least as great as the right side of (3.7.4). We notice that

$$\ln L(x_1, \ldots, x_T; \theta) = \sum_{t=1}^{T} \ln f(x_t; \theta)$$

and since the sample observations are independent and identically distributed

$$E\left(\frac{\partial^2 \ln L(x_1, \ldots, x_T; \theta)}{\partial \theta^2}\right) = TE\left(\frac{\partial^2 \ln f(x_t; \theta)}{\partial \theta^2}\right). \qquad (3.7.5)$$

when θ is a *vector* of parameters we have in place of the right hand side of (3.7.4) the inverse of the matrix

$$R(\theta) = -E\left(\frac{\partial^2 \ln L(x_1, \ldots, x_T; \theta)}{\partial \theta \partial \theta'}\right)$$

and $R(\theta)$ is known as the information matrix.

When we consider examples in which the sample observations are not necessarily independent and identically distributed we must work explicitly with the joint probability density $f(x_1, \ldots, x_T; \theta)$ of the sample observations. The concept of efficiency embodied in the equality (3.7.4) then carries over as before but we do not get the simplification in the form of the right hand side of (3.7.4) that results from (3.7.5) in the independent and identically distributed case (see Cramér, 1946, pp. 496—497, for a discussion of this generalisation).

The given model (3.7.1—2) is an instance of the seemingly unrelated regression model (3.4.1) above, and the efficient estimator (according to the above sense) in that model is given by (3.4.2). This estimator is linear and it depends on the knowledge of the disturbance covariance matrix Σ. To verify that (3.4.2) does, indeed, yield an efficient estimator we need only note that, under the normality assumption of the problem, $\hat{\beta}$ as given by (3.4.2) is the maximum likelihood estimator of β and the result follows from a theorem in Malinvaud (1970, Theorem 2, p. 175).

Remark As Malinvaud (1970, p. 176) comments, we have in this case the stronger result due to Rao (1965) that the estimator is efficient in the wider class of *all* unbiased estimators.

Efficient estimators exist only under very restrictive conditions (see, for instance, Cramér, 1946, p. 480) and in most cases of interest in econometrics we cannot expect that these conditions will be satisfied. For example, in the present model (3.7.1—2) we have seen in the last paragraph that the efficient estimator of the coefficients depends on the knowledge of the covariance matrix Σ; but, in many cases, the knowledge of Σ is not readily available and this estimator is, therefore, not operational. This means that we cannot normally rely upon the criterion of efficiency to discriminate between different estimators. Ideally, we would like to be able to derive the finite sample distributions of the different estimators we are considering and measure directly their relative degreees of concentration about the true parameter value. But, in most cases, it is a formidable task to extract the exact form of the finite sample distribution of an econometric estimator. On the other hand, many estimators (when suitably standardised) do have limiting normal distributions (see Solution 2.16) and it is possible to compare two different estimators by using the variances (or covariance matrices) of their limiting distributions. The concept of "asymptotic efficiency" is, loosely speaking, based on such a comparison.

We consider the class of consistent estimators whose limiting distribution as the sample size $T \to \infty$ is normal [in a rigorous theory we require also that the convergence to normality be uniform over compact sub-sets of the admissible parameter space (Dhrymes, 1970, p. 129 and Rao, 1963)]. Then, within this class, an asymptotically efficient estimator is an estimator whose asymptotic variance (or covariance matrix in the case of a parameter vector) attains the limit of the Cramér–Rao lower bound. More specifically, in the case we considered earlier of independent and identically distributed sample observatons [leading to the joint density (3.7.3)], the limit of the Cramér–Rao lower bound is

$$\lim_{T \to \infty} \{-T/E\,[\partial^2 \ln L(x_1, \ldots, x_T; \theta)/\partial\theta^2]\}$$
$$= -1/E\,[\partial^2 \ln f(x_t; \theta)/\partial\theta^2]$$

Note that the earlier formula for the Cramér–Rao lower bound, given by the right side of (3.7.4), has here been standardised with respect to the sample size T because we are concerned with the limiting distribution of $\sqrt{T}(\hat{\theta} - \theta)$ where $\hat{\theta}$ is our estimate of θ.

Remark We should not leave our discussion of asymptotic efficiency without some mention of the fact that there is by no means universal agreement about the right criteria for asymptotic efficiency. In fact, many different criteria have recently been suggested and the reader is recommended to consult the interesting articles by Rao (1960), Schmetterer (1966) and Wolfowitz (1966) for further details; recent discussions in the econometric literature are contained in Rothenberg (1973) and Madansky (1976). The type of criterion we have employed above is often referred to as BAN (or best asymptotically normal); i.e. in the class of estimators whose asymptotic distribution is normal we seek an estimator which has the smallest asymptotic variance. Several difficulties arise in this approach. The first is that BAN estimators do not, in general, exist unless we further restrict the class of estimators (usually by requiring uniform convergence to the limiting normal distribution, where uniform is taken to apply to the true position of the unknown parameter in the parameter space — we then talk of a CUAN estimator or an estimator which is consistent and uniformly asymptotically normal); an alternative approach which does not require us to further restrict the class of estimators we are considering is to accept that a BAN estimator need not exist everywhere in the parameter space but to show that the set of points in the parameter space at which we can do better is negligible (strictly speaking, is a set of Lebesgue measure zero). The latter approach is successfully used by Bahadur (1964).

A second difficulty with the BAN criterion is that we may well wish to consider alternative estimators whose limiting distributions are not necessarily normal; and the BAN criterion excludes such estimators as possible competitors. It becomes more difficult to compare the degree of concentration in the limiting distributions of two estimators if we have to deal with distributions other than the normal. The reader is referred to the recent article by Wolfowitz (1966) for a successful investigation of this problem.

Finally, we bring the reader's attention to the fact that most situations of interest in econometrics relate to the case where the sample observations are non-identically distributed and where we are dealing with a vector of parameters. The relevant statistical theory underlying the various concepts of asymptotic efficiency has not always been developed for this case. In this respect, the recent work by Barnett (1976) is very helpful. Barnett deals explicitly with the maximum likelihood estimator of a vector of parameters in the case of non-identically distributed observations arising from a multiple equation non-linear regression model (we will be considering such models in Chapter 5); and he shows how the proofs in Bahadur (1964) can be used to support the BAN criterion applied to the maximum likelihood estimator in this context.

Part (b) Asymptotically efficient estimates of α, β and γ in the given model are obtained by the following two-step procedure (compare Malinvaud, 1970, pp. 294–295):

(i) Estimate α, β and γ by using ordinary least squares on each equation and construct the sample moment matrix of residuals from these regressions.

$$\Sigma^* = \begin{bmatrix} s_1^2 & s_{12} \\ s_{22} & s_2^2 \end{bmatrix} = \frac{1}{T} \begin{bmatrix} \sum_{t=1}^{T} u_{1t}^{*2} & \sum_{t=1}^{T} u_{1t}^* u_{2t}^* \\ \sum_{t=1}^{T} u_{2t}^* u_{1t}^* & \sum_{t=1}^{T} u_{2t}^{*2} \end{bmatrix}$$

where $u_{1t}^* = y_{1t} - \alpha^* x_{1t}$, $u_{2t}^* = y_{2t} - \beta^* x_{1t} - \gamma^* x_{2t}$, and α^*, β^* and γ^* are the ordinary least squares estimates.

(ii) Estimate α, β and γ by Zellner's method as in (3.4.2) above but with the estimated covariance matrix Σ^* from step (i) in place of Σ.

We denote the estimates that result from step (ii) by $\alpha^{**}, \beta^{**}, \gamma^{**}$ and, as in (3.4.2), the Zellner estimates which *do use* Σ by $\hat{\alpha}, \hat{\beta}, \hat{\gamma}$. Then, since Σ^* converges in probability to Σ (Dhrymes, 1970, pp. 157–158),

$$\sqrt{T}\begin{bmatrix} \alpha^{**} - \alpha \\ \beta^{**} - \beta \\ \gamma^{**} - \gamma \end{bmatrix} \quad \text{and} \quad \sqrt{T}\begin{bmatrix} \hat{\alpha} - \alpha \\ \hat{\beta} - \beta \\ \hat{\gamma} - \gamma \end{bmatrix}$$

have the same limiting normal distribution (see Solution 2.16 and Dhrymes, 1970, p. 165). In particular, the covariance matrix of this limiting distribution is

$$V = \operatorname*{plim}_{T \to \infty} \left[\frac{1}{T} X'(\Sigma^{*-1} \otimes I)X \right]^{-1}$$

where

$$X = \begin{bmatrix} X_1 & 0 \\ 0 & X_2 \end{bmatrix}, \quad X_1' = [x_{11}, \ldots, x_{1T}] \quad \text{and}$$

$$X_2' = \begin{bmatrix} x_{11}, \ldots, x_{1T} \\ x_{21}, \ldots, x_{2T} \end{bmatrix}$$

Hence, writing $\Sigma^{*-1} = [(s^{ij})]$, we have

$$V = \operatorname*{plim}_{T \to \infty} \begin{bmatrix} s^{11} \dfrac{X_1'X_1}{T} & s^{12} \dfrac{X_1'X_2}{T} \\ s^{21} \dfrac{X_2'X_1}{T} & s^{22} \dfrac{X_2'X_2}{T} \end{bmatrix}^{-1}$$

which, by Slutsky's theorem (see p. 100 and Dhrymes, 1970, p. 111) is

$$\begin{bmatrix} \sigma^{11} \displaystyle\lim_{T \to \infty} \dfrac{X_1'X_1}{T} & \sigma^{12} \displaystyle\lim_{T \to \infty} \dfrac{X_1'X_2}{T} \\ \sigma^{21} \displaystyle\lim_{T \to \infty} \dfrac{X_2'X_1}{T} & \sigma^{22} \displaystyle\lim_{T \to \infty} \dfrac{X_2'X_2}{T} \end{bmatrix}$$

where $\Sigma^{-1} = [(\sigma^{ij})]$.

With the given data, (3.7.6) becomes

$$\begin{bmatrix} 2\sigma^{11} & 2\sigma^{12} & \sigma^{12} \\ 2\sigma^{21} & 2\sigma^{22} & \sigma^{22} \\ \sigma^{21} & \sigma^{22} & \sigma^{22} \end{bmatrix}^{-1}$$

The question concentrates on the asymptotic variance of $\sqrt{T}(\alpha^{**} - \alpha)$ and $\sqrt{T}(\gamma^{**} - \gamma)$. The former is given by

$$v_{11} = \frac{\begin{vmatrix} 2\sigma^{22} & \sigma^{22} \\ \sigma^{22} & \sigma^{22} \end{vmatrix}}{\Delta} = \frac{(\sigma^{22})^2}{\Delta}$$

where

$$\Delta = \begin{vmatrix} 2\sigma^{11} & 2\sigma^{12} & \sigma^{12} \\ 2\sigma^{21} & 2\sigma^{22} & \sigma^{22} \\ \sigma^{21} & \sigma^{22} & \sigma^{22} \end{vmatrix} = 2\sigma^{22}[\sigma^{22}\sigma^{11} - (\sigma^{12})^2]$$

But

$$\Sigma = \begin{bmatrix} \sigma_1^2 & \rho\sigma_1\sigma_2 \\ \rho\sigma_1\sigma_2 & \sigma_2^2 \end{bmatrix} = \begin{bmatrix} \sigma^{11} & \sigma^{12} \\ \sigma^{12} & \sigma^{22} \end{bmatrix}^{-1}$$

$$= \frac{1}{\sigma^{11}\sigma^{22} - (\sigma^{12})^2} \begin{bmatrix} \sigma^{22} & -\sigma^{12} \\ -\sigma^{12} & \sigma^{11} \end{bmatrix} \tag{3.7.7}$$

so that

$$\sigma^{22}/[\sigma^{22}\sigma^{11} - (\sigma^{12})^2] = \sigma_1^2 \tag{3.7.8}$$

and thus

$$v_{11} = \sigma_1^2/2$$

In the same way we find the asymptotic variance of $\sqrt{T}(\gamma^{**} - \gamma)$:

$$v_{33} = \begin{vmatrix} 2\sigma^{11} & 2\sigma^{12} \\ 2\sigma^{21} & 2\sigma^{22} \end{vmatrix}/\Delta$$

$$= \frac{4[\sigma^{11}\sigma^{22} - (\sigma^{12})^2]}{2\sigma^{22}[\sigma^{11}\sigma^{22} - (\sigma^{12})^2]} = \frac{2}{\sigma^{22}}.$$

Using (3.7.8) and the fact that $\sigma_1^2\sigma_2^2(1 - \rho^2) = 1/[\sigma^{11}\sigma^{22} - (\sigma^{12})^2]$, obtained by taking determinants of (3.7.7) we see that

$$v_{33} = \frac{2\sigma_1^2\sigma_2^2(1 - \rho^2)}{\sigma_1^2} = 2\sigma_2^2(1 - \rho^2)$$

Turning now to the ordinary least squares estimates α^* and γ^*, we know that the variance of the limiting distribution of $\sqrt{T}(\alpha^* - \alpha)$ is given by (see Solution 2.16)

$$\sigma_1^2 \lim_{T \to \infty} \left(\frac{X_1'X_1}{T} \right)^{-1} = \sigma_1^2/2$$

and the variance of the limiting distribution of $\sqrt{T}(\gamma^* - \gamma)$ is given by

$$\sigma_2^2 \left[\lim_{T \to \infty} \left(\frac{X_2' X_2}{T} \right)^{-1} \right]_{22} = \sigma_2^2 \left[\begin{pmatrix} 2 & 1 \\ 1 & 1 \end{pmatrix}^{-1} \right]_{22} = 2\sigma_2^2.$$

We note in particular that $2\sigma_2^2 > v_{33} = 2\sigma_2^2(1 - \rho^2)$ when $\rho \neq 0$ but that $\sigma_1^2/2 = v_{11}$. Thus, the asymptotic variance of $\sqrt{T}(\alpha^* - \alpha)$ and $\sqrt{T}(\alpha^{**} - \alpha)$ is the same, whereas the asymptotic variance of $\sqrt{T}(\gamma^* - \gamma)$ is greater than that of $\sqrt{T}(\gamma^{**} - \gamma)$ provided the errors on the equations are correlated.

The reason for this is that all prior restrictions on the given system are contained in equation 1. When we estimate this equation by least squares we take account of this restriction and do not neglect any prior information by ignoring equation 2. On the other hand, when we estimate equation 2 by least squares we fail to take account of the prior restriction on equation 1 and these estimates are therefore not as efficient asymptotically as β^{**} and γ^{**}.

Solution 3.8

The given model is a case of the multiple equation model (3.0.1). The coefficient matrix $A = [(a_{ij})]$ here has the form

$$A = \begin{bmatrix} \alpha & \beta \\ \beta & \gamma \end{bmatrix}$$

so that the model involves the cross equation restriction $\alpha_{12} = \alpha_{21} = \beta$. The best linear unbiased estimates of α, β and γ are then obtained by constrained generalised least squares (see Theil, 1971, pp. 282–289; and for the particular example of cross equation constraints in the multivariate model see Theil, 1971, pp. 312–317).

The general formula for the constrained generalised least squares estimator is a little complicated and it is worthwhile casting the model in the framework of (3.0.3) so that the constraint is incorporated and generalised least squares can be applied directly. We can do this by writing equations (3.8.1–2) in the form

$$y_t = X_t \delta + u_t \tag{3.8.3}$$

where $y_t' = (y_{1t}, y_{2t})$, $u_t' = (u_{1t}, u_{2t})$, $\delta' = (\alpha, \beta, \gamma)$ and

$$X_t = \begin{bmatrix} x_{1t} & x_{2t} & 0 \\ 0 & x_{1t} & x_{2t} \end{bmatrix}.$$

The system (3.8.3) is now an example of the general linear model discussed in Question 2.12 and by Malinvaud (1970, pp. 289–296). We note that the covariance matrix of u_t is given by

$$\Omega = \begin{bmatrix} \sigma^2 & 0 \\ 0 & \sigma^2 \end{bmatrix} = \sigma^2 I$$

and the best linear unbiased estimator of δ is (Malinvaud, 1970b, p. 293)

$$\hat{\delta} = \left(\frac{1}{T} \sum_{t=1}^{T} X_t' \Omega^{-1} X_t \right)^{-1} \left(\frac{1}{T} \sum_{t=1}^{T} X_t' \Omega^{-1} y_t \right) \tag{3.8.4}$$

which, from the form of $\Omega^{-1} = (1/\sigma^2)\, I$, reduces to

$$\left(\frac{1}{T} \sum_{t=1}^{T} X_t' X_t \right)^{-1} \left(\frac{1}{T} \sum_{t=1}^{T} X_t' y_t \right) \tag{3.8.5}$$

Now

$$\frac{1}{T} \sum_{t=1}^{T} X_t' X_t = \frac{1}{T} \sum_{t=1}^{T} \begin{bmatrix} x_{1t} & 0 \\ x_{2t} & x_{1t} \\ 0 & x_{2t} \end{bmatrix} \begin{bmatrix} x_{1t} & x_{2t} & 0 \\ 0 & x_{1t} & x_{2t} \end{bmatrix}$$

$$= \frac{1}{T} \sum_{t=1}^{T} \begin{bmatrix} x_{1t}^2 & x_{1t}x_{2t} & \\ x_{2t}x_{1t} & x_{2t}^2 + x_{1t}^2 & x_{1t}x_{2t} \\ 0 & x_{2t}x_{1t} & x_{2t}^2 \end{bmatrix}$$

and, using the given data, this matrix becomes

$$\begin{bmatrix} 10 & 5 & 0 \\ 5 & 10+20 & 5 \\ 0 & 5 & 20 \end{bmatrix} = \begin{bmatrix} 10 & 5 & 0 \\ 5 & 30 & 5 \\ 0 & 5 & 20 \end{bmatrix}.$$

Similarly, we find

$$\frac{1}{T} \sum_{t=1}^{T} X_t' y_t = \frac{1}{T} \sum_{t=1}^{T} \begin{bmatrix} x_{1t}y_{1t} \\ x_{2t}y_{1t} + x_{1t}y_{2t} \\ x_{2t}y_{2t} \end{bmatrix} = \begin{bmatrix} 20 \\ 45+25 \\ 20 \end{bmatrix} = \begin{bmatrix} 20 \\ 70 \\ 20 \end{bmatrix}.$$

Returning to (3.8.5) we now have

$$\delta = \begin{bmatrix} \hat{\alpha} \\ \hat{\beta} \\ \hat{\gamma} \end{bmatrix} = \begin{bmatrix} 10 & 5 & 0 \\ 5 & 30 & 5 \\ 0 & 5 & 20 \end{bmatrix}^{-1} \begin{bmatrix} 20 \\ 70 \\ 20 \end{bmatrix}$$

$$= \frac{1}{5250} \begin{bmatrix} 575 & -100 & 25 \\ -100 & 200 & -50 \\ 25 & -50 & 275 \end{bmatrix} \begin{bmatrix} 20 \\ 70 \\ 20 \end{bmatrix} = \begin{bmatrix} 500/525 \\ 1100/525 \\ 250/525 \end{bmatrix}.$$

Remark The estimates $\hat{\alpha}$, $\hat{\beta}$ and $\hat{\gamma}$ obtained above are different from the estimates we would obtain by the application of ordinary least squares to each equation of (7.8.1–2). Indeed, the use of ordinary least squares in this way will, in general, produce two different estimates of the parameter β, one from each of the two regressions (the reader is encouraged to verify this in the present case by using the given data); and, moreover, the ordinary least squares estimates will not be the best linear unbiased estimates. We should emphasize that this is true in the present case despite the fact that the errors on the two equations (7.8.1) and (7.8.2) *are uncorrelated* (compare the point we made earlier in Part (c) of Solution 3.1). Thus, when there are parameter restrictions across equations we need to employ some form of generalised least squares on the system of equations as a whole if we are to obtain the best linear unbiased estimates; and this is true even when the errors on the different equations are uncorrelated.

Solution 3.9

Part (a) The given system is another example of the model (3.1.1) in which the coefficient matrix A is constrained. As before we can proceed either by using constrained generalised least squares (see the references we gave in Solution 3.8) or by recasting the model so that the constraints are explicitly incorporated. Taking the latter approach we set up the system as

$$\begin{bmatrix} y_{1t} \\ y_{2t} \end{bmatrix} = \begin{bmatrix} x_{1t} & x_{2t} \\ x_{3t} & x_{3t} \end{bmatrix} \begin{bmatrix} \alpha \\ \beta \end{bmatrix} + \begin{bmatrix} u_{1t} \\ u_{2t} \end{bmatrix}$$

or $y = X_t \delta + u$ in notation similar to that of (3.8.3). The best linear unbiased estimates of α and β are then given by (Malinvaud, 1970b, p. 293):

$$\begin{bmatrix} \hat{\alpha} \\ \hat{\beta} \end{bmatrix} = \left(\frac{1}{T} \sum_{t=1}^{T} X_t' \Omega^{-1} X_t \right)^{-1} \left(\frac{1}{T} \sum_{t=1}^{T} X_t' \Omega^{-1} y_t \right) \qquad (3.9.1)$$

$$= \left(\frac{1}{T} \sum_{t=1}^{T} X_t' X_t \right)^{-1} \left(\frac{1}{T} \sum_{t=1}^{T} X_t' y_t \right)$$

$$= \left(\frac{1}{T} \sum_{t=1}^{T} \begin{bmatrix} x_{1t}^2 + x_{3t}^2 & x_{1t} x_{2t} + x_{3t}^2 \\ x_{2t} x_{1t} + x_{3t}^2 & x_{2t}^2 + x_{3t}^2 \end{bmatrix} \right)^{-1}$$

$$\times \left(\frac{1}{T} \sum_{t=1}^{T} \begin{bmatrix} x_{1t} y_{1t} + x_{3t} y_{2t} \\ x_{2t} y_{1t} + x_{3t} y_{2t} \end{bmatrix} \right).$$

The second step above follows from the form of $\Omega = \sigma^2 I_2$ which results in the cancellation of the $(1/\sigma^2)$ which occurs in each of the factors on the right hand side of (3.9.1) above. Using the given data, we now get

$$\begin{bmatrix} \hat{\alpha} \\ \hat{\beta} \end{bmatrix} = \begin{bmatrix} 2+4 & 1+4 \\ 1+4 & 7 \end{bmatrix}^{-1} \begin{bmatrix} 3+7 \\ 4+7 \end{bmatrix}$$

$$= \begin{bmatrix} 6 & 5 \\ 5 & 7 \end{bmatrix}^{-1} \begin{bmatrix} 10 \\ 11 \end{bmatrix}$$

$$= \frac{1}{17} \begin{bmatrix} 7 & -5 \\ -5 & 6 \end{bmatrix} \begin{bmatrix} 10 \\ 11 \end{bmatrix} = \begin{bmatrix} 15/17 \\ 16/17 \end{bmatrix}.$$

Since the best linear unbiased estimator of γ is $\hat{\gamma} = \hat{\alpha} + \hat{\beta}$ we have

$$\hat{\gamma} = 31/17.$$

Part (b)

$$\text{var}(\hat{\gamma}) = \text{var}(\hat{\alpha} + \hat{\beta})$$
$$= \text{var}(\hat{\alpha}) + 2\,\text{cov}(\hat{\alpha}, \hat{\beta}) + \text{var}(\hat{\beta})$$

Hence to find $\text{var}(\hat{\gamma})$ we need the covariance matrix of $(\hat{\alpha}, \hat{\beta})$, which is given by (see Malinvaud, 1970, p. 293)

$$\frac{1}{T} \left(\frac{1}{T} \sum_{t=1}^{T} X_t' \Omega^{-1} X_t \right)^{-1} = \frac{\sigma^2}{T} \left(\frac{1}{T} \sum_{t=1}^{T} X_t' X_t \right)^{-1}$$

$$= \frac{\sigma^2}{T} \begin{bmatrix} 6 & 5 \\ 5 & 7 \end{bmatrix}^{-1} = \frac{\sigma^2}{17T} \begin{bmatrix} 7 & -5 \\ -5 & 6 \end{bmatrix}.$$

Thus

$$\text{var}(\hat{\gamma}) \;=\; \frac{\sigma^2}{17T}\,(7 - 10 + 6) \;=\; \left(\frac{3}{17}\right)\frac{\sigma^2}{T}$$

Solution 3.10

The model (3.10.1) is an example of a multiple equation regression model in which the dependent variables are constrained. The constraints are

$$i'y_h \;=\; M_h \qquad (h = 1, \ldots, H) \tag{3.10.2}$$

and result from the fact that the commodity set is exhaustive in that it includes every commodity including savings) purchased by households in the given period. Models of this type have been used in many empirical applications (see especially Prais and Houthakker, 1955 and Stone, 1954); and some of the technical details of statistical inference in such models are treated in McGuire et al. (1968).

Part (a) Since $i'y_h = M_h$ and M_h is a scalar it follows that

$$i'y_h \;=\; (i'\beta)\,M_h + i'u_h \;=\; M_h \tag{3.10.3}$$

and taking expectations we obtain

$$i'\beta M_h \;=\; M_h$$

so that

$$i'\beta \;=\; 1 \tag{3.10.4}$$

Part (b) From (3.10.3) and (3.10.4) we have

$$M_h + i'u_h \;=\; M_h$$

so that $i'u_h = 0$. Hence

$$Vi \;=\; E(u_h u_h')\,i \;=\; E(u_h u_h' i) \;=\; 0$$

and i lies in the null space of V (see Halmos, 1958, p. 88 for the definition of the term null space). Since $i \neq 0$ the columns of V are linearly dependent and V is singular.

   If the rank of V is $n - 1$ then the nullity (or dimension of the null space) of V must be unity since

   rank + nullity = number of columns of $V = n$

see Halmos (1958, p. 90). But the non-zero vector i lies in the null space of V so that i is a basis of this space.

Part (c) We let $u_h^{(i)}$ be the vector obtained from u_h by deleting the ith component and set $V^{(i)} = E(u_h^{(i)} u_h^{(i)'})$. Hence, $u_h^{(i)}$ is the error vector on the sub-system of the given model obtained by deleting the ith equation.

Let $a = (a_i)$ be any $(n-1)$-component column vector for which $a'V^{(i)}a = 0$. Then

$$a'V^{(i)}a = E(a'u_h^{(i)}u_h^{(i)'}a) = E(a'u_h^{(i)})^2 = 0$$

so that $a'u_h^{(i)} = 0$. Hence

$$a'u_h^{(i)} + 0.u_{hi} = 0$$

or

$$a^{*'}u_h = 0$$

where $a^{*'} = (a_1, a_2, \ldots, a_{i-1}, 0, a_i, \ldots, a_{n-1})$. It now follows that

$$Va^* = E(u_h u_h')\,a^* = E(u_h u_h' a^*) = 0$$

so that a^* lies in the null space of V. But this sub-space is spanned by the vector i and, therefore, $a^* = \lambda i$ for some scalar λ. Since the ith component of a^* is zero, λ must also be zero and thus $a = 0$. It follows that $V^{(i)}$ is non-singular.

The constrained generalised least squares estimator of β is obtained by minimising with respect to the elements of β the quadratic form

$$Q^{(i)}(\beta) = \sum_{h=1}^{H} u_h^{(i)'} V^{(i)-1} u_h^{(i)}$$

subject to the restriction (3.10.4).

A general proof that this estimator is invariant with respect to the choice of equation deleted from the system is given in McGuire et al. (1968, pp. 1205–1206). In the present example we note that $Q^{(i)}(\beta)$ does not depend on β_i since $u_h^{(i)}$ has components $y_{hj} - M_h\beta_j$ for $j \neq i$. Hence, the constraint $i'\beta = 1$ can be neglected in estimation. Moreover, since the same regressor M_h occurs in each equation of the sub-system, generalised least squares is equivalent to the application of least squares to each equation in turn (see Solutions 3.1, Dhrymes. 1970, p. 161; Theil, 1971, pp. 309–310; or Goldberger 1964, p. 263). This leads to the estimates

$$\hat{\beta}_j = \left(\sum_{h=1}^{H} M_h^2\right)^{-1} \left(\sum_{h=1}^{H} M_h y_{hj}\right) \qquad (j \neq i)$$

and then

$$\hat{\beta}_i = 1 - \sum_{j \neq i} \hat{\beta}_j = 1 - \left(\sum_{h=1}^{H} M_h^2\right)^{-1}\left[\sum_{h=1}^{H} M_h \left(\sum_{j \neq i} y_{hj}\right)\right]$$

Using (3.10.2) this becomes

$$\hat{\beta}_i = 1 - \left(\sum_{h=1}^{H} M_h^2\right)^{-1} \sum_{h=1}^{H} M_h (M_h - y_{hi})$$

$$= \left(\sum_{h=1}^{H} M_h^2 \right)^{-1} \sum_{h=1}^{H} M_h \left(M_h y_{hi} \right)$$

$$= \left(\sum_{h=1}^{H} M_h^2 \right)^{-1} \left(\sum_{h=1}^{H} M_h y_{hi} \right) \qquad (3.10.5)$$

The above estimators will be the same whichever equation we choose to neglect initially. Furthermore, from (3.10.5) we see that $\hat{\beta}_i$ is the same as the least squares estimator of β_i obtained from the ith equation. It follows that an unconstrained least squares regression on each equation of the model leads to estimates of the coefficients which satisfy the constraint $i'\beta = 1$. This can, of course, be seen directly from the formula

$$\hat{\beta} = \left(\sum_{h=1}^{H} M_h^2 \right)^{-1} \left(\sum_{h=1}^{H} M_h y_h \right)$$

and the dependent variable constraint

$$i'y_h = M_h$$

Solution 3.11

Part (a) The given model is another example in which the dependent variables are constrained to satisfy a linear relation. Applying ordinary least squares to each equation we obtain

$$\hat{\delta}_i = (Z'Z)^{-1} Z' y_i$$

so that the calculated values of y_i are given by

$$\hat{y}_i = Z\hat{\delta}_i = Z(Z'Z)^{-1} Z' y_i$$

Using (3.11.1), we now have

$$\sum_{i=1}^{n} a_i \hat{y}_i = Z(Z'Z)^{-1} Z' \left(\sum_{i=1}^{n} a_i y_i \right) = 0$$

so that the calculated values of y_i do indeed satisfy the constraint.

Part (b) If the constraint on the dependent variables were changed to (3.11.2) then

$$\sum_{i=1}^{n} a_i \hat{y}_i = Z(Z'Z)^{-1} Z' \left(\sum_{i=1}^{n} a_i y_i \right)$$

$$= Z(Z'Z)^{-1} Z' b$$

which equals b if and only if b lies in the range space of Z. For if b lies in the range space of Z, then $b = Z\gamma$ for some $(m + 1)$ − component column vector γ; and clearly $Z(Z'Z)^{-1}Z'(Z\gamma) = Z\gamma$. This proves the sufficient condition. To prove the necessary condition we note that, if $b = Z(Z'Z)^{-1}Z'b$, then $b = Zc$ where $c = (Z'Z)^{-1}Z'b$, so that b lies in the range space of Z.

Solution 3.12

Part (a) Aggregating equation (3.12.1) over the n households we obtain

$$\sum_{i=1}^{n} y_{it} = \sum_{j=1}^{k} \sum_{i=1}^{n} \beta_{ij}x_{ijt} + \sum_{i=1}^{n} u_{it}$$

or

$$\bar{y}_t = \sum_{j=1}^{k} \bar{\beta}_{jt}\bar{x}_{jt} + \bar{u}_t \tag{3.12.3}$$

where

$$\bar{\beta}_{jt} = \sum_{i=1}^{n} \beta_{ij}x_{ijt} / \sum_{i=1}^{n} x_{ijt} = \sum_{i=1}^{n} \beta_{ij}\lambda_{ijt} \tag{3.12.4}$$

and $\lambda_{ijt} = x_{ijt}/\bar{x}_{jt}$ which is the proportion of x_{ijt} in the aggregate $\bar{x}_{jt}$. Equation (3.12.2) equals (3.12.3) and hence is a valid linear aggregation of (3.12.1) if $\bar{\beta}_{jt} = \beta_j$ for all j, t. Two conditions are sufficient to ensure this holds but neither is necessary. First, if $\beta_{ij} = \beta_j$ for all i, j, then $\bar{\beta}_{jt} = \beta_j$. In other words, if the micro-equations have the same coefficients, then the macro-equation (3.12.2) is a valid aggregation. Second, if λ_{ijt} does not depend upon time (i.e. $\lambda_{ijt} = \lambda_{ij}$ for all ijt) then again $\bar{\beta}_{jt} = \beta_j$, but now β_j is a weighted average of the n coefficients β_{ij} with weights λ_{ij} for all i, j (i.e. $\beta_j = \sum_{i=1}^{n} \beta_{ij}\lambda_{ij}$).

Part (b) Equation (3.12.1) can be written for the ith household at time t as

$$y_{it} = x'_{it}\delta_i + u_{it} \qquad (i = 1, \ldots, n; t = 1, \ldots, T) \tag{3.12.5}$$

where $x'_{it} = (x_{i1t}, \ldots, x_{ikt})$, $\delta'_i = (\beta_{i1}, \ldots, \beta_{ik})$. Combining all households at time t into one equation we have

$$y_t = X_t\delta + u_t \qquad (t = 1, \ldots, T) \tag{3.12.6}$$

where $y'_t = (y_{1t}, \ldots, y_{nt})$, $u'_t = (u_{1t}, \ldots, u_{nt})$, $\delta' = (\delta'_1, \ldots, \delta'_n)$,

$$X_t = \begin{bmatrix} x'_{1t} & 0 & . & . & 0 \\ . & . & . & . & . \\ 0 & 0 & . & . & x'_{nt} \end{bmatrix}$$

and the u_t are distributed as independent $N(0, \Sigma)$ variables with

$$\Sigma = \begin{bmatrix} \sigma_{11} & \cdot & \cdot & \sigma_{1n} \\ \cdot & \cdot & \cdot & \cdot \\ \sigma_{n1} & \cdot & \cdot & \sigma_{nn} \end{bmatrix}$$

We can now write the null hypothesis $\beta_{ij} = \beta_j$ alternatively as $\delta_i = \beta$ for all $i = 1, \ldots, n$ where $\beta' = (\beta_1, \ldots, \beta_k)$. In this case equation (3.12.6) can be rewritten as

$$y_t = Z_t \beta + u_t \qquad (t = 1, \ldots, T) \tag{3.12.7}$$

where $Z_t' = (x_{1t}, \ldots, x_{nt})$. Thus on the null hypothesis, H_0, equation (3.12.7) is correct but on the alternative hypothesis, H_1, we require (3.12.6).

For all three cases (i)–(iii) we can use a likelihood ratio test (see pp. 65–6). The log likelihood function can be written in each case and for each equation as

$$L = -\tfrac{1}{2} nT \ln (2\pi) + T \ln |\Sigma|^{-1/2} - \sum_{t=1}^{T} u_t' \Sigma^{-1} u_t / 2 \tag{3.12.8}$$

On H_0 we obtain

$$L_0 = c + T \ln |\Sigma|^{-1/2} - \sum_{t=1}^{T} (y_t - Z_t \beta)' \, \Sigma^{-1} (y_t - Z_t \beta)/2, \quad (3.12.9)$$

and on H_1

$$L_1 = c + T \ln |\Sigma|^{-1/2} - \sum_{t=1}^{T} (y_t - X_t \delta)' \, \Sigma^{-1} (y_t - X_t \delta)/2 \tag{3.12.10}$$

where $c = -\tfrac{1}{2} nT \ln (2\pi)$. The likelihood ratio test is then given by

$$l = 2(\hat{L}_1 - \hat{L}_0) \tag{3.12.11}$$

where $\hat{L}_0$ is L_0 evaluated using the maximum likelihood estimator (MLE) of β (and Σ where appropriate) and $\hat{L}_1$ is L_1 evaluated using the MLE of δ (and Σ).

The limiting distribution of l is a $\chi^2_{k(n-1)}$ distribution since δ has nk elements and β only k elements.

Case (i) In this case $\Sigma = \sigma^2 I$. The MLE's of β and δ are thus the OLS estimators

$$b = \left(\sum_{t=1}^{T} Z_t' Z_t \right)^{-1} \sum_{t=1}^{T} Z_t' y_t \tag{3.12.12}$$

and

$$d = \left(\sum_{t=1}^{T} X_t' X_t \right)^{-1} \sum_{t=1}^{T} X_t' y_t \tag{3.12.13}$$

The MLE of σ^2 on H_0 is $s_0^2 = \Sigma_{t=1}^T \hat{u}_t'\hat{u}_t/nT$, where $\hat{u}_t = y_t - Z_t b$ and the MLE of σ^2 on H_1 is $s_1^2 = \Sigma_{t=1}^T u_t^{*'}u_t^*/nT$, where $u_t^* = y_t - X_t d$. Substituting in (3.12.9) and (3.12.10) for the MLE's just obtained we find that

$$\hat{L}_0 = c - nT \ln s_0 - nT/2$$

and

$$\hat{L}_1 = c - nT \ln s_1 - nT/2,$$

hence

$$l = 2nT(\ln s_0 - \ln s_1). \tag{3.12.14}$$

Case (ii) For Σ known, the MLE's of β and δ are respectively the GLS estimators

$$\hat{\beta} = \left(\sum_{t=1}^T Z_t'\Sigma^{-1}Z_t\right)^{-1} \sum_{t=1}^T Z_t'\Sigma^{-1}y_t \tag{3.12.15}$$

and

$$\hat{\delta} = \left(\sum_{t=1}^T X_t'\Sigma^{-1}X_t\right)^{-1} \sum_{t=1}^T X_t'\Sigma^{-1}y_t. \tag{3.12.16}$$

It follows that

$$\hat{L}_0 = c + T \ln |\Sigma|^{-1/2} - \sum_{t=1}^T (y_t - Z_t\hat{\beta})'\, \Sigma^{-1}(y_t - Z_t\hat{\beta})/2 \tag{3.12.17}$$

$$\hat{L}_1 = c + T \ln |\Sigma|^{-1/2} - \sum_{t=1}^T (y_t - X_t\hat{\delta})\, \Sigma^{-1}(y_t - X_t\hat{\delta})/2 \tag{3.12.18}$$

and hence

$$l = \sum_{t=1}^T (y_t - Z_t\hat{\beta})'\, \Sigma^{-1}(y_t - Z_t\hat{\beta})$$

$$- \sum_{t=1}^T (y_t - X_t\hat{\delta})'\, \Sigma^{-1}(y_t - X_t\hat{\delta}) \tag{3.12.19}$$

Case (iii) For Σ unknown the above approach requires that we estimate each model obtaining the MLE's of β and Σ on H_0 and δ and Σ on H_1. We then substitute these estimators into (3.12.11) to obtain the test statistic

$$l = T(\ln|\hat{\Sigma}_0| - \ln|\hat{\Sigma}_1|) + \sum_{t=1}^T (y_t - Z_t\hat{\beta})\,\hat{\Sigma}_0^{-1}(y_t - Z_t\hat{\beta}) \tag{3.12.20}$$

$$- \sum_{t=1}^T (y_t - X_t\hat{\delta})\,\hat{\Sigma}_1^{-1}(y_t - X_t\hat{\delta})$$

$$= T(\ln|\hat{\Sigma}_0| - \ln|\hat{\Sigma}_1|)$$

where
$$\hat{\Sigma}_0 = T^{-1} \sum_{t=1}^{T} (y_t - Z_t\hat{\beta})(y_t - Z_t\hat{\beta})'$$
and
$$\hat{\Sigma}_1 = T^{-1} \sum_{t=1}^{T} (y_t - X_t\hat{\delta})(y_t - X_t\hat{\delta})'$$

are the MLE's of Σ on H_0 and H_1, respectively.

The estimators $\hat{\beta}$ and $\hat{\delta}$ are obtained from (3.12.15) and (3.12.16) as before except that Σ is replaced by $\hat{\Sigma}_0$ and $\hat{\Sigma}_1$, respectively. A disadvantage of this test is that the MLE's require full iteration until convergence.

CHAPTER 4

Further aspects of the linear model

0. INTRODUCTION

In this chapter additional problems connected with the linear models of chapters 2 and 3 are discussed. The notation used is the same as in these previous chapters.

1. QUESTIONS

Question 4.1

(a) For the linear model

$$y_t = x_{1t}\beta_1 + x_{2t}\beta_2 + u_t \qquad (t = 1, \ldots, T) \tag{4.1.1}$$

where the variables are measured as deviations about their means, $E(u_t) = 0$, $E(u_t^2) = \sigma^2$ and $E(u_t u_s) = 0$ for $t \neq s$, show that the multiple correlation coefficient satisfies the equation

$$R^2 = 1 - \frac{s^2}{m_{yy}} \tag{4.1.2}$$

where s^2 is an estimator of σ^2.

(b) Show that an estimator of the variance of b_i, the OLS estimator of β_i, can be written

$$\hat{\text{var}}(b_i) = \frac{T^{-1}(1 - R^2)m_{yy}}{(1 - r)^2 m_{ii}} \qquad (i = 1, 2) \tag{4.1.3}$$

where r is the correlation coefficient of x_1 and x_2, m_{yy} and m_{ii} are sample second moments of y and x_i, respectively.

(c) Show why (4.1.3) is useful in explaining the effects of multicollinearity.

Question 4.2

For the linear model

$$y = X\beta + u \tag{4.2.1}$$

where u is $N(0, \sigma^2 I_T)$:

(a) Express the variance of b, the OLS estimator of β, in terms of the eigenvalues and eigenvectors of $X'X$.

(b) Explain how this expression can be used to demonstrate the effects of multicollinearity.

(c) Show how a regression of y on the principal components of X can be used to derive a test for multicollinearity.

Question 4.3

(a) Obtain an expression for the bias of the OLS estimator of β_1 in the linear model

$$y = X_1 \beta_1 + u_1 \tag{4.3.1}$$

if the true model is

$$y = X_1 \beta_1 + X_2 \beta_2 + u \tag{4.3.2}$$

where X_1 is a $T \times k$ matrix, X_2 is a $T \times k_2$ matrix and $E(u) = 0$.

(b) What, if anything, can be said about the magnitude and direction of the bias?

(c) If the residuals from the regression of X_1 on X_2 are denoted by X^*, prove that the least squares estimator of β_1 in

$$y = X^* \beta_1 + u^* \tag{4.3.3}$$

is unbiased

(University of London B Sc. (Econ) examinations, 1971)

Question 4.4

Consider the linear model

$$y = X_1 \beta_1 + X_2 \beta_2 + u \tag{4.4.1}$$

where $E(u) = 0$ and $E(uu') = \sigma^2 I$. Suppose that an extraneous unbiased estimator b_1 exists for the $k_1 \times 1$ coefficient vector β_1, that the covariance matrix of b_1 is V_1 and that b_1 is uncorrelated with u.

(a) Derive the covariance matrix of the conditional regression estimator of β_2 obtained from a regression of $y - X_1 b_1$ on X_2.

(b) Compare the covariance matrix obtained in Part (a) with the covariance matrix of the unrestricted OLS estimator of β_2 obtained from (4.4.1)

(c) Show how a more efficient estimator of β_2 than those obtained in parts (a) and (b) can be derived.

(d) Explain why these results may be useful in combatting multicollinearity.

Question 4.5

The true model is defined by

$$y = X_1\beta_1 + u \tag{4.5.1}$$

with $E(u) = 0, E(uu') = \sigma^2 I_T$ but an investigator mistakenly assumes that it is

$$y = X_1\beta_1 + X_2\beta_2 + v \tag{4.5.2}$$

where X_1 and X_2 are $T \times 1$ and $T \times k$ respectively.

(a) Prove that the OLS estimator of β_1 from (4.5.2) is unbiased but inefficient.

(b) If $\hat{v}$ denotes the vector of residuals from (4.5.2), show that $\hat{v}'\hat{v}/(T-1-k)$ is an unbiased estimator of σ^2.

Question 4.6

(a) Show how it is possible to take account of seasonal variation in the linear model by using dummy variables and to obtain estimates of all of the seasonal dummies.

(b) The following regression was estimated using 16 quarterly observations (t ratios are in parentheses)

$$Y_t = 70.7 - 0.90t + 0.43S_{1t} + 6.55S_{2t} - 2.83S_{3t} \quad (R^2 = 0.68)$$
$$(3.7) \quad (0.27) \quad (3.37) \quad (3.40) \quad (3.37)$$

$$(4.6.1)$$

where $S_{it} = 1$ in the ith quarter and zero otherwise. Estimate the seasonal variation. Interpret your results.

Question 4.7

Show that if a set of variables is deseasonalised by the use of dummy variables, a multiple regression of the deseasonalised data will lead to the same coefficients as the use of multiple regression with the original data plus dummy variables as additional independent variables.

Question 4.8

It is thought that the relationship between y and a single explanatory variable x can be represented by two linear segments which intersect at x_A.

(a) Stating carefully any assumptions that you make, describe how you would estimate this relationship.

(b) Test the hypothesis of the relationship above against the alternative of two disjoint segments which do not necessarily intersect at x_A.

(c) Test the model of part (a) above against the alternative of a linear model which is a single segment.

Question 4.9

For the linear equation

$$y_t = x_t\beta + u_t \qquad (t = 1, \ldots, T) \tag{4.9.1}$$

where $E(u_t) = 0$, $E(u_t^2) = ax_t^2$, $E(u_t u_s) = 0$ for $t \neq s$ and $\Sigma_{t=1}^{T} x_t^2 = T$, prove that the OLS estimator of β is unbiased but inefficient and that its variance formula yields a downwards biased estimate of the true variance.

Question 4.10

Consider the linear model

$$y_t = x_t\beta + u_t \tag{4.10.1}$$

where x_t is non-stochastic with $\lim_{T \to \infty} T^{-1} \Sigma_{t=1}^{T} x_t^2 = m_{xx}$ which is finite, non-zero and $\lim_{T \to \infty} T^{-1} \Sigma_{t=1}^{T} x_t x_{t-s} = \alpha^s m_{xx}$ for all s with $|\alpha| < 1$. u_t is a disturbance with $E(u_t) = 0$ and $E(u_t u_{t-s}) = \rho^s \sigma_u^2$ for all s.

(a) Derive the asymptotic variance of b, the OLS estimator of β.

(b) Show that if $\alpha = \rho$ then the asymptotic efficiency of b is equal to $(1 - \rho^2)/(1 + \rho^2)$.

(Adapted from University of London examinations, M Sc. (Econ) 1970)

Question 4.11

For the linear model

$$y_t = x_t'\beta + u_t \qquad (t = 1, \ldots, T) \tag{4.11.1}$$

with

$$u_t = \rho u_{t-1} + e_t \qquad |\rho| < 1 \tag{4.11.2}$$

where the e_t are independent $N(0, \sigma^2)$, show how the Cochrane–Orcutt estimators of β and ρ are related to the maximum likelihood estimators of β and ρ.

Question 4.12

For the following linear model

$$y_t = x_t'\beta + u_t \qquad (t = 1, \ldots, T) \tag{4.12.1}$$

where $X' = (x_1, \ldots x_T)$ is a matrix of observations of non-random variables and $\lim_{T \to \infty} T^{-1} X'X$ is finite non-singular and

$$u_t = \rho u_{t-1} + e_t \qquad |\rho| < 1 \tag{4.12.2}$$

$$E(e_t) = 0, E(e_t^2) = \sigma^2 \text{ and } E(e_t e_s) = 0 \text{ for } t \neq s,$$

(a) Show that the probability limit of the Durbin–Watson statistic is $2(1 - \rho)$.
(b) Find the limiting distribution of the suitably standardised Durbin–Watson statistic when $\rho = 0$.

Question 4.13

Consider the linear model

$$\begin{bmatrix} y_1 \\ y_2 \\ y_3 \end{bmatrix} = \begin{bmatrix} X_1 \\ X_2 \\ X_3 \end{bmatrix} \beta + \begin{bmatrix} u_1 \\ u_2 \\ u_3 \end{bmatrix} \tag{4.13.1}$$

where y_3 represents missing observations on y, X_2 represents missing observations on the X variables, the random errors u_i are independently distributed $N(0, \sigma^2 I_{T_i})$, y_i and u_i are $T_i \times 1$ vectors and X_i are $T_i \times K$ matrices $(i = 1, 2, 3)$.

Derive and compare the properties of the following estimators of β:
(a) using OLS with only the complete observations for y and X;
(b) using OLS with X_2 replaced by a zero matrix and the observations corresponding to y_3 and X_3 dropped;
(c) using OLS on the complete model with both y_3 and X_2 replaced by zeros; and
(d) treating y_3 and X_2 as unknown parameters and using the maximum likelihood estimators of y_3, X_2 and β.

Question 4.14

For the linear model

$$y_{it} = \alpha_{it} + x_{it}'\beta + u_{it} \qquad (i = 1, \ldots, N; \quad t = 1, \ldots, T) \tag{4.14.1}$$

where β is a $k \times 1$ parameter vector, x_{it} is non-stochastic, $E(u_{it}^2) = \sigma^2$ and

$E(u_{it}u_{js}) = 0$ for $i = j, t = s$, there are observations for T time periods across N cross-sectional units. Suppose $\alpha_{it} = \theta_i + \psi_t$ and $\theta_1 = \psi_1 = 0$.
(a) Derive an estimator of the coefficients θ_i, ψ_t and β.
(b) Obtain test statistics for the hypotheses
    (i) $H_0: \alpha_{it} = 0, \beta \neq 0$ against $H_A : \alpha_{it} \neq 0, \beta \neq 0$
    (ii) $H_1: \theta_i = 0, \psi_t, \beta \neq 0$ against H_A.
    (iii) H_0 against H_1.
(c) For the model:

$$y_{it} = \theta_i + \beta_1 + \beta_2 x_{it} + u_{it} \qquad (i = 1, \ldots, 3; \quad t = 1, \ldots, 4)$$

$$(4.14.2)$$

the following observations are available:

cross-section units:

		y	x	y	x	y	x
time periods:	1	5	0	12	3	10	2
	2	7	1	15	5	11	3
	3	8	2	16	6	14	5
	4	9	2	16	7	14	4

(i) Estimate (4.14.2) and
(ii) test the hypothesis

$$H_0: \theta_2 = \theta_3 = 0, \beta_1, \beta_2 \neq 0 \quad \text{against} \quad H_A: \theta_2, \theta_3, \beta_1, \beta_2 \neq 0.$$

Question 4.15

Consider the following error (or variance) components model

$$y_{it} = x_{it}'\beta + e_{it} \qquad (i = 1, \ldots, N; \quad t = 1, \ldots, T) \qquad (4.15.1)$$

where β is a $k \times 1$ parameter vector, $k \leq NT$, x_{it}' is non-stochastic,

$$e_{it} = u_i + v_t + w_{it} \qquad (4.15.2)$$

with the u_i independent $N(0, \sigma_u^2)$, the v_t independent $N(0, \sigma_v^2)$ and the w_{it} independent $N(0, \sigma_w^2)$ variables. It is also assumed that u_i, v_t and w_{it} are mutually independent.
(a) Interpret the model, comparing it with the covariance model in Question (4.14).
(b) Explain how you would estimate the model when σ_u^2/σ_w^2 and σ_v^2/σ_w^2 are (i) known and (ii) unknown.

Question 4.16

Consider the following model

$$y_{it} = \alpha + x'_{it}\beta + u_i + v_t + w_{it} \qquad (i = 1, \ldots, N; \quad t = 1, \ldots, T)$$

$$(4.16.1)$$

where $E(w_{it}) = 0$, $E(w_{it}^2) = \sigma_w^2$, $E(w_{it}w_{js}) = 0$ for $i \neq j$ or $t \neq s$, β is a $k \times 1$ parameter vector, x_{it} is non-stochastic, $k \leq NT$ and $\Sigma_{it}x_{it} = 0$.

(a) Interpret (4.16.1) when u_i and v_t

(i) are constants,

(ii) are random variables with $E(u_i) = 0$, $E(u_i^2) = \sigma_u^2$, $E(u_iu_j) = 0$ for $i \neq j$, $E(v_t) = 0$, $E(v_t^2) = \sigma_v^2$, $E(v_tv_s) = 0$ for $(t \neq s)$ and u_i, v_t and w_{it} are independently distributed.

(b) You may assume the following:

1. $\displaystyle \lim_{N, T \to \infty} \frac{X'X}{NT}$ is finite non-singular,

2. $(\sigma_w^2 I_{NT} + \sigma_u^2 A + \sigma_v^2 B)^{-1} = \sigma_w^{-2}(I_{NT} - \gamma_1 A - \gamma_2 B + \gamma_3 J_{NT})(4.16.2)$

where $A = I_N \otimes J_T$, $B = J_N \otimes I_T$, J_P is a $P \times P$ matrix whose elements are all unity

$$\gamma_1 = \frac{\sigma_u^2}{\sigma_w^2 + T\sigma_u^2}, \quad \gamma_2 = \frac{\sigma_v^2}{\sigma_w^2 + N\sigma_v^2} \quad \text{and}$$

$$\gamma_3 = \gamma_1 \gamma_2 \left[1 + \frac{\sigma_w^2}{\sigma_w^2 + N\sigma_v^2 + T\sigma_u^2}\right]$$

3. $I_{NT} - F(F'F)^{-1}F' = I_{NT} - \dfrac{1}{T}A - \dfrac{1}{N}B + \dfrac{1}{NT}J_{NT}$ \qquad (4.16.3)

where $F = (I_N \otimes i_T \vdots i_N \otimes I_T)$ and i_P denotes a $P \times 1$ vector of ones,

4. σ_w^2, σ_u^2 and σ_v^2 are known.

Prove that

(i) the difference between the covariance matrices of the estimators of β obtained from the covariance and the error components models is positive semi-definite,

(ii) these two estimators are asymptotically equivalent if $N \to \infty$ and $T \to \infty$ in such a way that $N = aT$, where a is a positive constant.

Question 4.17

The behaviour of the ith micro-unit at time t is assumed to be explained by the model

$$y_{it} = x'_{it}\beta_i + z'_{it}\gamma + u_{it} \qquad (i = 1, \ldots, N; \quad t = 1, \ldots, T)$$

$$(4.17.1)$$

where β_i is a $k \times 1$ parameter vector and γ is an $l \times 1$ parameter vector, x_{it} and z_{it} are non-stochastic, $E(u_{it}^2) = \sigma^2$ and $E(u_{it}u_{js}) = 0$ for $i \neq j$ or $t \neq s$.

The corresponding macro-model is assumed to be

$$\bar{y}_t = \bar{x}'_t\beta + \bar{z}'_t\bar{\gamma} + v_t \qquad (4.17.2)$$

where $\bar{y}_t = \Sigma_{i=1}^{N} y_{it}$, $\bar{x}_t = \Sigma_{i=1}^{N} x_{it}$, $\bar{z}_t = \Sigma_{i=1}^{N} z_{it}$ and $\bar{\beta}$ and $\bar{\gamma}$ are coefficient vectors.

(a) Under what conditions does (4.17.2) represent the correct macro-model for (4.17.1)?

(b) Assuming that these conditions for aggregation hold, how would you estimate $\bar{\beta}$ and $\bar{\gamma}$ in (4.17.2)?

(c) Obtain an expression for the bias of these estimators when these conditions do not hold.

(d) Given data on the micro-variables y_{it}, x_{it} and z_{it} derive a test for the perfect aggregation of (4.17.1).

Question 4.18

The following regression was run across countries in order to test the hypothesis that variations in output per man (Q/L) in the iron and steel industries of different countries are explained by differences in the money wage rate (W):

$$\ln \frac{Q}{L} = 0.363 + 0.811 \ln W + \hat{u}, \qquad R^2 = 0.936 \qquad (4.18.1)$$
$$(0.051)$$

where $\hat{u}$ is the residual error and the figure in parentheses is the standard error.

(a) Test this hypothesis.

(b) It has been suggested that the equation above is mis-specified because it excludes the effects of variations in efficiency between countries which raise output per man and are positively correlated with money wages. How might this affect your conclusions?

2. SUPPLEMENTARY QUESTIONS

Question 4.19

Consider the linear model

$$y_t = x_{1t}\beta_1 + x_{2t}\beta_2 + u_t \qquad (t = 1, \ldots, 10)$$

where $E(u_t) = 0$, $E(u_t^2) = 1$, $E(u_t u_s) = 0$ for $t \neq s$ and the moment matrix of the variables is

	x_1	x_2	y
x_1	10	1	2
x_2	1	20	5
y	2	5	10

Suppose tht the following extraneous information is available

$$\begin{bmatrix} -1 \\ 1 \end{bmatrix} = \begin{bmatrix} 2 & 1 \\ 0 & 1 \end{bmatrix} \begin{bmatrix} \beta_1 \\ \beta_2 \end{bmatrix} + \begin{bmatrix} e_1 \\ e_2 \end{bmatrix}$$

where e_1 and e_2 are random variables with zero means, $E(e_1^2) = 1$, $E(e_2^2) = 2$ and $E(e_1 e_2) = 1$.

(a) Compute the unrestricted OLS estimators of β_1 and β_2 and their covariance matrix.

(b) Using the extraneous information, compute more efficient estimators of β_1 and β_2 and verify numerically that they are more efficient.

Question 4.20

In the model

$$y = X\beta + u \tag{4.20.1}$$

X is a non-random $T \times k$ matrix of rank k and u is a normally distributed vector of random disturbances with mean vector zero and covariance matrix $\sigma^2 I$.

(a) If D is a known $k \times l$ matrix of rank $l < k$ and

$$K = \{\beta; \beta = D\gamma \quad \text{for some} \quad \gamma\}$$

obtain a test statistic for the null hypothesis

$$H_0 : \beta \epsilon K$$

against the alternative

$$H_1 \beta \notin K$$

(b) X is now partitioned into $X = [X_1 \vdots X_2]$ where X_1 is $T \times q$ and X_2 is $T \times (k - q)$ and the following new variables are defined

$$g_1 = X_1 t_1 \qquad g_2 = X_2 t_2$$

where t_1 and t_2 are known vectors (g_1 and g_2 may be regarded as observations on aggregates of the variables in X_1 and X_2, respectively). Using these new variables, the following new model is constructed

$$y = g_1 \alpha_1 + g_2 \alpha_2 + u \qquad\qquad (4.20.2)$$

where α_1 and α_2 are scalar parameters.

Show how to apply the theory of Part (a) to test whether the new model (4.20.2) is appropriate.

(Adapted from University of Essex MA examinations 1976)

Question 4.21

Explain how a set of dummy variables can be used to test whether there is any difference in the constant terms of a multiple regression equation in different sub-populations. Show how the equations can be estimated by using deviations from arithmetic means, and consider how appropriate significance tests can be computed when this is done. Can similar techniques be employed when the errors are serially correlated with a known covariance matrix?

(University of London M Sc (Econ) examinations, 1976.)

Question 4.22

Consider the two-equation model

$$y_{1,t} = b_1 + b_2 x_{1,t} + b_3 x_{2,t} + u_{1,t}$$
$$y_{2,t} = b_4 + b_5 x_{3,t} + b_6 x_{4,t} + u_{2,t} \qquad (t = 1, \ldots, 20)$$

where $E(u_{i,t}) = 0$ $(i = 1, 2)$ and $E(u_{i,t} u_{j,t}) = \sigma_{ij}$. The above equations can be written in system form as

$$\begin{bmatrix} y_1 \\ y_2 \end{bmatrix} = \begin{bmatrix} X_1 & 0 \\ 0 & X_2 \end{bmatrix} \begin{bmatrix} \beta_1 \\ \beta_2 \end{bmatrix} + \begin{bmatrix} u_1 \\ u_2 \end{bmatrix}$$

where y_1 is a (20×1) vector, X_1 a (20×3) matrix, u_1 a (20×1) vector etc or, more compactly as

$$y = X\beta + u$$

where $E(uu') = \Phi$. Application of the Aitken estimator to the two equations gives

$$y_{1,t} = -27.7 + 0.038 x_{1,t} + 0.139 x_{2,t}$$
$$y_{2,t} = -1.3 + 0.058 x_{3,t} + 0.064 x_{4,t}.$$

It is desired to test the hypotheses $b_2 = b_5$ and $b_3 = b_6$

(a) Write the restrictions on the system equations in the form $R\beta = r$.

(b) If $[R(X'\Phi^{-1}X)^{-1}R']^{-1} = \begin{bmatrix} 9959.6 & 960.2 \\ 960.2 & 670.0 \end{bmatrix}$ compute the

Lagrangean multipliers for each restriction and their covariance matrix. Hence, provide a test on each of the restrictions separately and a joint test for the validity of both.

Question 4.23

(a) In the model

$$y = X\beta + u$$

y is $T \times 1$, X is a fixed $T \times k$ matrix of rank k and u is $N(0; \sigma^2 I)$. Let F denote the F-statistic used to test $H_0: \beta = 0$ against $H_1: \beta \neq 0$ and let $F(l)$ denote the statistic used to test $H_0(l): l'\beta = 0$ against $H_1(l): l'\beta \neq 0$. Prove that

$$\max_{l \in N} F(l) = kF$$

where $N = \{l : l'(Z'Z)^{-1}l = 1\}$ is a normalisation set,

(b) For the special case of the model in Part (a),

$$y_t = \beta_1 x_{1t} + \beta_2 x_{2t} + u_t \qquad (t = 1, \ldots, T)$$

the following data on sums of squares and cross-products were obtained for a sample size $T = 27$:

	y	x_1	x_2
y	1106	34	25
x_1	34	2	1
x_2	25	1	2

(i) Test the hypothesis

$$H_0: \binom{\beta_1}{\beta_2} = 0 \quad \text{against} \quad H_1: \binom{\beta_1}{\beta_2} \neq 0$$

at the 5% significance level.

(ii) Determine by a simultaneous comparisons procedure whether it is possible to say at *a significance level of at most 5%* that one or both the least squares estimates $\hat{\beta}_1$ and $\hat{\beta}_2$ of β_1 and β_2 are significantly different from zero.

(University of Essex MA examinations, 1977.)

Question 4.24

B_t denotes the number of bankruptcies occurring during period t amongst a (large) number of retailers in existence at the start of period t. The average rate of interest on hire purchase credit during period t is denoted by r_t. It is known that, conditional on r_t, B_t has a Poisson distribution with parameter $\lambda_t = \alpha + \beta r_t$.

(a) Derive the regression function of B_t on r_t.

(b) Explain why an ordinary least squares regression applied to the equation

$$B_t = \alpha + \beta r_t + u_t$$

where u_t is a random disturbance, yields inefficient estimators of α and β.

(c) Suppose T independent observations are available on B_t and r_t. Derive the likelihood function for α and β and find the equations whose solution yields the maximum likelihood estimators of α and β.

(Adapted from University of Birmingham B Soc.Sc. examinations, 1977.)

Question 4.25

The model

$$y_t = \beta_0 + \beta_1 X_t + \beta_2 D_{2t} + \beta_3 D_{3t} + \beta_4 D_{4t} + u_t$$

was estimated by ordinary least squares (OLS) from quarterly time series data, when

D_{2t} = 1 in quarter 2, 0 otherwise.

D_{3t} = 1 in quarter 3, 0 otherwise.

D_{4t} = 1 in quarter 3, 0 otherwise.

Show that $\hat\beta_1$, the OLS estimate of β_1, is equivalent to the coefficient of x_t^* in the regression $y_t^* = \alpha + \beta x_t^* + w_t$ where y_t^* is the residual in the regression of y_t on D_{2t}, D_{3t}, D_{4t} and a constant and x_t^* is the residual in the regression of x_t on D_{2t}, D_{3t}, D_{4t} and a constant. Give an interpretation and suggest a practical use for this result.

(University of London M Sc. (Econ) examinations, 1977.)

Question 4.26

It is thought that the relationship between y and a single explanatory variable x can be represented by three linear segments, intersecting in turn at $x = x_A$ and $x = x_B$. Describe the necessary computations and construct appropriate tests to carry out the following analyses.

(a) Test the restriction that the three linear segments join at $x = x_A$ and $x = x_B$ against the unrestricted alternative of three disjoint linear segments.

(b) Test the null hypothesis 'the relation between y and x is linear' against the alternative 'the relation is piecewise linear, segments intersecting at $x = x_A$ and $x = x_B$ in turn'. State carefully any assumptions that you make.

(University of London, B Sc. (Econ) examinations, 1975.)

Question 4.27

After the linear model

$$y_t = x_t'\beta + u_t$$

where $E(u_t) = 0$, $E(u_t^2) = \sigma^2$ and $E(u_t u_s) = 0$ for $t \neq s$ has been estimated from a sample of T observations, a further n observations become available $(n < k)$, and it is desired to test whether these additional observations satisfy the same linear model as the original sample.

(a) Develop an appropriate F-statistic for this purpose, stating carefully any assumptions that you make.

(b) In the case $n = 1$, develop an appropriate t-statistic for testing the hypothesis that the single new observation obeys the same linear relation as the original sample.

(c) If $n = 1$, show that the tests of parts (a) and (b) are equivalent. (You may use the relation

$$Q_{T+1} = Q_T + \frac{(y_{T+1} - x_{T+1}'\hat{\beta})^2}{1 + x_{T+1}'(X'X)^{-1}x_{T+1}}$$

where Q_T and Q_{T+1} are the residual sums of squares in regressions based on T and $T + 1$ observations respectively, y_{T+1} and x_{T+1} represent the new observation and $X' = (x_1, x_2, \ldots, x_T)$.)

(University of London B Sc. (Econ) examinations, 1975.)

Question 4.28

(a) Quarterly observations in the period 1953(3)–1965(4) are available on the following variables:

I_t = gross investment in quarter t

Y_t = gross domestic product in quarter t

C_t = gross consumption expenditure in quarter t

r_t = long term interest rate in quarter t

All variables are seasonally adjusted and in current prices. Suppose the relationship (4.28.1) were fitted using ordinary least squares (OLS) with the results shown in Table 1.

$$I_t = \beta_0 + \beta_1 Y_t + \beta_2 (C_t - C_{t-1}) + \beta_3 r_{t-2} + \beta_4 I_{t-1} + u_t \qquad (4.28.1)$$

Table 1

Coefficient	β_0	β_1	β_2	β_3	β_4
Estimate	6.166	0.060	0.502	−3.300	0.663
Standard Error		0.018	0.249	1.813	0.097

$R^2 = 0.947$, sum of squared residuals $= 106.32$
$d = 1.95$ (Durbin–Watson statistic).
No. of observations $= 47$

(from Moroney and Mason 1972).

(i) Test $H_0: \rho = 0$ against $H_1: \rho > 0$ where $u_t = \rho u_{t-1} + e_t$.
(ii) Test $H_0: \beta_3 = 0$ against $H_1: \beta_3 < 0$.
(b) Suppose there were some doubt concerning the effectiveness of the deseasonalisation techniques applied to the variables in (a). To ascertain whether any seasonal effect remained one might consider estimating the coefficients of the following equation:

$$I_t = \beta_0 + \beta_1 Y_t + \beta_2 (C_t - C_{t-1}) + \beta_3 r_{t-2} + \beta_4 I_{t-1} + \gamma_1 D_{1t}$$
$$+ \gamma_2 D_{2t} + \gamma_3 D_{3t} + u_t \qquad (4.28.2)$$

where $D_{it} = 1$ if observation number t relates to quarter i.
         $= $ otherwise.
Suppose the results of OLS estimation were as shown in Table 2.

Table 2

Coefficient	β_0	β_1	β_2	β_3	β_4	γ_1	γ_2	γ_3
Estimate	6.050	0.058	0.510	−3.100	0.652	1.170	0.820	−0.010
Standard error		0.020	0.230	1.810	0.010	0.600	0.500	0.010

$R^2 = 0.983$, sum of squared residuals $= 87.24$
$d = 1.98$
No. of observations $= 47$

(i) Test $H_0: \gamma = 0$ against $H_1: \gamma \neq 0$ where $\gamma' = (\gamma_1, \gamma_2, \gamma_3)$.
(ii) Why are only three seasonal dummies included when there are four quarters whose separate effects have to be explained?

(Adapted from University of Birmingham M Soc.Sc. examinations, 1974.)

Question 4.29

Consider the linear model

$$y_t = x_t\beta + u_t \qquad (t = 1, \ldots, T)$$

where

$$u_t = \rho u_{t-1} + e_t$$

the e_t are independent $N(0, \sigma^2)$. Also, $|\rho| < 1$, $u_0 = 0$ and $(x_1 \ldots x_T)$ are fixed in repeated samples. Carefully explain the principles of using Monte Carlo simulation methods to study the finite sample distribution of the maximum likelihood estimator $(\hat{\beta}, \hat{\rho}, \hat{\sigma}^2)$ of (β, ρ, σ^2). Include a brief description of how to investigate the following hypotheses:
(a) $E(\hat{\beta}) = \beta$
(b) $E[\hat{\rho} - E(\hat{\rho})]^2 = (1 - \rho^2)/T$
(c) the size of the test: reject H_0: $\beta = 0$ if $|\hat{\beta}|/\sqrt{\text{var}(\hat{\beta})} > 2$ is 0.05.
(d) $\hat{\beta}$ is more efficient than the ordinary least squares estimator of β.

(University of London B Sc. (Econ) examinations, 1977.)

Question 4.30

From a sample of observations on Y_t and X_t an investigator calculates the following moments in terms of deviations about means, the entries in the table (m_{ij}) being based on 102 sums of squares or cross products so that, for example, $m_{32} = \Sigma_{t=2}^{103} (Y_{t-1} - \bar{Y})(X_t - \bar{X}) = 74$ where $\bar{Y} = \frac{1}{102}\Sigma_{t=2}^{103} Y_{t-1}$ and $\bar{X} = \frac{1}{102}\Sigma_{t=2}^{103} X_t$.

	Y_t	X_t	Y_{t-1}	X_{t-1}
Y_t	150			
X_t	100	100		
Y_{t-1}	123	74	138	
X_{t-1}	82	75	92	90

(a) Estimate α in $Y_t = \alpha X_t + U_t (t = 2, \ldots T)$ and test H_0: $\alpha = 0$. Is it useful to test H_0: $\alpha = 1$?
(b) Letting $\hat{U}_t = Y_t - \alpha X_t (t = 1, \ldots, T)$ the estimate of P in $\hat{U}_t = P\hat{U}_{t-1} + V_t$ is $\hat{P} = 0.955$ and so you decide to reformulate the equation as

$$(Y_t - Y_{t-1}) = \alpha(X_t - X_{t-1}) + E_t \qquad (t = 2, \ldots, T).$$

Re-estimate α and now test H_0: $\alpha = 1$.
(c) Suggest an economic interpretation for Y_t and X_t where such null hypotheses occur.

(University of London, M Sc. (Econ) examinations, 1977.)

Question 4.31

(a) What are the essential features of a good numerical minimisation algorithm? Explain in detail why and under what conditions the Newton—Raphson algorithm is superior to the steepest descent algorithm.
(b) Describe and justify your choice of a computationally efficient algorithm to obtain statistical estimates of ρ and the k parameters in β, which are consistent and asymptotically efficient, for the linear model

$$y = X\beta + u$$

when the errors u are generated by a first order autoregressive process with serial correlation coefficient ρ. (Assume that the $T \times k$ matrix X consists of T observations on k "fixed" regressors.)

(University of London M Sc. (Econ) examinations, 1977.)

Question 4.32

It is required to test the multiple regression estimates of the equation

$$y_{ht} = \beta_0 + \sum_{i=1} \beta_i x_{iht} + \gamma_h + \delta_t + u_{ht}$$

from a sample of panel data for a set of households, $h = 1, \ldots, H$, $t = 1, \ldots, T$.
    Assuming first that γ_h and δ_t are non-stochastic, show how the equation can be estimated using covariance-transformed variables, and show how it is possible using these estimates to test the following alternative hypotheses:
    (i) that all $\gamma_h = 0$,
    (ii) that all γ_h and $\delta_t = 0$,
    (iii) that β_i depends on h, but that otherwise the above equation is
        valid.
    Show how an F-ratio test can also be derived by taking (i) as null hypothesis and taking (iii) as alternative hypothesis. Discuss the relationship between this F-ratio test and the preceding tests.
    Comment on the case where the γ_h and δ_t are assumed to be stochastic.

(University of London M Sc. (Econ) examinations, 1977)

Question 4.33

An investigator tentatively hypothesises the following relationship for the aggregate demand for money M_t at time t:

$$M_t = \beta_1 Y_t + \beta_2 I_t + u_t \qquad (4.33.1)$$

where Y_t is money national income and I_t is the rate of interest. He estimates (4.33.1) by ordinary least squares from a time-series of 50 observations for which $\bar{M}/\bar{Y} = 4$ and the correlations between M_t and t and Y_t and t are 0.995 and 0.980 respectively and obtains

$$M_t = 2Y_t - 4I_t \qquad R^2 = 0.990 \quad DW = 0.5 \qquad (4.33.2)$$
$$ (0.05)\,(30)$$

(standard errors in parentheses). Since the coefficient of I_t is "insignificant" he drops that variable, but because of the low DW (Durbin–Watson) statistic, he decides to include M_{t-1}. Re-estimation by OLS produces

$$\hat{M}_t = 1.0\,Y_t + 0.7M_{t-1} \qquad R^2 = 0.996 \quad DW = 2.1 \qquad (4.33.3)$$
$$\phantom{\hat{M}_t =} (0.04)\ (0.10)$$

which the investigator accepts as a "satisfactory" relationship. Critically appraise this entire "model building" exercise. Justify all your criticisms in the light of both econometric theory and the empirical evidence reported.

(University of London B Sc. (Econ) examinations, 1977.)

3. SOLUTIONS

Solution 4.1

Part (a) R^2 is defined as the ratio of the explained to the actual variance of y. Writing equation (4.1.1) more compactly as

$$y = X\beta + u \qquad (4.1.4)$$

where $X = (x_1, x_2), \beta' = (\beta_1, \beta_2)$, the explained variance of y is $T^{-1}b'X'Xb$ where b is the OLS estimator of β. Hence,

$$R^2 = \frac{b'X'Xb}{y'y} \qquad (4.1.5)$$

Substituting in (4.1.5) for $b = (X'X)^{-1}X'y$ and simplifying we have

$$R^2 = \frac{y'X(X'X)^{-1}X'y}{y'y} = \frac{y'y - y'[I - X(X'X)^{-1}X']y}{y'y}$$

$$= 1 - \frac{s^2}{m_{yy}}$$

where $s^2 = T^{-1}y'[I - X(X'X)^{-1}X']\,y$ is an estimator of σ^2. We note that s^2 is not an unbiased estimator of σ^2.

Part (b) We know that an estimate of the covariance matrix of b is given by

$$s^2(X'X)^{-1} = \frac{s^2}{T}\begin{pmatrix} m_{11} & m_{12} \\ m_{21} & m_{22} \end{pmatrix}^{-1}$$

$$= \frac{s^2}{T(m_{11}m_{22} - m_{12}^2)}\begin{bmatrix} m_{22} & -m_{12} \\ -m_{12} & m_{11} \end{bmatrix}$$

Therefore,

$$\text{vâr}(b_i) = \frac{s^2 m_{jj}}{T(m_{11}m_{22} - m_{12}^2)} \qquad (\text{for } i \neq j)$$

$$= \frac{s^2}{Tm_{ii}(1 - r^2)} \tag{4.1.6}$$

where

$$r^2 = m_{12}^2/(m_{11}m_{22}). \qquad \text{From (4.1.2)}$$
$$s^2 = (1 - R^2)m_{yy}. \tag{4.1.7}$$

Hence substituting (4.1.7) and (4.1.6) we obtain the required result

$$\text{vâr}(b_i) = \frac{T^{-1}(1 - R^2)m_{yy}}{(1 - r^2)m_{ii}}$$

Part (c) As the degree of collinearity between x_1 and x_2 increases r^2 increases, approaching unity for perfect collinearity. But as $r^2 \to 1$, from equation (4.1.3) we see that $\text{vâr}(b_i) \to \infty$. Thus multi-collinearity will result in large values of the variance of the OLS estimates, that is, in very imprecise estimates.

Solution 4.2

Part (a) From the definition of eigenvalues and eigenvectors we have for $i = 1, \ldots, k$

$$X'XQ_i = \lambda_i Q_i$$

or

$$X'XQ = Q\Lambda$$

where

$$Q = (Q_1 \ldots Q_k), \quad \Lambda = \begin{bmatrix} \lambda_1 & & 0 \\ & \ddots & \\ 0 & & \lambda_k \end{bmatrix}$$

and

$$Q'Q = QQ' = I_k$$

Q_i is known as the ith eigenvector and λ_i the corresponding eigenvalue. In this case $\lambda_i \geqslant 0$ for all i (Theil, 1971, pp. 26–28) It follows that

$$X'X = Q\Lambda Q'$$

and

$$(X'X)^{-1} = Q\Lambda^{-1}Q'$$

if $\lambda_i > 0$ for all i. Consequently, we can write the covariance matrix of b as

$$\sigma^2(X'X)^{-1} = \sigma^2 Q\Lambda^{-1}Q' = \sigma^2 \sum_{i=1}^{k} \lambda_i^{-1}Q_iQ_i' \qquad (4.2.2)$$

which is our required result:

Part (b) Perfect collinearity between two or more explanatory variables implies that at least one $\lambda_i = 0$. More precisely, if r explanatory variables are linearly independent and hence the remaining $k - r$ can be formed as linear combinations of these r, then the rank of X and of $X'X$ will be r and there will be $k - r$ zero eigenvalues. Near collinearity means that one or more eigenvalues will be small, nearly zero, and so their reciprocals will be very large. The contribution of these terms in equation (4.2.2) will dominate, leading to a large covariance matrix of b. This is one observable effect of the presence of multicollinearity. Another is unstable coefficient values due to rounding error problems in inverting $X'X$. When there is multicollinearity, the pivotal condensation methods of inverting a matrix will be using pivotal elements which are just rounding errors. To see this, let $k = 2$ and let $x_{2t} = \alpha x_{1t} + e_t$ be the regression of x_2 on x_1, then

$$X'X = T\begin{bmatrix} m_{11} & m_{12} \\ m_{21} & m_{22} \end{bmatrix} = T\begin{bmatrix} m_{11} & am_{11} \\ am_{11} & a^2m_{11} + m_{ee} \end{bmatrix}$$

$$= Tm_{11}\begin{bmatrix} 1 & a \\ a & a^2 + \theta \end{bmatrix}$$

where $m_{ij} = T^{-1}\sum_{t=1}^{T}x_{it}x_{jt}$ for $i, j = 1, 2$, $m_{ee} = T^{-1}\sum_{t=1}^{T}e_t^2$ and $\theta = m_{ee}/m_{11}$. After pivotal reduction of $X'X$ using the top left hand element of $X'X$ as the pivot we obtain the matrix

$$Tm_{11}\begin{bmatrix} 1 & a \\ -a & \theta \end{bmatrix}$$

If we now pivot on the element θ we obtain the inverse of $X'X$. Suppose, however, that x_1 and x_2 are nearly collinear then, apart from rounding errors, θ will be close to zero and hence either we shall not be able to perform this second pivotal reduction or, if we can, the elements of

$(X'X)^{-1}$ will be large, as they will reflect the attempt to divide by a near zero number.

Part (c) There are k principal components of X obtained from $C = XQ$; the ith principal component is $C_i = XQ_i$ and $C = (C_1 \ldots C_k)$. Recalling that $QQ' = I$ we can insert QQ' in equation (4.2.1) to obtain

$$y = XQQ'\beta + u$$

$$ = C\delta + u \tag{4.2.3}$$

where $\delta = Q'\beta$ is a length k column vector of coefficients of the k principal components. Equation (4.2.3) can also be written as

$$y = \sum_{i=1}^{k} C_i \delta_i + u \tag{4.2.4}$$

Equation (4.2.4) explains y by a linear model in which the principal components $C_i (i = 1, \ldots, k)$ are the explanatory variables.

Consider the explained sum of squares in the regression of y on c_1, $C_2, \ldots, C_k$; it is obtained from the decomposition

$$y'y = d'C'Cd + \hat{u}'\hat{u}$$

where d is the OLS estimator of δ, $u'u$ is the residual sum of squares and $d'C'Cd$ is the explained sum of squares. But

$$C'C = Q'X'XQ = \Lambda$$

hence

$$d'C'Cd = d'\Lambda d = \sum_{i=1}^{k} \lambda_i d_i^2$$

From this it can be seen that the principal components corresponding to the smallest eigenvalues have the least explanatory power; those corresponding to zero eigenvalues have no contribution to make to explaining variations in y.

This suggests that a possible test for multicollinearity is to use the hypothesis that a sub-set of the δ_i are zero against the alternative that they are non-zero. Conventional F or t tests result. We may note that if there is perfect collinearity and hence $\lambda_i = 0$ $(i = r + 1, \ldots, k)$ then the corresponding $\delta_i = Q_i'\beta = 0$. We should also note that even though we may accept the presence of multicollinearity using this test, it may still be possible to invert $X'X$ and hence obtain OLS estimates of β.

Solution 4.3

Part (a) The OLS estimator of β_1 obtained from (4.3.1) is

$$b_1 = (X_1'X_1)^{-1}X_1'y_1$$

$$= \beta_1 + (X_1'X_1)^{-1}\, X_1'(X_2\beta_2 + u)$$

As $E(u) = 0$ and X_1 and X_2 are fixed we can show that

$$E(b_1) = \beta_1 + (X_1'X_1)^{-1}\, X_1'X_2\beta_2$$

Thus the bias expression required is

$$E(b_1) - \beta_1 = (X_1'X_1)^{-1}\, X_1'X_2\beta_2 \qquad (4.3.4)$$

Part (b) In general it is difficult to say much about the magnitude and direction of the bias. Let us, therefore, consider the special case where X_1 and X_2. It is clear from (4.3.5) that the bias is greater in absolute size variables are measured as deviations about their means. The bias can now be written as

$$\text{bias} = m_{12}\beta_2/m_{11}$$

$$= r\beta_2\,(m_{22}/m_{11})^{1/2} \qquad (4.3.5)$$

where $m_{ij} = T^{-1}\sum_{t=1}^{T} x_{it}x_{jt}$ for $i, j = 1, 2$ and r is the correlation between X_1 and X_2. It is clear from (4.3.5) that the bias is greater in absolute size the greater is r, β_2 and m_{22}/m_{11}. The sign of the bias depends on the sign of $r\beta_2$. This result suggests the following generalisation: the greater the correlation between the excluded and the included variables and the greater the variance of the excluded relative to the included variables, the greater the bias.

Part (c) Let b_1^* be the OLS estimator of β_1 obtained from equation (4.3.3), then

$$b_1^* = (X^{*\prime}X^*)^{-1}\, X^{*\prime}y$$

Substituting the correct expression for y from (4.3.2) we obtain

$$b_1^* = (X^{*\prime}X^*)^{-1}\, X^{*\prime}(X_1\beta_1 + X_2\beta_2 + u)$$

By construction

$$X^* = X_1 - P_2X_1 = (I - P_2)X_1$$

where $P_2 = X_1(X_1'X_1)^{-1}X_1'$. Consequently,

$$X^{*\prime}X_1 = X_1'(I - P_2)X_1 \quad \text{and} \quad X^{*\prime}X_2 = X_1'(I - P_2)X_2 = 0$$

Therefore,

$$b_1^* = [X_1'(I - P_2)X_1]^{-1}\, [X_1'(I - P_2)X_1\beta_1 + X_1'(I - P_2)u]$$

$$= \beta_1 + [X_1'(I - P_2)X_1]^{-1}\, X_1'(I - P_2)u$$

Thus $E(b_1^*) = \beta_1$ and b_1^* is an unbiased estimator of β_1. In other words, we can obtain an unbiased estimator of the coefficients of a sub-set of variables by regressing y on the residuals from a regression of this sub-set on the other regressor variables.

Solution 4.4

Part (a) From equation (4.4.1) we can write

$$y - X_1 b_1 = X_2 \beta_2 + \tilde{u} \tag{4.4.2}$$

where $\tilde{u} = u - X_1(b_1 - \beta_1), E(\tilde{u}) = 0$ and

$$
\begin{aligned}
E(\tilde{u}\tilde{u}') &= E[u - X_1(b_1 - \beta_1)] \ [u - X_1(b_1 - \beta_1)]' \\
&= E(uu') + X_1 E(b_1 - \beta_1)(b_1 - \beta_1)' X_1' \\
&= \sigma^2 I + X_1 V_1 X_1'
\end{aligned}
$$

The vector of regression coefficients of $y - X_1 b_1$ on X_2 is

$$b_2 = (X_2'X_2)^{-1} X_2'(y - X_1 b_1) \tag{4.4.3}$$

Substituting (4.4.2) into (4.4.3) yields

$$b_2 = \beta_2 + (X_2'X_2)^{-1} X_2'\tilde{u} \tag{4.4.4}$$

Since X_2 is non-stochastic and $E(\tilde{u}) = 0, E(b_2) = \beta_2$ and the covariance matrix of b_2 is

$$
\begin{aligned}
E(b_2 - \beta_2)(b_2 - \beta_2)' &= (X_2'X_2)^{-1} X_2' E(\tilde{u}\tilde{u}') X_2 (X_2'X_2)^{-1} \\
&= \sigma^2 (X_2'X_2)^{-1} + (X_2'X_2)^{-1} X_2'X_1 V_1 X_1'X_2(X_2'X_2)^{-1} \\
&= V_2.
\end{aligned}
$$

Part (b) The OLS estimator of β_2 obtained form (4.4.1) is given in Question (2.7) as

$$\hat{\beta}_2 = (X_2'Q_1 X_2)^{-1} X_2'Q_1 y$$

where $Q_1 = I - X_1(X_1'X_1)^{-1}X_1'$. The covariance matrix of $\hat{\beta}_2$ is

$$
\begin{aligned}
\hat{V}_2 &= \sigma^2 (X_2'Q_1 X_2)^{-1} = \sigma^2 (X_2'X_2)^{-1} \\
&\quad - \sigma^2 (X_2'X_2)^{-1} X_2'X_1 (X_1'Q_2 X_1)^{-1} X_1'X_2 (X_2'X_2)^{-1}
\end{aligned}
\tag{4.4.5}
$$

where $Q_2 = I - X_2(X_2'X_2)^{-1}X_2'$. We can compare V_2 with $\hat{V}_2$ by considering

$$\hat{V}_2 - V_2 = (X_2'X_2)^{-1} X_2'X_1 [\sigma^2(X_1'Q_2 X_1)^{-1} - V_1] X_1'X_2(X_2'X_2)^{-1}$$

The difference $\hat{V}_2 - V_2$ is positive semi-definite and hence b_2 is at least as efficient as β_2 if $\sigma^2 (X_1'Q_2 X_1)^{-1} - V_1$ is positive semi-definite. In other words, the more precise the extraneous estimator, the smaller is V_1 and hence the more efficient is b_2 relative to β_2. There is, of course, no guarantee that $\hat{V}_2 - V_2$ is positive semi-definite. If, due to an imprecise estimator $b_2, \sigma^2 (X_1'Q_2 X_1)^{-1} - V_1$ is negative semi-definite, then β_2 is more efficient than b_2.

Part (c) An alternative method of combining the extraneous information with the sample information (4.4.1) is as follows. Let

$$b_1 = \beta_1 + e_1 \tag{4.4.6}$$

then from the given information on b_1, e_1 is an error term with $E(e_1) = 0$, $E(e_1 e_1') = V_1$ and $E(e_1' u) = 0$. Equations (4.4.1) and (4.4.6) can be combined to form the single equation

$$\begin{bmatrix} y \\ b_1 \end{bmatrix} = \begin{bmatrix} X_1 & | & X_2 \\ \hline I & | & 0 \end{bmatrix} \begin{bmatrix} \beta_1 \\ \beta_2 \end{bmatrix} + \begin{bmatrix} u \\ e_1 \end{bmatrix}$$

which can be written more compactly as

$$y^* = X^* \beta + u^* \tag{4.4.7}$$

where

$$y^{*\prime} = (y', b_1'), \quad X^* = \begin{bmatrix} X_1 & | & X_2 \\ \hline I & | & 0 \end{bmatrix}, \quad \beta' = (\beta_1', \beta_2'), \quad u^{*\prime} = (u', e_1').$$

$$E(u^*) = 0$$

and

$$E(u^* u^{*\prime}) = \begin{bmatrix} \sigma^2 I & | & 0 \\ \hline 0 & | & V_1 \end{bmatrix} = \Omega$$

An efficient estimator β^* of β is obtained by applying generalised least squares to (4.4.7). From Question 2.12 we have, therefore,

$$\beta^* = (X^{*\prime} \Omega^{-1} X^*)^{-1} X^{*\prime} \Omega^{-1} y^* \tag{4.4.8}$$

$$= \left\{ \begin{bmatrix} X_1' & | & I \\ \hline X_2' & | & 0 \end{bmatrix} \begin{bmatrix} \sigma^{-2} I & | & 0 \\ \hline 0 & | & V_1^{-1} \end{bmatrix} \begin{bmatrix} X_1 & | & X_2 \\ \hline I & | & 0 \end{bmatrix} \right\}^{-1}$$

$$\begin{bmatrix} X_1' & | & I \\ \hline X_2' & | & 0 \end{bmatrix} \begin{bmatrix} \sigma^{-2} I & | & 0 \\ \hline 0 & | & V_1^{-1} \end{bmatrix} \begin{bmatrix} y \\ b_1 \end{bmatrix}$$

$$= \begin{bmatrix} \sigma^{-2} X_1' X_1 + V_1^{-1} & | & \sigma^{-2} X_1' X_2 \\ \hline \sigma^{-2} X_2' X_1 & | & \sigma^{-2} X_2' X_2 \end{bmatrix}^{-1} \begin{bmatrix} \sigma^{-2} X_1' y + V_1^{-1} b_1 \\ \sigma^{-2} X_2' y \end{bmatrix} \tag{4.4.9}$$

Substituting (4.4.7) into (4.4.8)

$$\beta^* = \beta + (X^{*\prime} \Omega^{-1} X^*)^{-1} X^* \Omega^{-1} u^*$$

hence $E(\beta^*) = \beta$ and the covariance matrix of β^* is

$$(X^{*\prime}\Omega^{-1}X^*)^{-1} = \left[\begin{array}{c|c} \sigma^{-2}X_1'X_1 + V_1^{-1} & \sigma^{-2}X_1'X_2 \\ \hline \sigma^{-2}X_2'X_1 & \sigma^{-2}X_2'X_2 \end{array} \right] \qquad (4.4.10)$$

Using the result in question (2.1) on the inverse of a partitioned matrix, the covariance matrix of β_2^*, the estimate of β_2, can be shown to be the bottom right-hand element of (4.4.10) which is

$$V_2^* = \sigma^2(X_2'X_2)^{-1} + (X_2'X_2)^{-1}X_2'X_1HX_1'X_2(X_2'X_2)^{-1},$$

where

$$\begin{aligned} H &= \sigma^2[(X_1'X_1 + \sigma^2 V_1^{-1}) - X_1'X_2(X_2'X_2)^{-1}X_2'X_1]^{-1} \\ &= \sigma^2[X_1'Q_2X_1 + \sigma^2 V_1^{-1}]^{-1} \end{aligned}$$

Comparing V_2^* with V_2 we obtain

$$V_2 - V_2^* = (X_2'X_2)^{-1}X_2'X_1(V_1 - H)X_1'X_2(X_2'X_2)^{-1}$$

which is positive semi-definite if $V_1 - H$ is positive semi-definite.

Using the result that $B^{-1} - A^{-1}$ is positive semi-definite if $A - B$ is positive semi-definite and B is positive definite (Goldberger, 1964, p. 38) we can deduce that, since V_1^{-1} is positive definite, $V_1 - H$ is positive semi-definite if $H^{-1} - V_1^{-1}$ is positive semi-definite. But

$$H^{-1} - V_1^{-1} = (\sigma^{-2}X_1'Q_2X_1 + V_1^{-1}) - V_1^{-1} = \sigma^{-2}X_1'Q_2X_1$$

which is positive semi-definite. Hence $V_1 - H$ and $V_2 - V_2^*$ are both positive semi-definite, implying that β_2^* is at least as efficient as the conditional regression estimator b_2.

Comparing V_2^* with $\hat{V}_2$ we consider

$$\hat{V}_2 - V_2^* = (X_2'X_2)^{-1}X_2'X_1[\sigma^2(X_1'Q_2X_1)^{-1} - H]X_1'X_2(X_2'X_2)^{-1}$$

which is positive semi-definite if $\sigma^2(X_1'Q_2X_1)^{-1} - H$ is positive semi-definite, or using the above result, if $H^{-1} - \sigma^{-2}X_1'Q_2X_1$ is positive semi-definite. But

$$H^{-1} - \sigma^{-2}X_1'Q_2X_1 = (\sigma^{-2}X_1'Q_2X_1 + V_1^{-1}) - \sigma^{-2}X_1'Q_2X_1 = V_1^{-1}$$

which is positive semi-definite. Hence $\hat{V}_2 - V_2^*$ is positive semi-definite, implying that β_2^* is also at least as efficient as the unrestricted OLS estimator $\hat{\beta}_2$.

The estimator β_2^* is due to Durbin (1953). See also Goldberger (1964, pp 258–261).

Part (d) Suppose that the X_1 variables are collinear, then the moment matrix $X_1'X_1$ is singular. As a result, the unrestricted OLS estimators of β_1 and β_2 cannot be obtained. However, given an extraneous estimator of β_1, we can use the conditional regression estimator equation (4.4.3) or the more efficient estimator equation (4.4.9) due to Durbin. Durbin's method can easily be extended to cover the case where X is collinear and extraneous information is available on β_1 and/or β_2.

Another *ad hoc* way of overcoming multicollinearity is to use ridge regression (see Hoerl and Kennard, 1970). This consists of adding terms to the leading diagonal of the moment matrix of the explanatory variables, i.e. to the $X'X$ matrix, to achieve a non-singular matrix. Suppose, however, that we set b_1, the extraneous estimator of β_1, equal to zero and restrict V_1 to be a diagonal matrix, then (4.4.9) can be written

$$\beta^* = \begin{bmatrix} X_1'X_1 + \sigma^2 V_1^{-1} & | & X_1'X_2 \\ \hline X_2'X_1 & | & X_2'X_2 \end{bmatrix}^{-1} \begin{bmatrix} X_1'y \\ X_2'y \end{bmatrix} \tag{4.4.11}$$

But (4.4.11) has the same form as the ridge regression estimator. We may therefore, interpret ridge regression as a special case of the estimator β^*. From an econometric point of view, the artificial nature of this 'extraneous' information does not commend the ridge regression technique.

Solution 4.5

Part (a) Re-write equation (4.5.2) more compactly as

$$y = X\beta + v \tag{4.5.3}$$

where $X = (X_1 \vdots X_2)$ and $\beta' = (\beta_1', \beta_2')$. The OLS estimator b of β is clearly unbiased since X is fixed and, because $\beta_2 = 0$, $v = u$ and hence $E(v) = 0$. Thus

$$E \begin{bmatrix} b_1 \\ b_2 \end{bmatrix} = \begin{bmatrix} \beta_1 \\ 0 \end{bmatrix}$$

where $b' = (b_1', b_2')$ and hence $E(b_1) = \beta_1$ as required.

The efficiency of this estimator of β_1 is measured by comparing $\text{var}(b_1)$ with $\text{var}(\hat{\beta}_1)$, where $\hat{\beta}_1$ is the OLS estimator of β_1 obtained from (4.5.1); $\hat{\beta}_1$ is also unbiased. Now the covariance matrix of b is

$$\sigma^2 (X'X)^{-1} = \sigma^2 \begin{bmatrix} X_1'X_1 & X_1'X_2 \\ X_2'X_1 & X_2'X_2 \end{bmatrix}^{-1}$$

$$= \sigma^2 \left[\begin{array}{c|c} (X_1'X_1)^{-1} + (X_1'X_1)^{-1}X_1'X_2(X_2'Q_1X_2)^{-1}X_2'X_1(X_1'X_1)^{-1} & \\ \hline -(X_2'Q_1X_2)^{-1}X_2'X_1(X_1'X_1)^{-1} & \end{array} \right.$$

$$\left. \begin{array}{c} -(X_1'X_1)^{-1}X_1'X_2(X_2'Q_1X_2)^{-1} \\ \hline (X_2'Q_1X_2)^{-1} \end{array} \right] \tag{4.5.4}$$

where $Q_1 = I - X_1(X_1'X_1)^{-1}X_1'$. (See Question 2.1 for further details of this result). Thus V_1, the variance of b_1, is the top left-hand element of the partitioned matrix on the right hand side of (4.5.4). Now the variance of $\hat{\beta}_1$ is $\hat{V}_1 = \sigma^2(X_1'X_1)^{-1}$, hence

$$V_1 = \hat{V}_1 + (X_1'X_1)^{-1}X_1'X_2(X_2'Q_1X_2)^{-1}X_2'X_1(X_1'X_1)^{-1} \tag{4.5.5}$$

The last term of (4.5.5) is positive semi-definite since $(X_2'Q_1X_2)^{-1}$ is positive semi-definite. Consequently, $\hat{\beta}_1$ is at least as efficient an estimator of β_1 as b_1.

Part (b) By definition

$$\hat{v} = y - Xb$$
$$= [I - X(X'X)^{-1}X']y$$

We may substitute for y from (4.5.1) since it is the correct expression for y and, noting that $X_1 = X(X'X)^{-1}X'X_1$, we obtain

$$\hat{v} = [I - X(X'X)^{-1}X']u$$

and hence

$$\hat{v}'\hat{v} = u'[I - X(X'X)^{-1}X']u.$$

Now

$$E(\hat{v}'\hat{v}) = E\{u'[I - X(X'X)^{-1}X']u\}.$$

But $\hat{v}'\hat{v}$ is a scalar and so

$$E(\hat{v}'\hat{v}) = E(\text{tr}\{u'[I - X(X'X)^{-1}X']\,u\})$$
$$= E(\text{tr}\{[I - X(X'X)^{-1}X']\,uu'\})$$

$$= \sigma^2\,\text{tr}\,[I - X(X'X)^{-1}X']$$
$$= \sigma^2\,\{\text{tr}\,I - \text{tr}\,[X(X'X)^{-1}X']\}$$
$$= \sigma^2\,\{T - \text{tr}\,[(X'X)^{-1}X'X]\}$$
$$= \sigma^2(T - 1 - k).$$

Thus $\hat{v}'\hat{v}/(T - 1 - k)$ is unbiased for σ^2.

These results suggest that we should consider eliminating variables with zero coefficients and re-estimating our model to get more efficient estimates of the non-zero coefficients. *Prima facie* it would seem sensible to eliminate variables whose coefficients are not significantly different from zero. When eliminating these variables it is important to exercise care in the choice of the significance level of the test, for the smaller the significance level, the greater the probability of eliminating a variable whose true coefficient is non-zero. We must be especially careful because multi-collinearity, for example, can lead us to remove variables whose true coefficients are non-zero; and we would then have biased estimates of the remaining coefficients.

Solution 4.6

Part (a) Consider the quarterly model

$$y_t = \alpha + x_t\beta + \sum_{i=1}^{4} S_{it}\delta_i + u_t \qquad (t = 1, \ldots, T) \qquad (4.6.2)$$

where $S_{it} = 1$ in the ith quarter and 0 otherwise. Since the seasonal variation should contribute nothing to the constant term over time

$$\sum_{i=1}^{4} \delta_i = 0 \qquad (4.6.3)$$

In matrix form equation (4.6.1) becomes

$$
\begin{bmatrix} y_1 \\ y_2 \\ y_3 \\ y_4 \\ y_5 \\ \vdots \\ y_T \end{bmatrix}
=
\begin{bmatrix}
1 & x_1 & 1 & 0 & 0 & 0 \\
1 & x_2 & 0 & 1 & 0 & 0 \\
1 & x_3 & 0 & 0 & 1 & 0 \\
1 & x_4 & 0 & 0 & 0 & 1 \\
1 & x_5 & 1 & 0 & 0 & 0 \\
\vdots & \vdots & \vdots & & & \\
1 & x_T & 0 & 0 & 0 & 1
\end{bmatrix}
\begin{bmatrix} \alpha \\ \beta \\ \delta_1 \\ \delta_2 \\ \delta_3 \\ \delta_4 \end{bmatrix}
=
\begin{bmatrix} u_1 \\ u_2 \\ . \\ . \\ . \\ \\ u_T \end{bmatrix}
\qquad (4.6.4)
$$

or

$$y = X\theta + u \qquad (4.6.5)$$

Equation (4.6.5) cannot be estimated as it stands since X is not of full column rank: the first and the last four columns of X are linearly dependent. We must, therefore, impose the constraint given by equation (4.6.3). This can be done in several ways, either (i) by dropping one of the linearly dependent columns, or (ii) by substituting for one of the δ_i using (4.6.3), or (iii) by using restricted least squares with the constraint (see Question 2.5):

$$0 = (0 \quad 0 \quad 1 \quad 1 \quad 1 \quad 1)\theta$$

The disadvantage of (iii) is that it involves a more complicated method of estimation than OLS; (i) and (ii) enable OLS to be used but only (ii) preserves the original coefficients.

Using (ii), therefore, we substitute in (4.6.2) $\delta_4 = -(\delta_1 + \delta_2 + \delta_3)$ to get

$$y_t = \alpha + x_t \beta + \sum_{i=1}^{3} (S_{it} - S_{4t}) \delta_i + u_t.$$

Thus (4.6.4) becomes

$$
\begin{bmatrix} y_1 \\ y_2 \\ y_3 \\ y_4 \\ y_5 \\ \vdots \\ y_T \end{bmatrix}
=
\begin{bmatrix}
1 & x_1 & 1 & 0 & 0 \\
1 & x_2 & 0 & 1 & 0 \\
1 & x_3 & 0 & 0 & 1 \\
1 & x_4 & -1 & -1 & -1 \\
1 & x_5 & 1 & 0 & 0 \\
\vdots & \vdots & \vdots & \vdots & \vdots \\
1 & x_T & -1 & -1 & -1
\end{bmatrix}
\begin{bmatrix} \alpha \\ \beta \\ \delta_1 \\ \delta_1 \\ \delta_2 \\ \delta_3 \end{bmatrix}
+
\begin{bmatrix} u_1 \\ u_2 \\ u_3 \\ u_4 \\ u_5 \\ \vdots \\ u_T \end{bmatrix}
\qquad (4.6.6)
$$

which we can estimate by OLS. δ_4 is estimated by

$$d_4 = -(d_1 + d_2 + d_3)$$

where d_i is the OLS estimator of $\delta_i (i = 1, 2, 3)$.

Whilst method (i) does not preserve the original coefficients they can, nonetheless, be readily derived when this method is used. To show this, let us drop δ_4, say, then (4.6.2) becomes

$$y_t = \alpha^* + x_t \beta + \sum_{i=1}^{3} S_{it} \delta_i^* + u_t \qquad (4.6.7)$$

Equating terms with (4.6.2) we obtain

$$\alpha^* + \delta_i^* = \alpha + \delta_i \qquad (i = 1, 2, 3) \qquad (4.6.8)$$

and

$$\alpha^* = \alpha + \delta_4 \qquad (4.6.9)$$

We can derive α and δ_i from (4.6.8) and (4.6.9) as follows: from (4.6.8),

$$3\alpha^* + \sum_{1}^{3} \delta_i^* = 3\alpha + \sum_{1}^{3} \delta_i$$

and, using (4.6.3) and (4.6.9), this becomes

$$3(\alpha + \delta_4) + \sum_1^3 \delta_i^* = 3\alpha - \delta_4$$

or, simplifying,

$$\delta_4 = -\tfrac{1}{4} \sum_1^3 \delta_i^*. \tag{4.6.10}$$

Hence,

$$\alpha = \alpha^* - \tfrac{1}{4} \sum_1^3 \delta_i^* \tag{4.6.11}$$

and

$$\delta_i = \delta_i^* - \tfrac{1}{4} \sum_1^3 \delta_i^* \qquad (i = 1, 2, 3) \tag{4.6.12}$$

Given estimates of α^* and δ_i^*, equations (4.6.10)–(4.6.12) enable us to obtain estimates of α and δ_i.

Part (b) Method (i) above has been used in equation (4.6.1). The coefficients of S_{it} in (4.6.1) are estimates of $\delta_i^* (i = 1, 2, 3)$. We may obtain estimates d_i of the seasonal coefficients δ_1 from (4.6.10) and (4.6.12). Thus $d_1 = -0.61, d_2 = 5.51, d_3 = -3.87, d_4 = 1.04$, and the estimate of α is seen to be 69.3. (*Note:* $\Sigma_1^4 d_i = -0.01$ which differs from zero due to rounding errors; keeping more significant figures would have made Σd_i closer to zero.)

As the coefficient of the variable t in (4.6.1) is not significant even at a 20% level of significance, these results indicate that there is no trend to Y_t. There is only seasonal variation around the mean of Y_t which is 69.3. In quarter 1, Y_t takes the expected value 68.7; in quarter 2, 74.8; in quarter 3, 65.4; in quarter 4, 68.3.

Solution 4.7

Consider the linear model

$$y_t = \sum_{i=1}^k x_{ti}\beta_i + \sum_{j=1}^4 S_{jt}\delta_j + u_t \qquad (t = 1, \ldots, T) \tag{4.7.1}$$

where $s_{jt} = 1$ in the jth quarter and zero otherwise. Recall that $\Sigma_1^4 \delta_j = 0$ (See Question 4.6). Equation (4.7.1) may be written in matrix notation as

$$y = X\beta + S\delta + u \tag{4.7.2}$$

where

$$X = (x_{ti}), S = (s_{tj}), \beta' = (\beta_1 \beta_2, \ldots, \beta_k), \delta' = (\delta_1, \ldots, \delta_4).$$

Let Q be a matrix which deseasonalises (4.7.2). In other words, Q is chosen so that $QS = 0$. A suitable matrix Q is

$$Q = I_T - S(S'S)^{-1}S'$$

If there are exactly m years of data $(T = 4m)$ then $S'S = mI_4$ and hence

$$Q = I_T - \frac{1}{m}\begin{bmatrix} 1 & 0 & 0 & 0 & 1 & \cdots & 0 \\ 0 & 1 & 0 & 0 & 0 & \cdots & 0 \\ \cdot & \cdot & \cdot & \cdot & \cdot & \cdots & \cdot \\ \cdot & \cdot & \cdot & \cdot & \cdot & \cdots & \cdot \\ 0 & 0 & 0 & 1 & 0 & \cdots & 1 \end{bmatrix} \qquad (4.7.3)$$

Now

$$\begin{aligned} Qy &= QX\beta + QS\delta + Qu \\ &= QX\beta + Qu \end{aligned}$$

or,

$$y_s = X_s\beta + u_s \qquad (4.7.4)$$

where $y_s = Qy$, $X_s = QX$ and $u_s = Qu$ are deseasonalised variables. Thus (4.7.4) is the deseasonalised model corresponding to (4.7.2). The problem is reduced to showing that the OLS estimator of β obtained from (4.7.4) is identical to that obtained from (4.7.2). From (4.7.3)

$$y_s = Qy = \begin{bmatrix} y_1 - \bar{y}_1 \\ y_2 - \bar{y}_2 \\ \cdot \\ \cdot \\ y_T - \bar{y}_4 \end{bmatrix}$$

where $\bar{y}_i$ is the mean of the y_t in the ith quarter. The variables X_s are similarly defined. Thus all of the deseasonalised variables have simply had the appropriate quarterly means subtracted in each period from the original variable.

The OLS estimator of β obtained from the deseasonalised model (4.7.3) is

$$b_s = (X_s'X_s)^{-1}X_s'y_s$$

or, substituting for y_s and X_s,

$$b_s = (X'QX)^{-1}X'Qy. \qquad (4.7.5)$$

Using equation (4.7.2), the OLS estimator of β is obtained from

$$\begin{bmatrix} b \\ d \end{bmatrix} = \begin{bmatrix} X'X & X'S \\ S'X & S'S \end{bmatrix}^{-1} \begin{bmatrix} X'y \\ S'y \end{bmatrix} \tag{4.7.6}$$

From earlier results (Question 2.9), solving (4.7.6) for b gives

$$b = (X'QX)^{-1}X'Qy \tag{4.7.7}$$

which is identical to equation (4.7.5) and completes our proof.

Solution 4.8

Part (a) The relationship between y and x is assumed to satisfy

$$y_t = \alpha_1 + x_t\beta_1 + u_t \qquad (x_t \leqslant x_A) \tag{4.8.1}$$

$$y_t = \alpha_2 + x_t\beta_2 + u_t \qquad (x_A \leqslant x_t; \quad t = 1, \ldots, T) \tag{4.8.2}$$

with $E(u_t) = 0$, $E(u_t u_s) = \sigma^2 (t = s)$, $= 0(t \neq s)$. We also assume that $x_1 \leqslant x_2 \leqslant \ldots \leqslant x_A \leqslant \ldots \leqslant x_T$ and that we observe x_A.
We can rewrite (4.8.2) as

$$y_t = (\alpha_1 + \gamma) + x_t(\beta_1 + \delta) + u_t. \tag{4.8.3}$$

At the point of intersection, (4.8.1) and (4.8.3) are equal hence

$$\alpha_1 + x_A\beta_1 = \alpha_1 + \gamma + x_A(\beta_1 + \delta)$$

or

$$\gamma + x_A\delta = 0 \tag{4.8.4}$$

Equations (4.8.1) and (4.8.3) may be written compactly using dummy variables as

$$y_t = \alpha_1 + x_t\beta_1 + D_t\gamma + (D_t x_t)\delta + u_t \tag{4.8.5}$$

where $D_t = 0(t \leqslant A)$ and $D_t = 1(t > A)$. We can estimate (4.8.5) using restricted least squares, with (4.8.4) forming the linear restriction, (see Question 2.5). Alternatively, we can eliminate γ from (4.8.5) using (4.8.4) to obtain

$$y_t = \alpha + x_t\beta_1 + (D_t x_t - D_t x_A)\delta + u_t \tag{4.8.6}$$

Equation (4.8.6) can be estimated by OLS. The matrix of regressors has the form

$$X = \begin{bmatrix} 1 & x_1 & 0 \\ 1 & x_2 & 0 \\ \cdot & \cdot & \cdot \\ \cdot & \cdot & \cdot \\ 1 & x_A & 0 \\ 1 & x_{A+1} & x_{A+1} - x_A \\ \cdot & \cdot & \cdot \\ \cdot & \cdot & \cdot \\ 1 & x_T & x_T - x_A \end{bmatrix}$$

Part (b) If the relationship has two unrestricted disjoint segments with the break still at x_A, then equation (4.8.5) holds without the restriction (4.8.4) necessarily being satisfied. We wish to test for the validity of this restriction. One way of performing the test would be to estimate equation (4.8.5) and use the estimates of γ and δ obtained to estimate the restriction $\gamma + x_A \delta$. We would then test the restriction by testing whether or not this estimate was significantly different from zero. For further details see Question (2.5).

Alternatively, we can use a likelihood ratio test (Question 2.3) which is based on estimates of equations (4.8.5) and (4.8.6). If $L(H_0)$ is the maximum value of the likelihood function on the null hypothesis H_0 [equation (4.8.6)], $L(H_1)$ is the corresponding value on the alternative hypothesis H_1 [equation (4.8.5)] and the ratio of these likelihoods is $\lambda = L(H_0)/L(H_1)$ with $0 \leqslant \lambda \leqslant 1$ then we use the result that $-2 \ln \lambda$ has a limiting χ^2 distribution with, in this case, one degree of freedom due to the single restriction (4.8.4). (Theil, 1971, p. 396).

If the u_t are independent $N(0, \sigma^2)$ then

$$L(H_i) = (2\pi\hat{\sigma}_i^2)^{-T} \exp(-\hat{u}_i'\hat{u}_i/2\hat{\sigma}_i^2)$$
$$= (2\pi\hat{\sigma}_i^2)^{-T} \exp(-\tfrac{1}{2}T)$$

as $\hat{\sigma}_i^2 = \hat{u}_i'\hat{u}_i/T$, where ̂ denotes a maximum likelihood estimator and $i = 0, 1$. Thus

$$-2\ln\lambda = 2T\ln(\hat{\sigma}_0^2/\hat{\sigma}_1^2) \qquad (4.8.7)$$

which involves the ratio of the error variance of (4.8.6) to that of (4.8.5). We reject H_0 if $-2 \ln \lambda \geqslant \chi_1^2(\alpha)$, where α is our significance level.

Since it was not specified in the question as to whether the break point in the unrestricted case occurs at x_A we may wish to generalise the alternative to the case of an undetermined break point. Again we can employ a likelihood ratio test, but this time we must enlarge the parameter space over which we maximise the likelihood function associated with equation (4.8.5) by adding a separate parameter x_A. We can do this by choosing a value for x_A, forming equation (4.8.5), and then obtaining the error variance of the resulting equation. We repeat this for all possible values of x_A ($x_A = x_1, x_2, \ldots, x_T$). We choose that value of x_A and the corresponding equation which has the minimum error variance, for this will be the value which maximises the likelihood function. We compute our test statistic using (4.8.7) once more. This time, as we have dropped two restrictions on H_0, we have two degrees of freedom.

Part (c) If a continuous linear model is the correct relationship between y and x, then γ and δ in equation (4.8.5) will be zero. We can test this by a conventional F-test applied to (4.8.5).

Solution 4.9

Equation (4.9.1) can be written in matrix notation as

$$y = X\beta + u \qquad (4.9.2)$$

where X is a $T \times 1$ vector, $E(u) = 0$ and $E(uu') = \Sigma = \sigma^2 \, \text{diag} \{x_1^2, \ldots, x_T^2\}$.

The OLS estimator of β is

$$b_{\text{OLS}} = (X'X)^{-1}X'y = \beta + (X'X)^{-1}X'u$$

hence $E(b_{\text{OLS}}) = \beta$ and the covariance matrix of b_{OLS} is

$$
\begin{aligned}
V_{\text{OLS}} &= E(b_{\text{OLS}} - \beta)(b_{\text{OLS}} - \beta)' \\
&= (X'X)^{-1}X'E(uu')X(X'X)^{-1} \\
&= (X'X)^{-1}X'\Sigma X(X'X)^{-1}
\end{aligned}
$$

In the present case $X'X = T$ and $X' \Sigma X = \sigma^2 \Sigma_1^T x_t^4$. Thus

$$V_{\text{OLS}} = \sigma^2 \Sigma x_t^4 / T^2 \qquad (4.9.3)$$

The generalised least squares estimator of β is (see Theil, 1971, p. 238 and Question 2.12)

$$b_{\text{GLS}} = (X'\Sigma^{-1}X)^{-1}X'\Sigma^{-1}y$$

with covariance matrix

$$V_{\text{GLS}} = (X'\Sigma^{-1}X)^{-1}$$

In this case,

$$V_{\text{GLS}} = \sigma^2 / T \qquad (4.9.4)$$

We can now examine the efficiency of b_{OLS} compared to b_{GLS} using the ratio

$$\frac{V_{GLS}}{V_{OLS}} = \frac{\sigma^2/T}{\sigma^2 \Sigma x_t^4/T^2} = \frac{T}{\Sigma x_t^4} \tag{4.9.5}$$

Using the Cauchy inequality,

$$\Sigma a_i^2 \Sigma b_i^2 \geqslant (\Sigma a_i b_i)^2$$

and letting $a_i = x_i^2$ and $b_i = 1$ we obtain

$$\Sigma x_t^4 . \Sigma 1 \geqslant (\Sigma x_t^2)^2$$

or

$$\Sigma x_t^4 . T \geqslant T^2$$

or

$$\Sigma x_t^4 \geqslant T$$

Thus the ratio (4.9.5) is $\leqslant 1$ and so GLS is at least as efficient as OLS.

Suppose we assume incorrectly that $\Sigma = \sigma^2 I$. Then we would wrongly use the formula

$$V^* = \sigma^2 (X'X)^{-1}$$

to compute the variance of b_{OLS}. In this case

$$V^* = \sigma^2/T. \tag{4.9.6}$$

This happens to equal V_{GLS} obtained above but, of course, we must remember that (4.9.6) is an incorrect expression. Hence we see that comparing V_{OLS} with V^* gives us the same result as comparing V_{OLS} with V_{GLS}, i.e.,

$$V^*/V_{OLS} = V_{GLS}/V_{OLS} \leqslant 1$$

Thus V^* is a downwards biased estimator of the true variance of b_{OLS}.

Solution 4.10

Part (a) Writing (4.10.1) in matrix notation we have

$$y = X\beta + u \tag{4.10.2}$$

with X a $T \times 1$, $E(u) = 0$ and $E(uu') = \Sigma$ where (see Theil, 1971, p. 252)

$$= \sigma_u^2 \begin{bmatrix} 1 & \rho & . & . & \rho^{T-1} \\ \rho & 1 & . & . & \rho^{T-2} \\ . & & . & . & . \\ \rho^{T-1} & . & . & . & 1 \end{bmatrix}$$

From question (4.9), the variance of b the OLS estimator of β is given by

$$\text{var}(b) = (X'X)^{-1}X'\Sigma X(X'X)^{-1} \tag{4.10.3}$$

The question asks for the asymptotic variance of b, that is, for the variance of the limiting distribution of $\sqrt{T}(b-\beta)$. From the answer to question (2.16) we find that this is given by

$$\lim_{T \to \infty} T \text{var}(b) = \lim_{T \to \infty} \frac{X'X^{-1}}{T} \cdot \lim_{T \to \infty} \frac{X'\Sigma X}{T} \cdot \lim_{T \to \infty} \frac{X'X^{-1}}{T} \tag{4.10.4}$$

Now

$$X' \Sigma X = \sigma_u^2(x_1, \ldots, x_T) \begin{bmatrix} 1 & \rho & . . & \rho^{T-1} \\ \rho & 1 & . . & \rho^{T-2} \\ . . & & . . & . \\ \rho^{T-1} & . & . , & 1 \end{bmatrix} \begin{bmatrix} x_1 \\ . \\ . \\ . \\ x_T \end{bmatrix}$$

$$= \sigma_u^2 \left(\sum_{t=1}^{T} x_t^2 + 2\rho \sum_{t=2}^{T} x_t x_{t-1} + 2\rho^2 \sum_{t=3}^{T} x_t x_{t-2} + \ldots + 2\rho^{T-1} x_1 x_T \right)$$

Using the given assumptions

$$\lim_{T \to \infty} T^{-1}X'\Sigma X = \sigma_u^2 m_{xx}(1 + 2\rho\alpha + 2\rho^2\alpha^2 + \ldots)$$

$$= \sigma_u^2 m_{xx}(1 + \rho\alpha)/(1 - \rho\alpha) \tag{4.10.5}$$

From (4.10.4) and (4.10.5) it follows that

$$\lim_{T \to \infty} T \text{var}(b) = \frac{\sigma_u^2(1 + \rho\alpha)}{m_{xx}(1 - \rho\alpha)} \tag{4.10.6}$$

which is our required result.

Part (b) If $\alpha = \rho$ then (4.10.6) becomes $[\sigma_u^2(1 + \rho^2)]/[m_{xx}(1 - \rho^2)]$. The efficient estimator of β is the GLS estimator b^*. The variance of b^* is given by

$$\text{var}(b^*) = (X'\Sigma^{-1}X)^{-1}$$

and the variance of the limiting distribution of $\sqrt{T}(b_{GLS} - \beta)$ is $\lim_{T \to \infty}$ $T(X'\Sigma^{-1}X)^{-1}$. Using the result, (Theil, 1971, p. 252) that

$$\Sigma^{-1} = \frac{1}{\sigma_u^2(1-\rho^2)} \begin{bmatrix} 1 & -\rho & 0 & . & . & 0 \\ -\rho & 1+\rho^2 & -\rho & . & . & 0 \\ . & . & . & . & . & . \\ 0 & . & . & . & . & 1 \end{bmatrix}$$

we can show that

$$X'\Sigma^{-1}X = \sigma_u^{-2}(1-\rho^2)^{-1}\left[(1+\rho^2)\sum_1^T x_t^2 - 2\rho \sum_2^T x_t x_{t-1} \right.$$

$$\left. + \rho^2(x_1^2 + x_T^2)\right].$$

Hence

$$\lim_{T \to \infty} T^{-1}X'\Sigma^{-1}X = \sigma_u^{-2}(1-\rho^2)^{-1}m_{xx}(1+\rho^2 - 2\rho\alpha)$$

and so

$$\lim_{T \to \infty} T \operatorname{var}(b^*) = \frac{\sigma_u^2(1-\rho^2)}{m_{xx}(1+\rho^2 - 2\rho\alpha)} \tag{4.10.7}$$

If $\rho = \alpha$ then (4.10.7) becomes σ_u^2/m_{xx}. Hence a measure of the asymptotic efficiency of b and b^* is obtained by the ratio of the variances of their limiting distributions and is given by

$$\lim_{T \to \infty} \frac{\operatorname{var}(b^*)}{\operatorname{var}(b)} = \frac{\sigma_u^2/m_{xx}}{\sigma_u^2(1+\rho^2)/m_{xx}(1-\rho^2)} = \frac{1-\rho^2}{1+\rho^2}$$

which we were required to prove.

Solution 4.11

The Cochrane–Orcutt estimator of β and ρ is obtained as follows. First we combine (4.11.1) and (4.11.2) to obtain

$$(y_t - \rho y_{t-1}) + (x_t' - \rho x_{t-1}')\beta = e_t \qquad (t = 2, \dots, T) \tag{4.11.3}$$

This can also be written as

$$(y_t - x_t'\beta) - \rho(y_{t-1} - x_{t-1}'\beta) = e_t \tag{4.11.4}$$

We now choose β and ρ to minimise $\sum_2^T e_t^2$ using the following iterative scheme:

stage 1: set $\rho = 0$ in (4.11.3) and minimise $\Sigma\, e_t^2$ with respect to β
alone. This is equivalent to using OLS on (4.11.1). Denote the resulting
estimator by $b(1)$.
stage 2: set $\beta = b(1)$ in (4.11.4) and minimise $\Sigma\, e_t^2$ with respect to ρ
alone. This is equivalent to replacing u_t in (4.11.2) by $y_t - X_t b(1)$ and
using OLS on the resulting equation. Denote the estimator of that we
obtain by $r(1)$.
stage 3: set $\rho = r(1)$ in (4.11.3) and minimise $\Sigma\, e_t^2$ with respect to β,
obtaining $b(2)$. This is equivalent to replacing y_t and x_t in (4.11.1) by
autoregressive tranformed variables and using OLS on the resulting
equation.
stages 4, 5, 6 . . . : these repeat steps 2 and 3. Iteration is continued
until the change in $\Sigma\, e_t^2$ is sufficiently small or until the largest
percentage change in any estimate is sufficiently small. If x_t is
exogenous, in particular, if x_t contains no lagged dependent variables,
then stages $4, 5, 6, \ldots$ are not necessary to obtain full asymptotic
efficiency. Iteration can stop at stage 3.

In order to derive the maximum likelihood estimators of β, ρ and σ^2,
we must first construct the appropriate likelihood function. If we assume
that $u_0 = 0$, then the log-likelihood function is

$$L(\beta, \rho, \sigma^2; y, x) = -\frac{T}{2} \ln 2\pi - \frac{T}{2} \ln \sigma^2 - \frac{1}{2\sigma^2} \sum_{t=1}^{T} e_t^2$$

$$= -\frac{T}{2} \ln 2\pi - \frac{T}{2} \ln \sigma^2 - \tfrac{1}{2}\left[\sum_{t=2}^{T} (y_t - \rho y_{t-1}\right.$$

$$\left. -x_t'\beta + x_{t-1}'\beta\rho)^2 + (y_1 - x_1'\beta)^2 \right] \qquad (4.11.5)$$

since the Jacobian of the transformation from $(e_1, \ldots, e_T)$ to
$(y_1, \ldots, y_T)$ is

$$\left| \frac{\partial(e_1, \ldots, e_T)}{\partial(y_1, \ldots, y_T)} \right| = \begin{vmatrix} 1 & 0 & 0 & .. & 0 \\ -\rho & 1 & 0 & .. & 0 \\ . & -\rho & 1 & .. & 0 \\ . & . & . & .. & . \\ 0 & . & . & .. & 1 \end{vmatrix} = 1$$

Remark Without the assumption that $u_0 = 0$, the log-likelihood function
is

$$L(\beta, \rho, \sigma^2; y, x) = -\frac{T}{2} \ln 2\pi + \tfrac{1}{2} \ln |\Sigma^{-1}|$$

$$-\tfrac{1}{2} (y_1 - x_1'\beta, \ldots, y_T - x_T')$$

$$\Sigma^{-1}(y_1 - x_1'\beta, \ldots, y_T - x_T'\beta)'$$

where Σ^{-1} is defined in Solution (4.10). But

$$
\Sigma^{-1} = \sigma^{-2}
\begin{bmatrix}
1 & -\rho & 0 & .. & 0 \\
-\rho & 1+\rho^2 & -\rho & .. & 0 \\
0 & -\rho & 1+\rho^2 & .. & 0 \\
. & . & . & .. & . \\
0 & . & . & .. & 1
\end{bmatrix}
= \sigma^{-2} RR'
$$

where

$$
R =
\begin{bmatrix}
\sqrt{1-\rho^2} & 0 & 0 & .. & 0 \\
-\rho & 1 & 0 & .. & 0 \\
0 & -\rho & 1 & .. & 0 \\
. & . & . & .. & . \\
0 & . & . & .. & 1
\end{bmatrix}
$$
(see for instance Dhrymes 1971, pp. 66–8)

It follows that $|\Sigma^{-1}| = \sigma^{-2T}$, $|R|^2 = \sigma^{-2T}(1-\rho^2)$ and hence the log-likelihood function can be written

$$
L(\beta, \rho, \sigma^2; y, x) = -\frac{T}{2} \ln 2\pi - \frac{T}{2} \ln \sigma^2 + \tfrac{1}{2} \ln (1-\rho^2)
$$

$$
-\frac{1}{2\sigma^2} \left[\sum_{t=2}^{T} (y_1 - \rho y_{t-1} - x_t'\beta + x_{t-1}'\beta\rho)^2 \right.
$$
$$
\left. + (1-\rho^2)(y_1 - x_1'\beta)^2 \right].
$$

Using this likelihood function to obtain the maximum likelihood estimators of β, ρ and σ^2 would result in slightly different first order conditions from those derived below and hence would produce slightly different numerical estimates. However, as the asymptotic properties of the two sets of estimators are identical, we shall work with the assumption that $u_0 = 0$.

$$
\frac{\partial L}{\partial \beta} = \frac{1}{\hat{\sigma}^2} \sum_{t=2}^{T} (x_t - \hat{\rho} x_{t-1})\hat{e}_t + \frac{1}{\sigma^2} x_1(y_1 - x_1'\hat{\beta}) = 0 \qquad (4.11.6)
$$

$$
\frac{\partial L}{\partial \rho} = \frac{1}{\hat{\sigma}^2} \sum_{t=2}^{T} (y_{t-1} - x_{t-1}'\hat{\beta})\hat{e}_t = 0 \qquad (4.11.7)
$$

$$
\frac{\partial L}{\partial \sigma^2} = -\frac{T}{2\hat{\sigma}^2} + \frac{1}{2\hat{\sigma}^4} \sum_{t=1}^{T} \hat{e}_t^2 = 0 \qquad (4.11.8)
$$

where $\hat{e}_t = y_t - \hat{\rho} y_{t-1} - x_t'\hat{\beta} + x_{t-1}'\hat{\beta}\hat{\rho}$ and $\hat{\ }$ denotes a MLE. Equations (4.11.6)–(4.11.8) are $k+2$ non-linear equations which can be solved for the unknowns $\hat{\beta}$, $\hat{\rho}$ and $\hat{\sigma}^2$.

Solving equations (4.11.6) and (4.11.7) for $\hat{\beta}$ and $\hat{\rho}$ we obtain

$$\hat{\beta} = \left[\sum_{t=2}^{T} (x_t - \hat{\rho}x_{t-1})(x_t - \hat{\rho}x_{t-1})' \right]^{-1}$$
$$\left[\sum_{t=2}^{T} (x_t - \hat{\rho}x_{t-1})(y_t - \hat{\rho}y_{t-1}) + x_1(y_1 - x_1'\hat{\beta}) \right] \quad (4.11.9)$$

and

$$\hat{\rho} = \left[\sum_{t=2}^{T} (y_{t-1} - x_{t-1}'\hat{\beta})^2 \right]^{-1} \sum_{t=2}^{T} (y_{t-1} - x_{t-1}'\hat{\beta})(y_t - x_t'\hat{\beta}) \quad (4.11.10)$$

Now the second term within braces in (4.11.9) is $0(T^{-1})$ in probability and the first is $0(T^{-1/2})$ in probability. Consequently, the asymptotic distribution of $\hat{\beta}$ does not depend upon this second term of (4.11.9) but only on the first term. (See Question (2.16) for further details of the use of orders in probability.)

Dropping the last term in (4.11.9) we can interpret $\hat{\beta}$ as the regression coefficients of $y_t - \hat{\rho}y_{t-1}$ on $x_t - \hat{\rho}x_{t-1}$. Similarly, from (4.11.10), $\hat{\rho}$ is the regression coefficient of $y_t - x_t'\beta$ on $y_{t-1} - x_{t-1}'\beta$. But these are the same estimators as derived from the C–0 estimator. In order to maximise the likelihood function, equations (4.11.9) and (4.11.10) must be fully iterated. Thus, apart from the omitted term, a fully iterated C–0 estimator is identical to the MLE. The limiting distributions of the C–0 and the MLE estimators are identical, hence the C–0 estimator is asymptotically efficient under the usual conditions (Solution 3.7).

To see why the non-iterated C–0 estimator, which stops after stage 3, is asymptotically efficient, we note first that $b(1)$ and $r(1)$ are consistent estimators of β and ρ, respectively. Further, $\sqrt{T}[b(1) - \beta]$ and $\sqrt{T}[r(1) - \rho]$ possess limiting distributions and hence are $0(1)$ in probability.

Consider now the estimator

$$b(2) = \left[\sum_{t=2}^{T} [x_t - r(1)x_{t-1}][x_t - r(1)x_{t-1}]' \right]^{-1}$$
$$\sum_{t=2}^{T} [x_t - r(1)x_{t-1}][y_t - r(1)y_{t-1}].$$

Using

$$y_t - r(1)y_{t-1} = [x_t - r(1)x_{t-1}]'\beta + u_t - r(1)u_{t-1}$$

we can show that

$$\sqrt{T}[b(2) - \beta] = T^{-1/2}V_1^{-1}\sum_{t=2}^{T}[x_t - r(1)x_{t-1}][u_t - r(1)u_{t-1}]$$

where

$$V_1 = T^{-1}\sum_{t=2}^{T}[x_t - r(1)x_{t-1}][x_t - r(1)x_{t-1}]'.$$

But since plim $r(1) = \rho$, the limiting distribution of $\sqrt{T}[b(2) - \beta]$ is the same as that of

$$T^{-1/2} \bar{V}_1^{-1} \sum_{t=2}^{T} [x_t - r(1) x_{t-1}] [u_t - r(1) u_{t-1}]$$

where $\bar{V}_1 = \text{plim } V_1$. Now

$$T^{-1/2} \sum_{t=2}^{T} [x_t - r(1) x_{t-1}] [u_t - r(1) u_{t-1}]$$

$$= T^{-1/2} \sum_{t=2}^{T} \{x_t - \rho x_{t-1} - [r(1) - \rho] x_{t-1}\}.$$

$$\{u_t - \rho u_{t-1} - [r(1) - \rho] u_{t-1}\}$$

$$= T^{-1/2} \sum_{t=2}^{T} (x_t - \rho x_{t-1})(u_t - \rho u_{t-1}) + D \qquad (4.11.11)$$

where D is a term of $0(T^{-1/2})$ in probability and the first term on the right hand side of (4.11.11) is $0(1)$ in probability. Thus asymptotically, D can be ignored. A similar argument can be made if we use $\hat{\beta}$ and $\hat{\rho}$ instead of $b(1)$ and $r(1)$. Again we would obtain $\bar{V}_1$ and (4.11.11) but now with a new D term which is also $0(T^{-1/2})$ in probability. We have shown, therefore, that $\sqrt{T}(\hat{\beta} - \beta)$ and $\sqrt{T}[b(2) - \beta]$ have the same limiting distribution. We can also show that $\sqrt{T}(\hat{\rho} - \rho)$ and $\sqrt{T}[r(2) - \rho]$ have the same limiting distribution where $r(2)$ is obtained from (4.11.10) using $b(1)$ and $r(1)$. Thus it is not necessary to fully iterate the C–O estimator to obtain full asymptotic efficiency in this case. Full iteration is required when x_t contains lagged values of y_t.

Solution 4.12

Part (a) The Durbin–Watson statistic is defined as

$$d = \sum_{t=2}^{T} (\hat{u}_t - \hat{u}_{t-1})^2 / \sum_{t=1}^{T} \hat{u}_t^2 \qquad (4.12.3)$$

where

$$\hat{u}_t = y_t - x_t' b \qquad (4.12.4)$$

is the tth OLS residual and b is the OLS estimator of β. Multiplying out (4.12.3) we obtain

$$d = \left(\sum_{t=2}^{T} \hat{u}_t^2 + \sum_{t=2}^{T} \hat{u}_{t-1}^2 - 2 \sum_{t=2}^{T} \hat{u}_t \hat{u}_{t-1} \right) \Big/ \sum_{t=1}^{T} \hat{u}_t^2. \qquad (4.12.5)$$

Introducing matrix notation for (4.12.4) and (4.12.5) we can write

$$\hat{u} = y - Xb \qquad (4.12.6)$$

and

$$d = 2\left(1 - \frac{\hat{u}'\hat{u}_{-1}}{\hat{u}'_{-1}\hat{u}_{-1}}\right) + R \qquad (4.12.7)$$

where $\hat{u}_{-1}$ is $\hat{u}$ lagged once and R is $O(T^{-1})$ in probability. (See Question (2.16) for a discussion of order in probability).

Writing (4.12.1) and (4.12.2) in matrix notation we obtain

$$y = X\beta + u \qquad (4.12.8)$$

and

$$u = \rho u_{-1} + e \qquad (4.12.9)$$

Substituting (4.12.8) and (4.12.9) into (4.12.6) we find that

$$\hat{u} = u - X(b - \beta) \qquad (4.12.10)$$

$$= \rho u_{-1} + e - X(b - \beta) \qquad (4.12.11)$$

$$= \rho \hat{u}_{-1} + e - (X - \rho X_{-1})(b - \beta) \qquad (4.12.12)$$

Pre-multiplying (4.12.12) by $\hat{u}'_{-1}$ we obtain

$$\hat{u}'_{-1}\hat{u} = \rho \hat{u}'_{-1}\hat{u}_{-1} + \hat{u}'_{-1}e - \hat{u}'_{-1}(X - \rho X_{-1})(b - \beta)$$

or

$$\frac{\hat{u}'_{-1}\hat{u}}{\hat{u}'_{-1}\hat{u}_{-1}} = \rho + \frac{\hat{u}'_{-1}e}{\hat{u}'_{-1}\hat{u}_{-1}} - \frac{\hat{u}'_{-1}(X - \rho X_{-1})(b - \beta)}{\hat{u}'_{-1}\hat{u}_{-1}}. \qquad (4.12.13)$$

Thus, from (4.12.7) and (4.12.13),

$$d = 2(1 - \rho) - 2\frac{\hat{u}'_{-1}e}{\hat{u}'_{-1}\hat{u}_{-1}} + 2\frac{\hat{u}'_{-1}(X - \rho X_{-1})(b - \beta)}{\hat{u}'_{-1}\hat{u}_{-1}} + R \quad (4.12.14)$$

Taking probability limits of (4.12.4), plim $R = 0$ and

$$\text{plim } d = 2(1 - \rho) - \frac{2 \text{ plim } T^{-1}\hat{u}'_{-1}e}{\text{plim } T^{-1}\hat{u}'_{-1}\hat{u}_{-1}}$$

$$+ \frac{2 \text{ plim } T^{-1}\hat{u}'_{-1}(X - \rho X_{-1}) \text{ plim } (b - \beta)}{\text{plim } T^{-1}\hat{u}'_{-1}\hat{u}_{-1}}. \qquad (4.12.15)$$

Now plim $T^{-1}\hat{u}'_{-1}\hat{u}_{-1} = \text{plim } T^{-1}\hat{u}'\hat{u} = \lim_{T \to \infty} T^{-1}E(\hat{u}'\hat{u})$. But from earlier results, $E(\hat{u}'\hat{u}) = (T - K)\sigma_u^2$. Hence, plim $T^{-1}\hat{u}'_{-1}\hat{u}_{-1} = \sigma_u^2$. Further, from (4.12.11),

$$e'\hat{u}_{-1} = e'[\rho u_{-2} + e_{-1} - X_{-1}(b - \beta)]$$

$$= \rho e' u_2 + e'e_{-1} - e'X_{-1}(b - \beta). \qquad (4.12.16)$$

Successive substitution into (4.12.9) reveals that

$$u = e + \rho e_{-1} + \rho^2 e_{-2} + \ldots$$

but since $E(e'e_{-r}) = 0$ for $r > 0$, we have $E(e'u_{-2}) = 0$ and $E(e'e_{-1}) = 0$. Thus

$$\text{plim } \frac{1}{T} e'\hat{u}_{-1} = \text{plim } \frac{e'X_{-1}}{T} \cdot \text{plim } (b - \beta) \qquad (4.12.17)$$

Finally, we note that X is fixed and b is consistent for β, hence (4.12.17) and the last term of (4.12.15) are zero, implying that plim $d = 2(1 - \rho)$, as required.

Part (b) When $\rho = 0$, plim $d = 2$, Hence we require the limiting distribution of $\sqrt{T}(d - 2)$. For $\rho = 0$, (4.12.14) simplifies to

$$d = 2 - 2 \frac{\hat{u}'_{-1}e}{\hat{u}'_{-1}\hat{u}_{-1}} + 2 \frac{\hat{u}'_{-1}X(b - \beta)}{\hat{u}'_{-1}\hat{u}_{-1}} + R \qquad (4.12.18)$$

or, using (4.12.10) and (4.12.16),

$$d = 2 - 2 \frac{e'_{-1}e}{\hat{u}'_{-1}\hat{u}_{-1}} - 2 \left\{ \frac{e'X_{-1}(b - \beta)}{\hat{u}'_{-1}\hat{u}_{-1}} + \frac{[u_{-1} - X(b - \beta)]'X(b - \beta)}{\hat{u}'_{-1}\hat{u}_{-1}} \right\}$$

$$+ R \qquad (4.12.19)$$

By Cramér's theorem, (See also Question 2.16) and using (4.12.19), we deduce that $\sqrt{T}(d - 2)$ converges to the same limiting distribution as $-2\sigma^{-2} T^{-1/2} e'_{-1}e$. For, even when multiplied by $\sqrt{T}$, the term in curly brackets has a probability limit of zero and hence can be ignored.

The limiting distribution of $T^{-1/2} e'_{-1}e$ is $N(0, \sigma^4)$ since

$$E(T^{-1/2} e'_{-1}e) = T^{-1/2} \sum_{t=1}^{T} E(e_t e_{t-1}) = 0$$

and

$$\text{var}(T^{-1/2} e'_{-1}e) = T^{-1}E\left[\left(\sum_t e_t e_{t-1} \right) \left(\sum_s e_s e_{s-1} \right) \right]$$

$$= T^{-1}E\left[\sum_t E(e_t^2) E(e_{t-1}^2) \right] = \sigma^4$$

Thus the limiting distribution of $\sqrt{T}(d - 2)$ is $N(0, 4)$.

Solution 4.13

Part (a) In this case the model becomes in effect

$$y_1 = X_1\beta + u_1 \qquad (4.13.2)$$

Provided $T_1 \geqslant K$ we can estimate (4.13.2) by OLS. The resulting estimator b_1 is clearly unbiased for β and has the covariance matrix

$$V_1 = \sigma^2(X_1'X_1)^{-1} \tag{4.13.3}$$

Part (b) The model now becomes

$$\begin{bmatrix} y_1 \\ y_2 \end{bmatrix} = \begin{bmatrix} X_1 \\ X_2 \end{bmatrix} \beta + \begin{bmatrix} u_1 \\ u_2 \end{bmatrix} \tag{4.13.4}$$

with $X_2 = 0$, b_2 the OLS estimator of β is, therefore,

$$
\begin{aligned}
b_2 &= (X_1'X_1 + X_2'X_2)^{-1}(X_1'y_1 + X_2'y_2) \\
&= (X_1'X_1)^{-1}X_1'y_1
\end{aligned} \tag{4.13.5}
$$

which is the same as b_1 and has the same covariance matrix.

Part (c) In this case the model reverts to (4.13.1) with $y_3 = 0$ and $X_2 = 0$. b_3 the OLS estimator of β is

$$
\begin{aligned}
b_3 &= (X_1'X_1 + X_2'X_2 + X_3'X_3)^{-1}(X_1'y_1 + X_2'y_2 + X_3'y_3) \\
&= (X_1'X_1 + X_3'X_3)^{-1}X_1'y_1.
\end{aligned} \tag{4.13.6}
$$

To find the properties of b_3 we substitute in (4.13.6) for y_1 obtaining,

$$b_3 = (X_1'X_1 + X_3'X_3)^{-1}(X_1'X_1\beta + X_1'u_1) \tag{4.13.7}$$

hence,

$$
\begin{aligned}
E(b_3) &= (X_1'X_1 + X_3'X_3)^{-1}X_1'X_1\beta \\
&= \beta - (X_1'X_1 + X_3'X_3)^{-1}X_3'X_3\beta.
\end{aligned} \tag{4.13.8}
$$

Thus b_3 is a biased estimator of β. The covariance matrix of b_3 is

$$V_3 = \sigma^2(X_1'X_1 + X_3'X_3)^{-1}X_1'X_1(X_1'X_1 + X_3'X_3)^{-1} \tag{4.13.9}$$

Part (d) The log likelihood function of (4.13.1) satisfies

$$
L \propto = \text{const.} - \frac{T}{2}\ln\sigma^2 - \frac{1}{2\sigma^2}u'u
$$

$$
\begin{aligned}
= \text{const.} - \frac{T}{2}\ln\sigma^2 - \frac{1}{2\sigma^2}[(y_1 - X_1\beta)'(y_1 - X_1\beta) \\
+ (y_2 - X_2\beta)'(y_2 - X_2\beta) + (y_3 - X_3\beta)'(y_3 - X_3\beta)]
\end{aligned}
$$

Treating σ^2 as known and differentiating with respect to the unknown β, y_3 and X_2 we obtain

$$
\begin{aligned}
\frac{\partial L}{\partial \beta} = -\frac{1}{\sigma^2}[(X_1'X_1\hat{\beta} + \hat{X}_2'\hat{X}_2\hat{\beta} + X_3'X_3\hat{\beta}) \\
- (X_1'y_1 + \hat{X}_2'y_2 + X_3'\hat{y}_3)] = 0
\end{aligned} \tag{4.13.10}
$$

$$\frac{\partial L}{\partial y_3} = -\frac{1}{\sigma^2}(\hat{y}_3 - X_3\hat{\beta}) = 0 \tag{4.13.11}$$

and

$$\frac{\partial L}{\partial X_2} = -\frac{1}{\sigma^2}(\hat{X}_2\hat{\beta}\hat{\beta}' - y_2\hat{\beta}') = 0 \tag{4.13.12}$$

To obtain (4.13.12) we have used the result (Theil, 1971, p. 32)

$$\frac{\partial}{\partial A}(y'Az) = yz' \tag{4.13.13}$$

and also

$$\frac{\partial(y'X'Xz)}{\partial X} = \frac{\partial[(Xy)'Xz]}{\partial X} + \frac{\partial[(Xz)'Xy]'}{\partial X} = 2Xyz' \tag{4.13.14}$$

where y and z are column vectors and A and X are matrices. Pre-multiplying (4.13.11) by X_3' gives

$$X_3'\hat{y}_3 = X_3'X_3\hat{\beta} \tag{4.13.15}$$

and hence the terms with subscript 3 drop out of (4.13.10). Since (4.13.12) implies that

$$y_2 = \hat{X}_2\hat{\beta}, \tag{4.13.16}$$

pre-multiplying (4.13.16) by $\hat{X}_2'$ reveals that terms with subscript 2 also disappear from (4.13.10). The maximum likelihood estimator of β is thus

$$\hat{\beta} = (X_1'X_1)^{-1}X_1'y_1 \tag{4.13.17}$$

which is the same as b_1, the OLS estimator of β obtained from using observations on y_1 and X_1 alone.

If σ^2 is unknown we must estimate it. Differentiating the likelihood function with respect to σ^2 we obtain

$$\frac{\partial L}{\partial \sigma^2} = -\tfrac{1}{2}T^{-1}\hat{\sigma}^{-2} + \tfrac{1}{2}\hat{\sigma}^{-4}[(y_1 - X_1\hat{\beta})'(y_1 - X_1\hat{\beta})$$

$$+ (y_2 - \hat{X}_2\hat{\beta})'(y_2 - \hat{X}_2\hat{\beta}) + (\hat{y}_3 - X_3\hat{\beta})'(\hat{y}_3 - \hat{X}_3\beta)]$$

$$= 0$$

But $y_2 = \hat{X}_2\hat{\beta}$ and $\hat{y}_3 = X_3\hat{\beta}$, therefore,

$$\hat{\sigma}^2 = T^{-1}(y_1 - X_1\hat{\beta})'(y_1 - X_1\hat{\beta})$$

which is the residual sum of squares obtained from the regression of y_1 on X_1 divided by T.

It is clear, therefore, that of these estimators of β, the best is the OLS estimator obtained using only the complete observations on y and X.

Solution 4.14

Part (a) Equation (4.14.1) is sometimes referred to as the *covariance* model and is frequently used to pool cross-section and time-series data for a linear model which has an intercept that varies both with cross-sections and time periods. To analyse the covariance model we first introduce dummy variables and then express the resulting model in matrix notation.

Introducing dummy variables for the intercept shifts of equation (4.14.1) we can write

$$y_{it} = \theta_2 z_{2t} + \ldots + \theta_N z_{Nt} + \phi_2 w_{i2} + \ldots + \phi_T w_{iT} + x'_{it}\beta + u_{it}$$

where

$$z_{it} = 1, \text{ for the } i\text{th cross-section} \quad (i = 2, \ldots, N)$$

$$= 0, \text{ otherwise}$$

$$w_{it} = 1, \text{ for the } t\text{th time period} \quad (t = 2, \ldots, T)$$

$$= 0, \text{ otherwise}$$

Using matrix notation (4.14.3) becomes

$$y = Z\theta + W\phi + X\beta + u \tag{4.14.4}$$

where

$$
y = \begin{pmatrix} y_{11} \\ y_{12} \\ . \\ . \\ . \\ y_{NT} \end{pmatrix}_{NT \times 1}, \quad
Z = \begin{pmatrix} 0 \\ I_{N-1} \end{pmatrix}_{N \times (N-1)} \otimes \begin{pmatrix} 1 \\ 1 \\ . \\ . \\ 1 \end{pmatrix}_{T \times 1}, \quad
W = \begin{pmatrix} 1 \\ 1 \\ . \\ . \\ 1 \end{pmatrix}_{N \times 1} \otimes \begin{pmatrix} 0 \\ I_{T-1} \end{pmatrix}_{T \times (T-1)},
$$

$$
X = \begin{pmatrix} x'_{11} \\ . \\ . \\ . \\ x'_{NT} \end{pmatrix}_{NT \times k}, \quad
u = \begin{pmatrix} u_{11} \\ u_{12} \\ . \\ . \\ u_{NT} \end{pmatrix}_{NT \times 1}, \quad
\theta = \begin{pmatrix} \theta_2 \\ . \\ . \\ . \\ \theta_N \end{pmatrix}_{(N-1) \times 1}, \quad
\phi = \begin{pmatrix} \phi_2 \\ .. \\ . \\ \phi_T \end{pmatrix}_{(T-1) \times 1}
$$

with $E(u) = 0$ and $E(uu') = \sigma^2 I_{NT}$. Thus the covariance model is seen to be a conventional linear model. As such θ, ϕ and β are estimable by OLS.

Part (b) From equation (4.14.4), the hypotheses H_0 to H_2 are clearly seen to involve the usual F-tests for sub-sets of coefficients. These are derived in question (2.3).

(i) The test statistic for $H_0: \theta = 0, \phi = 0, \beta \neq 0$ against $H_A: \theta, \phi, \beta \neq 0$ is

$$F = \frac{RSS_0 - RSS_A}{RSS_A} \cdot \frac{NT - N - T - k + 2}{N + T - 2} \tag{4.14.5}$$

where RSS_0 is the residual sum of squares on H_0 and is obtained from the regression of y on X; RSS_A is the residual sum of squares on H_A and is obtained from the regression of y on Z, W and X. The degrees of freedom are the number of observations less the number of estimated coefficients.

(ii) The test statistic for $H_1: \theta = 0, \phi, \beta \neq 0$ against H_A is

$$F = \frac{RSS_1 - RSS_A}{RSS_A} \cdot \frac{NT - N - T - k + 2}{N - 1} \tag{4.14.6}$$

where RSS_1 is the residual sum of squares on H_1 and is obtained from the regression of y on W and X.

(iii) The test statistic for H_0 against H_1 is

$$F = \frac{RSS_0 - RSS_1}{RSS_1} \cdot \frac{NT - T - k + 1}{N - 1} \tag{4.14.7}$$

Part (c)

(i) Expressed in matrix notation, (4.14.2) is

$$y = Z\theta + X\beta + u \tag{4.14.8}$$

where all variables are defined as for (4.14.4) but with $\phi = 0$, $x_{it} = (1, x_{it})$, $N = 3$ and $T = 4$. The OLS estimators of θ and β are obtained from the normal equations

$$\begin{bmatrix} Z'Z & Z'X \\ X'Z & X'Z \end{bmatrix} \begin{bmatrix} \hat{\theta} \\ \hat{\beta} \end{bmatrix} = \begin{bmatrix} Z'y \\ X'y \end{bmatrix} \tag{4.14.9}$$

Substituting for Z, X, N and T we obtain

$$\begin{bmatrix} 4 & 0 & 4 & \sum_t x_{2t} \\ 0 & 4 & 4 & \sum_t x_{3t} \\ 4 & 4 & 12 & \sum_{it} x_{it} \\ \sum_t x_{2t} & \sum_t x_{3t} & \sum_{it} x_{it} & \sum_{it} x_{it}^2 \end{bmatrix} \begin{bmatrix} \hat{\theta}_2 \\ \hat{\theta}_3 \\ \hat{\beta}_1 \\ \hat{\beta}_2 \end{bmatrix} = \begin{bmatrix} \sum_t y_{2t} \\ \sum_t y_{3t} \\ \sum_{it} y_{it} \\ \sum_{it} x_{it} y_{it} \end{bmatrix} \tag{4.14.10}$$

$$
\begin{bmatrix} 4 & 0 & 4 & 21 \\ 0 & 4 & 4 & 14 \\ 4 & 4 & 12 & 40 \\ 21 & 14 & 40 & 182 \end{bmatrix} \begin{bmatrix} \hat{\theta}_2 \\ \hat{\theta}_3 \\ \hat{\beta}_1 \\ \hat{\beta}_2 \end{bmatrix} = \begin{bmatrix} 59 \\ 49 \\ 137 \\ 539 \end{bmatrix} \qquad (4.14.10)
$$

Hence, the required OLS estimates are

$$
\begin{bmatrix} \hat{\theta}_2 \\ \hat{\theta}_3 \\ \hat{\beta}_1 \\ \hat{\beta}_2 \end{bmatrix} = \begin{bmatrix} 1.4697 & 0.7955 & 0.0530 & -0.2424 \\ 0.7955 & 0.8068 & -0.0795 & -0.1364 \\ 0.0530 & -0.0795 & 0.3447 & -0.0758 \\ -0.2424 & -0.1364 & -0.0758 & 0.0606 \end{bmatrix} \begin{bmatrix} 59 \\ 49 \\ 137 \\ 539 \end{bmatrix}
$$

$$
= \begin{bmatrix} 2.29 \\ 2.07 \\ 5.62 \\ 1.30 \end{bmatrix} \qquad (4.14.1)
$$

(ii) The test statistic for H_0: $\theta_2 = \theta_3 = 0, \beta_1, \beta_2 \neq 0$ against II_A: $\theta_2, \theta_3,$ $\beta_1, \beta_2 \neq 0$ is

$$
F = \frac{RSS_0 - RSS_A}{RSS_A} \cdot \frac{NT - N - k + 1}{N - 1}
$$

with $N = 3$, $T = 4$ and $k = 2$. Now

$$
RSS_A = \sum_{it} y_{it}^2 - (\hat{\theta}_2, \hat{\theta}_3, \hat{\beta}_1, \hat{\beta}_2) \left(\sum_t y_{2t}, \sum_t y_{3t}, \sum_{it} y_{it}, \sum_{it} x_{it} y_{it} \right)'
$$

$$
= 1713 - (2.29, 2.07, 5.62, 1.30) (59, 49, 137, 539)'
$$

$$
= 1713 - 1708.77 = 4.23
$$

RSS_0 is the residual sum of squares of the regression of y_{it} on x_{it} and a constant. Thus

$$
RSS_0 = \sum_{it} y_{it}^2 - \left(\sum_{it} y_{it}, \sum_{it} x_{it} y_{it} \right) \begin{bmatrix} NT & \sum_{it} x_{it} \\ \sum_{it} x_{it} & \sum_{it} x_{it}^2 \end{bmatrix}^{-1} \begin{bmatrix} \sum_{it} y_{it} \\ \sum_{it} x_{it} y_{it} \end{bmatrix}
$$

$$
= 1713 - (137, 539) \begin{bmatrix} 12 & 40 \\ 40 & 182 \end{bmatrix}^{-1} \begin{bmatrix} 137 \\ 539 \end{bmatrix}
$$

$$= 1713 - (137, 539) \begin{bmatrix} 182 & -40 \\ -40 & 12 \end{bmatrix} \begin{bmatrix} 137 \\ 539 \end{bmatrix} / 584$$

$$= 1713 - 1703.77 = 9.63.$$

Substituting these figures into the F-value we obtain

$$F = \frac{9.63 - 4.23}{4.23} \cdot \frac{12 - 3 - 2 + 1}{3 - 1} = \frac{5.40 \times 8}{4.23 \times 2} = 5.11.$$

Now F is distributed as $F_{2,8}$. But $F_{2,8}(0.05) = 4.46$ and $F_{2,8}(0.025) = 6.06$. Therefore, at the 5% level of significance H_0 is not rejected but at the 2.5% level it is rejected.

Solution 4.15

Part (a) Like the covariance model, the error (or variance) components model (Wallace and Hussain, 1969; Maddala, 1971; Nerlove, 1971 and Henderson, 1971) is used in pooling cross-section and time-series data. But, unlike the covariance model, it is assumed that the error term consists of three independent components: a cross-section term u_i, a term associated with time v_t, and a general term w_{it} which is common to both the cross section and the time series data. Thus, in the covariance model, the three error terms u_i, v_t and w_{it} can be thought of as having different means but the same variances, whereas in the error components model they have the same (zero) means but different variances.

It has been argued, however, that a major disadvantage of the covariance model is that the intercept dummy variables eliminate a large part of the variation among both the dependent and independent variables if the between cross-section and between time-period variation is high. Further, it is often difficult to interpret the dummy variables whose inclusion can also use up a large number of degrees of freedom. For these reasons the error components model is often the preferred model for bringing cross-section and time-series evidence to bear on a model. The relationship between the error components and the covariance model is discussed further in Question (4.16).

Part (b)
(i) Writing (4.15.1) and (4.15.2) in matrix notation we have

$$y = X\beta + e \tag{4.15.3}$$

where

$$y = \begin{bmatrix} y_{11} \\ y_{12} \\ \cdot \\ \cdot \\ \cdot \\ y_{NT} \end{bmatrix}, \quad X = \begin{bmatrix} x'_{11} \\ x'_{12} \\ \cdot \\ \cdot \\ x'_{NT} \end{bmatrix}, \quad e = \begin{bmatrix} e_{11} \\ e_{12} \\ \cdot \\ \cdot \\ e_{NT} \end{bmatrix} \quad \text{and} \quad e = Zu + w$$

$$(4.15.4)$$

where $u' = (u_1, \ldots, u_N; v_1, \ldots, v_T)$, $w' = (w_{11}, w_{12}, \ldots, w_{NT})$, $Z = (I_N \otimes i_T \vdots i_N \otimes I_T)$ and i_A is an $A \times 1$ vector of ones.

It follows from the assumptions on u_i, v_t and w_{it} that e is $N(0, \Omega)$ where

$$\Omega = E(ee') = ZE(uu')Z' + E(ww')$$
$$= \sigma_w^2 (ZAZ' + I_{NT})$$

$$(4.15.5)$$

and

$$A = \sigma_w^{-2} E(uu')$$

$$= \sigma_w^{-2} \begin{bmatrix} \sigma_u^2 I_N & 0 \\ \hline 0 & \sigma_v^2 I_T \end{bmatrix}.$$

$$(4.15.6)$$

If σ_u^2/σ_w^2 and σ_v^2/σ_w^2 are known, then Ω is known up to a factor of proportionality and hence GLS can be used to estimate (4.15.3). That is, if

$$\Omega = \sigma_w^2 \Omega^*$$

then the GLS estimator is

$$\hat{\beta}_{\text{GLS}} = (X'\Omega^{*-1}X)^{-1}X'\Omega^{*-1}y$$

$$(4.15.7)$$

(ii) If σ_u^2/σ_w^2 and σ_v^2/σ_w^2 are unknown then Ω^* is unknown too and the above estimator cannot be used or, at least not directly. One alternative approach is to use maximum likelihood estimation but this can be computationally fairly burdensome, as it involves the solution of non-linear equations.

A simpler alternative is to use a two-step estimator in which in the first step an estimate of β is obtained which is used to estimate u and hence σ_u^2/σ_w^2, σ_v^2/σ_w^2 and Ω^*. This latter estimate can be used in (4.15.7) instead of the unknown Ω^* to provide the second step estimator of β. We shall describe this estimator in further detail.

A possible first stage estimator of β is OLS on (4.15.3). The residuals of this equation are an estimator $\hat{e}$ of e, i.e. $\hat{e} = y - Xb$, where b is the OLS estimator of β. An estimator of u is now obtained through replacing e by $\hat{e}$ in equation (4.15.4) and regressing $\hat{e}$ on Z. The resulting estimator of u is

$$\hat{u} = (Z'Z)^{-1} Z' \hat{e}$$

Now $u' = (u_1, \ldots u_N, v_1, \ldots v_T)$ and $\hat{u}' = (\hat{u}_1, \ldots \hat{u}_N, \hat{v}_1, \ldots \hat{v}_T)$. We can, therefore, estimate σ_u^2 and σ_v^2 by

$$\hat{\sigma}_u^2 = \frac{1}{N} \sum_i \left(\hat{u}_i - \frac{1}{N} \sum_i \hat{u}_i \right)^2$$

and

$$\hat{\sigma}_v^2 = \frac{1}{T} \sum_t \left(\hat{v}_t - \frac{1}{T} \sum_t \hat{v}_t \right)^2$$

respectively. Finally, we can estimate $\hat{\sigma}_w^2$ by $\hat{\sigma}_w^2 = \hat{w}'\hat{w}/NT$, where $\hat{w}$ is the residual vector $\hat{w} = \hat{e} - Z\hat{u}$. We can now obtain estimates of σ_u^2/σ_w^2, σ_v^2/σ_w^2 and hence of Ω^* as required.

Solution 4.16

Part (a)
  (i) If u_i and v_t are constants then (4.16.1) is the covariance model
      discussed in question (4.14) with the modification that in (4.16.1),
      in contrast to (4.14.1), the N cross-section and T time-series effects
      are all included explicitly.
 (ii) If the u_i and v_t are random with the properties given, then we have
      the error components model of question (4.15).

Part (b) For either model we can write (4.16.1) in matrix notation as

$$y = Z\delta + Gu + Hv + w \tag{4.16.4}$$

where

$$y = \begin{bmatrix} y_{11} \\ y_{12} \\ . \\ . \\ . \\ y_{NT} \end{bmatrix}, \quad Z = \begin{bmatrix} 1 & x'_{11} \\ 1 & x'_{12} \\ . & . \\ . & . \\ . & . \\ 1 & x'_{NT} \end{bmatrix}, \quad G = I_N \otimes i_T, \quad H = i_N \otimes I_T,$$

$$w = \begin{bmatrix} w_{11} \\ w_{12} \\ . \\ . \\ w_{NT} \end{bmatrix}, \quad \delta = \begin{bmatrix} \alpha \\ \beta \end{bmatrix}, \quad u = \begin{bmatrix} u_1 \\ . \\ . \\ u_N \end{bmatrix}, \quad v = \begin{bmatrix} v_1 \\ . \\ . \\ v_T \end{bmatrix}.$$

We shall consider first the error components model. Denoting the disturbances of (4.16.4) by ϵ, where

$$\epsilon = Gu + Hv + w, \tag{4.16.5}$$

we obtain $E(\epsilon) = 0$ and

$$E(\epsilon\epsilon') = \Omega = \sigma_w^2 I_{NT} + \sigma_u^2 GG' + \sigma_v^2 HH'$$
$$= \sigma_w^2 I_{NT} + \sigma_u^2 A + \sigma_v^2 B \tag{4.16.6}$$

where we have used the fact that u, v and w are independently distributed. A and B are as defined in the question. We note that Ω satisfies equation (4.16.2).

As σ_w^2, σ_u^2 and σ_v^2 are known, the best linear unbiased estimator of δ is GLS giving

$$\hat{\delta} = (Z'\Omega^{-1}Z)^{-1} Z'\Omega^{-1}y \tag{4.16.7}$$

with covariance matrix

$$V_{\hat{\delta}} = (Z'\Omega^{-1}Z)^{-1}$$

$$= \left[\begin{array}{c|c} i_{NT}'\Omega^{-1}i_{NT} & i_{NT}'\Omega^{-1}X \\ \hline X'\Omega^{-1}i_{NT} & X'\Omega^{-1}X \end{array} \right]^{-1} \tag{4.16.8}$$

where $Z = (i_{NT} : X)$ and $X' = (x_{11}', \ldots, x_{NT}')$.
Using the result (4.16.2), we obtain

$$i_{NT}'\Omega^{-1}X = \sigma_N^{-2} i_{NT}'(I_{NT} - \gamma_1 A - \gamma_2 B + \gamma_3 J_{NT})X. \tag{4.16.9}$$

Each column of X sums to zero, hence $i_{NT}'X = 0$. Moreover, $J_{NT} = i_{NT}i_{NT}'$, $i_{NT}'A = Ti_{NT}'$ and $i_{NT}'B = Ni_{NT}'$. Therefore, $i'_{NT}\Omega^{-1}X = 0$ and so (4.16.7) is block diagonal. Consequently,

$$\hat{\alpha} = (i_{NT}'\Omega^{-1}i_{NT})^{-1} i_{NT}'\Omega^{-1}y$$

and

$$\hat{\beta} = (X'\Omega^{-1}X)^{-1} X'\Omega^{-1}y. \tag{4.16.10}$$

The covariance matrix of $\hat{\beta}$ is

$$V_{\hat{\beta}} = (X'\Omega^{-1}X)^{-1}$$
$$= \sigma_w^2 [X'(I_{NT} - \gamma_1 A - \gamma_2 B)X]^{-1}, \tag{4.16.11}$$

where we have used the result derived above that $J_{NT}X = 0$.
Turning now to the covariance model, the best linear unbiased estimator for (4.16.4) is OLS giving

$$\begin{bmatrix} d \\ \hat{u} \\ \hat{v} \end{bmatrix} = \begin{bmatrix} Z'Z & Z'F \\ F'Z & F'F \end{bmatrix}^{-1} \begin{bmatrix} Z'y \\ F'y \end{bmatrix} \qquad (4.16.12)$$

where $F = (G \vdots H)$ and hence is identical to that defined in the question. From Question (2.7) we obtain the OLS estimator for a sub-set of coefficients as

$$d = (Z'QZ)^{-1} Z'Qy \qquad (4.16.13)$$

where $Q = I_{NT} - F(F'F)^{-1} F'$ and hence satisfies (4.16.3). Furthermore, the covariance matrix of d is

$$V_d = \sigma_w^2 (Z'QZ)^{-1}$$

$$= \sigma_w^2 \begin{pmatrix} i'_{NT} Q i_{NT} & i'_{NT} QX \\ X'Q i_{NT} & X'QX \end{pmatrix}^{-1} \qquad (4.16.14)$$

Given the definition of Q, we can use our earlier results to show that $l'_{NT} QX = 0$ and hence V_d is block diagonal. Consequently, the OLS estimator of β is

$$b = (X'QX)^{-1} X'Qy \qquad (4.16.15)$$

with covariance matrix

$$V_b = \sigma_w^2 (X'QX)^{-1}$$

Using the definition of Q and the result $J_{NT} X = 0$ we obtain

$$V_b = \sigma_w^2 \left[X' \left(I_{NT} - \frac{1}{T} A - \frac{1}{N} B \right) X \right]^{-1} \qquad (4.16.16)$$

To prove (i) we note that if A and B are positive definite matrices and if $A - B$ is positive semi-definite, then $B^{-1} - A^{-1}$ is positive semi-definite (Goldberger, 1964, p.38).

We are asked to prove that $V_b - V_{\hat{\beta}}$ is a positive semi-definite matrix and by the result above this is satisfied if $V_{\hat{\beta}}^{-1} - V_b^{-1}$ is positive definite. But from (4.16.11) and (4.16.16),

$$V_{\hat{\beta}}^{-1} - V_b^{-1} = \sigma_w^2 \left[X'(I_{NT} - \gamma_1 A - \gamma_2 B)X - X' \left(I_{NT} - \frac{1}{T} A - \frac{1}{N} B \right) X \right]$$

$$= \sigma_w^2 X' \left[\left(\frac{1}{T} - \gamma_1 \right) A + \left(\frac{1}{N} - \gamma_2 \right) B \right] X \qquad (4.16.17)$$

Now

$$\frac{1}{T} - \gamma_1 = \frac{1}{T} - \frac{\sigma_u^2}{\sigma_w^2 + T\sigma_u^2} = \frac{\sigma_w^2}{T(\sigma_w^2 + T\sigma_u^2)}$$

and

$$\frac{1}{N} - \gamma_2 = \frac{\sigma_w^2}{N(\sigma_w^2 + N\sigma_v^2)}$$

which are both positive. Hence (4.16.7) is positive semi-definite, our required result.

To prove (ii), we require the covariance matrices of the limiting distributions of $\sqrt{NT}(\hat{\beta} - \beta)$ and $\sqrt{NT}(b - \beta)$. From (4.16.11) and the above results on γ_1 and γ_2 the former is

$$\lim_{N,T \to \infty} NTV_{\hat{\beta}} = \lim_{N,T \to \infty} \sigma_w^2 \left[\frac{X'X}{NT} - \gamma_1 \frac{X'AX}{NT} - \gamma_2 \frac{X'BX}{NT} \right]^{-1}$$

$$= \lim_{N,T \to \infty} \sigma_w^2 \left[\frac{X'X}{NT} - \frac{X'AX}{NT^2} - \frac{X'BX}{N^2T} + \frac{\sigma_w^2}{\sigma_w^2 + T\sigma_u^2} \frac{X'AX}{NT^2} \right.$$

$$\left. + \frac{\sigma_w^2}{\sigma_w^2 + N\sigma_v^2} \frac{X'BX}{N^2T} \right]^{-1},$$

$$(4.16.18)$$

and, from (4.16.16), the latter is

$$\lim_{N,T \to \infty} NTV_b = \lim_{N,T \to \infty} \sigma_w^2 \left[\frac{X'X}{NT} - \frac{X'AX}{NT^2} - \frac{X'BX}{N^2T} \right]^{-1} \qquad (4.16.19)$$

If N and $T \to \infty$ such that N/T is constant, then, given $\lim_{N,T \to \infty} X'X/NT$ is finite and non-singular, both (4.16.18) and (4.16.19) can be shown to reduce to $\lim_{N,T \to \infty} \sigma_w^2 (X'X/NT)^{-1}$. Thus, in this case, the two estimators $\hat{\beta}$ and b are asymptotically equivalent. Despite the remarks made in Question (4.15a) about the advantages of the error components model interpretation over the covariance interpretation, this result suggests that the *covariance* interpretation might be preferred. As the estimation procedures provide asymptotically equivalent estimators of β, we would choose between them on the grounds of computational ease. In this case, as the covariance estimator is an OLS estimator and the error components estimator is a GLS estimator, typically with unknown error covariance matrix, we would choose the covariance interpretation. A comparison of small sample properties may, however, lead to a different conclusion.

It is important to note, however, that in general the two estimators $\hat{\beta}$

and b will not have the same asymptotic distributions. If N/T is not constant as N and $T \to \infty$, or if either N or $T \to \infty$, then (4.16.18) and (4.16.19) will not be equal. For example, if N is fixed but $T \to \infty$ in such a way that $\lim_{T \to \infty} X'X/NT$, $\lim_{T \to \infty} X'AX/NT$ and $\lim_{T \to \infty} X'BX/NT$ are all finite then (4.16.18) becomes

$$\lim_{T \to \infty} \sigma_w^2 \left[\frac{X'X}{NT} - \frac{X'BX}{N^2 T} + \frac{\sigma_w^2}{\sigma_w^2 + N\sigma_v^2} \frac{X'BX}{N^2 T} \right]^{-1} \tag{4.16.20}$$

and (4.16.19) becomes

$$\lim_{T \to \infty} \sigma_w^2 \left[\frac{X'X}{NT} - \frac{X'BX}{N^2 T} \right]^{-1} \tag{4.16.21}$$

The difference (4.16.21) − (4.16.20) is a positive semi-definite matrix. In this case the two estimators $\hat{\beta}$ and b do not have the same asymptotic distributions.

Solution 4.17

Part (a) Aggregating (4.17.1) over the N micro-units we obtain

$$\sum_{i=1}^{N} y_{it} = \sum_{i=1}^{N} x'_{it}\beta_i + \sum_{i=1}^{N} z'_{it}\gamma + \sum_{i=1}^{N} u_{it}$$

or,

$$\bar{y}_t = \bar{x}'_t \bar{\beta}_t + \bar{z}'_t \bar{\gamma} + \bar{u}_t \tag{4.17.3}$$

where the jth element of $\bar{\beta}_t$, $\bar{\beta}_{tj} = \Sigma_i x_{itj}\beta_{ij}/\Sigma_i x_{itj}$ (x_{itj} is the jth element of the column vector x_{it}), $\bar{\gamma} = \gamma$ and $\bar{u}_t = \Sigma_{i=1}^{N} u_{it}$.

In other words, whereas the macro-coefficient $\bar{\gamma}$ of $\bar{z}_t$ in (4.17.3) equals the micro γ and corresponds to equation (4.17.2), the macro-coefficient $\bar{\beta}_t$ of x_t in (4.17.3) does not correspond to $\bar{\beta}$ in (4.17.2). As indicated by the subscript, t, $\bar{\beta}_t$ depends on time and is not, in general, constant as is required if (4.17.2) is to be a correct macro-representation of (4.17.1).

$\bar{\beta}_t$ is seen to be a weighted average of the micro-coefficients β_i, with weights equal to the corresponding x_{it}'s. In other words, $\bar{\beta}_t$ depends upon the distribution of x_{it} across micro-units. A change in this distribution from one time period to another will usually alter the weighted average of the β_i's. It follows that if the distribution of x_{it}'s is constant over time then (4.17.2) will be a correct macro-representation of (4.17.1).

Also, if $\beta_i = \beta$ for all i, i.e. the micro-units have identical β_i's, then $\bar{\beta}_t = \beta$ and hence (4.17.2) becomes a correct aggregation of (4.17.1) with $\bar{\beta} = \beta$. In this case, the distribution of the x_{it}'s is irrelevant. Clearly this condition is met for the term $z_{it}\gamma$.

Part (b) If $\bar{\beta}_t = \bar{\beta}$ then $v_t = \bar{u}_t$ and, since $E(\bar{u}_t) = \Sigma_{i=1}^{N} E(u_{it}) = 0$ and $E(\bar{u}_t \bar{u}_s) = E(\Sigma_{i=1}^{N} u_{it})(\Sigma_{j=1}^{N} u_{js}) = N\sigma^2$ for $t = s$ and zero for $t \neq s$, we can estimate (4.17.2) efficiently by OLS.

Part (c) When (4.17.2) is an incorrect aggregation of (4.17.1) it represents a mis-specification; from (4.17.3) it can be seen that v_t in (4.17.2) satisfies

$$v_t = \bar{x}_t'(\bar{\beta}_t - \bar{\beta}) + \bar{u}_t \tag{4.17.4}$$

and not $\bar{u}_t$. From question (4.3) we know that the bias in estimating (4.17.2) by OLS will be

$$E\begin{bmatrix} \bar{b} \\ \bar{c} \end{bmatrix} - \begin{bmatrix} \bar{\beta} \\ \bar{\gamma} \end{bmatrix} = \begin{bmatrix} \bar{X}'\bar{X} & \bar{X}'\bar{Z} \\ \bar{Z}'\bar{X} & \bar{Z}'\bar{Z} \end{bmatrix}^{-1} \begin{bmatrix} \sum_t E(\bar{x}_t v_t) \\ \sum_t E(\bar{z}_t v_t) \end{bmatrix}$$

where $\bar{b}$ and $\bar{c}$ are the OLS estimators of $\bar{\beta}$ and $\bar{\gamma}$, respectively, $\bar{X}' = (\bar{x}_1, \ldots, \bar{x}_T)$ and $\bar{Z}' = (\bar{z}_1, \ldots, \bar{z}_T)$. Thus the bias is

$$E\begin{bmatrix} \bar{b} \\ \bar{c} \end{bmatrix} - \begin{bmatrix} \bar{\beta} \\ \bar{\gamma} \end{bmatrix} = \begin{bmatrix} \bar{X}'\bar{X} & \bar{X}'\bar{Z} \\ \bar{Z}'\bar{X} & \bar{Z}'\bar{Z} \end{bmatrix}^{-1} \begin{bmatrix} \sum_t \bar{x}_t \bar{x}_t'(\bar{\beta}_t - \bar{\beta}) \\ \sum_t \bar{z}_t \bar{x}_t'(\bar{\beta}_t - \bar{\beta}) \end{bmatrix} \tag{4.17.5}$$

In general, therefore, both $\bar{b}$ and $\bar{c}$ will be biased estimators.

Part (d) The test we require is $H_0 : \beta_1 = \beta_2 = \ldots \beta_N = \beta$ against $H_1 : \beta_i$ not all equal. This is a conventional test of the equality of a sub-set of coefficients in different equations (see Question 2.6). On H_0, we write equation (4.17.1) as

$$\begin{bmatrix} y_{11} \\ y_{12} \\ \cdot \\ \cdot \\ \cdot \\ y_{NT} \end{bmatrix} = \begin{bmatrix} x_{11} & z_{11} \\ x_{12} & z_{12} \\ \cdot & \cdot \\ \cdot & \cdot \\ \cdot & \cdot \\ x_{NT} & z_{NT} \end{bmatrix} \begin{bmatrix} \beta \\ \gamma \end{bmatrix} + \begin{bmatrix} u_{11} \\ u_{12} \\ \cdot \\ \cdot \\ \cdot \\ u_{NT} \end{bmatrix}$$

or

$$y = W\theta + u \tag{4.17.6}$$

where $E(u) = 0$ and $E(uu') = \sigma^2 I_{NT}$. On H_1, equation (4.17.1) can be written as

$$y = \begin{bmatrix} x_{11} & 0 & . & . & 0 & z_{11} \\ 0 & x_{12} & . & . & 0 & z_{12} \\ . & . & . & . & . & . \\ 0 & . & . & . & x_{NT} & z_{NT} \end{bmatrix} \begin{bmatrix} \beta_1 \\ \beta_2 \\ . \\ . \\ \beta_N \\ \gamma \end{bmatrix} + u$$

or,

$$y = W^*\theta^* + u. \tag{4.17.7}$$

Our test statistic is, therefore,

$$F = \frac{RSS_0 - RSS_1}{RSS_1} \cdot \frac{NT - Nk - l}{k(N-1)}$$

where RSS_0 and RSS_1 are the residual sums of squares of (4.17.6) and (4.17.7), respectively. F is distributed as an $F_{k(N-1), NT-Nk-l}$. For an alternative approach to this test see Question 3.12(bii).

Solution 4.18

Part (a) We wish to test whether or not the coefficient of $\ln W$ in equation (4.18.1) is significantly different from zero. In the absence of any figure for the number of observations we shall use the limiting normal distribution for our test statistic. This is $0.811/0.051 = 15.9$, which is highly significant. We may conclude, therefore, that this evidence supports the hypothesis that variations in output per man in the iron and steel industries of different industries are explained by differences in the money wage rate. Equation (4.18.1) suggests that a 1% rise in money wages leads to a 0.81% rise in output per man.

Part (b) Denote the omitted variable by X. Then, if this variable enters linearly, the modified equation can be written as

$$\ln \frac{Q}{L} = \beta_0 + \beta_1 \ln W + \beta_2 X + u \tag{4.18.2}$$

with $\beta_1, \beta_2 > 0$ and $cov(\ln W, X) > 0$. If (4.18.2) is correct, the OLS estimates of (4.18.1) will be biased. Assuming X is fixed, the bias of b_1 the OLS estimator of β_1 in (4.18.1) is (see Question 4.3)

$$E(b_1) - \beta_1 = \frac{\beta_2 cov(\ln W, X)}{var(\ln W)}$$

which is clearly positive. Thus the estimate 0.811 can be expected in this case to overestimate β_1.

CHAPTER 5

Further stochastic models

0. INTRODUCTION

Many of the models discussed in earlier chapters differ from the type of model we may wish to use in practice in two respects. In the first place, they require the equations relating the observable variables to be linear in both variables and parameters. Second, they are limited by the condition that the explanatory variables in an equation are all exogenous. In the present chapter, our questions deal with a number of different stochastic models which relax one or other of these requirements. Most of our attention is devoted to non-linear regressions and models with errors in the variables.

1. QUESTIONS

Question 5.1

In the model

$$y_t = g_t(\alpha^0) + u_t \qquad (t = 1, \ldots, T) \tag{5.1.1}$$

y_t is a vector of n observable random variables, u_t is a vector of random disturbances and $g_t(\alpha)$ is a vector of known functions of the unknown $p \times 1$ parameter vector α whose true value is denoted by α^0. The elements of $g_t(\alpha)$ also depend on a vector x_t of m non-random exogenous variables.

The estimator $\alpha_T(S)$ is defined as the vector α which minimises the quadratic form

$$\sum_{t=1}^{T} [y_t - g_t(\alpha)]' S [y_t - g_t(\alpha)]$$

where S is a positive definite matrix. Discuss the conditions under which $\alpha_T(S)$ is a consistent estimator of α^0.

(Adapted from University of Essex MA examinations, 1973.)

Question 5.2

In the model (5.1.1) it is assumed that the disturbances u_t $(t = 1, \ldots, T)$ are serially independent, identically distributed normal vectors with zero mean vector and positive definite covariance matrix Ω.

(a) Show that the maximum likelihood estimator of α^0 minimises

$$\ln \det \left\{ \frac{1}{T} \sum_{t=1}^{T} [y_t - g_t(\alpha)] [y_t - g_t(\alpha)]' \right\}$$

considered as a function of α.

(b) Show that the maximum likelihood estimator of α can be regarded as a minimum distance estimator. Does this mean that we can deduce the asymptotic properties of maximum likelihood estimators in models such as this from the corresponding properties of minimum distance estimators?

Question 5.3

(a) In the context of the model (5.1.1) discuss the asymptotic sampling properties of the estimator $\alpha_T(S_T)$ that minimises

$$\sum_{t=1}^{T} [y_t - g_t(\alpha)]' S_T [y_t - g_t(\alpha)]$$

with respect to α, where S_T is a random symmetric matrix which tends in probability to a positive definite matrix S. State clearly any assumptions made about the functions $g_t(\alpha)$ and the disturbances u_t.

(b) Demonstrate that $\alpha_T(S_T)$ is asymptotically efficient in the class of minimum distance estimators when the matrix S_T tends in probability to Ω^{-1}, the inverse of the covariance matrix of the disturbances.

Question 5.4

(a) In the model

$$y_t = \alpha^0 x_{1t} + (\exp \alpha^0) x_{2t} + u_t \qquad (t = 1, \ldots, T) \qquad (5.4.1)$$

the y_t $(t = 1, \ldots, T)$ are observable random variables, the x_{it} are non-random, bounded quantities whose second moment matrix is non-singular and tends to a non-singular limit as $T \to \infty$ and the u_t $(t = 1, \ldots, T)$ are independent and identically distributed disturbances with mean zero and finite variance.

Show that $\hat{\alpha}$, the estimator of α^0 which minimises

$$\sum_{t=1}^{T} (y_t - \alpha x_{1t} - e^\alpha x_{2t})^2$$

is a consistent estimator of α^0.

(b) If the model (5.4.1) is replaced by

$$y_t = \alpha^0 + (\exp \alpha^0) t + u_t \qquad (t = 1, \ldots, T) \qquad (5.4.2)$$

is $\hat{\alpha}$ still consistent? Prove your result.

Question 5.5

An econometric model is described by the equation system

$$y_t = A(\alpha^0) x_t + u_t \qquad (t = 1, \ldots, T)$$

where y_t is an observable random n-vector, x_t is an observable non-random m-vector, u_t is a vector of disturbances and $A(\alpha^0)$ is an $n \times m$ matrix whose elements are known functions of the unknown p-vector of parameters α^0.

The matrix $A(\alpha^0)$ is first estimated by an unrestricted least squares regression and we denote by A^* the resulting matrix of regression coefficients. The minimum distance estimator α^{**} is now defined as the vector which minimises

$$T^{-1} \sum_{t=1}^{T} [y_t - A(\alpha) x_t]' (M_{uu}^*)^{-1} [y_t - A(\alpha) x_t] \qquad (5.5.1)$$

where

$$M_{uu}^* = T^{-1} \sum_{t=1}^{T} (y_t - A^* x_t)(y_t - A^* x_t)'$$

(a) Show that α^{**} minimises

$$\text{tr}\{[A^* - A(\alpha)]' (M_{uu}^*)^{-1} [A^* - A(\alpha)] M_{xx}\} \qquad (5.5.2)$$

where

$$M_{xx} = T^{-1} \sum_{t=1}^{T} x_t x_t'$$

(b) List a set of assumptions under which $\sqrt{T}(\alpha^{**} - \alpha^0)$ has a limiting normal distribution and write down the covariance matrix of this limiting distribution.

(c) Show that, if the assumptions in (b) are satisfied, $\sqrt{T} [A(\alpha^{**}) - A(\alpha^0)]$ also has a limiting normal distribution.

(d) If ψ^{**} represents the covariance matrix of the limiting distribution $\sqrt{T} \text{vec} [A(\alpha^{**}) - A(\alpha^0)]$ and ψ^* represents the covariance matrix of the limiting distribution of $\sqrt{T} \text{vec} [A^* - A(\alpha^0)]$ show that the matrix $\psi^* - \psi^{**}$ is positive semi-definite.

Question 5.6

The observable random variables y_t $(t = 1, \ldots, T)$ and non-random quantities x_{it} $(i = 1, 2; t = 1, \ldots, T)$ satisfy the relation

$$y_t = a_1 x_{1t} + a_2 x_{2t} + u_t$$

in which u_t is distributed independently of t with mean zero and variance σ^2 and u_s and u_t are independent if $s \neq t$. The parameters a_1 and a_2 satisfy the restriction $a_1^2 = a_2$. The x_{it} are bounded and the moment matrix

$$M_{xx} = \begin{bmatrix} \dfrac{1}{T}\sum_{t=1}^{T} x_{1t}^2 & \dfrac{1}{T}\sum_{t=1}^{T} x_{1t} x_{2t} \\[2mm] \hline \\[-2mm] \dfrac{1}{T}\sum_{t=1}^{T} x_{2t} x_{1t} & \dfrac{1}{T}\sum_{t=1}^{T} x_{2t}^2 \end{bmatrix}$$

is non-singluar and tends to a non-singular matrix $\bar{M}_{xx}$ as T tends to infinity.

(a) Describe an iterative procedure for obtaining estimates $\hat{a}_1$ and $\hat{a}_2$ that satisfy the restriction $\hat{a}_1^2 = \hat{a}_2$ and are such that $\sqrt{T}(\hat{a}_1 - a_1)$ and $\sqrt{T}(\hat{a}_2 - a_2)$ have limiting normal distributions whose variances are at least as small as those of the limiting distributions of $\sqrt{T}(a_1^* - a_1)$ and $\sqrt{T}(a_2^* - a_2)$ respectively where a_1^* and a_2^* are the unrestricted least squares estimates.

(b) Compare the variances of the limiting distributions of $\sqrt{T}(\hat{a}_1 - a_1)$ and $\sqrt{T}(a_1^* - a_1)$ when $a_1 = 0.5, a_2 = 0.25, \sigma^2 = 1$ and

$$\bar{M}_{xx} = \begin{bmatrix} 1 & 1 \\ 1 & 2 \end{bmatrix}$$

(University of Auckland MA examinations, 1969.)

Question 5.7

In the system

$$y_{1t} = a_{11} x_{1t} + a_{12} x_{2t} + u_{1t} \tag{5.7.1}$$
$$y_{2t} = a_{21} x_{1t} + a_{22} x_{2t} + u_{2t} \tag{5.7.2}$$

the y_{it} $(i = 1, 2; t = 1, \ldots, T)$ are observable random variables, the x_{it} $(i = 1, 2; t = 1, \ldots, T)$ are observable, non-random, bounded quantities whose second moment matrix converges as $T \to \infty$ to the finite, positive definite matrix $\bar{M}_{xx}$. The u_{it} $(i = 1, 2)$ are serially independent random disturbances which have the same bivariate normal distribution for each value of t with $E(u_{1t}) = E(u_{2t}) = 0$ and second moments given by $E(u_{1t}^2) = 2\sigma^2, E(u_{1t}u_{2t}) = \sigma^2, E(u_{2t}^2) = \sigma^2$ for all t, The a_{ij} are unknown parameters which satisfy the restriction

$$a_{11}a_{12} = 1 \qquad (5.7.3)$$

(a) Briefly outline a procedure for obtaining asymptotically efficient estimates of the coefficients $a_{ij}(i, j = 1, 2)$.

(b) Compare the covariance matrix of the limiting distribution of your estimates with that of the least squares estimates when the true values of the parameters are $a_{11} = 1, a_{12} = 1, a_{21} = 1, a_{22} = 2$ and

$$\bar{M}_{xx} = \begin{bmatrix} 1 & 1 \\ 1 & 2 \end{bmatrix}.$$

Question 5.8

Two unobservable economic variables Y_t and $X_t (t = 1, \ldots, T)$ are assumed to be related by the equation

$$Y_t = \alpha^0 + \beta^0 X_t \qquad (t = 1, \ldots, T) \qquad (5.8.1)$$

in which α^0 and β^0 are unknown parameters. Observable variables y_t and x_t are known to be related to Y_t and X_t according to

$$\left. \begin{aligned} y_t &= Y_t + u_t \\ x_t &= X_t + v_t \end{aligned} \right\} \qquad (t = 1, \ldots, T) \qquad \begin{aligned} (5.8.2) \\ (5.8.3) \end{aligned}$$

where u_t and v_t are serially independent random disturbances which are distributed independently of t and of Y_s and $X_s (s = 1, \ldots, T)$, with zero means and second moments given by

$$E(u_t^2) = \sigma^2, E(v_t^2) = \sigma^2, E(u_t v_t) = 0 \text{ for all } t.$$

(a) Show that, under certain conditions, an orthogonal regression of the y_t on the x_t yields consistent estimates of α^0 and β^0. Derive an explicit representation of these estimates in terms of the sample moments of the y_t and x_t.

(b) Find the orthogonal regression estimates of α^0 and β^0 given the sample means $\bar{y} = 100, \bar{x} = 25$ and the following sample second moment matrix in terms of deviations from means:

	y	x
y	5	2
x	2	2

Question 5.9

The observable random variables $y_{1t} (t = 1, \ldots, T)$ are assumed to be related to the unobservable non-random variables $y_{2t}^* (t = 1, \ldots, T)$ according to the relation

$$y_{1t} = y_{2t}^* \gamma + u_{1t} \qquad (5.9.1)$$

where γ is an unknown scalar parameter. Observable random variables $y_{2t} (t = 1, \ldots, T)$ are known to be related to the $y_{2t}^* (t = 1, \ldots, T)$ by the equation

$$y_{2t} = y_{2t}^* + u_{2t} \qquad (5.9.2)$$

and the y_{2t}^* are determined by

$$y_{2t}^* = x_t' \beta \qquad (t = 1, \ldots, T) \qquad (5.9.3)$$

where x_t is a vector of k non-random exogenous variables and β is a vector of unknown parameters. In (5.9.1) and (5.9.2) the u_{it} are random disturbances whose first and second moments are given by:

$$E(u_{1t}) = E(u_{2t}) = 0 \qquad (t = 1, \ldots, T)$$

$$\left. \begin{array}{l} E(u_{1t}^2) = \sigma_{11} \\ E(u_{2t}^2) = \sigma_{22} \end{array} \right\} \qquad (t = 1, \ldots, T)$$

$$E(u_{it} u_{js}) = 0 \qquad \text{for all } i, j, t \text{ and } s \text{ satisfying } i \neq j \text{ or } t \neq s.$$

It is further assumed that the limit as $T \to \infty$ of the matrix

$$M_{xx} = T^{-1} \sum_{t=1}^{T} x_t x_t'$$

exists and is positive definite.

(a) Show that a consistent estimator of γ is obtained from the regression of y_{1t} on $\hat{y}_{2t}$ where $\hat{y}_{2t}$ is the calculated value in the regression of y_{2t} on x_t.

(b) Can you suggest any improvements in the procedure described in Part (a).

Question 5.10

In the vintage production function

$$Q(t) = B e^{-\delta(1-\alpha)t} L(t)^\alpha \left[\int_{-\infty}^{t} e^{\sigma v} I(v) \, dv \right]^{1-\alpha}, \qquad \sigma = \delta + \frac{\lambda}{1-\alpha}$$

$$(5.10.1)$$

$Q(t)$ represents gross output at time t, $L(t)$ the total amount of labour employed at time t and $I(v)$ real gross investment at time v. B, α, δ and λ are unknown parameters. The parameter λ measures the proportional rate at which new technical knowledge is being embodied in new capital and is called the rate of embodied technical progress.

It has been suggested that λ can be estimated from the equation

$$\ln\left\{\left[\frac{dR(t)}{dt} + \delta R(t)\right]\Big/ I(t)\right\} = \left(\frac{1}{1-\alpha}\right)\ln(B) + \left(\frac{\lambda}{1-\alpha}\right)t \qquad (5.10.2)$$

where

$$R(t) = [Q(t)/L(t)^\alpha]^{1/(1-\alpha)}$$

by using extraneous estimates of α and δ to construct a time series for $(\Delta R + \delta R)/I$ where ΔR is a first difference approximation to the derivative $dR(t)/dt$.

(a) Indicate how the estimating equation (5.10.2) can be derived from (5.10.1).

(b) How satisfactory is this procedure for estimating λ? Can you suggest any improvements?

2. SUPPLEMENTARY QUESTIONS

Question 5.11

The observable random variables $y_t\,(t = 1, \ldots, T)$ and non-random quantities $x_{it}\,(i = 1, 2, 3; t = 1, \ldots, T)$ satisfy the relation

$$y_t = a_1 x_{1t} + a_2 x_{2t} + a_3 x_{3t} + u_t \qquad (5.11.1)$$

where u_t is a serially independent random disturbance with the same distribution for all t in which $E(u_t) = 0$ and $E(u_t^2) = \sigma^2$. The parameters a_1 and a_2 are known to satisfy the restriction

$$a_1 a_2 = a_3 \qquad (5.11.2)$$

It is assumed that the x_{it} are bounded and the sample second moment matrix of the x_{it} is non-singular and tends to a non-singular matrix $\bar{M}$ as the sample size $T \to \infty$.

(a) Suggest a procedure for obtaining estimates $\hat{\alpha}_1$, $\hat{\alpha}_2$ and $\hat{\alpha}_3$ of the parameters in (5.11.1) that satisfy the restriction (5.11.2) and are such that the $\sqrt{T}(\hat{a}_i - a_i)$ have limiting normal distributions whose variances are at least as small as those of the limiting distributions of the $\sqrt{T}(a_i^* - a_i)$, where the a_i^* are the ordinary least squares estimates of the a_i.

(b) Compare the variances of the limiting distributions of $\sqrt{T}(\hat{a}_1 - a_1)$ and $\sqrt{T}(a_1^* - a_1)$ when $a_1 = 2$, $a_2 = \frac{1}{2}$, $a_3 = 1$ and

$$\bar{M} = \begin{array}{c} \\ x_1 \\ x_2 \\ x_3 \end{array} \begin{array}{ccc} x_1 & x_2 & x_3 \\ \left[\begin{array}{ccc} 1 & 0 & 0 \\ 0 & 2 & 1 \\ 0 & 1 & 1 \end{array}\right] \end{array}.$$

Question 5.12

The unobservable non-random variables y_t^* and x_t^* $(t = 1, \ldots, T)$ satisfy exactly the relation

$$y_t^* = \beta x_t^*$$

where β is an unknown parameter. The observable random quantities y_t and x_t $(t = 1, \ldots, T)$ are known to be related to y_t^* and x_t^* respectively but involve measurement errors, so that

$$y_t = y_t^* + u_t \quad \text{and} \quad x_t = x_t^* + v_t$$

where u_t and v_t $(t = 1, \ldots, T)$ are random errors for which

$$E(u_t) = E(v_t) = 0 \qquad (t = 1, \ldots, T)$$
$$E(u_t^2) = E(v_t^2) = \sigma^2 \qquad (t = 1, \ldots, T)$$

and

$$E(u_t u_s) = 0 \qquad (t \neq s)$$

Show that the estimator of β defined by

$$b = \sum_{t=1}^{T} y_t x_t \Big/ \sum_{t=1}^{T} x_t^2$$

tends in probability to β as

$$s_{xx}^* = \sum_{t=1}^{T} x_t^{*2}$$

tends to infinity while T and σ^2 remain fixed. Comment on the significance of this result.

Question 5.13

An investigator wishes to estimate the model

$$y = X\beta + W\gamma + u \tag{5.13.1}$$

where y is a $T \times 1$ vector of observations on the endogenous variable, X is a matrix of observations on k non-random exogenous variables, W is a vector of values of another exogenous variable which is non-random but also unobservable and $u = (u_t)$ is a vector of random disturbances.

It is proposed to estimate the parameter vector β in (5.13.1) by two different methods:
(a) by omitting the unobservable variable W in (5.13.1) and regressing y on X to obtain $\hat{\beta}$;
(b) by introducing an observable proxy variable P for W and regressing y on X and P to obtain $\tilde{\beta}$, the vector of estimated coefficients of the k variables in X.

It is assumed that P is related to W by the equation

$$P = W\theta + v$$

where θ is an unknown parameter and $v = (v_t)$ is a vector of disturbances. It is further assumed that u and v are independent and

$$E(u_t) = E(v_t) = 0 \qquad (t = 1, \ldots, T)$$

$$\left.\begin{array}{l} E(u_t^2) = \sigma^2 \\ E(v_t^2) = \sigma_v^2 \end{array}\right\} \qquad (t = 1, \ldots, T)$$

$$E(u_t u_s) = E(v_t v_s) = 0 \qquad (t \neq s).$$

If

$$M_{XX} = \lim_{T \to \infty} \frac{X'X}{T}, M_{WW} = \lim_{T \to \infty} \frac{W'W}{T}, M_{XW} = \lim_{T \to \infty} \frac{X'W}{T}$$

are all finite and in addition $M_{WW} > 0$ and M_{XX} is positive definite, show that

$$\plim_{T \to \infty} (\hat{\beta} - \beta) = M_{XX}^{-1} M_{XW} \gamma$$

and

$$\plim_{T \to \infty} (\tilde{\beta} - \beta) = \frac{\sigma_V^2}{\theta^2 M_{WW}(1 - R_{WX}^2) + \sigma_V^2} M_{XX}^{-1} M_{XW} \gamma$$

where R_{WX}^2 is the limit in probability of the coefficient of determination in the auxiliary regression of W on X.

What conclusion can you draw from the large sample bias of $\hat{\beta}$ and $\tilde{\beta}$?

(Reference: Wickens, 1972; see also McCallum, 1972 and Aigner, 1975).

Question 5.14

In the system

$$Y_{1t} = \beta_1 X_{1t} + u_{1t}$$

$$Y_{2t} = \beta_2 X_{2t} + u_{2t}$$

$\{Y_{1t}, X_{1t}: t = 1, \ldots, T\}$ and $\{Y_{2t}, X_{2t}: t = 1, \ldots, T\}$ are true values of the same economic variables (Y and X) for two different microeconomic units 1 and 2, respectively. The $u_{it} (i = 1, 2; t = 1, \ldots, T)$ are random disturbances and the $\beta_i (i = 1, 2)$ are unknown parameters. Both X and Y are measured with error and the measured values of these variables are, for the two units,

$$y_{1t} = Y_{1t} + w_t \quad x_{1t} = X_{1t} + v_t \qquad (t = 1, \ldots, T)$$

and

$$y_{2t} = Y_{2t} - w_t \quad x_{2t} = X_{2t} - v_t \qquad (t = 1, \ldots, T)$$

where $w_t (t = 1, \ldots, T)$ and $v_t (t = 1, \ldots, T)$ are random measurement errors.

It is assumed that the X_{it} are non-random and that the second moment matrix

$$\frac{1}{T}\begin{bmatrix} \sum_{t=1}^{T} X_{1t}^2 & \sum_{t=1}^{T} X_{1t}X_{2t} \\ \sum_{t=1}^{T} X_{2t}X_{1t} & \sum_{t=1}^{T} X_{2t}^2 \end{bmatrix}$$

tends, as $T \to \infty$, to the positive definite matrix

$$\begin{bmatrix} m_{11} & m_{12} \\ m_{21} & m_{22} \end{bmatrix}.$$

The disturbances u_{it} are serially independent and for each value of t have the same distribution with $E(u_{it}) = 0\,(i = 1, 2)$, $E(u_{1t}^2) = \sigma_1^2$, $E(u_{1t}u_{2t}) = \sigma_{12}$ and $E(u_{2t}^2) = \sigma_2^2$. The measurement errors w_t and v_t are also serially independent and for each value of t have the same distribution with $E(w_t) = 0$, $E(w_t^2) = \sigma_w^2$, $E(v_t) = 0$ and $E(v_t^2) = \sigma_v^2$, respectively. It is further assumed that w_t and v_t are mutually independent and independent of the u_{it}.

If b_i is the coefficient in the regression of the y_{it} on the x_{it} $(i = 1, 2)$ and b is the coefficient in the regression of the aggregate variables $y_{1t} + y_{2t}$ on the aggregate variables $x_{1t} + x_{2t}$ verify that

$$\plim_{T \to \infty} b_i = \frac{\beta_i m_{ii}}{m_{ii} + \sigma_v^2} \qquad (i = 1, 2)$$

and

$$\plim_{T \to \infty} b = \gamma\beta_1 + (1 - \gamma)\beta_2$$

where

$$\gamma = \frac{m_{11} + m_{12}}{m_{11} + m_{22} + 2m_{12}}$$

(a) Do these results suggest that macro-equation regressions offer any advantages over micro-equation regressions when the micro-variables are subject to measurement error?

(b) Comment on any simplifications in the structure of the model that you may feel are unrealistic.

(Reference for an extensive analysis of this type of model: Aigner and Goldfeld, 1974)

Question 5.15

For the equation

$$y = X\beta + u \tag{5.15.1}$$

where $E(X'u) = 0$ and u is $N(0, \sigma^2 I_T)$, the set of available observations on X is the $T \times k$ matrix X^* with

$$X^* = X + V \tag{5.15.2}$$

$E(V) = 0$, $T^{-1}E(VV') = \Omega$ which is positive definite, $E(X'V) = 0$ and $E(V'u) = 0$.

(a) Show that the regression of y on X^* yields an inconsistent estimator of β.

(b) It is known that the X matrix satisfies

$$X = Z\pi'$$

where the $T \times n$ matrix Z is observable, $(T > n > k)$ and π is a $k \times n$ matrix of unknown coefficients. Show that a regression of X^* on Z yields a consistent estimator of π and hence obtain a consistent estimator $\hat{\Omega}$ of Ω. Derive an instrumental variable estimator $\hat{\beta}$ of β and if $\lim_{T \to \infty}(Z'Z/T)$ exists and is non-singular, prove that $\hat{\beta}$ is consistent for β.

(c) Show that

$$\frac{X^{*\prime}X^*}{T} = \hat{\pi}\left(\frac{Z'Z}{T}\right)\hat{\pi}' + \hat{\Omega}$$

and hence prove that

$$\hat{\beta} = (T^{-1}X^{*\prime}X^* - \hat{\Omega})^{-1}T^{-1}X^{*\prime}y$$

yields a consistent estimator of β.

(University of London BSc (Econ) examinations, 1977.)

Question 5.16

Consider the data generation process given by

$$y_t = \beta x_t + u_{1t} \qquad (t = 1, \ldots, T) \tag{5.16.1}$$

$$x_t = \gamma z_t + u_{2t} \tag{5.16.2}$$

where $E(x_t u_{1t}) = \alpha \neq 0$, $E(z_t u_{1t}) = E(z_t u_{2t}) = 0$, the z_t are independent $N(0, \delta)$, the u_{it} are independent $N(0, \sigma_{ii})$ for all t and $E(u_{1t}u_{2t}) = \alpha$.

(a) Derive the following population moments as functions of the parameters $(\alpha, \beta, \gamma, \delta, \sigma_{11}, \sigma_{22})$

$$E(z_t^2), \quad E(x_t^2), \quad E(x_t z_t),$$

$$E(y_t^2), \quad E(y_t x_t) \quad \text{and} \quad E(y_t z_t).$$

(b) Describe appropriate functions of these six population moments which are equal to each of the six parameters respectively. Explain how consistent estimators of these six parameters can be obtained using sample data.

(c) Let $x_t^* = x_t - kz_t$, where $k = E(x_t^2)/E(x_tz_t) = \text{plim}(\Sigma x_t^2/\Sigma x_tz_t)$, then show that $\hat{\alpha} = (1/T)\Sigma x_t^* y_t = (1/T)\Sigma x_t^* u_{1t}$ is a consistent estimator of α.
(d) Derive the limiting distribution of $\sqrt{T}\hat{\alpha}$ when $\alpha = 0$. [Note: $E(x_t u_{1t})$ $= 0$ if $\alpha = 0$].

(University of London BSc (Econ) examinations, 1977.)

3. SOLUTIONS

Solution 5.1

The given model (5.1.1) is a non-linear regression model with additive disturbances and the estimator $\alpha_T(S)$ is known as a minimum distance estimator of α^0. The asymptotic theory of regression in this type of model is developed in Malinvaud (1970a) and Jennrich (1969) and an excellent general treatment of the problem of statistical inference in non-linear regression models is given in Chapter 9 of Malinvaud (1970b). More recently, this type of model has been the subject of further discussion in Gallant (1975a and 1975b), Phillips (1976) and Barnett (1976). Our own discussion in this solution will touch on a number of aspects of the problem considered in these references but the reader is urged to consult these references for a complete discussion. It will be assumed that the reader is familiar with some of the basic concepts in modern analysis (such as neighbourhoods, closed sets, compactness and the notion of an infimum and supremum) and for further reference here the books by Rudin (1964) and Dieudonné (1969) are recommended.

Malinvaud (1970b) gives a simple and direct result in which $\alpha_T(S)$ is consistent under the following condition:

Condition 5.1.A *For every closed set ω which does not contain α^0*

(i) $P[\inf_{\alpha \in \omega} Q_T(\alpha) = 0]$ *tends to zero as* $T \to \infty$; *and*

(ii) $P\left(\sup_{\alpha \in \omega}\left\{\dfrac{1}{Q_T(\alpha)} \sum_{t=1}^{T} [g_t(\alpha) - g_t(\alpha^0)]'Su_t\right\} \geqslant \tfrac{1}{2}\right)$ *tends to zero*

   as $T \to \infty$, *where* $Q_T(\alpha) = \sum_{t=1}^{T} [g_t(\alpha) - g_t(\alpha^0)]' S [g_t(\alpha) - g_t(\alpha^0)]$.

Despite its generality, Malinvaud's result that $\alpha_T(S)$ is consistent under condition 5.1.A is not very helpful as it stands. For it does not spell out *precise* conditions on the functions $g_t(\alpha)$ and the disturbances u_t which will ensure the consistency of $\alpha_T(S)$. Such conditions are however, given in the articles by Malinvaud (1970a) and Jennrich (1969), although the latter deals only with the scalar model.

If we wish to make our conditions on the model more explicit than

Condition 5.1.A above then we must first detail our assumptions about the disturbances u_t and the possible domain of the parameter vector α. Our remaining conditions then concern the systematic component $g_t(\alpha)$. We note that the elements of the vector function $g_t(\alpha)$ are functions of the exogenous variable vector x_t as well as α so that any conditions on $g_t(\alpha)$ will also imply some conditions on the exogenous variables. We can now adopt an indirect approach involving conditions on the sequence of functions $g_t(\alpha)$ or a direct approach detailing sufficient conditions on the exogenous variable sequence x_t. Malinvaud (1970a) uses both approaches and this is one of the reasons why his article is so valuable. Jennrich (1969) uses the indirect approach and his elegant treatment of the problem has formed the basis of much later work (Hannan, 1971, Robinson, 1972, Phillips, 1976). As might be expected the indirect approach leads to simpler and more general conditions on the model.

Using the indirect approach, we note from Phillips (1976), that the following two conditions are sufficient for the consistency of $\alpha_T(S)$ in the present case:

Condition 5.1.B *(i) α^0 lies in a compact set Φ in p-dimensional Euclidean space.*
(ii) The disturbance vectors $\{u_t : t = 1, 2, \ldots\}$ are stochastically independent and identically distributed with zero mean and positive definite covariance matrix Ω.
(iii) The elements of $g_t(\ )$ are continuous functions on Φ.

Condition 5.1.C

(i) $\displaystyle \lim_{T \to \infty} \frac{1}{T} \sum_{t=1}^{T} g_t(\alpha) \, g_t(\beta)'$ *exists and the convergence is uniform*

for all $\alpha, \beta \in \Phi$.

(ii) $\displaystyle \lim_{T \to \infty} \frac{1}{T} \sum_{t=1}^{T} [g_t(\alpha) - g_t(\alpha^0)] \, [g_t(\alpha) - g_t(\alpha^0)]'$ *is positive definite*

for all $\alpha \neq \alpha^0$ in Φ.

Conditions 5.1.B and 5.1.C are, in fact, sufficient to establish that

$$P[\lim_{T \to \infty} \alpha_T(S) = \alpha^0] = 1 \tag{5.1.2}$$

(for a proof along the Jennrich lines see Phillips, 1976). This means that the sequence $\alpha_T(S)$ converges to α^0 with probability one; and (5.1.2) is a stronger result than

$$\underset{T \to \infty}{\text{plim}} \ \alpha_T(S) = \alpha^0 \tag{5.1.3}$$

Remark The concept behind convergence with probability one (or almost sure convergence as it is sometimes called) is discussed, for instance, in

Rao (1973, p. 110). The fact that this type of convergence implies convergence in probability [i.e. that (5.1.2) implies (5.1.3) in the present case] is demonstrated in the same reference. As Rao points out, the concept that underlies (5.1.2) is more profound than that underlying (5.1.3). For (5.1.2) tells us that those sequences $\{\alpha_T(S)\}$ which do not converge to α^0 (in the ordinary sense) have zero probability in the space of all realisations $\{y_1, y_2, \dots\}$ of the y_t process.

Turning to discuss Conditions 5.1.B and 5.1.C we see that 5.1.B is fairly conventional: 5.1.B (ii) is a classical assumption on the errors in the model; whereas 5.1.B (i) and 5.1.B (iii) ensure that the estimator $\alpha_T(S)$ exists and is a properly defined random vector (Lemma 2 in Jennrich, 1969). Condition 5.1.C involves the sequence of functions $g_t(\alpha)$ and, therefore, implicitly imposes conditions on the components of the model which make up the systematic part $g_t(\alpha)$. Moreover, part (ii) of Condition 5.1.C involves the identifiability of α^0 in $\{g_t(\alpha^0); t = 1, 2, \dots\}$. We can illustrate the implications of 5.1.C (i) and 5.1.C (ii) by taking the simple model in which

$$g_t(\alpha^0) = A(\alpha^0) x_t \qquad (5.1.4)$$

and $A(\alpha^0)$ is an $n \times m$ matrix whose elements are continuous functions of the more basic set of parameters α^0. Then, the following new condition is sufficient to ensure that 5.1.C (i) holds.

Condition 5.1.D

$$\lim \frac{1}{T} \sum_{t=1}^{T} x_t x_t' = \bar{M}_{xx} \text{ exists and is positive definite.}$$

Turning to 5.1.C (ii), we note that under (5.1.4)

$$\lim_{T \to \infty} \frac{1}{T} \sum \left[g_t(\alpha) - g_t(\alpha^0)\right] \left[g_t(\alpha) - g_t(\alpha^0)\right]'$$

$$= \left[A(\alpha) - A(\alpha^0)\right] \lim_{T \to \infty} \frac{1}{T} \sum_{t=1}^{T} x_t x_t' \left[A(\alpha) - A(\alpha^0)\right]'$$

$$= \left[A(\alpha) - A(\alpha^0)\right] \bar{M}_{xx} \left[A(\alpha) - A(\alpha^0)\right]' \qquad (5.1.5)$$

Now, when Condition 5.1.C (ii) holds, the matrix (5.1.5) is a zero matrix *only when* $\alpha = \alpha^0$. This means that if $\bar{M}_{xx}$ is non-singular (as it is under Condition 5.1.D) then the equation

$$A(\alpha) - A(\alpha^0) = 0$$

implies that $\alpha = \alpha^0$. In other words, the equation $A(\alpha) = A(\alpha^0)$ has the unique solution $\alpha = \alpha^0$; and the parameter vector α^0 is identifiable in the coefficient matrix A.

Details of direct conditions on the exogenous variables which, together with Condition 5.1.B, are sufficient for the consistency of $\alpha_T(S)$ are discussed in Malinvaud (1970a) and Gallant (1975). The main ideas behind these conditions are outlined in Malinvaud (1970b) p. 331.

Final Remarks
(a) Frequently we will be interested in estimators of the same type as $\alpha_t(S)$ but which minimise

$$\sum_{t=1}^{T} [y_t - g_t(\alpha)]' S_T [y_t - g_t(\alpha)]$$

where the matrix S_T is positive definite and dependent on T in such a way that S_T converges to a positive definite matrix S as $T \to \infty$. If $S_T \to S$ with probability one, then we have the same result for $\alpha_T(S_T)$ as for $\alpha_T(S)$ when Conditions 5.1.B and 5.1.C are satisfied (c.f. Phillips, 1976).
(b) Condition 5.1.C (ii) is stronger than is really necessary. To see this we need only consider the following two-equation model:

$$y_{1t} = \alpha x_{1t} + u_{1t} \tag{5.1.6}$$

$$y_{2t} = \alpha^2 x_{1t} + u_{2t} \tag{5.1.7}$$

5.1.C (ii) is now not satisfied because the matrix

$$\lim_{T \to \infty} \frac{1}{T} \sum_{t=1}^{T} [g_t(\alpha) \quad g_t(\alpha^0)]' [g_t(\alpha) - g_t(\alpha^0)]'$$

is in this case (under 5.1.D) just

$$m \begin{bmatrix} \alpha - \alpha^0 \\ \alpha^2 - \alpha^{02} \end{bmatrix} [\alpha - \alpha^0, \alpha^2 - \alpha^{02}]$$

where $m = \lim_{T \to \infty} T^{-1} \sum_{t=1}^{T} x_{1t}^2$. This matrix has rank unity and is not positive definite. On the other hand, it is a zero matrix *only when* $\alpha = \alpha^0$ and the estimator $\alpha_T(S)$ is certainly consistent [note also that an ordinary least squares regression on (5.1.6) will produce a consistent estimator but will neglect the information about the parameter α that is contained in (5.1.7)].

We can, in fact, replace condition 5.1.C (ii) by the alternative weaker condition 5.1.C (ii)*:

$$\lim_{T \to \infty} T^{-1} \sum_{t=1}^{T} [g_t(\alpha) - g_t(\alpha^0)] [g_t(\alpha) - g_t(\alpha^0)]'$$

is positive semi-definite for all $\alpha \neq \alpha^0$ in Φ and is a zero matrix only when $\alpha = \alpha^0$.

The result we gave earlier in (5.1.2) still holds.

Solution 5.2

Part (a) Since $u_1, u_2, \ldots, u_T$ are independent and normally distributed, their joint probability densisty is given by

$$\frac{1}{(2\pi)^{nT/2} [\det(\Omega)]^{T/2}} \exp\left(-\tfrac{1}{2} \sum_{t=1}^{T} u_t' \Omega^{-1} u_t\right) \qquad (5.2.1)$$

From (5.2.1) we derive the joint density of the endogenous variables $y_1, y_2, \ldots, y_T$ first by replacing u_t in (5.2.1) by its definition in terms of y_t [i.e. $u_t = y_t - g_t(\alpha^0)$] ; in Solution 5.1 we used the superscript in α^0 to emphasise the true position of α in the parameter space. In most cases, this will not be necessary and we will often drop the superscript. We then multiply (5.2.1) by the Jacobian of the transformation of the u_t into the y_t. Since

$$\frac{\partial u_t}{\partial y_t'} = I_n \quad \text{and} \quad \frac{\partial u_t}{\partial y_s'} = 0 \qquad (t \neq s)$$

the Jacobian is unity and the joint density of $y_1, \ldots, y_T$ is

$$\frac{1}{(2\pi)^{nT/2} [\det(\Omega)]^{T/2}} \exp\left\{-\tfrac{1}{2} \sum_{t=1}^{T} [y_t - g_t(\alpha)]' \Omega^{-1} [y_t - g_t(\alpha)]\right\}.$$

$$(5.2.2)$$

For given data on the variables, (5.2.2) considered as a function of the parameters contained in α and Ω is called the likelihood function. The maximum likelihood estimators of α and Ω are then obtained by maximising this function (or, equivalently, its logarithm) with respect to α and Ω. We write the logarithm of the likelihood function as

$$L(\alpha, \Omega) = -\frac{nT}{2} \ln(2\pi) - \frac{T}{2} \ln[\det(\Omega)]$$

$$-\tfrac{1}{2} \sum_{t=1}^{T} [y_t - g_t(\alpha)]' \Omega^{-1} [y_t - g_t(\alpha)]$$

$$= -\frac{nT}{2} \ln(2\pi) - \frac{T}{2} \ln[\det(\Omega)] - \frac{T}{2} \operatorname{tr}(\Omega^{-1} M)$$

where
$$M = (1/T) \sum_{t=1}^{T} [y_t - g_t(\alpha)] [y_t - g_t(\alpha)]'.$$

Thus maximising $L(\alpha, \Omega)$ is equivalent to minimising

$$\bar{L}(\alpha, \Omega) = \ln[\det(\Omega)] + \operatorname{tr}(\Omega^{-1} M) \qquad (5.2.3)$$

We can do this sequentially by first fixing α and minimising with respect to Ω. The resulting value of Ω will then itself be dependent on α and can be substituted back into $\bar{L}$ to give a function concentrated in terms of α.

This process is called concentrating the likelihood function and the justification of this stepwise procedure can be found in Koopmans and Hood (1953, pp. 156–158).

Differentiating (5.2.3) with respect to the elements ω_{ij} of Ω we obtain

$$\frac{\partial \bar{L}}{\partial \omega_{ij}} = \text{tr}\left(\Omega^{-1} \frac{\partial \Omega}{\partial \omega_{ij}}\right) - \text{tr}\left(\Omega^{-1} \frac{\partial \Omega}{\partial \omega_{ij}} \Omega^{-1} M\right) \tag{5.2.4}$$

$$(i, j = 1, \ldots, n)$$

Remark The right hand side of (5.2.4) is obtained by using the following two rules from matrix calculus:

Let $A = A(\lambda)$ be a square non-singular matrix of order n whose elements are differentiable functions of a scalar λ. Then

(i) $\dfrac{\partial}{\partial \lambda} [A^{-1}(\lambda)] = -A^{-1}(\lambda) \left[\dfrac{\partial A(\lambda)}{\partial \lambda}\right] A^{-1}(\lambda)$

and

(ii) $\dfrac{\partial}{\partial \lambda} \ln [\det A(\lambda)] = \text{tr}\left[A^{-1}(\lambda) \dfrac{\partial A(\lambda)}{\partial \lambda}\right]$

Rule (i) is established, for instance, in Malinvaud (1970b, pp. 196–197). There are a number of alternative forms of Rule (ii) in popular use (c.f. Fisk, 1967, pp. 147–148) but since these can cause confusion when A is symmetric as it is here, we outline the derivation of Rule (ii) in Appendix B (the reader is also referred to the helpful remarks in Theil, 1971, p. 32). Returning now to (5.2.4) we have

$$\frac{\partial \bar{L}}{\partial \omega_{ij}} = \text{tr}\left(\frac{\partial \Omega}{\partial \omega_{ij}} \Omega^{-1}\right) - \text{tr}\left(\frac{\partial \Omega}{\partial \omega_{ij}} \Omega^{-1} M \Omega^{-1}\right)$$

$$= \text{tr}\left[\frac{\partial \Omega}{\partial \omega_{ij}} (\Omega^{-1} - \Omega^{-1} M \Omega^{-1})\right]$$

From the symmetry of Ω we note that when $i \neq j$

$$\left(\frac{\partial \Omega}{\partial \omega_{ij}}\right)_{rs} = \begin{cases} 1 & \text{if } r = i, \quad s = j \\ 1 & \text{if } r = j, \quad s = i \\ 0 & \text{otherwise} \end{cases}$$

so that

$$\frac{\partial \bar{L}}{\partial \omega_{ij}} = (\Omega^{-1} - \Omega^{-1} M \Omega^{-1})_{ji} + (\Omega^{-1} - \Omega^{-1} M \Omega^{-1})_{ij}$$

$$= 2\,(\Omega^{-1} - \Omega^{-1}M\Omega^{-1})_{ij} \tag{5.2.5}$$

because of the symmetry of Ω^{-1} and M. When $i = j$ we have

$$\left(\frac{\partial \Omega}{\partial \omega_{ij}}\right)_{rs} = \begin{cases} 1 & \text{if } r = s = i \\ 0 & \text{otherwise} \end{cases}$$

so that

$$\frac{\partial \bar{L}}{\partial \omega_{ij}} = (\Omega^{-1} - \Omega^{-1}M\Omega^{-1})_{ii} \tag{5.2.6}$$

Setting the first order derivatives of $\bar{L}$ equal to zero, it follows from (5.2.5) and (5.2.6) that

$$\hat{\Omega}^{-1} = \hat{\Omega}^{-1}M\hat{\Omega}^{-1}$$

and hence the matrix

$$\hat{\Omega} = M$$

satisfies the first order conditions for a minimum of $\bar{L}$. The fact that $\bar{L}$ is a minimum for this value of $\hat{\Omega}$ is proved by Malinvaud (1970b, p. 339). Substituting $\hat{\Omega} = M$ into (5.2.3) we obtain the concentrated function

$$L^*(\alpha) = \ln\,[\det(M)] + n \tag{5.2.7}$$

The maximum likelihood estimator of α is now obtained by minimising (5.2.7) with respect to α and it is clear that the same result is obtained by minimising $\ln[\det(M)]$, which we were required to prove.

Part (b) If $\hat{\alpha}$ is the maximum likelihood estimator of α then from Part (a) we know that $\hat{\alpha}$ minimises $\ln[\det(M)]$; and the maximum likelihood estimator of Ω is

$$\hat{\Omega} = \frac{1}{T} \sum_{t=1}^{T} [y_t - g_t(\hat{\alpha})]\,[y_t - g_t(\hat{\alpha})]'. \tag{5.2.8}$$

By definition the pair $(\hat{\alpha}, \hat{\Omega})$ maximises $L(\alpha, \Omega)$, the logarithm of the likelihood function. Moreover, $\hat{\alpha}$ maximises $L(\alpha, \Omega)$ when $\Omega = \hat{\Omega}$. From the form of $L(\alpha, \Omega)$ it then follows that $\hat{\alpha}$ minimises

$$\sum_{t=1}^{T} [y_t - g_t(\alpha)]'\,\hat{\Omega}^{-1}\,[y_t - g_t(\alpha)] \tag{5.2.9}$$

In other words $\hat{\alpha} = \alpha_T(\hat{\Omega}^{-1})$ in the notation of question 5.1. Hence, $\hat{\alpha}$ can be regarded as a minimum distance estimator of α in which the distance or metric is defined by the matrix $\hat{\Omega}$.

However, this representation of $\hat{\alpha}$ is not very useful in determining the properties of $\hat{\alpha}$; and, in particular, in verifying that $\hat{\alpha}$ is consistent. For, $\hat{\Omega}$

itself depends on $\hat{\alpha}$ and, thus, in the absence of an independent theory which explains the behaviour of $\hat{\alpha}$ when T becomes large we cannot infer the asymptotic behaviour of the random matrix $\hat{\Omega}$. The latter is necessary if we are to appeal to the consistency of minimum distance estimators (recall our Final Remark (a) in Solution 5.1 above). Fortunately, an independent asymptotic theory for $\hat{\alpha}$ is readily available (see Phillips, 1976); in particular, we know that, under Conditions 5.1.B and 5.1.C which we discussed in Solution 5.1, $\hat{\alpha}$ converges to α^0 almost surely (and hence in probability) as $T \to \infty$.

We can also compare the pair of maximum likelihood estimators $(\hat{\alpha}, \hat{\Omega})$ with the pair of estimators obtained from the following iteration:
  (i) Find the minimum distance estimator $\alpha_T(S)$ taking any positive definite matrix for S (such as the identity matrix I)
 (ii) Estimate the covariance matrix Ω by constructing the second moment matrix of the residuals from the regression in (i):

$$M_{uu}^* = T^{-1} \sum_{t=1}^{T} \{y_t - g_t[\alpha_T(S)]\} \{y_t - g_t[\alpha_T(S)]\}' \qquad (5.2.10)$$

(iii) Find the new minimum distance estimator

$$\alpha_T(M_{uu}^{*-1}) \qquad (5.2.11)$$

(iv) Return to (ii) and continue the iteration from (ii) to (iii) and back again to (ii) until the procedure has converged (that is, until successive estimates of α are numerically the same at a given level of tolerance).

The above procedure is known as the iterated minimum distance (or iterated generalised least squares) procedure. It was suggested in Malinvaud (1970, pp. 337–338) and has more recently been considered by Phillips (1976) and Barnett (1976). Malinvaud suggested that we can expect the iteration in (iv) to be convergent and also observed that, upon convergence, the estimators from this procedure share the same property of interdependence exhibited by the pair of maximum likelihood estimators $(\hat{\alpha}, \hat{\Omega})$. Indeed, if we denote the estimators that emerge from the iteration in (iv) by $(\alpha^{**}, \Omega^{**})$ we have from (5.2.10) that

$$\Omega^{**} = T^{-1} \sum_{t=1}^{T} [y_t - g_t(\alpha^{**})] [y_t - g_t(\alpha^{**})]'$$

and

$$\alpha^{**} = \alpha_T(\Omega^{**-1})$$

from (5.2.11). These considerations suggest that the iterated minimum distance procedure (i)–(iv) may well provide a convenient route to the estimators $(\hat{\alpha}, \hat{\Omega})$. But, for this to be so it is important that the iteration in (iv) be convergent and that the point of convergence α^{**} yields a global maximum of the concentrated likelihood function (or, equivalently, a global minimum of $L^*(\alpha)$ defined in (5.2.7) above). Regularity conditions under which this is indeed the case are given in the article by Phillips (1976). Moreover, when the procedure is convergent and this convergence holds uniformly in T (note that to obtain α^{**} the iteration in (iv) is needed for every sample size T) Barnett (1976) has shown that the consistency of the maximum likelihood estimator can be deduced from the consistency of the minimum distance estimators of α obtained at each stage of the iteration in (iv).

Remark We have in this solution concentrated on the consistency properties of maximum likelihood and minimum distance estimators. We will consider other asymptotic properties in our next question.

Question 5.3

Part (a) The asymptotic sampling properties of $\alpha_T (S_T)$ or more precisely the limiting distribution of $\sqrt{T}[\alpha_T (S_T) - \alpha^0]$ are discussed by Malinvaud (1970b, pp. 331–336). In the first place, we require $\alpha_T (S_T)$ to be a consistent estimator of α^0. To this end we can assume that Conditions 5.1.B and 5.1.C of Solution 5.1 hold. We remark in passing that if for some reason $\alpha_T (S_T)$ is not a consistent estimator of α [for instance, there may be a specification error in the systematic component $g_t(\alpha)$] then we may still be able to discuss the asymptotic sampling properties of $\alpha_T (S_T)$ but we will need more information before doing so (such as the true specification of the model if $g_t(\alpha)$ is misspecified) and we may need to impose stronger conditions on the disturbances (such as the existence of fourth order moments — compare Solution 6.10 below).

Following Malinvaud (1970b), we construct a matrix z_t whose i, jth element is

$$z_{ijt} = \partial g_{it}(\alpha^0)/\partial \alpha_j$$

and we let

$$M_T (S) = \frac{1}{T} \sum_{t=1}^{T} Z_t' S Z_t$$

for any positive definite matrix S. We now impose two further conditions:

Condition 5.3.A *The parameter space Φ contains a neighbourhood V^0 of the vector α^0 of the true parameter values.*

Condition 5.3.B
  (i) *In the neighbourhood V^0 of α^0 the functions $g_{it}(\alpha)$ and their first three derivatives are uniformly bounded.*
  (ii) *For any positive definite matrix S the matrix $M_T (S)$ is positive definite and has a positive definite limit $M(S)$ as $T \to \infty$.*

Under conditions 5.1.B, 5.1.C, 5.3.A and 5.3.B and given that the matrix S_T tends in probability to the positive definite matrix S, Malinvaud (1970b, pp. 334–335) proves that the vector

$$\sqrt{T}[\alpha_T(S_T) - \alpha^0]$$

has a limiting normal distribution as $T \to \infty$. The mean of this limiting distribution is the zero vector, and the covariance matrix is

$$[M(S)]^{-1} M(S\Omega S) [M(S)]^{-1} \tag{5.3.1}$$

Part (b) When $S = \Omega^{-1}$ (so that S_T converges in probability to Ω^{-1}) we see that (5.3.1) reduces to

$$[M(\Omega^{-1})]^{-1}$$

To prove that $\alpha_T(S_T)$ is asymptotically efficient in the class of minimum distance estimators when S_T tends to Ω^{-1} in probability we must show that

$$[M(S)]^{-1} M(S\Omega S) [M(S)]^{-1} - [M(\Omega^{-1})]^{-1} \tag{5.3.2}$$

is a positive semi-definite matrix. To do this we first define T matrices $\{A_\tau : \tau = 1, \ldots, T\}$ by the equations

$$\left(\frac{1}{T}\sum_{t=1}^{T} Z_t'SZ_t\right)^{-1} Z_\tau'S = \left(\frac{1}{T}\sum_{t=1}^{T} Z_t'\Omega^{-1}Z_t\right)^{-1} Z_\tau'\Omega^{-1} + A_\tau$$

$$(\tau = 1, \ldots, T)$$

When α has p components, A_τ has dimension $p \times n$ for all τ. We note that

$$\frac{1}{T}\sum_{t=1}^{T} A_\tau Z_\tau = 0 \tag{5.3.3}$$

and also that

$$\left[\left(\frac{1}{T}\sum_{t=1}^{T} Z_t'SZ_t\right)^{-1} Z_\tau'S\right] \Omega \left[SZ_\tau\left(\frac{1}{T}\sum_{t=1}^{T} Z_t'SZ_t\right)^{-1}\right]$$

$$= \left[\left(\frac{1}{T}\sum_{t=1}^{T} Z_t\Omega^{-1}Z_t\right)^{-1} Z_\tau'\Omega^{-1}\right] \Omega \left[\Omega^{-1}Z_\tau\left(\frac{1}{T}\sum_{t=1}^{T} Z_t'\Omega^{-1}Z_t\right)^{-1}\right]$$

$$+ \left(\frac{1}{T}\sum_{t=1}^{T} Z_t'\Omega^{-1}Z_t\right)^{-1} Z_\tau'\Omega^{-1}\Omega A_\tau'$$

$$+ A_\tau\Omega\Omega^{-1}Z_\tau\left(\frac{1}{T}\sum_{t=1}^{T} Z_t'\Omega^{-1}Z_t\right)^{-1} + A_\tau\Omega A_\tau'. \tag{5.3.4}$$

Hence, summing (5.3.4) over $\tau = 1, \ldots, T$, dividing through by T, and using (5.3.3) we obtain

$$[M_T(S)]^{-1} \, M_T(S\Omega S) \, [M_T(S)]^{-1} \; = \; [M_T(\Omega^{-1})]^{-1} + \frac{1}{T} \sum A_t \Omega A_t'$$

We now let K be a non-singular matrix for which $\Omega = KK'$. (This is possible since Ω is positive definite). Then for any non-zero vector d with p components we note that

$$d'\left(\frac{1}{T} \sum_{t=1}^{T} A_t \Omega A_t'\right) d \; = \; \frac{1}{T} \sum_{t=1}^{T} d' A_t \Omega A_t' d$$

$$= \; \frac{1}{T} \sum_{t=1}^{T} d' A_t KK' A_t' d$$

$$= \; \frac{1}{T} \sum b_t' b_t$$

where $b_t = K' A_t' d$. But

$$b_t' b_t \; = \; \sum_{i=1}^{n} b_{it}^2 \geqslant 0$$

where b_{it} denotes the ith component of b_t. It follows that

$$d'\left(\frac{1}{T} \sum_{t=1}^{T} A_t' \Omega A_t\right) d \geqslant 0$$

for any non-zero vector d and hence

$$[M_T(S)]^{-1} \, M_T(S\Omega S) \, [M_T(S)]^{-1} - [M_T(\Omega^{-1})]^{-1}$$

is positive semi-definite. This holds for all finite T and therefore,

$$\lim_{T \to \infty} d' \{[M_T(S)]^{-1} \, M_T(S\Omega S) \, [M_T(S)]^{-1} - [M_T(\Omega^{-1})]^{-1}\} d \geqslant 0.$$

$$(5.3.5)$$

That is, the limit of a sequence of non-negative numbers must be non-negative, if that limit is known to exist. Here, the limit exists since $M_T(S)$ and $M_T(\Omega^{-1})$ are known to have non singular limits by 5.3.B (ii). We can write (5.3.5) as

$$d' \, [M(S)]^{-1} \, M(S\Omega S) \, [M(S)]^{-1} \, d - d' \, [M(\Omega^{-1})]^{-1} \, d \geqslant 0$$

so that the matrix (5.3.2) is positive semi-definite. It follows that $\alpha_T(S_T)$ is asymptotically efficient in the minimum distance class when $S_T \to \Omega^{-1}$ in probability.

Remark The above use of the term asymptotically efficient is a little different from that in Solution 3.7. Here, we consider a very specific class of estimators with which we are comparing $\alpha_T(S_T)$, where S_T tends in probability to Ω^{-1} (that is, the class of minimum distance estimators $\alpha_T(S_T)$ for which S_T tends in probability to an arbitrary positive definite matrix S). If we assume, however, that the disturbances u_t in the model (5.1.1) are normally distributed, then the estimator $\alpha_T(S_T)$, where $S_T \to \Omega^{-1}$ in probability, is asymptotically efficient in a more general class of estimators. It is, indeed, best asymptotically normal in the sense (and with the associated limitations of the definition) discussed in Solution 3.7. We need only verify that the asymptotic covariance matrix

$$[M(\Omega^{-1})]^{-1}$$

attains the limit of the Cramér-Rao (matrix) lower bound. That this is so is shown in Malinvaud (1970b, pp. 340–341).

Solution 5.4

Part (a) The model (5.4.1) is a single equation example of the general constrained linear model

$$y_t = A(\alpha^0) x_t + u_t \qquad (t = 1, \ldots, T) \tag{5.4.3}$$

where y_t is a vector of n endogenous variables, x_t is a vector of m exogenous variables and $A(\alpha^0)$ is a parameter matrix whose elements are functions of the basic parameter vector α, whose true value is denoted by α^0.

The model (5.4.3) is discussed in detail by Malinvaud (1970b, pp. 348–360). In particular, Malinvaud proves in his Theorem 3 on page 350 that, if S_T is a positive definite matrix which tends in probability to a positive definite matrix S, then the estimator $\alpha_T(S_T)$ which minimises

$$\sum_{t=1}^{T} [y_t - A(\alpha)x_t]' S_T [y_t - A(\alpha)x_t] \tag{5.4.4}$$

is a consistent estimator of α^0 provided the following conditions hold:

Condition 5.4.A (Malinvaud's Assumption 1 on page 331) *The disturbance vectors $u_t (t = 1, \ldots, T)$ are independently and identically distributed with zero mean vector and non-singular covariance matrix Ω.*

Condition 5.4.B (Malinvaud's Assumption 4 on page 349) *The exogenous variable vectors $x_t (t = 1, \ldots, T)$ are non-random bounded quantities for which the matrix $(1/T) \sum_{t=1}^{T} x_t x_t'$ is non-singular and tends to a non singular limit as $T \to \infty$.*

Condition 5.4.C (Malinvaud's Assumption 5 on page 349) $A^0 = A(\alpha^0)$ and α_T *is a sequence of vectors for which $A(\alpha_T)$ converges to A^0 then α_T converges to α^0.*

We see from the assumption made about the u_t and the x_{it} in (5.4.1) that Conditions 5.4.A and 5.4.B are both satisfied in the present case. Condition 5.4.C is essentially concerned with the identifiability of the true vector α^0 in the matrix $A^0 = A(\alpha^0)$. For, let us suppose there was a vector $\alpha^* \neq \alpha^0$ for which $A(\alpha^*) = A^0$. The vectors α^* and α^0 would then be indistinguishable in the true coefficient matrix A^0 and we would not be able to identify α^0 as the true vector. To show that this contradicts Condition 5.4.C we need only select the sequence $\alpha_T = \alpha^* (T = 1, 2, \ldots ,)$. For, $A(\alpha_T)$ then equals A^0 for all T and $A(\alpha_T)$ converges to A^0 as $T \rightarrow \infty$. But, since $\alpha_T \rightarrow \alpha^*$ as $T \rightarrow \infty$ and $\alpha^* \neq \alpha^0$ this contradicts Condition 5.4.C. Hence, if 5.4.C is to be satisfied it is necessary that α^0 is identifiable in the true coefficient matrix A^0.

In the present case $A(\alpha)$ is the vector

$$A(\alpha) = (\alpha, e^\alpha) \tag{5.4.5}$$

so that if $A(\alpha_T)$ converges to $A^0 = A(\alpha^0)$ it follows that

$$\alpha_T \rightarrow \alpha^0 \quad \text{and} \quad \exp \alpha_T \rightarrow \exp \alpha^0$$

Hence, Condition 5.4.C is satisfied in this case; and, therefore, $\hat{\alpha}$ is a consistent estimator of α^0 in (5.4.1).

Part (b) In the new model (5.4.2) the vector x_t of (5.4.3) is now

$$x_t' = (1, t)$$

and therefore

$$T^{-1} \sum_{t=1}^{T} x_t x_t' = T^{-1} \sum_{t=1}^{T} \begin{bmatrix} 1 & t \\ t & t^2 \end{bmatrix}$$

$$= \frac{1}{T} \begin{bmatrix} T & T(T+1)/2 \\ T(T+1)/2 & T(T+1)(2T+1)/6 \end{bmatrix}$$

Although M_{xx} is non-singular for fixed T it is clear that this matrix does not converge to a finite matrix as $T \rightarrow \infty$. Thus, Condition 5.4.B is not satisfied and if we are to establish that the estimator $\hat{\alpha}$ is consistent, we cannot rely directly on Malinvaud's Theorem 3 on page 350, as we did in Part (a). However, what we can do is appeal directly to Condition 5.1.A, which as we have seen in Solution 5.1 is sufficient to ensure that $\hat{\alpha}$ is consistent.

First of all we define

$$Q_T(\alpha) = \sum_{t=1}^{T} (\alpha + (\exp \alpha)t - \alpha^0 - (\exp \alpha^0)t)^2$$

$$= \sum_{t=1}^{T} \left\{ [\alpha - \alpha^0, \exp \alpha - \exp \alpha^0] \begin{bmatrix} 1 \\ t \end{bmatrix} \right\}^2$$

$$= \sum_{t=1}^{T} [\alpha - \alpha^0, \exp \alpha - \exp \alpha^0] \begin{bmatrix} 1 \\ t \end{bmatrix} [1, t] \begin{bmatrix} \alpha - \alpha^0 \\ \exp \alpha - \exp \alpha^0 \end{bmatrix}$$

$$= [\alpha - \alpha^0, \exp \alpha - \exp \alpha^0]$$

$$\begin{bmatrix} T & \frac{1}{2}T(T+1) \\ \frac{1}{2}T(T+1) & \frac{1}{6}T(T+1)(2T+1) \end{bmatrix} \begin{bmatrix} \alpha - \alpha^0 \\ \exp \alpha - \exp \alpha^0 \end{bmatrix} \quad (5.4.6)$$

and also

$$V_T(\alpha) = \frac{1}{Q_T(\alpha)} \sum_{t=1}^{T} [\alpha + (\exp \alpha)t - \alpha^0 - (\exp \alpha^0)t] \, u_t$$

$$= \frac{1}{Q_T(\alpha)} [\alpha - \alpha^0, \exp \alpha - \exp \alpha^0] \begin{bmatrix} \sum_{t=1}^{T} u_t \\ \sum_{t=1}^{T} t u_t \end{bmatrix} \quad (5.4.7)$$

Then $\hat{\alpha}$ will be consistent if we can verify that

(i) $P[\inf_{\alpha \in \omega} Q_T(\alpha) - 0] \to 0$ (as $T \to \infty$)

and

(ii) $P[\sup_{\alpha \in \omega} V_T(\alpha) \geq \frac{1}{2}] \to 0$ (as $T \to \infty$)

where ω is any closed set which does not contain α^0 (Malinvaud, 1970b, Lemma on p. 330).

To verify (i) we first note the representation of $Q_T(\alpha)$ as a quadratic form in (5.4.6). This gives us the inequality

$$Q_T(\alpha) \geq \lambda_T [\alpha - \alpha^0, \exp \alpha - \exp \alpha^0] \begin{bmatrix} \alpha - \alpha^0 \\ \exp \alpha - \exp \alpha^0 \end{bmatrix} \quad (5.4.8)$$

where λ_T is the smaller eigenvalue of the matrix

$$N_T = \begin{bmatrix} T & \frac{1}{2}T(T+1) \\ \frac{1}{2}T(T+1) & \frac{1}{6}T(T+1)(2T+1) \end{bmatrix} \quad (5.4.9)$$

Remark The inequality (5.4.8) follows from the fact that if x is an n-vector and A is a symmetric $n \times n$ matrix then

$$x'Ax \geq \lambda_m x'x \quad \text{for all } x$$

where λ_m is the smallest eigenvalue of A (see, for instance, Rao, 1973, p. 62). It now follows from (5.4.8) that

$$\inf_{\alpha \in \omega} Q_T(\alpha) \geqslant \lambda_T \inf_{\alpha \in \omega} [(\alpha - \alpha^0)^2 + (\exp \alpha - \exp \alpha^0)^2]$$

and, since ω is closed and does not contain α^0, we know that

$$\inf_{\alpha \in \omega} (\alpha - \alpha^0)^2 \geqslant \epsilon > 0$$

where ϵ is a small positive quantity. Then

$$P[\inf_{\alpha \in \omega} Q_T(\alpha) = 0] \leqslant P(\lambda_T \epsilon = 0) = P(\lambda_T = 0)$$

But $\lambda_T > 0$ for all $T > 1$ since the matrix (5.4.9) is positive definite for $T > 1$. Hence

$$P[\inf_{\alpha \in \omega} Q_T(\alpha) = 0] = 0 \qquad (T = 2, 3, \ldots)$$

and (i) is verified.

We now turn to (ii) and first of all introduce the matrix

$$D_T = \begin{bmatrix} T^{1/2} & 0 \\ 0 & T^{3/2} \end{bmatrix}$$

Using (5.4.6) and (5.4.9) we write $Q_T(\alpha)$ as

$$Q_T(\alpha) = [\alpha - \alpha^0, \exp \alpha - \exp \alpha^0] \, D_T D_T^{-1} N_T D_T^{-1} D_T$$

$$\times \begin{bmatrix} \alpha - \alpha^0 \\ \exp \alpha - \exp \alpha^0 \end{bmatrix}$$

But

$$D_T^{-1} N_T D_T^{-1} = \begin{bmatrix} 1 & \frac{1}{2}(T+1)/T \\ \frac{1}{2}(T+1)/T & \frac{1}{6}(T+1)(2T+1)/T^2 \end{bmatrix} = K_T,$$

say, so that

$$Q_T(\alpha) = [T^{1/2}(\alpha - \alpha^0), T^{3/2}(\exp \alpha - \exp \alpha^0)] \, K_T$$

$$\times \begin{bmatrix} T^{1/2}(\alpha - \alpha^0) \\ T^{3/2}(\exp \alpha - \exp \alpha^0) \end{bmatrix}$$

and

$$Q_T(\alpha) \geqslant \mu_T \left[T^{1/2}(\alpha - \alpha^0), T^{3/2}(\exp \alpha - \exp \alpha^0) \right]$$

$$\times \begin{bmatrix} T^{1/2}(\alpha - \alpha^0) \\ T^{3/2}(\exp \alpha - \exp \alpha^0) \end{bmatrix} \tag{5.4.10}$$

where μ_T is the smaller eigenvalue of K_T. Thus, from (5.4.7) and (5.4.10) we have

$$|V_T(\alpha)| \leqslant \frac{1}{\mu_T \left[T(\alpha - \alpha^0)^2 + T^3 (\exp \alpha - \exp \alpha^0)^2 \right]}$$

$$\times \left| [\alpha - \alpha^0, \exp \alpha - \exp \alpha^0] \, D_T D_T^{-1} \begin{bmatrix} \sum_{t=1}^{T} u_t \\ \sum_{t=1}^{T} t u_t \end{bmatrix} \right|$$

$$\leqslant \frac{\| [T^{1/2}(\alpha - \alpha^0), T^{3/2}(\exp \alpha - \exp \alpha^0)] \| \, \| (T^{-1/2} \Sigma_{t=1}^{T} u_t, T^{-3/2} \Sigma_{t=1}^{T} t u_t) \|}{\mu_T \left[T(\alpha - \alpha^0)^2 + T^3 (\exp \alpha - \exp \alpha^0)^2 \right]} \tag{5.4.11}$$

where by $\|a\|$ for some vector $a = (a_i)_{n \times 1}$ we mean the Euclidean distance $(a'a)^{1/2}$. [The last inequality (5.4.11) above is then obtained by Cauchy's inequality (Hardy, 1952, p. 34): $|b'a| \leqslant (b'b)^{1/2} (a'a)^{1/2}$]. From (5.4.11) we now obtain

$$|V_T(\alpha)| \leqslant \frac{\left[(T^{-1/2} \Sigma_{t=1}^{T} u_t)^2 + (T^{-3/2} \Sigma_{t=1}^{T} t u_t)^2 \right]^{1/2}}{\mu_T \left[T(\alpha - \alpha^0)^2 + T^3 (\exp \alpha - \exp \alpha^0)^2 \right]^{1/2}}$$

$$= \frac{\left[(T^{-1} \Sigma_{t=1}^{T} u_t)^2 + (T^{-2} \Sigma_{t=1}^{T} t u_t)^2 \right]^{1/2}}{\mu_T \left[(\alpha - \alpha^0)^2 + T^2 (\exp \alpha - \exp \alpha^0)^2 \right]^{1/2}}$$

so that

$$\sup_{\alpha \in \omega} |V_T(\alpha)| < \frac{\left[(T^{-1} \Sigma_{t=1}^{T} u_t)^2 + (T^{-2} \Sigma_{t=1}^{T} t u_t)^2 \right]^{1/2}}{\mu_T \epsilon}$$

where ϵ is now defined by

$$\epsilon = \left[\inf_{\alpha \in \omega} (\alpha - \alpha^0)^2 \right]^{1/2}$$

It follows that

$$P[\sup_{\alpha \in \omega} V_T(\alpha) \geqslant \tfrac{1}{2}] \leqslant P\left[\left(T^{-1} \sum_{t=1}^{T} u_t \right)^2 + \left(T^{-2} \sum t u_t \right)^2 \geqslant \tfrac{1}{4} \mu_T^2 \epsilon^2 \right]$$

which, by Tchebycheff's theorem (Cramer, 1946, p. 182; see also solution 2.15), is less than

$$\frac{E\left[(T^{-1} \Sigma_{t=1}^{T} u_t)^2 + (T^{-2} \Sigma_{t=1}^{T} t u_t)^2 \right]}{\mu_T^2 \epsilon^2 / 4}$$

$$= \frac{T^{-2}(T\sigma^2) + T^{-4}(\sigma^2 \Sigma_{t=1}^T t^2)}{\mu_T^2 \epsilon^2/4}$$

$$= \frac{T^{-1}\sigma^2 + \frac{1}{2} T^{-3}(T+1)(2T+1)\sigma^2}{\frac{1}{4}\mu_T^2 \epsilon^2} \tag{5.4.12}$$

Now μ_T is the smaller characteristic root of K_T and from the definition of K_T it is clear that K_T is positive definite for $T > 1$ and tends to the positive definite limit

$$\begin{pmatrix} 1 & \frac{1}{2} \\ \frac{1}{2} & \frac{1}{3} \end{pmatrix}$$

as $T \to \infty$. Hence μ_T is positive for all T and has a positive limit as $T \to \infty$.

It follows that (5.4.12) tends to zero as $T \to \infty$ and, therefore,

$$P(\sup_{\alpha \in \omega} V_T(\alpha) \geqslant \tfrac{1}{2}) \to 0$$

as $T \to \infty$. This verifies (ii). Since (i) and (ii) both hold in the present case, $\hat{\alpha}$ is consistent by Malinvaud's Lemma.

Solution 5.5

Part (a) We write

$$y_t - A(\alpha)x_t = y_t - A^*x_t + [A^* - A(\alpha)] x_t$$

so that

$$T^{-1} \sum_{t=1}^T [y_t - A(\alpha)x_t]'(M_{uu}^*)^{-1} [y_t - A(\alpha)x_t]$$

$$= T^{-1} \sum_{t=1}^T (y_t - A^*x_t)'(M_{uu}^*)^{-1}(y_t - A^*x_t)$$

$$+ 2T^{-1} \sum_{t=1}^T (y_t - A^*x_t)'(M_{uu}^*)^{-1} [A^* - A(\alpha)] x_t$$

$$+ T^{-1} \sum_{t=1}^T x_t' [A^* - A(\alpha)]'(M_{uu}^*)^{-1} [A^* - A(\alpha)] x_t.$$

Now, since the trace of a scalar equals the scalar itself, we have

$$T^{-1} \sum_{t=1}^{T} (y_t - A^* x_t)'(M_{uu}^*)^{-1}(y_t - A^* x_t)$$

$$= T^{-1} \sum_{t=1}^{T} \text{tr} \left[(y_t - A^* x_t)'(M_{uu}^*)^{-1}(y_t - A^* x_t) \right]$$

$$= T^{-1} \sum_{t=1}^{T} \text{tr} \left[(M_{uu}^*)^{-1}(y_t - A^* x_t)(y_t - A^* x_t)' \right]$$

$$= \text{tr} \left\{ (M_{uu}^*)^{-1} \left[T^{-1} \sum_{t=1}^{T} (y_t - A^* x_t)(y_t - A^* x_t)' \right] \right\}$$

$$= \text{tr} \left[(M_{uu}^*)^{-1} M_{uu}^* \right]$$

$$= n.$$

In a similar way we find that

$$2T^{-1} \sum_{t=1}^{T} (y_t - A^* x_t)'(M_{uu}^*)^{-1}(A^* - A(\alpha)) x_t$$

$$= 2T^{-1} \text{tr} \left\{ (M_{uu}^*)^{-1} [A^* - A(\alpha)] \sum_{t=1}^{T} x_t (y_t - A^* x_t)' \right\}$$

$$= 0$$

since

$$\sum_{t=1}^{T} x_t (y_t - A^* x_t)' = \sum_{t=1}^{T} x_t y_t' - \left(\sum_{t=1}^{T} x_t x_t' \right) A^* = 0$$

from the definition of A^* [see (3.1.2) above]. Finally

$$T^{-1} \sum_{t=1}^{T} x_t' [A^* - A(\alpha)]'(M_{uu}^*)^{-1}[A^* - A(\alpha)] x_t$$

$$= \text{tr} \{ [A^* - A(\alpha)]'(M_{uu}^*)^{-1}[A^* - A(\alpha)] M_{xx} \}$$

and thus (5.5.1) equals (5.5.2) plus a constant which does not depend on α. It follows that the minimisation of (5.2.2) with respect to α is equivalent to the minimisation of (5.5.1).

Part (b) We make the following assumption in addition to Conditions 5.4.A, 5.4.B and 5.4.C:

Condition 5.5.A (Malinvaud's Assumption 6 on page 349) *The set of possible values of the parameter vector α contains a neighbourhood of α^0*

in which the functions $a_{ij}(\alpha)$, where $A(\alpha) = a_{ij}(\alpha)$, have bounded derivatives up to the third order. The vector α^0 is not a singular point of $A(\alpha)$, which requires that the $p \times nm$ matrix

$$\frac{\partial\,(\mathrm{vec}\,A(\alpha^0))'}{\partial\alpha}$$

have full rank ($= p < nm$).

Remark We refer the reader at this point to Appendix B for a discussion of the notation of matrix and vector differentiation that we are using.

Under Conditions 5.4.A, 5.4.B, 5.4.C and 5.5.A, Malinvaud (1970b Theorems 4 and 5 on pages 352 and 355) proves that $\sqrt{T}(\alpha^{**} - \alpha^0)$ has a limiting normal distribution with mean vector zero and covariance matrix which is the inverse of the matrix whose (i, j)th element is

$$\mathrm{tr}\left[\frac{\partial A(\alpha^0)'}{\partial\alpha_i}\,\Omega^{-1}\,\frac{\partial A(\alpha^0)}{\partial\alpha_j}\,\bar{M}\right] \tag{5.5.3}$$

where $\bar{M} = \lim_{T \to \infty} M_{xx}$. But from Appendix A (in particular, property (ii) on page 496) we see that (5.5.3) can be written as

$$\frac{\partial[\mathrm{vec}\,A(\alpha^0)]}{\partial\alpha_i}{}'\,(\Omega^{-1} \otimes \bar{M})\,\frac{\partial\,\mathrm{vec}\,A(\alpha^0)}{\partial\alpha_j}$$

and thus the covariance matrix of the limiting distribution of $\sqrt{T}(\alpha^{**} - \alpha^0)$ is

$$\left\{\left(\frac{\partial\,[\mathrm{vec}\,A(\alpha^0)]}{\partial\alpha}{}'\right)(\Omega^{-1} \otimes \bar{M})\left(\frac{\partial\,\mathrm{vec}\,A(\alpha^0)}{\partial\alpha'}\right)\right\}^{-1}$$

Part (c) In view of Condition 5.5.A we can write $A(\alpha)$ in a neigbourhood of $\alpha = \alpha^0$ in the form

$$A(\alpha) \;=\; A(\alpha^0) + \sum_{i=1}^{P}\frac{\partial A(\alpha^0)}{\partial\alpha_i}\,(\alpha_i - \alpha_i^0)$$

$$+ \sum_{i=1}^{P}\sum_{j=1}^{P}\frac{\partial^2 A(\tilde{\alpha})}{\partial\alpha_i\partial\alpha_j}\,(\alpha_i - \alpha^0)\,(\alpha_j - \alpha^0)$$

where each element of $\tilde{\alpha}$ lies between the corresponding elements of α and α^0. Since α^{**} is a consistent estimator of α^0 under the stated conditions (see Solution 5.4) it follows that

$$\sqrt{T}[A(\alpha^{**}) - A(\alpha^0)] \ = \ \sum_{i=1}^{P} \frac{\partial A(\alpha^0)}{\partial \alpha_i} \sqrt{T}(\alpha_i^{**} - \alpha_i^0)$$

$$+\frac{1}{\sqrt{T}} \sum_{i=1}^{P} \sum_{j=1}^{P} \frac{\partial^2 A(\tilde{\alpha})}{\partial \alpha_i \partial \alpha_j} \sqrt{T}(\alpha_i^{**} - \alpha^0) \sqrt{T}(\alpha_j^{**} - \alpha_j^0). \tag{5.5.4}$$

But $\sqrt{T}(\alpha_i^{**} - \alpha_i^0)$ has a limiting normal distribution as $T \to \infty$ (Part (b) above) for all i and the elements of

$$\frac{\partial^2 A(\tilde{\alpha})}{\partial \alpha_i \partial \alpha_j}$$

are bounded in probability as $T \to \infty$ (since α^{**} is itself consistent and $\tilde{\alpha}$ lies between α^{**} and α^0 in this case). Thus the last term on the right hand side of (5.5.4) tends to zero in probability (see Proposition 4 on page 370 of Malinvaud, 1970b).

It now follows that $\sqrt{T}[A(\alpha^{**}) - A(\alpha^0)]$ has the same limiting distribution as the first term on the right hand side of (5.5.4) (see Proposition 5 on page 370 of Malinvaud, 1970b). But this term is a linear combination of random quantities [the $\sqrt{T}(\alpha_i^{**} - \alpha_i^0); i = 1, \ldots, p$] which have limiting normal distributions so that the limiting distribution of $\sqrt{T}[A(\alpha^{**}) - A(\alpha^0)]$ is also normal. Note that we can write (5.5.4) in the form

$$\sqrt{T} \,\mathrm{vec}\,[A(\alpha^{**}) - A(\alpha^0)] \ = \ \sum_{i=1}^{P} \frac{\partial \,\mathrm{vec}\,A(\alpha^0)}{\partial \alpha_i} \sqrt{T}(\alpha_i^{**} - \alpha_i^0) + o_p(1)$$

where $o_p(1)$ denotes a term which tends in probability to zero. More simply

$$\sqrt{T} \,\mathrm{vec}\,[A(\alpha^{**}) - A(\alpha^0)] \ = \ \left\{ \frac{\partial \,\mathrm{vec}\,A(\alpha^0)}{\partial \alpha} \right\} \sqrt{T}(\alpha^{**} - \alpha^0) + o_p(1)$$

and thus $\sqrt{T} \,\mathrm{vec}[A(\alpha^{**}) - A(\alpha^0)]$ has a limiting normal distribution with mean vector zero and covariance matrix

$$\left(\frac{\partial \,\mathrm{vec}\,A(\alpha^0)}{\partial \alpha'} \right) \left\{ \left(\frac{\partial \,[\mathrm{vec}\,A(\alpha^0)]'}{\partial \alpha} \right) (\Omega^{-1} \otimes \bar{M}) \left(\frac{\partial \,\mathrm{vec}\,A(\alpha^0)}{\partial \alpha'} \right) \right\}^{-1} \left(\frac{\partial \,[\mathrm{vec}\,A(\alpha^0)]'}{\partial \alpha} \right)$$

$$\tag{5.5.5}$$

Remark We observe that, in view of Condition 5.5.A, the matrix (5.5.5) has rank p which is less than nm, i.e. (5.5.5) has the same rank as the matrix $\partial \operatorname{vec} A(\alpha^0)/\partial \alpha'$. This means that the limiting distribution of $\sqrt{T}\operatorname{vec}[A(\alpha^{**}) - A(\alpha^0)]$ is a *singular* normal distribution (see, for instance, Cramer, 1946, p. 312 for a discussion of the singular normal distribution); and the covariance matrix of this limiting distribution is positive semi-definite.

Part (d) From (5.5.5) we know that the covariance matrix of the limiting distribution of $\sqrt{T}\operatorname{vec}[A(\alpha^{**}) - A(\alpha^0)]$ can be written as

$$\psi^{**} = B'[B(\Omega^{-1} \otimes \bar{M})B']^{-1}B$$

where

$$B = \frac{\partial[\operatorname{vec} A(\alpha^0)]'}{\partial \alpha}$$

Moreover, the covariance matrix of the limiting distribution of $\sqrt{T}[A^* - A(\alpha^0)]$ is

$$\psi^* = \Omega \otimes \bar{M}^{-1} \tag{5.5.6}$$

(c.f. Malinvaud, 1970b, pages 209 and 225). Thus

$$
\begin{aligned}
\psi^* - \psi^{**} &= \Omega \otimes \bar{M}^{-1} - B'[B(\Omega^{-1} \otimes \bar{M})B']^{-1}B \\
&= \psi^* - \psi^*(\psi^{*-1}B^{-1})\,[(B\psi^{*-1})\,\psi^*(\psi^{*-1}B')^{-1}] \\
&\quad (B\psi^{*-1})\,\psi^* \\
&= \psi^* - \psi^*C'(C\psi^*C')^{-1}C\psi^* \tag{5.5.7}
\end{aligned}
$$

where

$$C = B\psi^{*-1}.$$

We now consider the partitioned matrix

$$
\begin{aligned}
\Phi &= \begin{bmatrix} \psi^* & \psi^*C' \\ C\psi^* & C\psi^*C' \end{bmatrix} \\
&= \begin{bmatrix} I & 0 \\ 0 & C \end{bmatrix} \begin{bmatrix} \psi^* & \psi^* \\ \psi^* & \psi^* \end{bmatrix} \begin{bmatrix} I & 0 \\ 0 & C' \end{bmatrix} \tag{5.5.8}
\end{aligned}
$$

We can write

$$
\begin{bmatrix} \psi^* & \psi^* \\ \psi^* & \psi^* \end{bmatrix} = \begin{bmatrix} 1 & 1 \\ 1 & 1 \end{bmatrix} \otimes \psi^*
$$

which is positive semi-definite since ψ^* is positive definite (by assumption on Ω and $\bar{M}$) and

$$\begin{bmatrix} 1 & 1 \\ 1 & 1 \end{bmatrix}$$

is positive semi-definite. (The Kronecker product of two positive semi-definite matrices is itself positive semi-definite; c.f. Dhrymes, 1970, page 155). It follows from (5.5.8) that Φ is also positive semi-definite.

From (5.5.7) we now have

$$\psi^* - \psi^{**} = [I \vdots - \psi^* C'(C\psi^* C')^{-1}] \; \Phi \begin{bmatrix} I \\ \cdots \\ -(C\psi^* C')^{-1} C\psi^* \end{bmatrix}$$

$$= K\Phi K', \text{ say.} \qquad (5.5.9)$$

But Φ is positive semi-definite so it follows from the form of (5.5.9) that $\psi^* - \psi^{**}$ is positive semi-definite as required.

Final Remark We observe that whereas ψ^{**} is positive semi-definite [see the Remark at the end of Part (c)], ψ^* is positive definite. Thus, the limiting distribution of the unconstrained estimator A^* is non-singular while that of the constrained estimator $A(\alpha^{**})$ is singular. This is as we would expect; because in the latter case we are confining the matrix A to the subset of nm-dimensional Euclidean space defined by the equations $A = A(\alpha)$ where α is a p-dimensional vector.

Solution 5.6

Part (a) The model (5.6.1) is a single equation instance of the constrained linear model (5.4.3). The constraint $a_1^2 = a_2$ is simple to parameterise in this case, so that we can write (5.6.1) as

$$y_t = a_1 x_{1t} + a_1^2 x_{2t} + u_t \qquad (5.6.2)$$

and the coefficients in (5.6.2) are now simple functions of the parameter $a_1 = \alpha$, say. Let us now write (5.6.2) as

$$y_t = a(\alpha)' x_t + u_t \qquad (5.6.3)$$

and it is clear that we can estimate α by minimising

$$L(\alpha) = \sum_{t=1}^{T} [y_t - a(\alpha)' x_t]^2$$

Since the model (5.6.1) involves only a single equation we need not weight the quadratic form $L(\alpha)$ [compare (5.5.1)] as any such weighting leads only to the addition of a positive scalar coefficient to $L(\alpha)$, which will not affect the estimate of α we finally obtain.

Rather than directly minimising $L(\alpha)$ we can use the following iterative procedure:

(i) estimate $a(\alpha)$ by an unrestricted least squares regression on (5.6.3) to obtain the vector of regression coefficients a^*;

(ii) estimate α by minimising $[a^* - a(\alpha)]' M_{xx} [a^* - a(\alpha)]$. As shown in Part (a) of Solution 5.5 the estimate $\hat{\alpha}$ obtained from (i) and (ii) is the same as that obtained by directly minimising $L(\alpha)$.

Once we have found $\hat{\alpha}$ we estimate a_1 and a_2 by $\hat{a}_1 = \hat{\alpha}$, $\hat{a}_2 = \hat{\alpha}^2$. Then, as shown in Solution 5.5, $\sqrt{T}(\hat{a}_1 - a_1)$ and $\sqrt{T}(\hat{a}_2 - a_2)$ have limiting normal distributions centred on zero with variances that are at least as small as those of the limiting distributions of $\sqrt{T}(a_1^* - a_1)$ and $\sqrt{T}(a_2^* - a_2)$.

Part (b) We now consider the case where

$$a_1 = 0.5, \quad a_2 = 0.25, \quad \sigma^2 = 1 \text{ and } \bar{M}_{xx} = \begin{bmatrix} 1 & 1 \\ 1 & 2 \end{bmatrix}$$

The covariance matrix of the limiting distribution of $\sqrt{T}(a^* - a)$ is given by

$$\sigma^2 \bar{M}_{xx}^{-1} = \begin{bmatrix} 2 & -1 \\ -1 & 1 \end{bmatrix} \tag{5.6.4}$$

and that of $\sqrt{T}[a(\hat{\alpha}) - a]$ is given by

$$\frac{\partial a(\alpha^0)}{\partial \alpha} \left[\frac{\partial a(\alpha^0)'}{\partial \alpha} (\sigma^{-2} \bar{M}_{xx}) \frac{\partial a(\alpha^0)}{\partial \alpha} \right]^{-1} \frac{\partial a(\alpha^0)'}{\partial \alpha} \tag{5.6.5}$$

where

$$\frac{\partial a(\alpha^0)}{\partial \alpha} = \begin{bmatrix} 1 \\ 2\alpha^0 \end{bmatrix} = \begin{bmatrix} 1 \\ 1 \end{bmatrix}$$

since $\alpha^0 = 0.5$. Thus (5.6.5) becomes

$$\begin{bmatrix} 1 \\ 1 \end{bmatrix} \left\{ (1, 1) \begin{pmatrix} 1 & 1 \\ 1 & 2 \end{pmatrix} \begin{pmatrix} 1 \\ 1 \end{pmatrix} \right\}^{-1} [1, 1]$$

$$= \tfrac{1}{5} \begin{bmatrix} 1 \\ 1 \end{bmatrix} [1, 1]$$

$$= \tfrac{1}{5} \begin{bmatrix} 1 & 1 \\ 1 & 1 \end{bmatrix}$$

Comparing (5.6.4) and (5.6.6) we see that the variance of the limiting distribution of $\sqrt{T}(a_1^* - a_1)$ is 2, whereas the variance of the limiting distribution of $\sqrt{T}(\hat{a}_1 - a_1)$ is 1/5.

Remark It is worth noting that (5.6.4) takes the same value regardless of the true values of a_1 and a_2 whereas (5.6.5) depends explicitly on the value of the true parameter α^0. As a result, the (asymptotic) variance reduction that is gained by the use of $a(\hat{\alpha})$ rather than a^* can vary considerably with changes in the value of α^0. The reader may for example like to try the above calculation again with the alternative value $\alpha^0 = -0.5$ giving $a_1 = -0.5$ and $a_2 = 0.25$.

Solution 5.7

Part (a) We denote the matrix of coefficients in the system (5.7.1.2) by

$$A = \begin{bmatrix} a_{11} & a_{12} \\ a_{21} & a_{22} \end{bmatrix}$$

Then the following three-stage procedure produces asymptotically efficient estimates of A (see Malinvaud, 1970b, pp. 355–358):
   (i) Calculate the matrix A^* of unrestricted least squares estimates of A
   (ii) Calculate the sample second moment matrix of residuals from the regression in (i). That is, calculate

$$M_{uu}^* = \frac{1}{T} \sum_{t=1}^{T} u_t^* u_t^{*\prime}$$

where $u_t^* = y_t - A^* x_t$, $y_t' = (y_{1t}, y_{2t})$ and $x_t' = (x_{1t}, x_{2t})$.
   (iii) Calculate the matrix A^{**} which minimises

$$\operatorname{tr}\left[(A^* - A)'(M_{uu}^*)^{-1}(A^* - A)M_{xx}\right] \tag{5.7.4}$$

subject to the restriction (5.7.1), where $M_{xx} = T^{-1}\sum_{t=1}^{T} x_t x_t'$.
   Under the assumptions given in the question, A^{**} is an asymptotically efficient estimator of A (see Theorem 6 of Malinvaud, 1970b, p. 356)

Remark Rather than minimise (5.7.4) subject to the restriction (5.7.3), we can reparameterise the model by writing A explicitly in the form

$$A = \begin{bmatrix} a_{11} & 1/a_{11} \\ a_{21} & a_{22} \end{bmatrix} = A(\alpha)$$

where $\alpha' = (a_{11}, a_{21}, a_{22})$. Then $A^{**} = A(\alpha^{**})$, where α^{**} is the vector which minimises

$$\text{tr}\{[A^* - A(\alpha)]' (M_{uu}^*)^{-1} [A^* - A(\alpha)] M_{xx}\}$$

with respect to α.

Part (b) In view of the above remark the limiting distribution of $\sqrt{T}(A^{**} - A)$ is the same as that of $\sqrt{T}[A(\alpha^{**}) - A]$. But the covariance matrix of the limiting distribution of $\sqrt{T}\,\text{vec}\,[A(\alpha^{**}) - A]$ is given by

$$\left(\frac{\partial\, \text{vec}\, A(\alpha^0)}{\partial \alpha'}\right)\left\{\left(\frac{\partial\, [\text{vec}\, A(\alpha^0)]\,'}{\partial \alpha}\right) (\Omega^{-1} \otimes \bar{M}_{xx})\right.$$

$$\left. \times \left(\frac{\partial\, \text{vec}\, A(\alpha^0)}{\partial \alpha'}\right)\right\}^{-1} \left(\frac{\partial\, [\text{vec}\, A(\alpha^0)]\,'}{\partial \alpha}\right) \qquad (5.7.5)$$

(see (5.5.5) above). In the present case

$$\Omega = \sigma^2 \begin{bmatrix} 2 & 1 \\ 1 & 1 \end{bmatrix} \qquad \bar{M}_{xx} = \begin{bmatrix} 1 & 1 \\ 1 & 2 \end{bmatrix}$$

and

$$\alpha^0{}' = (1, 1, 2).$$

Moreover

$$\frac{\partial\, \text{vec}\, A(\alpha)'}{\partial \alpha} = \begin{bmatrix} 1 & -1/a_{11}^2 & 0 & 0 \\ 0 & 0 & 1 & 0 \\ 0 & 0 & 0 & 1 \end{bmatrix}$$

so that (5.7.5) becomes

$$\begin{bmatrix} 1 & 0 & 0 \\ -1 & 0 & 0 \\ 0 & 1 & 0 \\ 0 & 0 & 1 \end{bmatrix} \left(\sigma^{-2} \begin{bmatrix} 1 & -1 & 0 & 0 \\ 0 & 0 & 1 & 0 \\ 0 & 0 & 0 & 1 \end{bmatrix} \begin{bmatrix} 1 & 1 & -1 & -1 \\ 1 & 2 & -1 & -2 \\ -1 & -1 & 2 & 2 \\ -1 & -2 & 2 & 4 \end{bmatrix}\right.$$

$$\times \left\{ \begin{bmatrix} 1 & 0 & 0 \\ -1 & 0 & 0 \\ 0 & 1 & 0 \\ 0 & 0 & 1 \end{bmatrix}^{-1} \begin{bmatrix} 1 & -1 & 0 & 0 \\ 0 & 0 & 1 & 0 \\ 0 & 0 & 0 & 1 \end{bmatrix} \right.$$

$$= \sigma^2 \begin{bmatrix} 1 & 0 & 0 \\ -1 & 0 & 0 \\ 0 & 1 & 0 \\ 0 & 0 & 1 \end{bmatrix} \begin{bmatrix} 1 & 0 & 1 \\ 0 & 2 & 2 \\ 1 & 2 & 4 \end{bmatrix}^{-1} \begin{bmatrix} 1 & -1 & 0 & 0 \\ 0 & 0 & 1 & 0 \\ 0 & 0 & 0 & 1 \end{bmatrix}$$

$$= \tfrac{1}{2}\sigma^2 \begin{bmatrix} 1 & 0 & 0 \\ -1 & 0 & 0 \\ 0 & 1 & 0 \\ 0 & 0 & 1 \end{bmatrix} \begin{bmatrix} 4 & 2 & -2 \\ 2 & 3 & -2 \\ -2 & -2 & 2 \end{bmatrix} \begin{bmatrix} 1 & -1 & 0 & 0 \\ 0 & 0 & 1 & 0 \\ 0 & 0 & 0 & 1 \end{bmatrix}$$

$$= \sigma^2 \begin{bmatrix} 2 & -2 & 1 & -1 \\ -2 & 2 & -1 & 1 \\ 1 & -1 & 3/2 & -1 \\ -1 & 1 & -1 & 1 \end{bmatrix} \qquad (5.7.4)$$

On the other hand the covariance matrix of the limiting distribution of $\sqrt{T}\,\mathrm{vec}\,(A^* - A)$ is given by

$$\Omega \otimes \bar{M}_{xx}^{-1}$$

[see (5.5.6) above] which, in this case, is

$$\sigma^2 \begin{bmatrix} 4 & -2 & 2 & -1 \\ -2 & 2 & -1 & 1 \\ 2 & -1 & 2 & -1 \\ -1 & 1 & -1 & 1 \end{bmatrix} \qquad (5.7.5)$$

Subtracting (5.7.4) from (5.7.5) it is easy to see that the resulting matrix

$$\sigma^2 \begin{bmatrix} 2 & 0 & 1 & 0 \\ 0 & 0 & 0 & 0 \\ 1 & 0 & \tfrac{1}{2} & 0 \\ 0 & 0 & 0 & 0 \end{bmatrix}$$

is positive semi-definite, as theory suggests (see solution 5.5, Part (c)). Taking the diagonal elements of the matrices (5.7.4) and (5.7.5), we see that the variance of the limiting distribution of $\sqrt{T}(a_{ij}^{**} - a_{ij})$ is less than that of $\sqrt{T}(a_{ij}^{*} - a_{ij})$ for the components a_{11} and a_{21}. The variances are equal in the case of a_{12} and a_{22}.

Remark Since the constraint (5.7.3) involves coefficients of the first equation, it is not surprising that the non-linear regression leads to an efficiency gain (asymptotically) for one of the coefficients of this equation. The fact that there is an asymptotic efficiency gain from the non-linear regression in the case of a coefficient of the second equation is important and is the result of the inter-equation disturbance correlation. The reader may like to try the same question again with

$$\Omega = \sigma^2 \begin{bmatrix} 2 & 0 \\ 0 & 1 \end{bmatrix}.$$

Question 5.8

Part (a) The given model is a single-equation errors-in-variables model. We know that in such models, least squares regression does not, in general, provide consistent estimates (see, for instance, Malinvaud, 1970b, pp. 379—380). Thus it is proposed in the question to use an orthogonal regression.

The perpendicular distance of the point (y_t, x_t) from the line

$$y = \alpha + \beta x$$

is given by

$$\left| \frac{y_t - \alpha - \beta x_t}{\sqrt{1 + \beta^2}} \right|$$

(see, for instance, Brown and Manson, 1950). Thus, the orthogonal regression estimates of α^0 and β^0 in (5.8.1) are obtained by minimising with respect to α and β the sum of squares

$$\sum_{t=1}^{T} \left(\frac{y_t - \alpha - \beta x_t}{\sqrt{1 + \beta^2}} \right)^2 = \left(\frac{1}{1 + \beta^2} \right) \sum_{t=1}^{T} (y_t - \alpha - \beta x_t)^2 \qquad (5.8.4)$$

We can now concentrate (5.8.3) as a function of β. Setting to zero the first derivative of (5.8.4) with respect to α we get

$$-\left(\frac{2}{1+\beta^2}\right) \sum_{t=1}^{T} (y_t - \alpha - \beta x_t) = 0$$

so that

$$\alpha = \bar{y} - \beta \bar{x} \tag{5.8.5}$$

where

$$\bar{y} = T^{-1} \sum_{t=1}^{T} y_t \quad \text{and} \quad \bar{x} = T^{-1} \sum_{t=1}^{T} x_t$$

when (5.8.3) attains its minimum. Next we concentrate (5.8.4) as a function of β by substituting (5.8.5) into (5.8.4). We obtain as the new expression to be minimised

$$\left(\frac{1}{1+\beta^2}\right) T^{-1} \sum_{t=1}^{T} \left[(y_t - \bar{y}) - \beta(x_t - \bar{x})\right]^2$$

$$= \left(\frac{1}{1+\beta^2}\right)(m_{yy} - 2\beta m_{yx} + \beta^2 m_{xx}) \tag{5.8.6}$$

where

$$m_{yy} = T^{-1} \sum_{t=1}^{T} (y_t - \bar{y})^2, \qquad m_{yx} = T^{-1} \sum_{t=1}^{T} (y_t - \bar{y})(x_t - \bar{x})$$

$$\text{and} \quad m_{xx} = T^{-1} \sum_{t=1}^{T} (x_t - \bar{x})^2.$$

We can write (5.8.6) as

$$\frac{1}{1+\beta^2} [1, \quad -\beta] \begin{bmatrix} m_{yy} & m_{yx} \\ m_{yx} & m_{xx} \end{bmatrix} \begin{bmatrix} 1 \\ -\beta \end{bmatrix} \tag{5.8.7}$$

which is at least as great as

$$\frac{\lambda_m}{1+\beta^2} [1, \quad -\beta] \begin{bmatrix} 1 \\ -\beta \end{bmatrix} = \left(\frac{\lambda_m}{1+\beta^2}\right)(1+\beta^2) = \lambda_m \tag{5.8.8}$$

where λ_m is the smaller of the two eigenvalues of the matrix in (5.8.7). Moreover, (5.8.8) is attained when β takes on the value ($\hat{\beta}$, say) for which

$$\begin{bmatrix} m_{yy} & m_{yx} \\ m_{yx} & m_{xx} \end{bmatrix} \begin{bmatrix} 1 \\ -\hat{\beta} \end{bmatrix} = \lambda_m \begin{bmatrix} 1 \\ -\hat{\beta} \end{bmatrix}. \tag{5.8.9}$$

that is, when $(1, -\hat{\beta})$ is the eigenvector corresponding to λ_m. From the first equation in (5.8.9) we have

$$m_{yy} - \hat{\beta} m_{yx} = \lambda_m$$

so that

$$\hat{\beta} = (m_{yy} - \lambda_m)/m_{yx}. \tag{5.8.10}$$

To find $\hat{\beta}$ we now need only find λ_m. But λ_m is the smaller of the roots of the equation

$$\begin{vmatrix} m_{yy} - \lambda & m_{yx} \\ m_{yx} & m_{xx} - \lambda \end{vmatrix} = 0$$

That is

$$\lambda^2 - (m_{xx} + m_{yy})\lambda - (m_{yx}^2 - m_{xx} m_{yy}) = 0$$

from which we have

$$\lambda = \frac{m_{xx} + m_{yy} \pm [(m_{xx} + m_{yy})^2 + 4(m_{yx}^2 - m_{xx}m_{yy})]^{1/2}}{2}$$

$$= \frac{m_{xx} + m_{yy} \pm [(m_{xx} - m_{yy})^2 + 4m_{yx}^2]^{1/2}}{2}$$

Clearly

$$\lambda_m = \frac{m_{xx} + m_{yy} - [(m_{xx} - m_{yy})^2 + 4m_{yx}^2]^{1/2}}{2}$$

so that from (5.8.10) we obtain

$$\hat{\beta} = \frac{m_{yy} - m_{xx} + [(m_{yy} - m_{xx})^2 + 4m_{yx}^2]^{1/2}}{2m_{yx}} \tag{5.8.11}$$

and, hence, from (5.8.5)

$$\hat{\alpha} = \bar{y} - \hat{\beta}\bar{x}. \tag{5.8.12}$$

The estimates $\hat{\alpha}$ and $\hat{\beta}$ can alternatively be thought of as being obtained by a weighted regression. To define the latter we introduce the notation

$$z_t = \begin{bmatrix} y_t \\ x_t \end{bmatrix} \qquad Z_t = \begin{bmatrix} Y_t \\ X_t \end{bmatrix} \quad \text{and} \quad w_t = \begin{bmatrix} u_t \\ v_t \end{bmatrix}.$$

We let $\Omega = E(w_t w_t')$. The model comprising (5.8.1–3) can now be written as

$$(1, -\beta^\circ) Z_t = \alpha^\circ$$

$$z_t = Z_t + w_t$$

and a weighted regression is obtained by minimising the quadratic form

$$\sum_{t=1}^{T} (z_t - Z_t)' \, \Omega^{-1} (z_t - Z_t) \qquad\qquad (5.8.13)$$

But, by assumption, in the present case

$$\Omega = \begin{bmatrix} \sigma^2 & 0 \\ 0 & \sigma^2 \end{bmatrix}$$

so that (5.8.13) becomes

$$\frac{1}{\sigma^2}\sum_{t=1}^{T} (y_t - Y_t)^2 + \frac{1}{\sigma^2}\sum_{t=1}^{T} (x_t - X_t)^2$$

$$= \frac{1}{\sigma^2}\sum_{t=1}^{T} (y_t - \alpha - \beta X_t)^2 + \frac{1}{\sigma^2}\sum_{t=1}^{T} (x_t - X_t)^2. \qquad (5.8.14)$$

The weighted regression then amounts to minimising (5.8.14) with respect to α, β and $X_1, \ldots, X_T$. Concentrating (5.8.13) first in terms of α and β we set the derivatives of (5.8.14) with respect to the X_t equal to zero giving

$$\left(-\frac{\beta}{\sigma^2}\right)(y_t - \alpha - \beta X_t) - \frac{1}{\sigma^2}(x_t - X_t) = 0 \qquad (t = 1, \ldots, T).$$

Thus

$$x_t - X_t = -\beta(y_t - \alpha - \beta X_t) \qquad\qquad (5.8.15)$$

or

$$(1 + \beta^2)X_t = x_t + \beta y_t - \beta\alpha$$

so that

$$X_t = \left(\frac{1}{1 + \beta^2}\right)(x_t + \beta y_t - \beta\alpha). \qquad\qquad (5.8.16)$$

From (5.8.15) we see that (5.8.13) can be written as

$$\frac{1}{\sigma^2}\sum_{t=1}^{T} (1 + \beta^2)\,(y_t - \alpha - \beta X_t) = \left(\frac{1 + \beta^2}{\sigma^2}\right)\sum_{t=1}^{T} (y_t - \alpha - \beta X_t)^2$$

which, using (5.8.16), becomes

$$\left(\frac{1+\beta^2}{\sigma^2}\right) \sum_{t=1}^{T} \left[y_t - \alpha - \frac{\beta}{1+\beta^2}(x_t + \beta y_t - \beta\alpha)\right]^2$$

$$= \frac{1}{\sigma^2}\left(\frac{1}{1+\beta^2}\right) \sum_{t=1}^{T} [y_t(1+\beta^2) - \alpha(1+\beta^2) - \beta(x_t + \beta y_t - \beta\alpha)]^2$$

$$= \frac{1}{\sigma^2}\left(\frac{1}{1+\beta^2}\right) \sum_{t=1}^{T} (y_t - \alpha - \beta x_t)^2.$$

Thus, minimisation of (5.8.13) is, in the present case, equivalent to the minimisation of (5.8.4) so that $\hat{\alpha}$ and $\hat{\beta}$ can be thought of as being obtained by a weighted regression. It follows that $\hat{\alpha}$ and $\hat{\beta}$ will in this case have the properties of weighted regression estimators. A detailed discussion of weighted regression and its properties in the context of models with errors in variables is given by Malinvaud (1970b, pp. 383–394). Malinvaud (Proposition 1 on page 387) proves, in particular, that a weighted regression in this context leads to consistent estimates provided the following additional assumption is satisfied.

Assumption 5.8.A (Malinvaud's Assumption 3 on page 377). *The unknown vectors Z_t all satisfy the equation $(1, -\beta^0)' Z_t = \alpha^0$. The matrix*

$$M_{ZZ} = T^{-1} \sum_{t=1}^{T} (Z_t - \bar{Z})(Z_t - \bar{Z})',$$

where $\bar{Z} = T^{-1} \sum_{t=1}^{T} Z_{t'}$ is of rank 1. As $T \to \infty$, $\bar{Z}$ tends to a finite limit and M_{ZZ} tends to a finite matrix of rank 1.

Remark 1 It is implicitly assumed in Assumption 5.8.A that the sequence $\{Z_t\}$ involves non-random quantities. We note that since this sequence must satisfy the equation $(1, -\beta^0)' Z_t = \alpha^0$, it follows that

$$(1, -\beta^0)'(Z_t - \bar{Z}) = 0$$

and hence M_{ZZ} cannot have full rank. Moreover, if we let

$$v = \lim_{T \to \infty} \frac{1}{T} \sum_{t=1}^{T} (X_t - \bar{X})^2$$

then it is clear from the fact that $Y_t - \bar{Y} = \beta^0 (X_t - \bar{X})$ that M_{ZZ} tends to the limit matrix

$$v \begin{bmatrix} \beta^{02} & \beta^0 \\ \beta^0 & 1 \end{bmatrix}.$$

Remark 2 Under the further assumption that u_t and v_t are both normally distributed we can deduce from the form of the likelihood function (and, in particular, the presence of the quadratic form (5.8.13) in the exponent of the likelihood function) that $\hat\alpha$ and $\hat\beta$ are in this case also the maximum likelihood estimates (c.f. Malinvaud, 1970b, p. 387).

Part (b) From the formulae (5.8.10) and (5.8.11) above we have

$$\hat\beta \;=\; \frac{5-2+\sqrt{9+16}}{4} \;=\; \frac{8}{4} \;=\; 2$$

and

$$\hat\alpha \;=\; 100 - 2 \times 25 \;=\; 50.$$

Solution 5.9

The model in the question is a regression model with a single unobservable independent variable. This type of model has been the subject of a number of recent investigations and the reader is referred particularly to Zellner (1970), Goldberger (1972a and 1972b) and Griliches (1974).

Part (a) Introducing the notation $y_1' = (y_{11}, \ldots, y_{1T}), y_2' = (y_{21}, \ldots, y_{2T})$ and $X' = (x_1, \ldots, x_T)$ we see that (5.9.1) and (5.9.2) can be written as

$$y_1 = (X\beta)\,\gamma + u_1 \tag{5.9.4}$$

$$y_2 = X\beta + u_2 \tag{5.9.5}$$

where $u_1' = (u_{11}, \ldots, u_{1T})$ and $u_2' = (u_{21}, \ldots, u_{2T})$. From (5.9.5) we have

$$X'y_2 = X'X\beta + X'u_2$$

or

$$\left(\frac{X'y_2}{T}\right) = \left(\frac{X'X}{T}\right)\beta + \left(\frac{X'u_2}{T}\right).$$

But the covariance matrix of $X'u_2/T$ is

$$\sigma_{22}\frac{X'X}{T^2} = \sigma_{22}\frac{M_{xx}}{T}$$

which, in view of the stated assumption about M_{xx}, tends to zero as $T \to \infty$. Thus, by Tchebycheff's Theorem (c.f. the solution to 2.15 above)

$$\operatorname*{plim}_{T\to\infty}\left(\frac{X'y_2}{T}\right) = \left(\lim_{T\to\infty}\frac{X'X}{T}\right)\beta = \bar M_{xx}\beta, \tag{5.9.6}$$

say. Now, from the regression of y_2 on X we obtain the vector of calculated values

$$\hat y_2 = X\hat\beta = X(X'X)^{-1}X'y_2$$

and from the regression of y_1 on $\hat{y}_2$ we have the estimator of γ given by

$$\hat{\gamma} = \frac{\hat{y}_2' \hat{y}_1}{\hat{y}_2' \hat{y}_2}. \tag{5.9.7}$$

But

$$y_1 = \hat{y}_2 \gamma + (X\beta)\gamma - \hat{y}_2 \gamma + u_1$$
$$= \hat{y}_2 \gamma + X(\beta - \hat{\beta})\gamma + u_1 \tag{5.9.8}$$

Substituting (5.9.8) into (5.9.7 we have

$$\hat{\gamma} = \gamma + \left[\frac{\hat{y}_2' X (\beta - \hat{\beta})}{\hat{y}_2' \hat{y}_2} \right] \gamma + \frac{\hat{y}_2' u_1}{\hat{y}_2' \hat{y}_2}. \tag{5.9.9}$$

Now

$$\hat{y}_2' \hat{y}_2 = y_2' X (X'X)^{-1} X' y_2$$

and

$$\hat{y}_2' X = y_2' X$$

so that we can write the second term on the right side of (5.9.9) as

$$\left[\frac{y_2' X (\beta - \hat{\beta})}{y_2' X (X^1 X)^{-1} X^1 y_2} \right] \gamma = \left[\left(\frac{y_2' X}{T} \right) (\beta - \hat{\beta}) \middle/ \left(\frac{y_2' X}{T} \right) \left(\frac{X'X}{T} \right)^{-1} \left(\frac{X' y_2}{T} \right) \right] \gamma \tag{5.9.10}$$

But, it follows from (5.9.6) that $\hat{\beta}$ is a consistent estimator of β and

$$\plim_{T \to \infty} \left(\frac{y_2' X}{T} \right) \left(\frac{X'X}{T} \right)^{-1} \left(\frac{X' y_2}{T} \right) = \beta' \bar{M}_{xx} \bar{M}_{xx}^{-1} \bar{M}_{xx} \beta = \beta' \bar{M}_{xx} \beta$$

which is positive for $\beta \neq 0$. Hence (5.9.10) tends to zero in probability as $T \to \infty$. Similarly we have

$$\frac{\hat{y}_2' u_1}{\hat{y}_2' \hat{y}_2} = \frac{y_2' X (X'X)^{-1} X' u_1}{y_2' X (X'X)^{-1} X' y_2} = \left(\frac{y_2' X}{T} \right) \left(\frac{X'X}{T} \right)^{-1} \left(\frac{X' u_1}{T} \right) \middle/$$
$$\left(\frac{y_2' X}{T} \right) \left(\frac{X'X}{T} \right)^{-1} \left(\frac{X' y_2}{T} \right). \tag{5.9.11}$$

But $X' u_1 / T$ tends to zero in probability for the same reason as does $X' u_2 / T$ and, it follows, therefore, that

$$\plim_{T \to \infty} \frac{\hat{y}_2' u_1}{\hat{y}_2' \hat{y}_2} = 0.$$

Since the last two terms in (5.9.9) have now been shown to tend to zero in probability as $T \to \infty$ it follows that $\hat{\gamma}$ is a consistent estimator of γ.

Part (b) The procedure in Part (a) involves two steps, in which the regression of y_2 on X provides calculated values $\hat{y}_2$ which are used as instruments for the y_2^* in (5.9.1). Thus, the procedure is essentially an instrumental variables method of estimation where the regression of y_2 on X in the first step is designed to provide instruments for use in the second step. However, it could be argued that the procedure fails to take account of all our information about the structure of the system. Writing (5.9.4) and (5.9.5) as

$$y_1 = X\delta + u_1 \qquad (\delta = \beta\gamma) \tag{5.9.12}$$

$$y_2 = X\beta + u_2 \tag{5.9.13}$$

we see that a number of cross-equation parameter restrictions are implied by the fact that the vector δ in (5.9.12) is proportional to the vector β in (5.9.13). In this case, we would expect to obtain more precise estimates of β and γ by estimating (5.9.12) and (5.9.13) jointly. Furthermore, we should take into account in our estimation that there is zero covariance between the disturbances of the two equations. Zellner (1970) considers these points and develops a procedure based on generalised least squares applied to the joint system.

$$\begin{bmatrix} y_1 \\ y_2 \end{bmatrix} = \begin{bmatrix} X\delta \\ X\beta \end{bmatrix} + \begin{bmatrix} u_1 \\ u_2 \end{bmatrix} \tag{5.9.1}$$

where the covariance matrix of the vector of disturbances on (5.9.14) is

$$\begin{bmatrix} \sigma_{11}I_T & 0 \\ 0 & \sigma_{22}I_T \end{bmatrix}.$$

We minimise with respect to β and γ

$$[(y_1 - X\delta)', (y_2 - X\beta)] \begin{bmatrix} \dfrac{1}{\sigma_{11}}I & 0 \\ 0 & \dfrac{1}{\sigma_{22}}I \end{bmatrix} \begin{bmatrix} y_1 - X\delta \\ y_2 - X\beta \end{bmatrix}$$

$$= \frac{1}{\sigma_{11}}(y_1 - X\beta\gamma)'(y_1 - X\beta\gamma) + \frac{1}{\sigma_{22}}(y_2 - X\beta)'(y_2 - X\beta).$$

Zellner takes two cases. The first, when the ratio $\lambda = \sigma_{11}/\sigma_{22}$ is known and the second, when there is no prior knowledge of σ_{11} and σ_{22}. In the first, we can obtain an explicit solution to the problem conditional on the given value of λ. In the second, Zellner suggests that we use the same solution and estimate the ratio λ by

$$\hat{\lambda} = \frac{T^{-1}(y_1 - X\hat{\delta})'(y_1 - X\hat{\delta})}{T^{-1}(y_2 - X\hat{\beta})'(y_2 - X\hat{\beta})} = \frac{\hat{\sigma}_{11}}{\hat{\sigma}_{22}},$$

say, where $\hat{\sigma}_{11}$ and $\hat{\sigma}_{22}$ are estimates of σ_{11} and σ_{22} obtained from the residuals of the regressions of y_1 on X and y_2 on X respectively.

In the first case, the estimators obtained are maximum likelihood estimators when the disturbances are normally distributed. Maximum likelihood estimators in the more general case where u_{1t} and u_{2t} are contemporaneously correlated [that is $E(u_{1t}u_{2t}) = \sigma_{12} \neq 0$, whereas $E(u_{1t}u_{2s}) = 0, t \neq s$] are considered by Goldberger (1972a) and Wickens (1976). The asymptotic variances of these estimators do not seem to have appeared in the literature. Since the estimator of γ involves quadratic terms in the observation vectors y_1 and y_2 (see Zellner, 1970, page 444) these asymptotic variances will depend on the fourth moments of the disturbances u_{1t} and u_{2t} (compare the derivations in Malinvaud, 1970b, pp. 390–391).

Solution 5.10

The model of production which leads to (5.10.1) was first developed by Solow (1960). It is based on the hypothesis that new technical knowledge affects production by being incorporated in new captial equipment. In this sense, technical progress is said to be embodied and is distinct from what is usually disembodied technical progress which, in Solow's words, "floats down from the outside" and thus affects production without being incorporated in new equipment.

In deriving (5.10.1) Solow distinguishes between capital of different vintages. Thus, $K_v(t)$ represents capital services at time t which are obtained from vintage v equipment ($v \leqslant t$). Similarly, $L_v(t)$ represents labour services at time t that are working with vintage v equipment and $Q_v(t)$ is the output produced at time t from vintage v equipment, i.e. $K_v(t)$, with labour services $L_v(t)$. More specifically, $Q_v(t)$ is assumed to be determined by

$$Q_v(t) = Be^{\lambda v}L_v(t)^\alpha K_v(t)^{1-\alpha} \qquad (5.10.3)$$

so that the technical relation between $L_v(t)$, $K_v(t)$ and $Q_v(t)$ is Cobb–Douglas and improvements in technology take place at the time (v) when capital is installed or built. This means that there is a once and for all improvement in the technology that is incorporated in capital of vintage v represented by the factor $e^{\lambda v}$ in (5.10.3). This improvement takes place instantaneously at time v and capital of this vintage cannot then benefit from further technical advances that take place at a later time. If $I(v)$ represents the actual investment in vintage v equipment at time v, then we write

$$K_v(t) = e^{-\delta(t-v)}I(v) \qquad (5.10.4)$$

so that the efficiency of vintage v equipment is assumed to decline exponentially at a rate δ over time.

Total output $Q(t)$ is the sum total of output produced from equipment of all vintages so that

$$Q(t) = \int_{-\infty}^{t} Q_v(t)\,dv. \tag{5.10.5}$$

Similarly, the total amount of labour employed at time t is given by

$$L(t) = \int_{-\infty}^{t} L_v(t)\,dv. \tag{5.10.6}$$

Solow then derives the final form of the production function (5.10.1) from equations (5.11.3) to (5.11.6) together with the profit maximising assumption that in competitive labour markets labour is allocated to work with capital of different vintages in such a way that its marginal productivity is the same in every use.

Part (a) It is difficult to make direct use of (5.10.1) in empirical work because of the complicated non-linear way in which the parameters α, δ and λ enter the equation. In particular, not only is the component of the model

$$\int_{-\infty}^{t} e^{\sigma v} I(v)\,dv \qquad \left(\sigma = \delta + \frac{\lambda}{1-\alpha}\right)$$

unobservable, but it is defined directly in terms of the unknown parameters. To overcome these difficulties Solow devised an ingenious procedure for transforming the model into an estimable form. He introduced the new variable

$$R(t) = \left(\frac{Q(t)}{L(t)^\alpha}\right)^{1/(1-\alpha)} \tag{5.10.7}$$

so that from (5.10.1) we have

$$R(t) = B^{1/(1-\alpha)} e^{-\delta t} \int_{-\infty}^{t} e^{\sigma v} I(v)\,dv$$

and then by differentiation we obtain

$$\frac{dR(t)}{dt} = -\delta R(t) + B^{1/(1-\alpha)} e^{(\alpha-\delta)t} I(t).$$

Since $\alpha - \delta = \lambda/(1-\alpha)$ we therefore have

$$\frac{dR(t)/dt + \delta R(t)}{I(t)} = B^{1/(1-\alpha)} e^{\lambda t/(1-\alpha)}. \tag{5.10.8}$$

from which we obtain (5.10.2) by taking logarithms.

Given that α and δ can be estimated extraneously the left hand side of (5.11.8) can be calculated approximately by replacing $dR(t)/dt$ by the first difference $\Delta R(t) = R(t) - R(t-1)$ and constructing a series for $R(t)$ from time series for $Q(t)$ and $L(t)$ and then using (5.10.7) to find $R(t)$ from the extraneous estimate of α. Once this has been done, the slope coefficient $\lambda/(1-\alpha)$ is readily estimated from (5.10.2) from which we derive an estimate of λ using the extraneous estimate of α.

Part (b) In spite of the fact that this procedure is very ingenious it is far from satisfactory (Solow himself was undoubtedly aware of this as is clear from section 4 of his paper.) This is so for a number of reasons. First of all the procedure leads to estimates of λ which are conditional on the extraneous estimates of α and δ. These latter estimates will themselves be subject to sampling error which will lead to a further source of variation in the estimate of λ obtained from (5.10.2). To see this we need only note that if $\hat{b}$ is the estimated coefficient of t in the regression on (5.10.2) then our estimate of λ is

$$\hat{\lambda} = \hat{b}(1 - \hat{\alpha})$$

where $\hat{\alpha}$ is the extraneous estimate of α. The sampling variation of $\hat{\lambda}$ then depends on that of $\hat{b}$ and $\hat{\alpha}$. To use (5.10.2) for statistical inference about λ we should at least have some measure of the sampling variation of $\hat{\alpha}$.

Moreover, in the production function (5.10.1) it is implicitly assumed that there is no disembodied technical progress at all. It may seem more acceptable to start with a model in which there is both embodied and disembodied technical progress. This leads us to a function of the form

$$Q(t) = Be^{[\mu - \delta(1-\alpha)]t} L(t)^\alpha \left[\int_{-\infty}^{t} e^{\upsilon v} I(v)\,dv \right]^{1-\alpha} \tag{5.10.9}$$

where μ is the rate of disembodied technical progress. We then find the following equation in place of (5.10.2):

$$\ln\left[\frac{dR(t)}{dt} + \left(\delta - \frac{\mu}{1-\alpha} \right) R(t)/I(t) \right] = \frac{1}{1-\alpha}\ln B + \frac{\mu + \lambda}{1-\alpha}t.$$

Thus, when μ is positive rather than zero, we would expect the estimate of λ obtained from the regression on (5.10.2) to be biased upwards.

These points were considered by Wickens (1970) who, in addition, developed a procedure for estimating the function (5.10.1) more directly than Solow. Working with (5.10.9) rather than (5.10.1), Wickens transformed the model into the form

$$\ln[Q(t)/L(t)] \ = \ \ln B + [\mu - \delta(1-\alpha)]\,t + (1-\alpha)\ \ln\left[\int_{-\infty}^{t} e^{\sigma v} I(v)\,dv/L(t)\right]$$

$$(5.10.10)$$

To treat the non-linearity in the last term of (5.10.10), Wickens suggests that we use the following approximation

$$\ln\left[\int_{-\infty}^{t} e^{\sigma v} I(v)\,dv/L(t)\right] \ = \ \ln\left[\int_{-\infty}^{t} e^{\bar{\sigma}v} I(v)\,dv/L(t)\right] \qquad (5.10.11)$$

$$+ (\sigma - \bar{\sigma})\left(L(t)/\int_{-\infty}^{t} e^{\bar{\sigma}v} I(v)\,dv\right)\left(\int_{-\infty}^{t} v e^{\bar{\sigma}v} I(v)\,dv/L(t)\right)$$

which is based on the first two terms of the Taylor expansion of

$$\ln\left[\int_{-\infty}^{t} e^{\sigma v} I(v)\,dv/L(t)\right] \qquad (5.10.12)$$

about its value at $\sigma = \bar{\sigma}$, where $\bar{\sigma}$ represents an initial estimate of σ. (Note that the second term on the right side of (5.10.11) is obtained by differentiating (5.10.12) with respect to σ and treating it as a function of a function) Substituting (5.10.11) into (5.10.10) we obtain the equation.

$$\ln[Q(t)/L(t)] \ = \ \ln B + [\mu - \delta(1-\alpha)]\,t \qquad (5.10.13)$$

$$+ (1-\alpha)\ \ln\left[\int_{-\infty}^{t} e^{\bar{\sigma}v} I(v)\,dv/L(t)\right]$$

$$+ (1-\alpha)(\sigma - \bar{\sigma})\ \ln\left[\int_{-\infty}^{t} v e^{\bar{\sigma}v} I(v)\,dv/\int_{-\infty}^{t} e^{\bar{\sigma}v} I(v)\,dv\right]$$

This equation is non-linear in parameters and linear in the logarithms of the following variables:

$$\frac{Q(t)}{L(t)}, \quad \int_{-\infty}^{t} e^{\bar{\sigma}v} I(v)\,dv/L(t) \quad \text{and} \quad \int_{-\infty}^{t} v e^{\bar{\sigma}v} I(v)\,dv/\int_{-\infty}^{t} e^{\bar{\sigma}v} I(v)\,dv \ (5.10.14)$$

Using the initial estimate $\bar{\sigma}$, Wickens shows how the last two variables can be computed from observations of $L(t)$ and observations (over unit time periods) of $I(v)$. The coefficients of the variables on the right side of (5.10.13) can then be estimated by ordinary least squares. Wickens proposes an iterative procedure in which we now use these estimated coefficients to compute a new estimate of σ and hence recalculate the last two variables of (5.10.14). We should then estimate (5.10.13) again and iterate in this way until the estimates of σ from successive iterations have converged.

This procedure has the great advantage of not requiring extraneous estimates of some parameters as in the Solow method. We can then estimate the standard errors of the estimated coefficients of (5.10.13). One final remark should be made. Since we have in this equation introduced disembodied technical progress through the parameter μ, we note that, apart from the constant in (5.10.13), there are three coefficients and four parameters $[\mu, \delta, \alpha$ and $\lambda;$ since $\sigma = \delta + \lambda/(1 - \alpha)]$. We will not as a result be able to separately identify μ, δ and λ so that these parameters cannot be specifically estimated from the regression. This does not, however, prevent us from drawing some inferences about λ and the reader is referred to Wickens (1970) for further details on this.

Appendix

A. THE VEC( ) OPERATOR

Definition *If A is an $n \times m$ matrix and a_i' denotes the ith row of A then we write*

$$\text{vec}(A) = \begin{bmatrix} a_1 \\ a_2 \\ \cdot \\ \cdot \\ \cdot \\ a_n \end{bmatrix}.$$

Clearly $\text{vec}(A)$, which is an $nm \times 1$ vector, is an alternative representation of the elements of the matrix A. This alternative representation is particularly useful in algebraic manipulations when A is a random matrix, for the second moment properties of the elements of A can often be more conveniently analysed when these elements are arranged in vector form (so that there is a matrix of second moments) than when the elements are arranged in a rectangular array. A simple example is the least squares estimator $A^* = M_{yx} M_{xx}^{-1}$ of A in the multiple equation regression model $y_t = A x_t + u_t$ (see Solutions 3.1, 3.2 and 3.3). In this case, the covariance matrix of $\text{vec}(A^*)$ is given by

$$E[\text{vec}(A^*) - \text{vec}(A)][\text{vec}(A^*) - \text{vec}(A)]' = T^{-1} \Omega \otimes M_{xx}^{-1}$$

where Ω is the covariance matrix of the disturbance vector u_t (see Goldberger, 1964, p. 209, and Malinvaud, 1970, p. 209).

The main properties of the vec operation which we find useful are as follows:

Property (i) $\text{vec}(ABC) = (A \otimes C') \text{vec}(B)$

where A, B and C are rectangular arrays of dimension $n \times m$, $m \times p$ and $p \times q$ respectively.

Proof We let $D = ABC$ and write $A = [(a_{ij})]$, $B = [(b_{ij})]$, $C = [(c_{ij})]$ and $D = [(d_{ij})]$. Then

$$d_{ij} = \sum_{k=1}^{m} \sum_{l=1}^{p} a_{ik} b_{kl} c_{lj}$$

$$= \sum_{k} \sum_{l} a_{ik} c'_{jl} b_{kl}$$

where c'_{jl} is the (j, l)th element of C'. The matrix D has dimension $n \times q$ so that there are q elements in each row of D and therefore the $(iq + j)$th element of $\text{vec}(D)$ is $d_{ij} = \sum_{k} \sum_{l} a_{ik} c'_{jl} b_{kl}$. But

$$A \otimes C' = \begin{bmatrix} a_{11} C' & a_{12} C' & \cdots & a_{1m} C' \\ a_{21} C' & a_{22} C' & \cdots & a_{2m} C' \\ \cdot & \cdot & \cdots & \\ a_{nl} C' & a_{n2} C' & \cdots & a_{nm} C' \end{bmatrix}$$

so that the $(iq + j)$th row of $A \otimes C'$ is the jth row of

$$[a_{i1} C' a_{i2} C' \ldots a_{im} C']$$

That is

$$[a_{i1}(c'_{j1}, c'_{j2}, \ldots, c'_{jp}), \ldots, a_{im}(c'_{j1}, c'_{j2}, \ldots, c'_{jp})] \tag{A.1}$$

Now since

$$B = \begin{bmatrix} b_{11} & b_{12} & \cdots & b_{1p} \\ \cdot & \cdot & & \cdot \\ \cdot & \cdot & & \cdot \\ \cdot & \cdot & & \cdot \\ b_{m1} & b_{m2} & & b_{mp} \end{bmatrix}$$

$$\text{vec}(B) = \begin{bmatrix} b_{11} \\ b_{12} \\ \vdots \\ b_{1p} \\ b_{21} \\ \vdots \\ b_{mp} \end{bmatrix} \tag{A.2}$$

and the $(iq + j)$th element of $(A \otimes C')\,\text{vec}(B)$ is the scalar product of (A.1) and (A.2). That is

$$\sum_k \sum_l a_{ik} c'_{jl} b_{kl}$$

Thus $\text{vec}(D)$ and $(A \otimes C')\,\text{vec}(B)$ have the same $(iq + j)$th elements and since this holds for all i and j we have

$$\text{vec}(D) = (A \otimes C')\,\text{vec}(B)$$

Remark It follows immediately from Property (i) that

$$\text{vec}(AB) = (A \otimes I)\,\text{vec}(B)$$

and

$$\text{vec}(BC) = (I \otimes C')\,\text{vec}(B)$$

Property (ii) $\text{tr}(A'C) = [\text{vec}(A)]'\,[\text{vec}(C)]$

Proof

$$\text{tr}(A'C) = \sum_i \sum_j a'_{ij} c_{ji}$$

where a'_{ij} is the (i, j)th element of A' and c_{ji} is the (j, i)th element of C. Hence

$$\text{tr}(A'C) = \sum_i \sum_j a_{ji} c_{ji}$$

$$= [\text{vec}(A)]'\,[\text{vec}(C)]$$

where a_{ji} is the (j, i)th element of A.

Property (iii) $\text{tr}(A'BCD) = [\text{vec}(A)]'(B \otimes D')\,\text{vec}(C)$

where A', B, C and D are conformable matrices.

Proof From (ii) above it follows that

$$\text{tr}(A'BCD) = [\text{vec}(A)]'\,\text{vec}(BCD)$$

$$= [\text{vec}(A)]'\,(B \otimes D')\,\text{vec}(C)$$

and the last line follows from (i) above.

Final Remark The vec( ) operation as defined above is not the only way of rearranging the elements of a matrix into a long vector. Another way which is in common use (c.f. Marcus, 1964) is to stack the columns of a matrix. Thus, if A is $n \times m$ and we write A in the form $A = [A_1, A_2, \ldots, A_m]$, where A_i denotes the ith column of A we can define

$$\overline{\mathrm{vec}}\,(A) \;=\; \begin{bmatrix} A_1 \\ A_2 \\ \vdots \\ A_m \end{bmatrix} \;=\; \begin{bmatrix} a_{11} \\ a_{21} \\ \vdots \\ a_{n1} \\ a_{12} \\ a_{22} \\ \vdots \\ a_{nm} \end{bmatrix}$$

Since the columns of A are the rows of A' and $\mathrm{vec}\,(A')$ stacks the rows of A' it follows immediately that

$$\overline{\mathrm{vec}}\,(A) \;=\; \mathrm{vec}\,(A')$$

From this relationship between the $\overline{\mathrm{vec}}\,(\ )$ and $\mathrm{vec}\,(\ )$ operations we can deduce the main rules for operating with $\overline{\mathrm{vec}}\,(\ )$ on matrix products. For example, the rule corresponding to Property (i) above is

$$\overline{\mathrm{vec}}\,(ABC) \;=\; (C' \otimes A)\,\overline{\mathrm{vec}}\,(B)$$

since

$$\overline{\mathrm{vec}}\,(ABC) \;=\; \mathrm{vec}[(ABC)'] \;=\; \mathrm{vec}\,(C'B'A')$$
$$=\; (C' \otimes A)\,\mathrm{vec}\,(B')$$
$$=\; (C' \otimes A)\,\overline{\mathrm{vec}}\,(B).$$

B. MATRIX CALCULUS NOTATION

Definition *If α is a $p \times 1$ vector then by $\partial/\partial\alpha$ (sometimes written $d/d\alpha$) we mean the $p \times 1$ vector operator $(\partial/\partial\alpha_i)$.*

If $a = a(\alpha)$ is a scalar function of the elements of α, $b = b(\alpha)$ is an n-vector $[b_i(\alpha)]$ whose elements $b_i(\alpha)$ are functions of α and $A = A(\alpha)$ is an $n \times m$ matrix $[a_{ij}(\alpha)]$ whose elements $a_{ij}(\alpha)$ are functions of α, then we use the following notation

$$\frac{\partial a}{\partial \alpha} = \begin{bmatrix} \dfrac{\partial a(\alpha)}{\partial \alpha_1} \\ \vdots \\ \dfrac{\partial a(\alpha)}{\partial \alpha_p} \end{bmatrix}, \quad \frac{\partial a}{\partial \alpha'} = \begin{bmatrix} \dfrac{\partial a(\alpha)}{\partial \alpha_1}, & \cdots, & \dfrac{\partial a(\alpha)}{\partial \alpha_p} \end{bmatrix}$$

$$\frac{\partial^2 a}{\partial \alpha \partial \alpha'} = \left[\left(\frac{\partial^2 a(\alpha)}{\partial \alpha_i \partial \alpha_j} \right)_{ij} \right]_{p \times p}$$

$$\frac{\partial b}{\partial \alpha_i} = \begin{bmatrix} \dfrac{\partial b_1(\alpha)}{\partial \alpha_i} \\ \dfrac{\partial b_n(\alpha)}{\partial \alpha_i} \end{bmatrix} , \quad \frac{\partial b'}{\partial \alpha_i} = \left[\frac{\partial b_1(\alpha)}{\partial \alpha_i} , \dots , \frac{\partial b_n(\alpha)}{\partial \alpha_i} \right],$$

$$\frac{\partial b'}{\partial \alpha} = \left[\left(\frac{\partial b_j(\alpha)}{\partial \alpha_i} \right)_{ij} \right]_{p \times n} , \quad \frac{\partial b}{\partial \alpha'} = \left[\left(\frac{\partial b_i(\alpha)}{\partial \alpha_j} \right)_{ij} \right]_{n \times p} ,$$

$$\frac{\partial A}{\partial \alpha_i} = \left[\left(\frac{\partial a_{kl}(\alpha)}{\partial \alpha_i} \right)_{kl} \right]_{n \times m} ,$$

$$\frac{\partial \operatorname{vec}(A)}{\partial \alpha_i} = \begin{bmatrix} \dfrac{\partial a_{11}(\alpha)}{\partial \alpha_i} \\ \dfrac{\partial a_{12}(\alpha)}{\partial \alpha_i} \\ \cdot \\ \cdot \\ \cdot \\ \dfrac{\partial a_{1m}(\alpha)}{\partial \alpha_i} \\ \dfrac{\partial a_{21}(\alpha)}{\partial \alpha_i} \\ \cdot \\ \cdot \\ \cdot \\ \dfrac{\partial a_{nm}(\alpha)}{\partial \alpha_i} \end{bmatrix}_{nm \times 1} , \quad \frac{\partial [\operatorname{vec}(A)]'}{\partial \alpha} = \begin{bmatrix} \dfrac{\partial \operatorname{vec}(A)}{\partial \alpha_1}' \\ \cdot \\ \cdot \\ \cdot \\ \dfrac{\partial \operatorname{vec}(A)}{\partial \alpha_p}' \end{bmatrix}_{p \times nm}$$

and

$$\frac{\partial \operatorname{vec}(A)}{\partial \alpha'} = \left[\frac{\partial \operatorname{vec}(A)}{\partial \alpha_1} , \dots , \frac{\partial \operatorname{vec}(A)}{\partial \alpha_n} \right]$$

Most of the rules for operating in matrix calculus can be found in the main econometrics texts and will not be discussed here. We refer the reader to Goldberger (1964, pp. 39–44), Theil (1971, pp. 30–33), Malinvaud (1970b, pp. 196–198) and Fisk (1967, pp. 144–154). Dwyer (1967) and Neudecker (1968) are also useful references in this area. One rule we will find it useful to derive here is the following:

If $A = A(\lambda)$ is a square non-singular matrix of order n whose elements are differentiable functions of the scalar λ then

$$\frac{\partial}{\partial \lambda} \ln \det[A(\lambda)] = \mathrm{tr}\left[A^{-1}(\lambda) \frac{\partial A(\lambda)}{\partial \lambda}\right] \tag{B.1}$$

Proof We set $A = [(a_{pq})]$. Then

$$\frac{\partial \ln \det[A(\lambda)]}{\partial \lambda} = \frac{\partial \ln \det[A(\lambda)]}{\partial \det A(\lambda)} \frac{\partial \det A(\lambda)}{\partial \lambda}$$

$$= \frac{1}{\det A(\lambda)} \frac{\partial \det[A(\lambda)]}{\partial \lambda}$$

$$= \frac{1}{\det A(\lambda)} \sum_{p=1}^{n} \sum_{q=1}^{n} \frac{\partial \det[A(\lambda)]}{\partial a_{pq}} \frac{\partial a_{pq}}{\partial \lambda}$$

$$= \frac{1}{\det A(\lambda)} \sum_{p} \sum_{q} A_{pq} \frac{\partial a_{pq}}{\partial \lambda}$$

where A_{pq} is the cofactor of a_{pq} in A. Note that the last line follows because we have

$$\det A = \sum_{q=1}^{n} a_{iq} A_{iq}$$

and thus

$$\frac{\partial \det A}{\partial a_{pq}} = A_{pq}.$$

But

$$\frac{A_{pq}}{\det A} = (A^{-1})_{qp} \quad \text{and} \quad \frac{\partial a_{pq}}{\partial \lambda} = \left(\frac{\partial A}{\partial \lambda}\right)_{pq}$$

so that

$$\frac{\partial \ln \det[A(\lambda)]}{\partial \lambda} = \sum_{p} \sum_{q} (A^{-1})_{qp} \left(\frac{\partial A}{\partial \lambda}\right)_{pq} = \mathrm{tr}\left[A^{-1}(\lambda) \frac{\partial A(\lambda)}{\partial \lambda}\right]$$

as required.

Remark It is important to realise that rule (B.1) holds whether or not $A(\lambda)$ is a symmetric matrix. But, note that if $A(\lambda)$ is not symmetric and we set $\lambda = a_{ij}$, the (i, j)th element of A, then $\partial A(\lambda)/\partial\lambda$ has unity in the (i, j)th position and zeros elsewhere. The rule then tells us that

$$\frac{\partial \ln(\det A)}{\partial a_{ij}} = a^{ji}$$

the (i, j)th element of A'^{-1}. Thus

$$\frac{\partial \ln(\det A)}{\partial A} = A'^{-1}.$$

Bibliography

Aigner D.J. and Goldfeld S.M. (1974), 'Estimation and prediction from aggregate data when aggregates are measured more accurately than their components', *Econometrica*, 42, 113—134.

Amemiya T. (1966), 'Specification analysis in the estimation of parameters of a simultaneous equation model with autoregressive residuals', *Econometrica*, 34, 283—306.

Amemiya T. (1974), 'The nonlinear two-stage least-squares estimator', *Journal of Econometrics*, 2, 105—110.

Amemiya T. (1977), 'The maximum likelihood and the nonlinear three-stage least squares estimator in the general nonlinear simultaneous equation model', *Econometrica*, 45, 955—968.

Anderson T.W. (1971), *The Statistical Analysis of Time Series*, John Wiley, New York.

Anderson T.W. (1974), 'An asymptotic expansion of the distribution of the limited information maximum likelihood estimate of a coefficient in a simultaneous equation system', *Journal of the American Statistical Association*, 69, 565—573.

Ashenfelter O. and Heckman J. (1974), 'The estimation of income and substitution effects in a model of family labor supply', *Econometrica*, 42, 73—86.

Bahadur R.R. (1964), 'On Fisher's bound for asymptotic variances', *Annals of Mathematical Statistics*, 35, 1545—1552.

Barnett W.A. (1976), Maximum likelihood and iterated Aitken estimation of nonlinear systems of equations', *Journal of the American Statistical Association*, 71, 354—360.

Barten A.P. and Bronsard L.S. (1970), 'Two-stage least squares estimators with shifts in the structural form', *Econometrica*, 38, 938—941.

Bartlett M.S. (1966), *An Introduction to Stochastic Processes with Special Reference to Methods and Applications*, Cambridge University Press, London (2nd edn).

Basmann R.L. (1960), 'On finite sample distributions of generalised classical linear identifiability test statistics', *Journal of the American Statistical Association*, 55, 650—659.

Basmann R.L. (1974), 'Exact finite sample distributions of some econometric estimators and test statistics: a survey and appraisal', in Intriligator M.D. and Kendrick D. (eds) *Frontiers of Quantitative Economics* Vol II, North Holland, Amsterdam, Chap. 4, pp 209—271.

Bentzel R. and Hansen B. (1954), 'On recursiveness and interdependency in economic models', *Review of Economic Studies*, 22, 153—168.

Bergstrom A.R. (1962), 'The exact sampling distributions of least squares and maximum likelihood estimators of the marginal propensity to consume', *Econometrica*, 30, 480—490.

Bergstrom A.R. (1966), 'What is econometrics?', *The University of Auckland Gazette*, 8, 1—3.

Bergstrom A.R. (1967), *'The Construction and Use of Economic Models'*, English Universities Press, London.

Berndt E.R. and Savin N.E. (1977), 'Conflict among criteria for testing hypotheses in the multivariate regression model', *Econometrica*, **45**, 1263–1278.

Box G.E.P. and Jenkins G.M. (1970), *'Time Series Analysis Forecasting and Control'*, Holden Day, San Francisco.

Braithwaite R.B. (1968), *Scientific Explanation*, Cambridge University Press, London.

Breuch T. (1976), 'The relationship among three statistics for testing hypotheses in the linear regression model – an expository note', unpublished paper, Australian National University.

Brissimis S.N. (1976), 'Multiplier effects for higher than first-order linear dynamic econometric models', *Econometrica*, **44**, 593–596.

Brown J.T. and Manson C.W. (1950), *'The Elements of Analytical Geometry'*, Macmillan, London.

Byron R.P. (1970), 'The restricted Aitken estimation of sets of demand relations', *Econometrica*, **38**, 816–830.

Chatfield C. and Prothero D.L. (1973), 'Box–Jenkins seasonal forecasting: problems in a case study', *Journal of the Royal Statistical Society*, Series A, **136**, 295–315.

Chow G.C. (1960), 'Tests of equality between sets of coefficients in two linear regressions', *Econometrica*, **28**, 591–605.

Chow G.C. (1976), *Analysis and Control of Dynamic Economic Systems*, John Wiley, New York.

Christ C. (1975), 'Judging the performance of econometric models of the US', *International Economic Review*, **16**, 54–74.

Clark P. (1973), 'A subordinated stochastic process model with finite variance for speculative prices', *Econometrica*, **41**, 135–156.

Cochrane D. and Orcutt G. (1949), 'Application of least squares regression to relationships containing autocorrelated error terms', *Journal of the American Statistical Association*, **44**, 32–61.

Cooper R.L. (1972), 'The predictive performance of quarterly econometric models of the United States', in Hickman B.G. (ed.) *Econometric Models of Cyclical Behaviour*, Columbia University Press, New York, pp 813–916.

Court R.H. (1974), 'Three-stage least squares and some extensions where the structural disturbance covariance matrix may be singular', *Econometrica*, **42**, 547–558.

Cramer H. (1946), *Mathematical Methods of Statistics*, Princeton University Press, Princeton NJ.

Daniels H.E. (1956), 'The approximate distribution of serial correlation coefficients', *Biometrika*, **43**, 169–185.

Deistler M. (1975), 'z–Transform and identification of linear econometric models with autocorrelated errors', *Metrika*, **22**, 13–25.

Deistler M. (1976), 'The identifiability of linear econometric models with autocorrelated errors', *International Economic Review*, **17**, 26–45.

Dhrymes P.J. (1970), *Econometrics*, Harper and Row, New York.

Dhrymes P.J. (1971), *Distributed Lags: Problems of Estimation and Formulation*, Holden-Day, San Francisco.

Dhrymes P.J. et al. (1972), 'Criteria for evaluation of econometric models', *Annals of Economic and Social Measurement*, **1**, 291–324.

Dhrymes P.J. (1974), 'A note on an efficient two-step estimator', *Journal of Econometrics*, **2**, 301–304.

Dhrymes, P.J. and Erlat H. (1974), 'Asymptotic properties of full information estimators in dynamic autoregressive simultaneous equation models', *Journal of Econometrics*, **2**, 247–260.

Dieudonné J. (1969), *Foundations of Modern Analysis*, Academic Press, New York.

Doob J.L. (1953), *Stochastic Processes*, John Wiley, New York.

Durbin J. (1953), 'A note on regression when there is extraneous information about one of the coefficients', *Journal of the American Statistical Association*, **48**, 799—808.

Durbin J. (1970), 'Testing for serial correlation in least-squares regression when some of the regressors are lagged dependent variables', *Econometrica*, **38**, 410—421.

Durbin J. and Watson G.S. (1950), 'Testing for serial correlation in least squares regression I', *Biometrika*, **37**, 409—428.

Durbin J. and Watson G.S. (1951), 'Testing for serial correlation in least squares regression II', *Biometrika*, **38**, 159—178.

Dwyer P.S. (1967), 'Some applications of matrix derivatives in multivariate analysis', *Journal of the American Statistical Association*, **62**, 607—625.

Eckstein O. and Fromm G. (1968), 'The price equation', *American Economic Review*, **68**, 1159—1183.

Edwards D.A. and Moyal J.E. (1955), 'Stochastic differential equations', *Proceedings of the Cambridge Philosophical Society*, **51**, 663—677.

Fair R.C. (1970), 'The estimation of simultaneous equation models with lagged endogenous variables and first order serially correlated errors', *Econometrica*, **38**, 507—516.

Fair R.C. (1972), 'Efficient estimation of simultaneous equations with autoregressive errors by instrumental variables', *Review of Economics and Statistics*, **54**, 444—449.

Fair R.C. (1974), *A Model of Macroeconomic Activity, Volume 1 : The Theoretical Model*, Ballinger, Cambridge, Mass.

Fair R.C. and Kelejian H.H. (1974), 'Methods of estimation for markets in disequilibrium: a further study', *Econometrica*, **42**, 177—190.

Fisher F.M. (1966), *The Identification Problem in Econometrics*, McGraw-Hill, New York.

Fisher F.M. (1970), 'Tests of equality between sets of coefficients in two linear regressions: an expository note', *Econometrica*, **38**, 361—366.

Fishman G.S. (1969), *Spectral Methods in Econometrics*, Harvard University Press, Cambridge, Mass.

Fisk P.R. (1967), *Stochastically Dependent Equations*, Griffin, London.

Friedman M. (1953), 'The methodology of positive economics' in *Essays in Positive Economics*, University of Chicago Press, Chicago.

Gallant A.R. (1975a), 'Seemingly unrelated nonlinear regressions', *Journal of Econometrics*, **3**, 35—50.

Gallant A.R. (1975b), 'Nonlinear regression', *American Statistician*, **29**, 73—81.

Gantmacher F.R. (1959), *Theory of Matrices*, Chelsea, New York.

Godfrey L.G. and Poskitt D.S. (1975), 'Testing the restrictions of the Almon lag technique', *Journal of the American Statistical Association*, **70**, 105—108.

Godfrey L.G. and Wickens M.R. (1977), 'The estimation of incomplete models using subsystem LIML', Essex University Discussion paper, No. 99.

Goldberger A.S. (1964), *Econometric Theory*, John Wiley, New York.

Goldberger A.S. (1972a), 'Structural equation methods in the social sciences', *Econometrica*, **40**, 979—1002.

Goldberger A.S. (1972b), 'Maximum likelihood estimation of regressions containing unobservable independent variables', *International Economic Review*, **13**, 1—15.

Granger C.W.J. and Newbold P. (1973), 'Some comments on the evaluation of economic forecasts', *Applied Economics*, **5**, 35—47.

Granger C.W.J. and Newbold P. (1974), 'Spurious regressions in econometrics', *Journal of Econometrics*, **2**, 111—120.

Green H.A.J. (1971), *Consumer Theory*, Penguin, London.

Grenander U. and Rosenblatt M. (1957), *Statistical Analysis of Stationary Time Series*, John Wiley, New York.

Griliches Z. (1974), 'Errors in variables and other unobservables', *Econometrica*, **42**, 971—998.

Haavelmo T. (1944), 'The probability approach in econometrics, *Econometrica*, Supplement to Volume 12.

Halmos P. (1958), *Finite Dimensional Vector Spaces*, Van Nostrand, Princeton NJ.

Hannan E.J. (1969), 'The identification of vector mixed autoregressive moving average systems', *Biometrika*, **56**, 223–225.

Hannan E.J. (1970), *Multiple Time Series*, John Wiley, New York.

Hannan E.J. (1971), 'Non-linear time series regression', *Journal of Applied Probability*, **8**, 767–780.

Hardy G.H. (1952), *A Course of Pure Mathematics*, Cambridge University Press, London.

Hatanaka M. (1973), 'On the existence and the approximation formulae for the moments of the k-class estimators', *Economic Studies Quarterly*, **24**, 1–15.

Hatanaka M. (1974), 'An efficient two-step estimator for the dynamic adjustment model with autoregressive errors', *Journal of Econometrics*, **2**, 199–220.

Hatanaka M. (1976), 'Several efficient two-step estimators for the dynamic simultaneous equation model with autoregressive disturbances', *Journal of Econometrics*, **4**, 189–204.

Henderson C.R. (1971), 'Comment on "The use of error components models in combining cross section with time series data" ', *Econometrica*, **39**, 397–402.

Hendry D.F. (1971), 'Maximum likelihood estimation of systems of simultaneous regression equations with errors generated by a vector autoregressive process', *International Economic Review*, **12**, 257–272, plus 'Correction', **15**, 260.

Hendry D.F. (1976), 'The structure of simultaneous equations estimators', *Journal of Econometrics*, **4**, 51–88.

Hoerl A.E. and Kennard R.W. (1970), 'Ridge regression: biased estimation for non-orthogonal problems', *Technometrics*, **12**, 55–82.

Hood W.C. and Koopmans T.C. (eds) (1953), *Studies in Econometric Method*, John Wiley, New York.

Hurwicz L. (1950), 'Least squares bias in time series', in Koopmans T.C. (ed.), *Statistical Inference in Dynamic Economic Models*, John Wiley, New York, Chap. 16, pp 365–383.

Jennrich R.I. (1969), 'Asymptotic properties of non-linear least squares estimators', *Annals of Mathematical Statistics*, **40**, 633–643.

Johnston J. (1972), *Econometric Methods*, McGraw-Hill, New York (2nd edn).

Jorgenson D.W., Hunter J. and Nadiri M.I. (1970), 'The predictive performance of econometric models of quarterly investment behaviour', *Econometrica*, **38**, 213–254.

Kendall M.G. and Stuart A. (1969), *The Advanced Theory of Statistics*, Volume I, Griffin, London.

Klein L.R. (1962), *An Introduction to Econometrics*, Prentice-Hall, Englewood Cliffs NJ.

Koopmans T.C. (1957), *Three Essays on the State of Economic Science*, McGraw-Hill, New York.

Koopmans T.C. and Hood W.C. (1953), 'The estimation of simultaneous linear economic relationships', in Hood and Koopmans (1953), Chap. 6.

Laidler D.E. (1975), 'Expectations adjustment and the dynamic response of income to policy changes', Chapter 3, 65–81, in Laidler D.E., *Essays on Money and Inflation*, Manchester University Press, Manchester, Chap, 3, pp 65–81.

Lukacs E. and Laha R.G. (1964), *Applications of Characteristic Functions*, Griffin, London.

McGuire T.W., Farley J.W., Lucas R.E. (Jnr) and Ring L. Winston (1968), 'Estimation and inference for linear models in which subsets of the dependent variable are constrained', *Journal of the American Statistical Association*, **63**, 1201–1213.

MacDuffee C.C. (1933), *The Theory of Matrices*, Chelsea, New York.

Madansky A. (1976), *Foundations of Econometrics*, North Holland, Amsterdam.

Maddala G.S. (1971a), 'The use of variance components models in pooling cross-section and time-series data', *Econometrica*, 39, 341–358.

Maddala G.S. (1971b), 'Generalised least squares with an estimated covariance matrix', *Econometrica*, 39, 23–34.

Maddala G.S. and Nelson F.D. (1974), 'Maximum likelihood methods of markets in disequilibrium', *Econometrica*, 42, 1031–1044.

Malinvaud E. (1966), *Statistical Methods of Econometrics*, North-Holland, Amsterdam, (1st edn).

Malinvaud E. (1970a), 'The consistency of non-linear regressions', *Annals of Mathematical Statistics*, 41, 956–969.

Malinvaud E. (1970b), *Statistical Methods of Econometrics*, North Holland, Amsterdam, (2nd edn).

Mann H.B. and Wald A. (1943a), 'On the statistical treatment of linear stochastic difference equations', *Econometrica*, 11, 173–220.

Mann H.B. and Wald A. (1943b), 'On stochastic limit and order relationships', *Annals of Mathematical Statistics*, 14, 173–220.

Marcus M. and Mine H. (1964), *A Survey of Matrix Theory and Matrix Inequalities*, Allyn and Bacon, Boston.

Mariano R.S. (1973), 'Approximations to the distribution functions of the ordinary least squares and two-stage least squares estimators in the case of two included endogenous variables', *Econometrica*, 41, 67–77.

Mariano R.S. and Sawa T. (1972), 'The exact finite-sample distribution of the limited information maximum likelihood estimator in the case of two included endogenous variables', *Journal of the American Statistical Association*, 67, 159–163.

de Menil G. (1974), 'Aggregate price dynamics', *The Review of Economics and Statistics*, 56, 129–140.

Mikhail W.M. (1972), 'Simulating the small sample properties of econometric estimators', *Journal of the American Statistical Association*, 67, 620–624.

Moroney J.R. and Mason J.M. (1971), 'The dynamic impacts of autonomous expenditures and the monetary base on aggregate income', *Journal of Money, Credit and Banking*, 3, 793–814.

Nagar A.L. (1959), 'The bias and moment matrix of the general k–class estimators of the parameters in simultaneous equations', *Econometrica*, 27, 575–595.

Nelson C.R. (1972), 'The predictive performance of the FRB–MIT–PENN model of the US economy', *American Economic Review*, 62, 902–917.

Neudecker H. (1968), 'The Kronecker matrix product and some of its applications in econometrics', *Statistica Neerlandica*, 22, 69–82.

Nerlove M. (1971), 'A note on error components models', *Econometrica*, 39, 383–396.

Phillips P.C.B. (1972), 'The structural estimation of a stochastic differential equation system', *Econometrica*, 40, 1021–1041.

Phillips P.C.B. (1976), 'The iterated minimum distance estimator and the quasi-maximum likelihood estimator', *Econometrica*, 44, 449–460.

Phillips P.C.B. (1977), 'Approximations to some finite sample distributions associated with a first-order stochastic difference equation', *Econometrica*, 45, 463–485.

Pigou A.C. (1908), *Economic Science in Relation to Practice*, Macmillan, London.

Popper K.F. (1959), *The Logic of Scientific Discovery*, Hutchinson, London.

Popper K.F. (1963), *Conjectures and Refutations*, Routledge and Kegan Paul, London.

Prais S.J. and Houthakker H.S. (1955), *The Analysis of Family Budgets*, Cambridge University Press, London.

Preston A.J. and Wall K.D. (1973), 'An extended identification problem for state space representations of econometric models', Discussion Paper, Programme of Research into Econometric Methods, Queen Mary College, London.

Rao C.R. (1963), 'Criteria of estimation in large samples', *Sankhya, Series A*, 25, 189–206.

Robinson P.M. (1972), 'Non-linear regression for multiple time series', *Journal of Applied Probability*, **9**, 758—768.
Robinson P.M. (1976a), 'The estimation of linear differential equations with constant coefficients', *Econometrica*, **44**, 751—764.
Robinson P.M. (1976b), 'Instrumental variables estimation of differential equations', *Econometrica*, **44**, 765—776.
Rothenberg T.J. (1971), 'Identification in parametric models', *Econometrica*, **39**, 577—591.
Rothenberg T.J. (1973), *Efficient Estimation with a priori Information*, Yale University Press, New Haven.
Rothenberg T.J. and Leenders C.T. (1964), 'Efficient estimation of simultaneous equation systems', *Econometrica*, **32**, 57—76.
Rubin H. (1950), 'Consistency of maximum likelihood estimates in the explosive case', in Koopmans T.C. (ed.), *Statistical Inference in Dynamic Economic Models*, John Wiley, New York, Chap. 14, 356—364.
Rudin W. (1964), *Principles of Mathematical Analysis*, McGraw-Hill, New York.
Samuelson P.A. (1954), 'Report of the Evaluate Committee for Econometrica', *Econometrica*, **22**, 141—146.
Sargan J.D. (1964a), 'Three-stage least squares and full information maximum likelihood estimates', *Econometrica*, **32**, 77—81.
Sargan J.D. (1964b), 'Wages and prices in the United Kingdom: a study in econometric methodology', *Colston Papers*, **16**, Butterworths, London.
Sargan J.D. (1972), 'The identification and estimation of sets of simultaneous stochastic equations', mimeographed, London School of Economics (and Discussion Paper No. A1, LSE Econometrics Programme 1975).
Sargan J.D. (1974), 'The validity of Nagar's expansion for the moments of econometric estimators', *Econometrica*, **42**, 169—176.
Sargan J.D. (1975), 'Gram Charlier approximations applied to t-ratios of k-class estimators', *Econometrica*, **43**, 327—346.
Sargan J.D. (1976), 'Some discrete approximations to continuous time stochastic models', in Bergstrom A.R. (ed.) *Statistical Inference in Continuous Time Economic Models*, North Holland, Amsterdam, Chap. 3, pp 27—79.
Schmetterer L. (1966), 'On the asymptotic efficiency of estimates', in David F.N. (ed.) *Research Papers in Statistics*, (Festschrift for J. Neyman), John Wiley, London, 1966, 301—316.
Schmidt P. (1976), *Econometrics*, Marcel Dekker, New York.
Schönfeld P. (1971), 'A useful central limit theorem for m-dependent variables', *Metrika*, **15**, 116—128.
Seber G.A.F. (1964), *The Linear Hypothesis: a General Theory*, Griffin, London.
Shenton L.R. and Johnson W.L. (1965), 'Moments of a serial correlation coefficient', *Journal of the Royal Statistical Society, Series B*, **27**, 308—320.
Schiller, R.J. (1973), 'A distributed lag estimator derived from smoothness priors', *Econometrica*, **41**, 775—788.
Simon H.A. (1953), 'Causal ordering and identifiability', in Hood and Koopmans (1953), Chap. 3, pp 49—74.
Smyth D.J. and Briscoe G. (1969), 'Investment plans and realisations in United Kingdom manufacturing', *Economica*, **36**, 277—293.
Stigum B.P. (1974), 'Asymptotic properties of dynamic stochastic parameter estimates', *Journal of Multivariate Analysis*, **4**, 351—381.
Stigum B.P. (1976), 'Least squares and stochastic difference equations', *Journal of Econometrics*, **4**, 349—370.
Stone R. (1954), 'Linear expenditure systems and demand analysis: an application to the pattern of British demand', *Economic Journal*, **64**, 511—527.
Theil H. (1958), *Economic Forecasts and Policy*, North Holland, Amsterdam.
Theil H. (1971), *Principles of Econometrics*, John Wiley, New York.

Theil H. and Boot J.C.G. (1962), 'The final form of econometric equation systems', *Review of the International Statistical Institute*, 30, 136—152.

Tichmarsh E.C. (1964), *The Theory of Functions*, Oxford University Press, London.

Trivedi P.K. and Pagan A.R. (1976), 'Polynomial distributed lags: a unified treatment', Australian National University, Working Papers in Economics and Econometrics, No. 34.

von Tunzelmann G.N. (1968), 'The new economic history: an econometric appraisal', *Explorations in Entrepreneurial History*, 2nd series, 5.

Wald A. (1943), 'Tests of statistical hypotheses concerning several parameters when the number of observations is large', *Transactions of the American Mathematical Society*, 54, 426—482.

Wallace T.D. and Hussain A. (1969), 'The use of error component models in combining cross-section and time series data', *Econometrica*, 37, 55—72.

Wallis K.F. (1977), 'Multiple time series and the final form of econometric models', *Econometrica*, 45, 1481—1498.

Wegge L. (1965), 'Identifiability criteria for systems of equations as a whole', *Australian Journal of Statistics*, 7, 67—77.

White J.S. (1958), 'The limiting distribution of the serial correlation coefficient in the explosive case', *Annals of Mathematical Statistics*, 29, 1188—1197.

Wickens M.R. (1969), 'The consistency and efficiency of generalised least squares in simultaneous equations systems with autocorrelated errors', *Econometrica*, 37, 651—659.

Wickens M.R. (1972), 'A note on the use of proxy variables', *Econometrica*, 40, 759—762.

Wickens M.R. (1976), 'Rational expectations and the efficient estimation of econometric models', Australian National University, Working Paper in Economics and Econometrics, No. 35.

Wickens M.R. (1977), 'The estimation of incomplete econometric models with autoregressive errors using subsystem estimators', Essex University Discussion Paper, No. 98.

Widder D.V. (1961), *Advanced Calculus*, Prentice Hall, Englewood Cliffs NJ.

Wold H. (1954), 'Causality and econometrics', *Econometrica*, 23, 162—177.

Wolfowitz J. (1965), 'Asymptotic efficiency of the maximum likelihood estimator', *Theory of Probability and its Applications*, 10, 247—254.

Wong E. (1971), *Stochastic Processes in Information and Dynamical Systems*, McGraw-Hill, New York.

Yaglom A.M. (1962), *An Introduction to the Theory of Stationary Random Functions*, Prentice-Hall, Englewood Cliffs NJ.

Zellner A. (1962), 'An efficient method of estimating seemingly unrelated regressions and tests for aggregation bias', *Journal of the American Statistical Association*, 57, 348-368.

Zellner A. (1970), 'Estimation of regression relationships containing unobservable independent variables', *International Economic Review*, 11, 441—454.

Zellner A. and Geisel M.S. (1970), 'Analysis of distributed lag models with applications to consumption function estimation', *Econometrica*, 38, 865—888.

Index